CHINA AND THE BRICS
Setting up a Different Kitchen

中国与金砖五国：另起炉灶

CHINA AND THE BRICS

Setting up a Different Kitchen

中国与金砖五国：另起炉灶

Editors

Srikanth Kondapalli

Priyanka Pandit

PENTAGON PRESS

China and the BRICS: Setting up a Different Kitchen
Editors: Srikanth Kondapalli and Priyanka Pandit

First Published in 2017

ISBN 978-81-8274-927-6

Disclaimer: The views expressed in this volume are of individual contributors and do not represent the viewpoint of the editors or publishers.

Published by
PENTAGON PRESS
206, Peacock Lane, Shahpur Jat
New Delhi-110049
Phones: 011-64706243, 26491568
Telefax: 011-26490600
email: rajan@pentagonpress.in
website: www.pentagonpress.in

Printed at Aegean Offset Printers, Greater Noida, U.P.

Contents

PART II: BILATERAL RELATIONS

List of Contributors

Srikanth Kondapalli is Professor in Chinese Studies at Jawaharlal Nehru University. He wrote two books (*China's Military: The PLA in Transition* in 1999 & *China's Naval Power* in 2001), two monographs, co-edited three volumes (*Asian Security & China* in 2004; *China and its Neighbours* in 2010 & *China's Military and India* in 2012) and a number of articles in journals and edited volumes – all on China. He can be contacted at srikondapalli@gmail.com

Priyanka Pandit is a researcher in Chinese political economy and her work focuses on China's policies towards state owned enterprises, as well as, its engagements with multilateral economic institutions. She was formerly a researcher at the Institute for Defence Studies and Analyses (IDSA), New Delhi and visiting fellow at the Jinan University, China. Her research has appeared in Journal of South East Asian Studies, International Studies (Sage), as well as in Jamestown Foundation, Asia Times etc. She is a recipient of Graduate Fellowship from the Indian Council of Social Science Research, New Delhi. She can be contacted at panditpriyanka5@gmail.com

Amrita Jash is the Editor-in-Chief at IndraStra Global, a New York based online research forum. Her PhD. thesis is "China's Perceptions of Japan: A Study of Historical Memories as an Agency, 2002-2012". She is a visiting faculty at the Department of Chinese, Sikkim Central University, a fellow at the South Asia Democratic Forum, Brussels, and a senior fellow at the BRICS Institute, New Delhi. Her research has appeared in two edited books, International Journals such as Review of Global Politics, Strategic Analysis, Yonsei Journal, China Report and Strategic Vision. She can be contacted at ajash108@gmail.com

Tilak Jha's PhD. thesis is on "*Chinese Print Media: Public Opinion and State-Market Dimensions, 2000-2013*" at the Jawaharlal Nehru University. He has more than a dozen national and international conferences and half a dozen papers and book chapters to his credit in reputed publications on China, media and related issues. He is also a regular contributor to national and international dailies. His research interests include Chinese media, India-China relations and China's South Asia policy. He can be contacted at tilakjha@gmail.com

Hu Xiaowen is an Assistant Professor at Yunnan Academy of Social Sciences and PhD scholar in Centre for East Asian Studies at Jawaharlal Nehru University. Her research interest is on Sino-Indian relations, the role of think-tanks and India's foreign policy. She published papers in reputed journals in China such as *Global Review, Southeast Asian studies, Southeast Asian and South Asian Studies, China Social Science News* etc., and has written for online websites in China such as Sina and Yunnan Information Weekly. She has led and joined a number of research projects on Think Tanks and China-India relations. She can be contacted at effiehu@hotmail.com.

Prachi Aggarwal is an Assistant Professor at Sanchi University of Buddhist Indic Studies. Her areas of interest are China's foreign policy, energy security, and international politics. As a Mandarin speaking research she has written for various columns and online websites and also published papers in reputed journals. Her recent work has been as an author of a book titled "**China's Energy Security the Domestic Discussion**" which was published in 2016 by Knowledge World Publishers at New Delhi. She can be contacted at 28.prachi@gmail.com

Kaushal Kishore Chandel is an Assistant Professor at Centre for Chinese and South East Asian Studies (CCSEAS), Jawaharlal Nehru University (JNU), New Delhi. His areas of interest are China's cyber warfare, cyber security and international cyber governance. He teaches Mandarin at the CCSEAS. His research has appeared in leading websites and he has a book chapter titled "Taiwan's National Cybersecurity Strategy". He can be contacted at kaykayjnu@gmail.com

Shaheli Das is a Junior Fellow at Observer Research Foundation. Her research interests include China's foreign policy, China-Brazil relations and Chinese military strategy. She has published in various journals and magazines. Some of her publications include "Uncertain Trajectory in the South China Sea" in

The Strategic Vision for Taiwan Security Journal and "Inch Towards Miles" for Australian Security Magazine. She can be contacted at shaheli02@gmail.com

Sakshi Anand, former full-time **Assistant Professor** at the Centre for Far East Languages, Central University of Jharkhand. She holds the prestigious Confucius scholarship for the study of Chinese language. Her area of interest includes foreign policy, China-Russia relationship, International Organisations. She can be contacted at sakshianand4u@gmail.com

Sriparna Pathak is a Consultant at the Policy Planning and Research Division at the Ministry of External Affairs, New Delhi. She earned her PhD from the Centre for East Asian Studies, Jawaharlal Nehru University in 2015. She has previously worked with the Observer Research Foundation in Kolkata and New Delhi respectively, UNICEF India and the Centre for Armed Forces Historical Research. She has also been a recipient of the MHRD scholarship for studying Mandarin at Beijing Language and Culture University (2011-13). Her areas of interest are China's domestic economy, trade and economic relations between India and China and China's economic linkages with the world. She has previously written extensively on these issues in newspapers, journals and books. She can be contacted at sriparnapathak@gmail.com

Zhang Yang, former Visiting Faculty at Centre for Far East Languages, Centre University of Jharkhand, Ranchi and teaches remedial classes at the Centre for Chinese and South East Asian Studies (CCSEAS), JNU. He has studied in Capital Normal University, Beijing, University of Delhi and National Taiwan University. His areas of research are East Asian culture and philosophy, with a focus on China-India relations. He is part of The *Juxtapose Project*, Oxford (A multi-disciplinary international annul forum on China-India comparative studies). He can be contacted at zhangyang0086@gmail.com.

Abhishek Kumar Darbey's PhD thesis is on Sino-African relations at JNU. His areas of interest are China's Foreign Aid, China-Africa Relations and China's Military. He has compiled two volumes of Directories on PLA published by Center for China Analysis & Strategy in 2014 titled "**PLA Directory-2014**" & "**PLA Directory Military Region -2014**" and has written articles for journals. He can be contacted at abhishekdarbey@gmail.com

Acronyms

AFP	Agence France-Presse
AIIB	Asian Infrastructure Investment Bank
ANC	African National Congress
AP	Associated Press
APEC	Asia-Pacific Economic Cooperation
AU	African Union
BASIC	Brazil, South Africa, India and China
BNC	Bi-National Commission
BRICS	Brazil, Russia, India, China and South Africa
BRICS-TERN	BRICS Trade & Economic Research Network
BPC	BRICS Policy Centre
BRC	BRICS Research Centre
BTTC	BRICS Think Tanks Council
CBRC	China Banking Regulatory Commission
CCCWS	China Centre for Contemporary World Studies
CCIEE	China Centre for International Economic and Exchange
CCP	Chinese Communist Party
CCPIT	China Council for the Promotion of International Trade
CCTV	China Central Television
CII	Critical Information Infrastructure
CICA	Conference on Interaction and Confidence Building Measures
CMIM	Chiang Mai Initiative
CNI	Confederation of National Industry

CNSILG	Central Network Security and Informatization Leading Group
COP	Conference of Parties
COSBAN	China-Brazil-High-Level Coordination and Cooperation Committee
CPC	Communist Party of China
CPPCC	Chinese People's Political Consultative Conference
CRA	Contingent Reserve Arrangement
CSIRT	Computer Security Incident Response Teams
CSMEI	China Small and Medium Enterprise Investment Limited
DBO	Daulat Beg Oldi
EAS	East Asia Summit
EEU	Eurasian Economic Union
E&M	Entertainment and Media
ESPN	Entertainment and Sports Programming Network
EU	European Union
EURODAD	European Network on Debt and Development
FDI	Foreign Direct Investment
FGV	Fundação Getulio Vargas
FICCI	Federation of Indian Chambers of Commerce and Industry
FOCAC	Forum on China-Africa Cooperation
G4	Brazil, India, Germany and Japan
G5	Mexico, Brazil, China, India and South Africa
G8	Group of 8
G20	Group of Twenty
GDP	Gross Domestic Product
GNI	Gross National Income
HSRC	Human Sciences Research Council
IADB	Inter-American Development Bank
IBSA	India, Brazil, South Africa
IBRD	The International Bank for Reconstruction and Development
ICANN	Internet Corporation for Assigned Names and Numbers
ICT	Information and Communication Technology
ICBC	Industrial and Commercial Bank of China

IFI	International Financial Institutions
IGO	Intergovernmental Organisations
IGN	Inter-governmental negotiations
IMF	International Monetary Fund
IPEA	Institute for Applied Economic Research
IPR	Intellectual Property Right
ITU	International Telecommunication Union
JeM	Jaish-e-Mohammed
KIIO	Key Information Infrastructure Operators
LAC	Line of Actual Control
MDGs	Millennium Development Goals
MERCOSUL	Southern Common Market: Mercado Comun del Sur/ Mercado Comum do Sul
MFN	Most Favored Nation
MNC	Multi-National Corporation
MoU	Memorandum of Understanding
MTV	Music Television
NAM	Non-Aligned Movement
NATO	North Atlantic Treaty Organization
NDB	New Development Bank
NEPAD	New Partnership for Africa's Development
NIHSS	National Institute of Humanities and Social Sciences
NPC	National People's Congress
NPT	Non Proliferation Treaty
NSG	Nuclear Suppliers Group
NWICO	New World Information and Communication Order
OAS	Organization of American States
ORF	Observer Research Foundation
PCPIR	Petroleum Chemicals and Petrochemical Investment Region
PLA	People's Liberation Army
PRC	People's Republic of China
PUC-Rio	Pontifical Catholic University of Rio de Janeiro
R&D	Research and Development
RMB	Renminbi
RT	Russia Today

RUMIGS	Research Unit for Media in the Global South
SADC	South African Development Community
SCO	Shanghai Cooperation Organization
SDT	Special and Differentiated Treatment
SOEs	State Owned Enterprises
UN	United Nations
UNASUL	Union of South American Nations
UNCAC	United Nation Convention against Corruption
UNCTAD	United Nations Conference on Trade and Development
UNFCCC	United Nations Framework Convention on Climate Change
UNGA	United Nations General Assembly
UNSC	United Nations Security Council
US	United States
USD	USA dollar
WHO	World Health Organization
WTO	World Trade Organization

List of Tables, Figures and Graphs

Tables

Figures

Graphs

Introduction

One of the most significant contemporary developments in international politics involves the growing importance of emerging powers within global governance. The emerging powers such as China, India, Brazil and Russia, already wield considerable influence in their own regions and have expanded their roles in various international institutions. They have also organized themselves in new institutional forms such as the G20, the India-Brazil-South Africa (IBSA) Dialogue Forum, the Brazil, South Africa, India, China (BASIC) group of countries, and the BRICS, suggesting their increasing influence and stature in global order. The emerging powers thus, presuppose a number of characteristics which raise important questions about their nature of rise, factors shaping their behaviour and the extent to which they will challenge existing institutions and practices, constituting the international economic order. While some scholars view the rise of emerging powers from a 'power shift' narrative, the others understand it as a shift from Western predominance to a more diverse international system, in which there is a deepening interdependence among the established and new actors.

Seeking greater roles, the rising powers have created new associations through which they can collectively negotiate and bargain the terms on which global governance takes place. BRICS, comprising of Brazil, Russia India, China and South Africa represent one of the prominent institutional manifestations of emerging powers to assert their interests and worldviews. BRIC(S) which officially came into being in the midst of global financial crisis, in 2009, aims at reforming the global economic order. The objective includes:

- reform of the Bretton Woods institutions and the international monetary system;
- the establishment and institutionalization of mechanisms to correct

terms of trade imbalances between the North and the South;

- strengthening coordination and cooperation among states in the energy field, including amongst producers and consumers of energy and transit states;
- the facilitation of technology transfer and the promotion of endogenous technological development;
- to ensure global food security;
- the extension of assistance to the 'least developed countries', as well as the strengthening of mutual economic, trade, financial, science and technological cooperation among the developing countries.

The motivation behind these reform objectives, are two-fold; first, to correct the historically inherited disparities and second, to reduce global dependence on the US dollar.

Although the idea of BRIC(S) dates back to the early 2000s, it began to be taken seriously after the financial crisis had hit the US economy in 2008, exposing the deep-rooted contradictions of the global economic system. The symptoms of which are the explosive growth of the financial system relative to manufacturing and the economy as a whole, and the proliferation of speculative and destabilising financial instruments of wealth accumulation, the rise of new economic centres, resource depletion and ecological crisis. The collapse of the British bank Northern Rock in August 2007 marked the starting point for the big financial landslides. This was followed by many 'falls' and 'crunches' which translated into a fully fledged economic crisis, spreading in all corners of the world, unsettling hedge funds, banks and stock markets as far away as Australia, Thailand Germany and also some parts in Asia.

It was not until September 2008 that the impact of financial crisis on world trade became evident. The rate of trade growth had already slowed from 6.4 percent in 2007 to 2.1 percent in 2008, but the 12.2 percent contraction in 2009 was without precedent in recent history[1]. The full impact of the crisis was felt across all regions of the global economy by the fourth quarter of 2008, with Europe experiencing a fall of 16 percent in the fourth quarter and Asia recording a fall of 5 percent in exports in the same period (see table 1). The economies in transition, Africa, Western Asia and Latin America and the Caribbean saw a significant rebound in their terms of trade, having suffered important losses in 2009 following trends in primary commodity prices. The predominantly manufactured exports in East and South Asia, in contrast, saw stagnant or slightly declining terms of trade in

2010, after a modest improvement during the global recession. Greater export diversification explains the mild fluctuations in the terms of trade among these economies.

Table I.1: World Trade Volumes of Goods and Services (During the Global Financial Crisis)

(Annual Percent Change)

					Projections	
	2007	*2008*	*2009*	*2010*	*2011*	*2012*
World Trade Volume (goods and services)	7.7	3.0	-10.7	12.8	7.5	5.8
Imports						
Advanced economies	5.2	0.6	-12.4	11.7	5.9	4.0
Emerging and developing economies	13.8	9.1	-8.0	14.9	11.1	8.1
Exports						
Advanced economies	6.8	2.1	11.9	12.3	6.2	5.2
Emerging and developing economies	10.2	4.7	-7.7	13.6	9.4	7.8

Source: World Economic Outlook, 2011.

The 2008 financial crisis accelerated shifts that began after 1997. Brazil, China, India and Russia offered financial packages to boost the economy. Between 2009 and 2010, two Chinese state-owned banks had lent more money to other developing countries than the World Bank. China also became an important contributor to the International Development Association. Brazil invested $10 billion in IMF bonds, which transformed its status from a debtor to creditor. As a domestic policy response to withstand the effects of financial crisis, they initiated fiscal stimulus measures and a move towards increasing domestic demand and consumption. Brazil's economic recovery was strong in 2010 and was one of the first countries to emerge from the crisis. The improved macroeconomic fundamentals which include reduction of fiscal and external imbalances, a less vulnerable public sector along with an increase in international reserves, supported Brazil to adopt countercyclical policies to mitigate the crisis impacts on finance as well as on the economic activities.

To counter the 7.8 percent contraction of the Russian economy in 2009, the government injected massive liquidity in the form of stimulus package, releasing more than $200 billion of its reserves for the support of major banks and government corporations. The oil revenues helped it to stabilize the funds but also monetize the deficit. Most importantly, Russia came out of the crisis without facing any major debt issues, unlike the advanced economies including the US and countries of EU.

In its efforts to contain the contagious effects of subprime meltdown, the Indian government responded through enacting three fiscal stimulus packages in the form of tax relief to boost consumption and increased expenditure on public projects to create employment and public assets, along with a number of monetary easing measures to maintain a comfortable rupee liquidity and to keep the credit mechanism in track.

China too, announced a massive fiscal stimulus plan worth Yuan 4 trillion to boost domestic demand and spur the slowing economy in the crisis period. One of the major responses to tackle the crisis domestically had been an increased emphasis on the state owned enterprises (SOEs) along with active public sector. A number of policy measures were also undertaken by the central government to improve the social safety net and to reduce corporate savings.

In South Africa, the government had undertaken a strong counter-cyclical fiscal and monetary policy so that government spending levels were maintained despite large drop in tax revenues. The Reserve Bank had reduced interest rates on four occasions and monthly meetings of Monetary Policy Committee were organised, to track the developments during the crisis.

Overall, the relatively high growth performance of BRICS countries during the recession stuck years, in contrast to the slow recovery in the United States and Europe, has enlivened the discussion on the role of BRICS in global governance.

Over the last decade, the discussion about BRICS largely focused on motivations of its formation and the implications it hold for the global order. Theoretical discussion on BRICS has primarily drawn from the mainstream theories of international relations (IR). Arguing from the realist paradigm, scholars view the BRICS formation as a challenge to US dominated economic order, which will inevitably lead to conflicts between the two in a competitive inter-state system. Some scholars even go on to describe the rise of BRICS as the rise of an Asian century, where West will be both less powerful and important in the global economic system. Seen from the perspective of national economies and international markets, the BRICS as a collective constitutes an economic and political powerhouse with the potential to reshape the liberal governance order.

Economic interdependency scholars suggest that the emerging economies are a product of the globalizing winds with most-favoured nation treatment, WTO, free trade areas, bilateral trade, investments and value chains expanding interactions and thereby blunting any political conflict with the developed world. They argue that the BRICS countries with their individual share of trade and investments with the developed western markets being higher than the intra-BRICS trade, their dependency create conditions for resolving any potential conflicts with the developed countries.

Constructivists suggest that the BRICS emphasis on norms build-up in the international relations, identity formation as emerging nations and the like have prospects for creating a niche for them in the longer run.

Classification of Views about BRICS

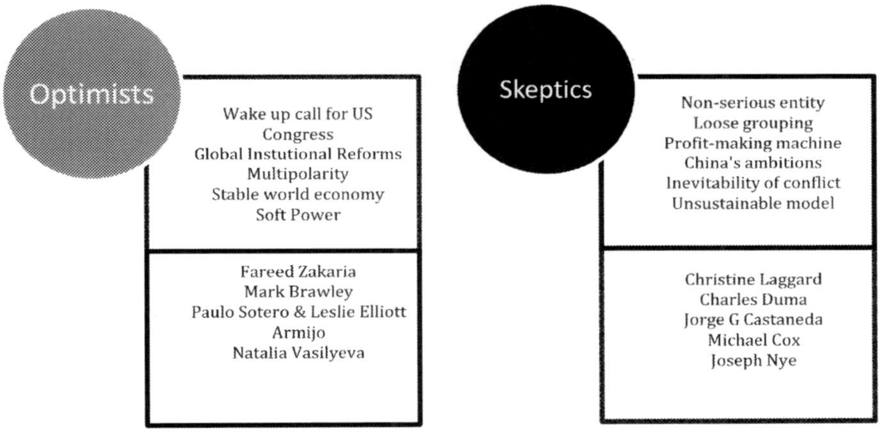

Scholars taking the historical materialist approach to explain the rise of BRICS have mainly proposed three arguments. First, the structure of global capitalism determines the forms of rivalries prevalent in the international system, which accordingly shapes behaviour of rising powers. Stephen (2014) argues "when economic expansion is dependent on territorial gain, territorialized conflicts with established powers emerge. When economic expansion is accommodated within a liberal world economy, conflicts shift to the management of the global economy". Second, BRICS countries' preferences for global governance depend on their nature of social formation that is, the dynamics between the state–society interactions. Finally, historical materialism emphasizes the role of social and class forces in the global political economy and how these forces are manifest through the inter-state system. The leading social forces integrate the rising powers into established transnational class mechanisms, further shaping its preference for global governance.

The BRICS have been involved in an accelerated integration into these globalised production and financial structures and the policies that the bloc has been pursuing, seek to further this integration. Also, the interests of the leading capitalists and elites in the BRICS countries lie in advancing the interests of TNCs and global financial institutions rather than pursuing local accumulation.

While analyzing the nuances of BRICS formation and its agenda, some analysts apply centre-periphery formulations in which the BRICS as a 'semi-peripheral states' are gradually replacing the 'centre powers'. For instance, the decline of the US dollar and its ability to provide exchange rate stability to countries that peg their currencies to it suggest the failure of the US to safeguard international monetary and fiscal stability and the emerging market economies like that of BRICS countries, especially China with its current account surplus, have a growing manufacturing capacity which increasingly supply to developed countries with manufactured goods.

However, the extant interpretation of BRICS formation and its implications for the global order have been centered on multi-polarity in global political economy. One set of scholars arguing within this framework believe that multi-polarity generates a higher premium on policy cooperation between sovereign states than a uni-polar system does and therefore, the BRICS countries would seek for greater multilateral cooperation with the established powers to collectively bring about a transformation in the global economic governance.

The other category of political economists argue that although the rise of BRICS signify multi-polarity in economic and financial affairs, but the significant differences in terms of preferences, beliefs and interests between the BRICS nations and the developed countries make cooperation both difficult to achieve and sustain. In their opinion, the newly empowered states would not prefer to compromise their interests in order to reach cooperative agreements with the developed countries. There are numerous evidences like the negotiation in the Doha rounds, exchange rate issues, climate change etc. which indicate that the multilateral cooperation between the inter-states have either stalled or failed to produce any significant outcomes.

Thus, it cannot be denied that the increase in relative capabilities of the BRICS nations have been a noticeable development in international circles and the traditional powers cannot help but acknowledge their presence. The slow recovery of the west from the global financial crisis have the major powers realized that the world economy and its institutional structures require a more coordinated response and this cannot be achieved alone by the G-7 countries.

Although the extant scholarship on BRICS suggest that the emerging economies desire a larger share in global governance in terms of greater voice, representation, leadership positions within the intergovernmental institutions, they so far have worked towards greater multilateral cooperation, while creating global influence for themselves. Since there exists considerable differences between the members of the BRICS bloc, constructing a common position on key issues of global governance becomes difficult than it may seem from the outside. Also, none of the BRICS states including China are ready to pay domestic costs that it would entail in revamping the global order.

From an Idea to a Reality

The acronym, BRIC (Brazil, Russia, India and China) was coined in 2001 by Goldman Sach economist, Jim O'Neill, who described in a report that the BRIC countries as an engine of new demand growth and spending power along with demographics, size of potential markets, recent growth rates, could become a much larger force in the world economy in the coming years and help stabilize the system and expand opportunities for transnational investors. According to forecasts made by Goldman Sachs, China will replace the U.S. economy and occupy the first place in the world, followed by that of India. Brazil's and Russia's economies will seriously compete with Japan's economy in the year 2050.

Fig. I.1: Forecast Rankings of the most Important Economies in 2050

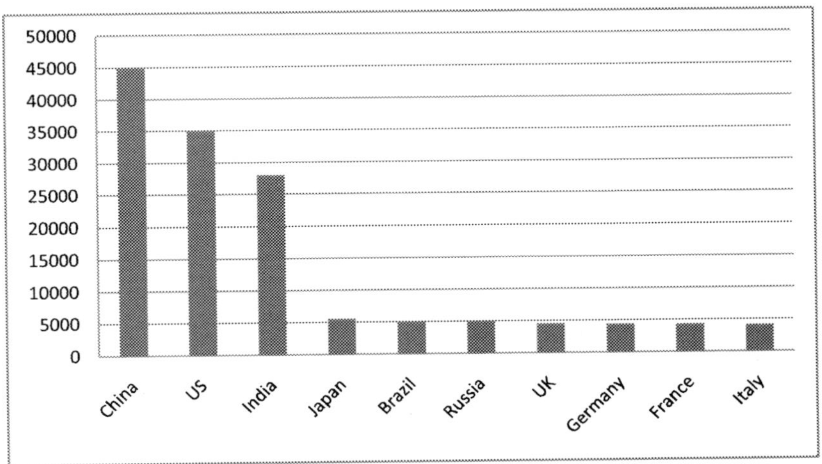

Source: Goldman Sachs, Dreaming with BRICs. The Path to 2050, 2003.

Fig. I.2: GDP per capita in US$ billion, PPP for BRICS

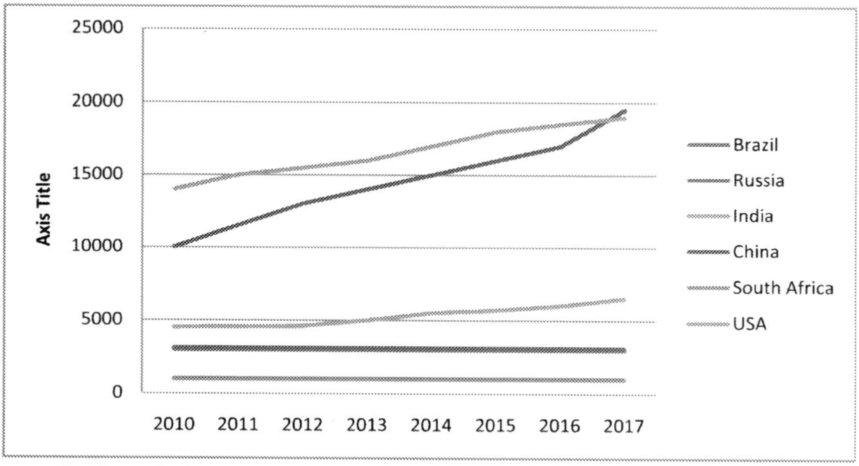

Source: Goldman Sachs.

The key assumption underlying the projections has been that the BRICs maintain policies and develop institutions that are supportive of growth and therefore the implications it hold for growth and economic activities in the world could be large. In O'Neill's view, China was to become the most important exporter of manufactured goods, India of services and Russia and Brazil of raw materials.

Today the BRICS is an inter-governmental, consultative, multilateral, trans-continental and emerging economies grouping. However, in the initial years, there was little initiative to institutionalize the interaction. The BRICS agenda had proved to be extensive and all-round in nature touching upon issues of global security, financial, market-related and the like, although these evolved over a period of time. From 2006, the BRIC nations began to take steps to formalise the group[2]. In September 2006, the first meeting of the BRIC foreign ministers took place, as a side event to the 61st UN General Assembly in New York. This was followed by a number of other meetings among representatives of the BRIC states. In the September 2007 and 2008 meetings, foreign ministers met once again in a side event to the 62nd UN General Assembly in New York, with next meetings of foreign ministers taking place in Russia (also see annexure 1.).

BRICS Timeline

2002

↓

BRIC, acronym created by Goldman Sachs analyst Jim O'Neill to indicate Brazil, Russia, India and China, which he assumed would be safe places for investors in the 21st century.

↓

2003

O'Neill and his colleagues produced a paper called "Dreaming with BRICS: The Path to 2050".

↓

2005

O'Neill explained why Korea and Mexico had not been included in BRIC.

↓

2008

Russia hosted the first formal BRIC summit, a meeting of BRIC foreign ministers in Yekaterinburg. BRIC leaders also met in Hokkaido, Japan (no documents issued from a meeting that took place during the G8 summit)

↓

2009

A formal gathering of all four BRIC heads of state, met in Yekaterinburg, Russia.

↓

2010

2nd BRIC Summit of Heads of State and Government were held at Brasilia, Brazil

↓

2011

The 3rd BRICS Summit was held in Sanya, Hainan, China under the theme *"Broad Vision, Shared Prosperity"*

↓

2012

The 4th BRICS Summit was held in Delhi, under the theme *"BRICS Partnership for Global Stability, Security and Prosperity".*

↓

2013

The 5th BRICS Summit was held in Durban, South Africa under the theme *"BRICS and Africa: Partnership for Development, Integration and Industrialization"*

↓

2014

The 6th BRICS Summit was held in Fortaleza, Brazil under the theme "Inclusive Growth: Sustainable Solutions".

↓

2015

7th BRICS Summit was held in Ufa, Russia under the theme "BRICS Partnership – a Powerful Factor of Global Development".

In June 2009, Russia hosted the first BRICS summit[3], which was attended by the heads of the state from four BRIC countries; Luiz Inácio Lula da Silva of Brazil, Dmitry Medvedev of Russia, Manmohan Singh of India and Hu Jintao of China. The first BRIC summit is important for many reasons. First, it institutionalized the informal BRIC group and laid the groundwork for BRIC(S) grouping. Second, although the first BRIC summit received less attention, as compared to the ninth summit of SCO, held a day earlier to the BRICS summit, it helped the member states to raise their international standing as a collective, enhancing their bargaining power than before in the international organizations. In fact, the act led to the initiation of 2010 IMF quota reform to increase the voting share of the developing countries. Third, the first summit also strengthened the intra-BRICs cooperation, encouraging the members to enter into agreements on issues such as food security, education, science and technology and health practices.

The main themes discussed during the Yekaterinburg summit (refer to annxure 1.2 &1.3) included the 2008 financial crisis, reform of the international financial institutions, major issues concerning the developing and less-developing countries, and also the socially vital areas where BRIC countries could strengthen their collaboration. The summit began by extending an emphasis to the role played by G20 in mitigating the negative effects of the economic crisis and delivered a warning against the global domination of the US dollar as the world's standard reserve currency. Few days before the summit, Russian President Dmitry Medvedev proposed that countries use a mix of regional reserve currencies to reduce reliance on the dollar.

The summit's joint declaration outlined the basis for BRICs formation which was to promote a more democratic and just multi-polar world order based on the rule of international law, equality, mutual respect, cooperation, coordinated action and collective decision-making of all states, envisioning a lead role for the UN in dealing with global challenges and threats. They proposed "to promote dialogue and cooperation among our countries in an incremental, proactive, pragmatic, open and transparent way". During this summit, Russia and China voiced their support for a greater role for Brazil and India in the UN by suggesting that they "understand and support their aspirations to play a greater role in the United Nations". Since then the BRICS statements subsequently mentioned this formulation without elaborating what the "greater role" would imply.

Broader issues such as diversification of energy resources, climate change problem, terrorism, the sustainability of the global economy, and an overall fairer global economic system were also discussed at the summit. On climate change issue they suggested to a "principle of common but differentiated responsibility".This resulted in a strong understanding among the BRICs nations that their contribution could make a significant difference in stepping up the multilateral efforts in achieving solutions to these problems. Particular emphasis was also laid on ending the informal agreement that the United States and Europe could appoint the World Bank president and IMF director, respectively. Rather, the BRIC took the position that those leadership positions should be appointed through "an open, transparent, and merit-based selection process" (Joint Statement of the BRIC Countries' Leaders 2009). However, at this stage, the BRIC nations clarified that they would work within the traditional structure of global governance by cooperating with the developed countries.

Along with a joint statement of the summit, a joint declaration on global food security was also issued by the BRICs states. The document outlines a number of issues of common understanding on food security. These include sharing of experiences in bio-fuel technology uses and ensuring sustainable production in accordance with the three pillars of sustainable development such as social, economic and environmental, to achieve the goal of global food security. They reiterated the importance to accelerate the Doha round of talks at the World Trade Organization (WTO) so that a fair and just agreement could be reached on the issue of reduction of agricultural subsidies. The document while emphasized the need to oppose protectionism, it made clear that the farmers from developing countries should receive adequate incentives for agricultural production.

In 2010, the ministers of agriculture of the BRIC nations met in Moscow (refer to annexure 4). They produced a joint declaration that focuses on establishing modes of coordinated action to pursue global food security. In the beginning of the declaration, there was a particular emphasis on family farming as one of the means to ensure sufficient production of grain, increase in living standards and the development of rural areas. Since BRICs countries are large agricultural producers, they play an important role in the global agriculture market. Therefore, to achieve the above objectives, they outlined few priority areas:

i) to establish an agricultural information database that would help countries compute supply and demand and establish grain reserves,
ii) development of a general strategy for ensuring access to food for the most vulnerable members of the population,

iii) to reduce the effects of global climate change on food security through comprehensive adaptive measures, including exchange of experience, best practices and public policies,

iv) to enhance cooperation in the field of agricultural technology and innovation.

An expert working group was set up to implement these measures, and it will meet on a regular basis, including through video conference. Thus, despite the criticism about the nature of BRICs grouping and marginal media attention, the first summit was a success. It not only formalized the experiment but also raised the individual stature of BRICs countries and they depicted themselves as responsible stakeholders in key issues of global governance.

The second BRIC summit[4] took place in April in 2010 in Brasilia and focused on strengthening intra-BRIC cooperation initiatives at different levels of government and civil society, including business and union representatives and think tanks (see annexures 2 & 3). The joint statement from this summit reiterated the importance of BRICs countries as engines of economic growth as well as in reducing imbalances in global economic development. It mentioned "a significant contribution from BRIC countries, have greatly increased resources available to the IMF". The declaration focused on increasing the voting quotas of the BRICS within the IMF and fostering greater involvement in the choice of leaders for the IMF and the World Bank. They also urged the Finance Ministers and Central Bank Governors to discuss modalities of cooperation in regional monetary arrangements, to facilitate local currency trade settlement arrangement between the BRICs countries. Rather than simply calling for reform in global economic governance, the BRICS also undertook an agreement to increase cooperation between major domestic financial institutions. In addition, the declaration suggested to "encouraging the dialogue among civilizations, cultures, religions and peoples".

In 2010, several BRICS banks—the National Bank for Economic and Social Development, the China Development Bank Corporation (CDB), the Export–import Bank of India (Exim Bank), and the State Corporation Bank for Development and Foreign Economic Affairs (Vnesheconombank)—agreed to cooperate in the global economy. A Memorandum of Cooperation was signed among BRIC Development Banks and the first edition of the BRIC Statistical publication was also released. This marked the first step towards developing multilateral financial cooperation within the BRICS countries, creating basic mechanisms for settling payments and financing investment projects in local currencies. Thus, in the year following the first BRICs summit, both intra-BRICs cooperation and cooperation on global affairs was taken to a higher level by the BRICs countries.

In the BRICs Foreign Ministers meeting in New York in 2010, it was agreed upon that South Africa may be invited to join BRIC. In December 2010, South Africa was officially invited to join the group at the next meeting of the heads of state, which would take place in April 2011 in Sanya on the island of Hainan, China[5].

The Sanya Summit[6] which commenced under the theme "*Broad Vision, Shared Prosperity*", focused on increasing engagement and cooperation with non-BRICS countries, ongoing international conflicts, climate change issues, and the host of socio-economic challenges facing the Least Developed Countries in Africa (see annexures 2 & 3). They also extended full support to an early accession of Russia to the WTO. With regard to international conflicts, BRICS expressed concerns for the ongoing turbulence in West Asia, the North African and West African regions and on issue of Libya, it sided with the African Union High-Level Panel Initiative on Libya on evolving a "peaceful means and dialogue". Its position on international conflict was that "the independence, sovereignty, unity and territorial integrity of each nation should be respected", although they added that the "legitimate aspirations of their peoples" be heard.

In terms of new areas of cooperation, the BRICS expressed support for nuclear energy in the future energy mix and also expanded cooperation on the development of clean energy and encouraged technical co-operation in this sector. Fifty of the 66 nuclear reactors currently under construction are in BRICS states. Other areas of cooperation included meetings between representatives of international organizations, meetings of experts in agriculture, meetings of the heads of national statistical institutions, and financial co-operation between the BRICS Development Banks. Other issues included the establishment of new areas of cooperation: BRICS Friendship Cities and Local Governments Cooperation Forum in 2011 in China; meetings of ministers of health; and support for joint research on economic and commercial issues and co-operation in the areas of culture and sport.

The joint declaration outlined support to several international agreements and international organizations such as the UN, the G20, the IMF, the Millennium Development Goals, the UN Framework Convention on Climate Change, the Kyoto Protocol, the Rio Declaration on Environment and Development, the Agenda 21, the Johannesburg Plan of Implementation, the NEPAD, and the WTO. Finally, the declaration also proposed a "BRICS-

UNESCO GROUP", aimed at developing common strategies within the mandate of the Organization.

New Delhi hosted the 4th Summit of Heads of Government in March 2012[7], under the theme *"BRICS Partnership for Global Stability, Security and Prosperity"*. While the first three summit meetings emphasized on the desirables for a new international political and security order, the New Delhi meeting for the first time emphasized on the financial aspect and made some concrete proposals in the direction of setting up the bank (see annexures 2 & 3). The main focus of the summit was global economic recovery, international stability, particularly security in the West Asia and North Africa, as well as a focus on climate change. The meeting called for a "comprehensive, just and lasting settlement of the Arab-Israeli conflict" and an "immediate end to all violence and violations of human rights in Syria". The Delhi Declaration exalted BRICS relatively quick recovery from the global financial crisis and expressed concerns about ineffectiveness of IMF to implement 2010 quota reforms. Emphasizing the need for a financial institution that would supplement the multilateral and regional financial institutions, BRICS began plans to establish a BRICS Development Bank. The BRICS Development Bank was designed to reduce the bureaucratic frustration that developing countries have faced in accessing funds from the Bretton Woods Institutions. Five banks of the BRICS states, viz., Brazilian Development Bank, the State Corporation Bank for Development and Foreign Economic Affairs of Russia, the Export-Import Bank of India, the China Development Bank and the Development Bank of Southern Africa have been identified for making credit available in local currencies and cut transaction costs among these states. The next step for the Development Bank is to make credit available for infrastructure projects, small and medium enterprises and for sustainable development of the BRICS states.[8] However, initially several debates indicated to differences among the BRICS states on several issues relating to the bank.[9] Nevertheless, the design and ethos of the BRICS bank was worked out further at the 5th summit, which took place in Durban in 2013. At the September 2013 8th summit meeting of the G-20 at St. Petersburg, Russian President announced formally – in the presence of the BRICS leaders- the $100 billion fund.[10] It was agreed that China's contribution to this fund will be 41 percent ($41 billion), while Russia, India and Brazil will each contribute $18 billion and South Africa $5 billion.[11]

The 5th BRICS summit[12], titled as "*BRICS and Africa—Partnerships for Integration and Industrialization*" largely focused on furthering institutional links between the BRICS members and on the role of the BRICS in the developing world (see annexures 2 & 3). In the eThekwini Declaration, there was a special mention of strengthening cooperation between the BRICS countries and the African continent. Subsequent meetings acquired this flavor of involving other emerging or developing countries in the region for the overall broad basing of the BRICS phenomenon in the international relations. Significantly, the meeting decided to "aim at progressively developing BRICS into a full-fledged mechanism of current and long-term coordination on a wide range of key issues of the world economy and politics". The 2013 Durban Declaration also demonstrated BRICS member states policy interest in cyberspace. The joint statement highlighted the "critical positive role the Internet plays" and the BRICS' belief that "it's important to contribute to and participate in a peaceful, secure, and open cyberspace." The 2013 summit, however, remains important particularly for agreeing formally to establish the BRICS Development Bank, with a focus on lending for infrastructural projects in the developing world. The summit also extended a positive nod to the creation of a Contingent Reserve Arrangement (CRA) amongst BRICS countries with an initial size of US$ 100 billion, as a safety net for the crisis.

During the 6th BRICS summit in Fortaleza in 2014[13], which signified the completion of one cycle of the BRICS, the bank was formally established (see annexures 2 & 3). Establishment of the bank suggested that unlike the Russia-India-China trilateral meetings which remained declarative and aspirational, the BRICS can move into a more concrete and constructive alternative. The bank, with its headquarter at Shanghai and first chair of the Board of Governors from Russia., would contribute to the efforts to eliminate infrastructure gaps and meet the sustainable-development needs of the BRICS member states and of other emerging and developing economies. With capital of $100 billion, including $50 billion of equally shared among the members, the bank would be one of the world's largest multilateral financial development institutions. The concept of a currency contingency fund was further developed. The Treaty for the establishment of the Contingent Reserve Arrangement was signed followed by the signing of the Memorandum of Understanding on Cooperation among BRICS Export Credit and Guarantees Agencies meant to improve the support for increasing trade opportunities among BRICS nations.

The BRICS countries expressed their commitment to the G20 goal of lifting collective GDP by more than 2 percent above the trajectory implied by current policies over the coming 5 years. New areas of economic cooperation were also discussed at the 6th summit, including the development of a BRICS Interbank Cooperation Mechanism, a BRICS Business Council, Strategy for Multilateral Economic Cooperation and the Roadmap for Investment

Cooperation, a BRICS Banking Forum, and a BRICS Exchanges Alliance. Driven by Russia, there was also a focus on increasing the inter-institutional relationship and trade among the BRICS in the area of energy resources. Russia also proposed to establish a BRICS Energy Association, a Fuel Reserve Bank, and a BRICS Energy Policy Institute. Also, the way BRICS leaders rallied behind Russia, facing isolation from the West over its role in Crimea and Ukraine indicated their heightened 'south-south' cooperation against the north.

The seventh BRICS Summit[14] was held under the theme ""*BRICS Partnership – a Powerful Factor of Global Development*" in Ufa, Russia. In the backdrop of the Ukraine-Crimea tussle and the European Union sanctions on Russia, the meeting provided an opportunity for Russia to showcase its skills (see annexures 2 & 3). The two financial institutions of BRICS, Development Bank and CRA entered into force during the Ufa Summit. It was also decided that BRICS would hold a meeting with the Heads of States and Governments of the countries of the Eurasian Economic Union and the Shanghai Cooperation Organization (SCO), as well as the Heads of observer States of the SCO. Putin said at Ufa that the coming together of the BRICS, SCO and EEU can provide a "powerful economic breakthrough". Russia concluded $400 billion gas supply deal in May 2014 and invited Greece to join the BRICS bank. An idea for a parliamentary forum among the BRICS members was also mooted.

In a step further to promote exports among the BRICS countries, the BRICS countries have agreed to the establishment of an annual BRICS ECA meeting and the inaugural of this new format was held on the sidelines of Ufa summit. It was during this summit, the BRICS countries, for the first time, blamed the US directly for failing to ratify the IMF 2010 reform package. Among new areas of cooperation, ICT including internet governance received greater focus among the BRICS states, who expressed their support for an open internet, without much unilateral interference. However, the BRICS lack joint proposal on either a code of conduct on cyber-security or on a new internet governance body.

Overview of BRICS Economies

The countries comprising the BRICS are not an obvious set. In fact they have dissimilar economic models, cultural traditions and political systems.[15] However, all of them possess modern industries, share strong ties with the global economy and provide investors with higher profit opportunities than the developed countries[16]. Each of the BRICS components has its own advantage, with Brazil and South Africa termed in common parlance as global resources base, Russia as global energy station, India as global office and China as global manufacturing base. BRICs' share as a destination for global FDI continues to rise and reports suggest that its importance to global equity markets would increase to around 10 per cent by 2020, depending on the extent of capital market development. Further, market capitalization in the BRICs economies have increased in the coming years with a large increase in capital market activity. The combined market capitalization of Chinese and Indian stocks rose to a record $6.4 trillion in December 2014, with the Shanghai Composite Index and India's S&P BSE Sensex Index recording their biggest annual gains in five years. Judged by market capitalization, the Chinese market stands out today The Shenzhen, Shanghai and Hong Kong stock markets had a market capitalization of $8.1 trillion at the end of 2015. The Shenzhen stock exchange is overwhelmingly dominated by SOEs which are the back bone of the Chinese economy, while the Shanghai is not fully opened to foreign investors.

Fig. I.3: Market Capitalization of BRICS Domestic Companies (Current US$)

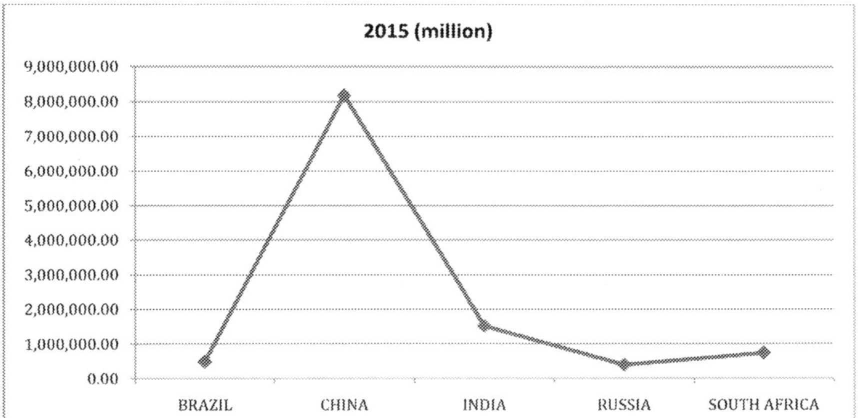

Source: World Federation of Exchanges Database.

The BRICS economies have shown impressive growth, increasing their share in world exports from 8 per cent in 2000 to 19 per cent in 2014. Their share of world trade of goods and services has also grown over time, with the U.S. as the BRICS's largest export market. In 2014 BRICS traded more than US$ 3 trillion in goods and imported over US$ 700 billion in services whilst exporting around US$ 500 billion. The U.S., Germany, and Japan continue to remain the leading sources of imports to the BRICS countries.

Fig. I.4: GDP per capita in US$ billion, PPP for BRICS

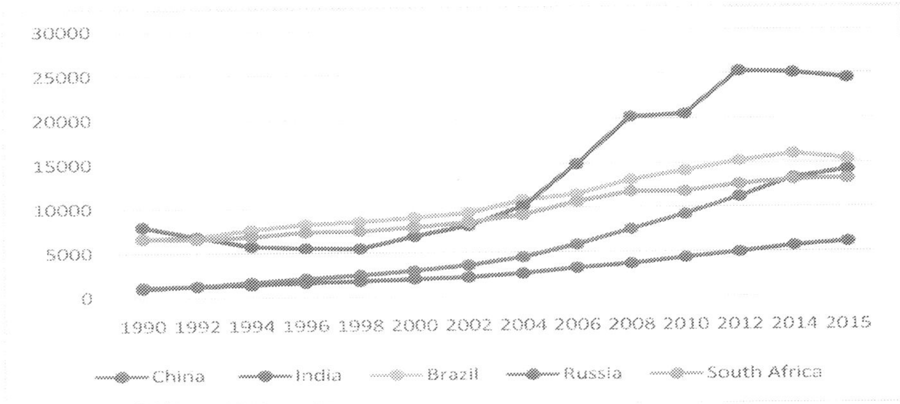

Source: World Bank.

Table I.2: Exports of Goods and Services (% of GDP)

Country	*1960*	*2015*
Brazil	7.1	13.0
China	4.3	22.4
India	4.4	NA
Russian Federation	NA	29.5
South Africa	30.6	30.9

Fig. I.5: Exports of Goods and Services

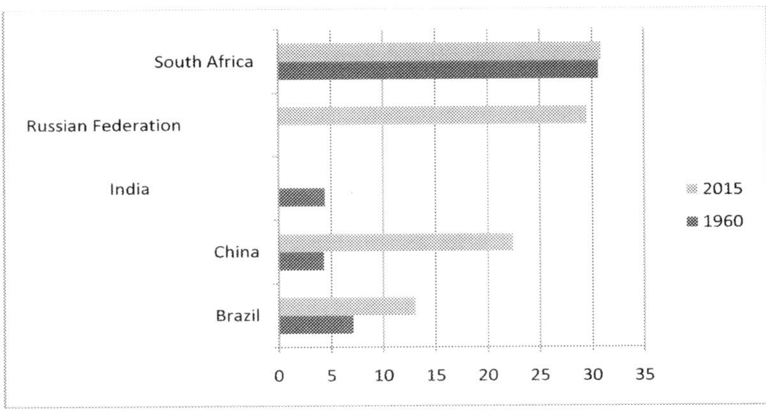

Source: World Bank.

Starting with a low base, the intra-BRICS trade is evolving gradually. China is the largest contributor to intra-BRICS exports, accounting for 51 percent of the total intra-BRICS trade (refer to annexure 6). Intra-BRICS trade increased from $593.5 billion in 2012 to $653 billion in 2014.[17] On the other hand, the intra-BRICS exports grew from $34 billion in 2001 to $244 billion in 2014 (see annexure 6). In merchandise trade, China remains the largest exporter and the second largest importer of merchandise goods in 2014. Russia, India and Brazil have also entered into the list of top 20 world merchandise exporters and importers[18].

The BRICS countries encompass 30 percent of the world's area and about 42 percent of the total population (see annexure 5). In 2015, they accounted for a total nominal GDP of $16.92 trillion, equivalent to 23.1 percent of world GDP. The demographic trends, labour supply dynamics seem to remain favourable for Brazil, India and South Africa (see annexure 5).

The working age population continues to expand in Brazil, India and South Africa, hence the possibility of reaping demographic dividend is present while China witnesses a declining trend with the number of its citizens aged 65 years and above, are increasing by 4 percent every year. Russia, on the other hand has faced negative demographic trends since 1990, with the population decreasing by 3.7 million. However, in the Human Development Index, Russia, Brazil and China are in the high HDI category (2014) with rankings of 57, 79 and 91 respectively, while India has the lowest Human Development Index (HDI) among all BRICS nations, with its life expectancy higher only than South Africa (refer to annexure 5).

Also being the growth centres, the BRICS countries together contributed about 38 percent of global carbon emissions in 2014. China by far, has the biggest share in the BRICS, which constitutes more than 24 percent of the global total, whereas Brazil and India remain below the world average. India despite being the fourth largest carbon emitter continues to be far behind the other three top big emitters in terms of per capita emission whereas Brazil relies more on the use of hydropower and biofuels. In case of Russia, although its emission levels had dropped significantly after 1990, it remains fourth largest emitter of green house gases. South Africa, on the other hand, does not follow the emission trajectory of developed countries but remains responsible for nearly half the CO_2 emissions in the entire African continent.

Table I.3: BRICS CO_2 Emissions (metric tons per capita)

Country	*1960*	*2011*
Brazil	0.6	2.2
China	1.2	6.7
India	0.3	1.7
Russian Federation	NA	12.6
South Africa	5.6	9.3

Source: *World Bank* Data.

Fig. I.6: BRICS CO_2 Emissions

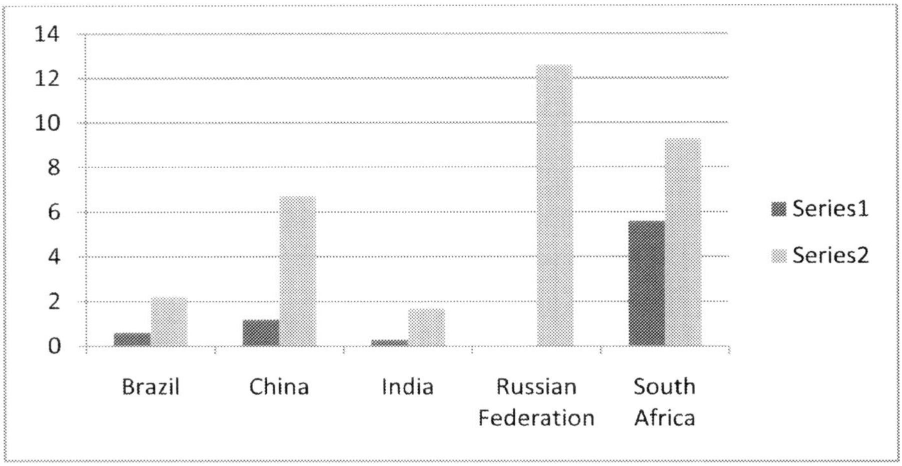

Brazil

Brazil, the largest country in South America has established itself as one of the significant emerging economies of the 21st century. Owing to its size and economy, it holds strong influence in the region, and aspires to join the ranks of major powers (see annexures 5, 6, 7 & 8). It is a key player in the south-south cooperation and actively participates in the international institutions and forums as a representative of the developing countries. It joined the G-20 group of Finance and Economy Ministers, in multilateral efforts to stabilize the global economy and reform the international monetary system, and it resulted in its inclusion in the Financial Stability Board and the Basel Committee. Thus, as a member of powerful multilateral forums like G-20 and BRICS, it enjoys outstanding edge.

BRAZIL
Major Economic Indicators (Year- 2015)

GDP Growth (%)	-3.8
Inflation, consumer prices (%)	9.0
Central Government Debt (% of GDP)	66.5
Gross Savings (% of GDP)	14
Total reserves (gold, current billion US$)	35.64

Source: World Bank national accounts data, and OECD National Accounts data files

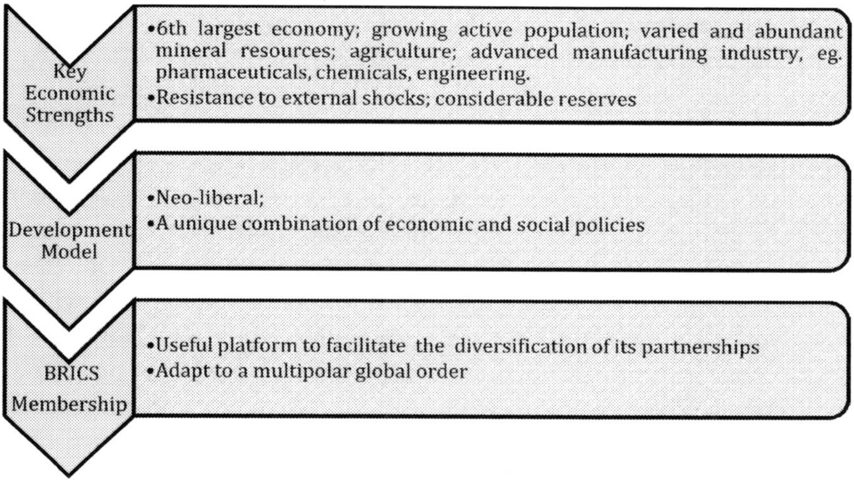

Fig. I.7: Inflation, Consumer Prices (annual %)

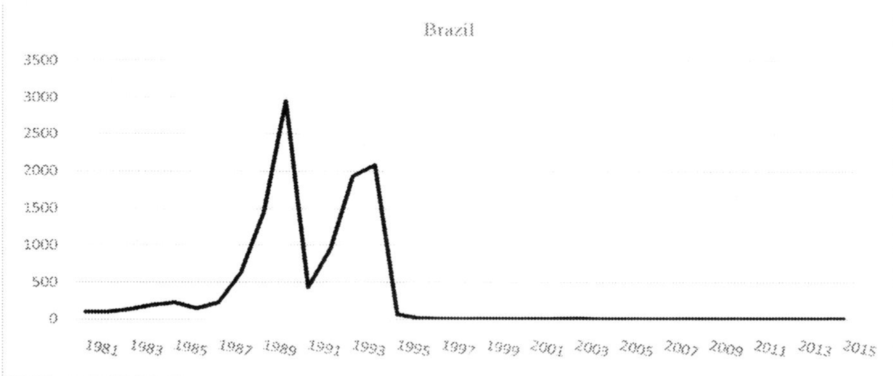

Source: *World Bank.*

Fig. I.8: Gross Savings (% of GDP)

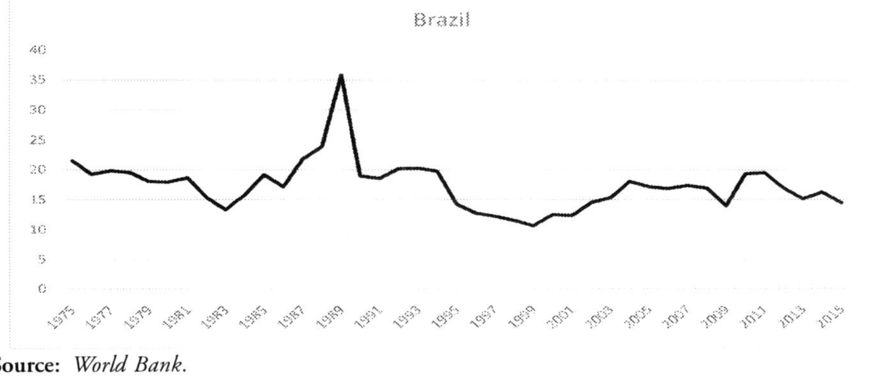

Source: *World Bank.*

Like other members of BRICS, it has taken good advantage of its size and natural resources to foster country's economic development. Primarily an agricultural country, it has diversified its economy with export of manufactured goods constituting almost 60 percent of its total exports. Brazil's agricultural sector is divided between field crop and livestock, 60 percent and 40 percent respectively. Both farm products and livestock have become competitive and hold good share in international markets. In its relations with other countries, especially the developing ones, Brazil has entered into numerous 'Technical Cooperation' (TC) agreements, which deal with the exchange of knowledge and practices, not monetary transfers. Although this is a traditional aspect of Brazilian foreign policy, the number of projects and countries involved has grown markedly over the past decade. Brazil's initiatives in the health sector have also given it considerable prominence in the international affairs. It has had a host of health related TCs with developing countries. It has worked consistently to combat HIV/Aids and advocated for an easy and cheap access to ARV drugs and was the first developing country to offer free ARV treatment to HIV/AIDS patients, despite an assessment by the World Bank that such a policy was not cost-effective.

Brazil is also known to be an active player in global environmental negotiations, hosting, for example, the UN Conference on Environment and Development in 1992. Lula's presidency strongly advocated for the developing countries, based on the principle 7 of the Rio Declaration 'common but differentiated responsibilities' over environmental commitments, and that the developed world should acknowledge the responsibility to reduce their emissions and the need to ensure the right of poor countries to develop.

Brazilian diplomacy under Lula worked on stimulating the debate on the use of biofuels, as carrying considerable potential for developing countries to promote sustainable development. To this regard, Brazil and the other BRIC leaders in its joint statement on global food security in 2009 emphasized the importance of sustainable bio-fuels which constitutes in their opinion, 'a driving force for social inclusion and income distribution mainly in the impoverished rural areas of developing and least developed countries'.

Thus, Brazil's pathway to power is through its active participation in international institutions as a means to democratize and augment the efficiency of organizations through effective bargaining strategies. Brazil's diplomacy since 1990s has advocated for a strong representation of developing countries and remains an important broker in many instances, on the international agenda. However, in the context of BRICS, Brazil needs to pull up its growth rates, its relative share of the world GDP and also its intensity of participation in international trade.

Russia

Like other BRICS countries, Russia's economy has undergone reforms after the Soviet collapse in the 1990s. The country experienced strong economic growth, averaging an annual growth rate of 6.7 percent from after the 1998 ruble collapse until 2007, with the most dynamic sectors including construction, transport and telecommunications, retail and wholesale trade, and financial services (see annexures 5, 6, 7 & 8). However, Russia's economic recovery has mostly been dependent on the earnings from its boom in earnings from oil and gas exports. Earnings from oil increased after the rise of world crude oil prices in the late 1990s and early 2000s.

RUSSIA

Major Economic Indicators (Year -2015)

GDP Growth (%)	-3.7
Inflation, consumer prices (%)	15.5
Central Government Debt (% of GDP)	17.70
Gross Savings (% of GDP)	26
Total reserves (gold, current billion US$)	36.80

Source: World Bank national accounts data, and OECD National Accounts data files

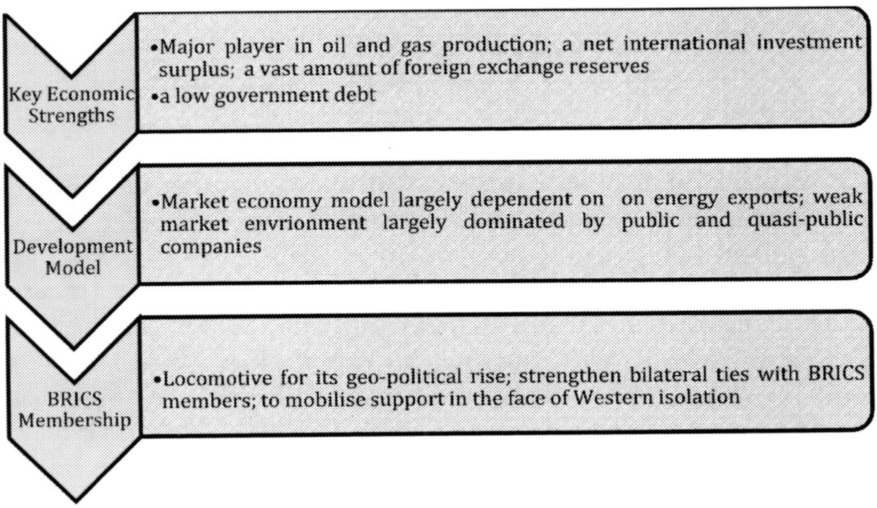

Fig. I.9: Inflation, Consumer Prices (annual %)

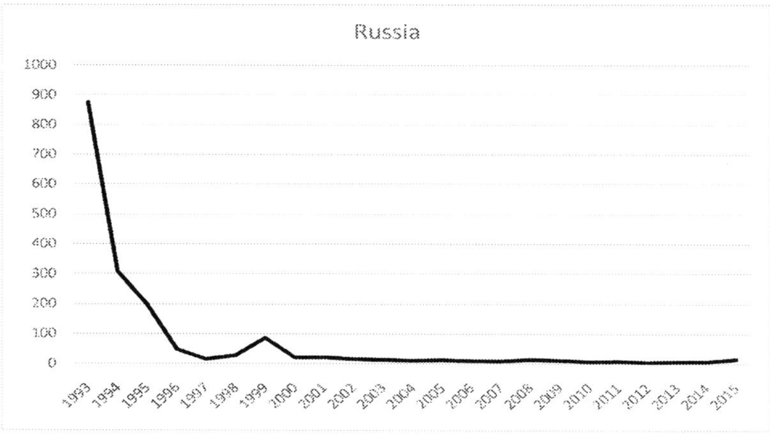

Source: *World Bank.*

Fig. I.10: Gross Savings (% of GDP)

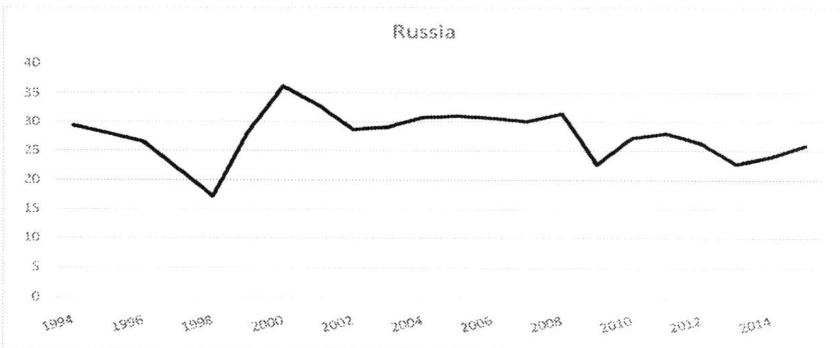

Source: *World Bank.*

Russia ranks in the world's top ten resource rich countries and oil and to a lesser extent gas contribute around 50 percent to the federal budget. Russia's resurgence and its desire to regain great power status in the post Soviet era, has been through a number of means. BRICS is one such means to assert itself in the international affairs. Its frustration with the West, especially US and EU coupled with an ailing domestic economy, has largely driven its interest behind the BRIC formation as it believes that BRICS have an immense potential to emerge as one of the main poles in multi-polar world order. In this regard, Russia's interests and policy priorities in the BRICS are best described in the document titled "Concept of participation of the Russian Federation in BRICS" prepared by the Foreign Ministry on the eve of the BRICS' Durban summit in March 2013.

Compared to the other BRICS economies, especially India and China, Russia's economic recovery after the financial crisis remains slow, and it faces significant challenges in terms of population decline, its growing budget deficit, continued reliance on energy exports, and domestic corruption. However, despite the economic slowdown, unemployment remains at a very low level, indicating a tight labour market and a shrinking working age population. Also, there is a lack of competitiveness and innovation in Russian business, with 10 percent Russian businesses engaged in technological, organisational or marketing innovation.

India

In order of rising global influence and also within BRICS, India comes second after China. India's economic growth, its increasing working age population, rising foreign exchange reserves and growing transnational activities of its firms, remain important sources of its rising power status in the world (see annexures 5, 6, 7 & 8). While economic growth has been high, India's share of world trade continues to be low. Domestic investment and consumption constitute the backbone of its economic growth and also act as a safety valve from global financial shocks.

India's economy is divided into three sectors: agriculture which accounts for a quarter of the gross national product, manufacturing constituting another quarter and the high-tech service sector, which now makes up fully half of the gross national product. In the post-crisis period, when the global economy is emerging from the sluggish performance, India finds an opportunity in the global manufacturing market, especially with costs of manufacturing going up in China. Most of Indian businesses import components and specialized inputs (such as specialized chemicals and additives) comprise whereas finished products and manufactured inputs dominate exports. West Asia and North Africa region forms the most attractive export market for Indian businesses, followed by Europe.

INDIA

Major Economic Indicators (Year -2015)

GDP Growth (%)	7.6
Inflation, consumer prices (%)	5.9
Central Government Debt (% of GDP)	67.20
Gross Savings (% of GDP)	29.01
Total reserves (gold, current billion US$)	35.33

Source: World Bank national accounts data, and OECD National Accounts data files

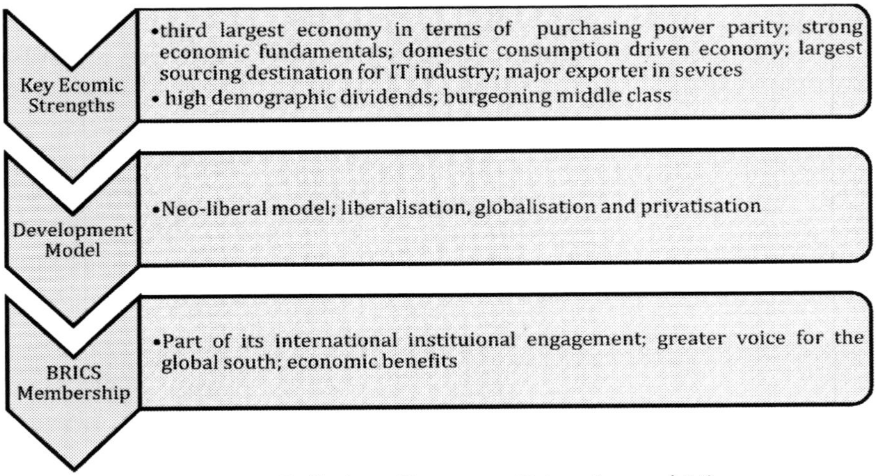

Fig. I.11: Inflation, Consumer Prices (annual %)

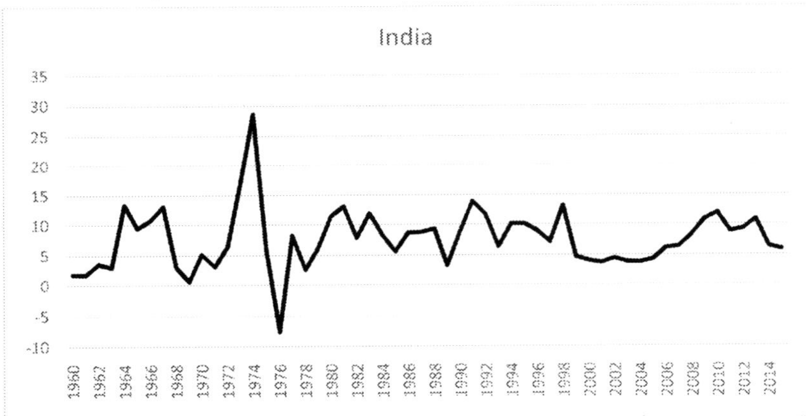

Source: *World Bank.*

Fig. I.12: Gross Savings (% of GDP)

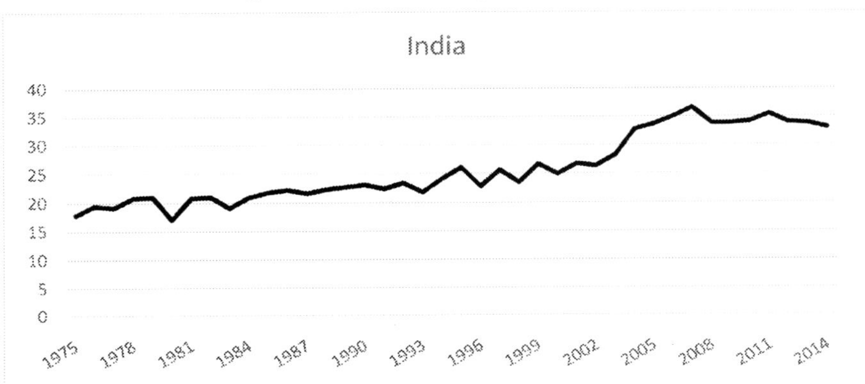

Source: *World Bank.*

India also has the second fastest growing service sector, contributing about 61 percent to India's GDP, 51 percent of FDI and 28 per cent of employment. Information technology, in which India leads the globe, has its major exporting destinations in the United States, United Kingdom and Europe. India has strengthened its cooperation with countries with abundant natural resources and advanced technological cooperation with the developed countries.

India's strong diplomatic efforts towards seeking an important role in international regimes, has also demonstrated its rise in power. In fact India has a never been a silent participant in the international institutions. Ranging from its active role in G77, NIEO and Non-Aligned Movement and presently, it's activism in the WTO, IBSA, BRICS, suggests that India is expanding its influence through multilateral diplomacy and has emerged as a seasoned player in these forums. With regard to its joining the "BRIC" in 2009, Indian Prime Minister Manmohan Singh said, "An important goal of BRIC countries is to reform the global governance mechanisms to reflect the current reality of the international community".

India has stepped up its cooperation with the BRICS countries. Also, as an effort to establish the democratic and accountable character of BRICS, the Ministry of External Affairs is funding a 'Civil BRICS' conference in October, which will run parallel to the 8th BRICS summit. However, the country remains plagued by its own problems. In addition to the common challenges of poverty, unemployment and corruption faced by developing countries in general, India suffers from a weak manufacturing base to meet the demands of its population, poor R&D infrastructure, inadequate health facilities and sustainable development issues.

China

After just one and half decade of reform, China had emerged as a new economic miracle in Asia. Over that period, the country had undergone a shift from a largely agrarian society to an industrial powerhouse. By 1995, China had become the world's tenth largest producer of export goods, the second largest recipient of foreign direct investment and was among the top ten trading nations of the world. By mid 1990s, American multinational corporations like General Motors, Coco Cola and Pepsi made an entry into the Chinese market as they became aware of the tremendous business opportunities offered by China at the dawn of opening up era. The gradual process of market liberalization brought about several changes in China's foreign trade regime, before it established itself as a major global exporter. It allowed for the reopening of the Shanghai stock exchange in December 1990 and following years of arduous negotiations, China entered the WTO in 2001, eventually leading to its integration with multilateral trading order. In 2010, China surpassed Japan to become the world's second largest economy.

CHINA
Major Economic Indicators (Year -2015)

GDP Growth (%)	6.9
Inflation, consumer prices (%)	1.4
Central Government Debt (% of GDP)	43.9
Gross Savings (% of GDP)	49
Total reserves (gold, current billion US$)	3405.25

Source: World Bank national accounts data, and OECD National Accounts data files.

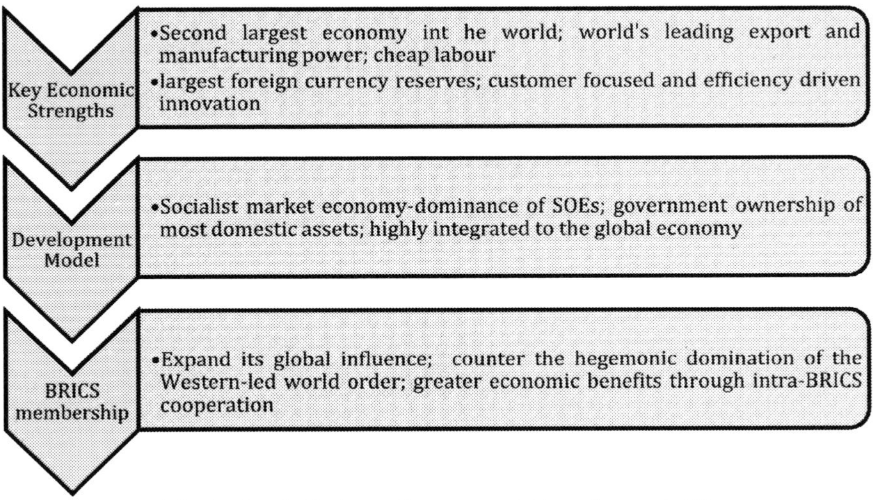

Fig. I.13: Inflation, Consumer Prices (annual %)

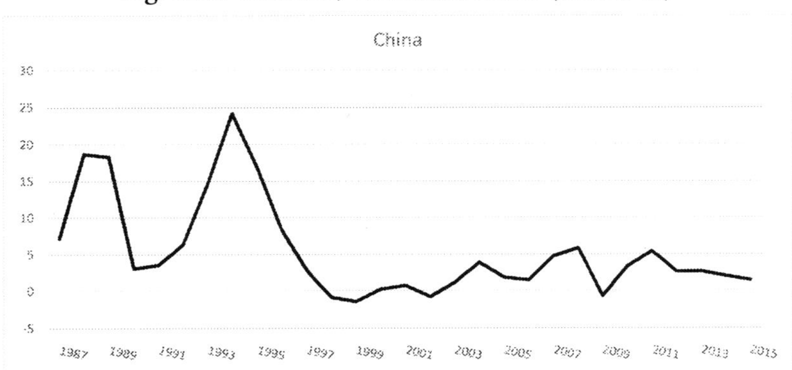

Source: *World Bank.*

Fig. I.14: Gross Savings (% of GDP)

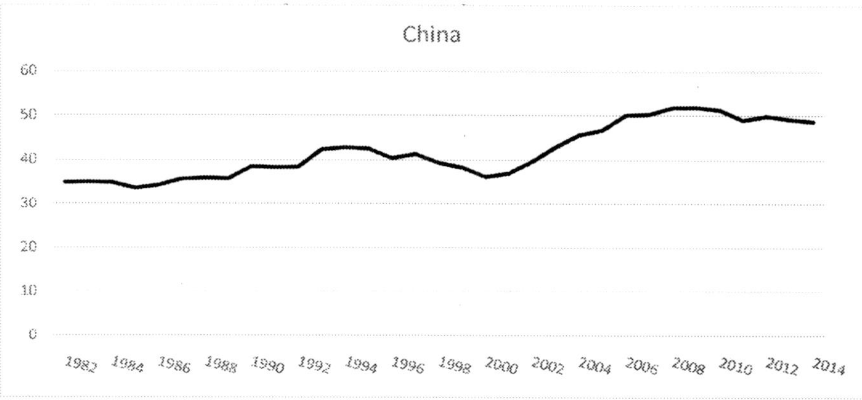

Source: *World Bank.*

China's population is the largest in the world, larger than the combined population of high income economies. As per the IMF statistics 2014, China surpassed 17 percent of the world GDP (based on purchasing parity) exceeding U.S.A's 16 percent GDP (see annexures 5, 6, 7 & 8). China's growth relies heavily on external demand and investment with much of that investment concentrated in manufacturing, followed by infrastructure and real estate sector.

China's growing economic power has led it to become increasingly involved in global economic affairs and policy initiatives. China's 'One-Belt One Road' project followed by the creation of two investment banks, Asian Infrastructure Investment Bank (AIIB), the BRICS Bank, in order to redirect the surplus and capital for regional infrastructure development as a means to improve trade and bilateral relations with ASEAN, Central Asian and European countries.

China also attaches a great importance to the BRICS grouping. China not only has a higher GDP, share in global trade and foreign exchange reserves, but also has raised the economic credentials of this diverse geopolitical grouping. In turn, BRICS has created a favourable external environment for China to pursue its interests as well as use the collective voice of BRICS to challenge the hegemonic leadership of the US in the global governance. Yet China remains a developing country (its per capita income is lower than the US) and its market reforms are incomplete. SOEs still continue to have a strong grip on the economy's most fundamental sectors.

As a major developing country, China faces certain development challenges. The level of market openness as well as general market competition needs to be improved. The development of legislative system is unable to meet the market economy's development needs. Besides, Chinese economy suffers from insufficient domestic consumption, weak demand for investment, limited natural resources and a growth driven by low costs rather than an innovation led model.

South Africa

Like other BRICS economies, South Africa has undergone a remarkable transformation since its democratic transition in 1994 but its economic performance over the decades has not been very impressive. Its economy ranks 32 out of 184 countries and comes in the category of middle-income economies of the world (see annexures 5, 6, 7 & 8). South Africa's per capital income is larger than that of both China and India, and it has one of the highest ratios of market capitalisation in the world. Its domestic economy has a well-developed tertiary sector, which accounted for more than 65 percent of the country's GDP in 2014. The tertiary sector is dominated by the financial services sector, largely driven by a strong banking system, trade comprising retail, wholesale and motor trade, and transport related services. However, the primary sector comprising of agriculture, fishing, mining and the share of the secondary sectors, particularly manufacturing, have maintained their modest share of GDP over time.

SOUTH AFRICA

Major Economic Indicators (Year -2015)

GDP Growth (%)	1.3
Inflation, consumer prices (%)	4.6
Central Government Debt (% of GDP)	50.1
Gross Savings (% of GDP)	15.4
Total reserves (gold, current $)	45.88

Source: World Bank national accounts data, and OECD National Accounts data files.

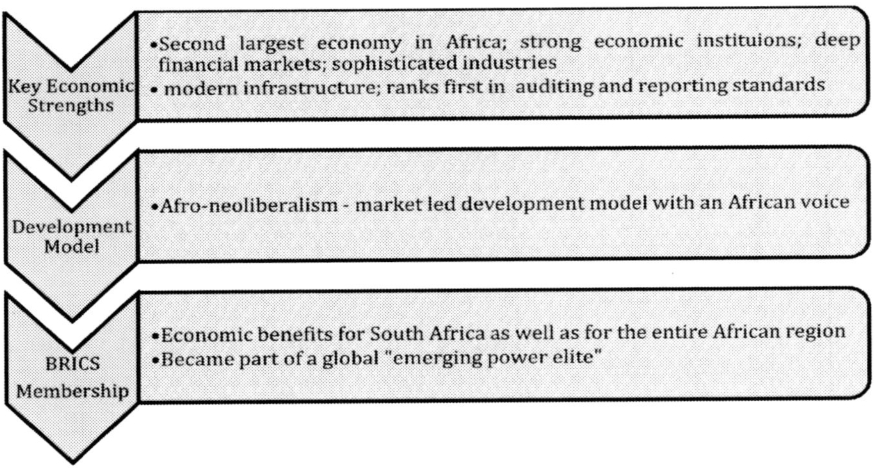

Fig. I.15: Inflation, Consumer Prices (annual %)

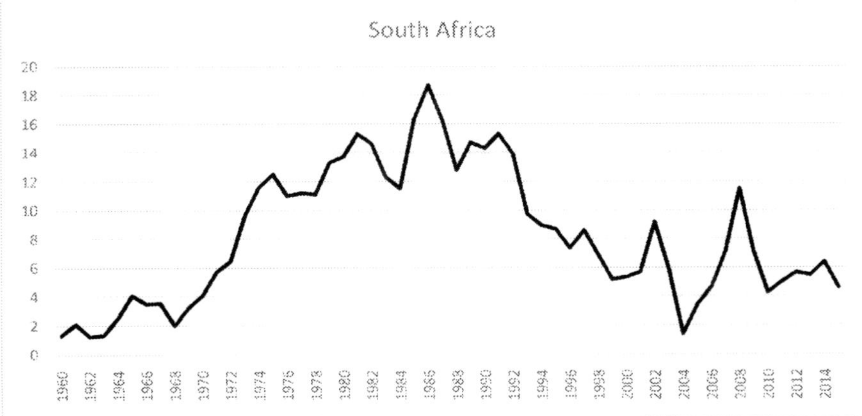

Source: *World Bank.*

Fig. I.16: Gross Savings (% of GDP)

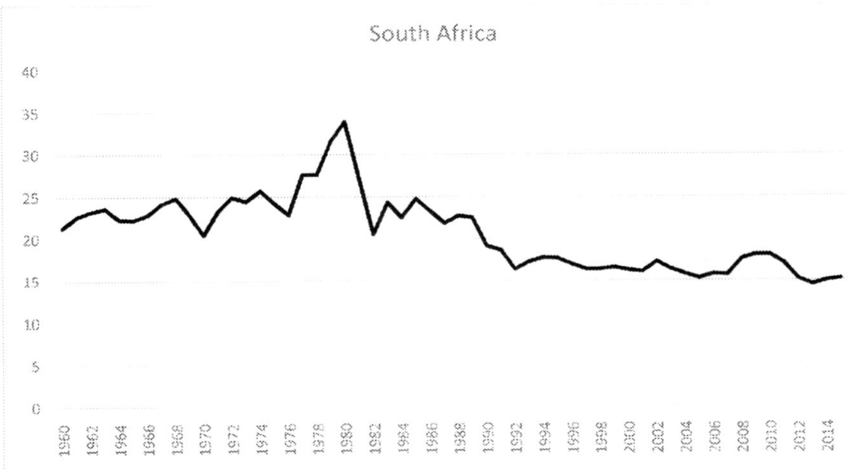

Source: *World Bank.*

Although the country is renowned for an abundance of mineral resources, accounting for a significant proportion of world production and reserves, South Africa's mining industry is far from being fully tapped. It is also the world's biggest producer of gold and platinum and one of the leading producers of base metals and coal. Its agro-processing sector has also been identified as a high growth potential, but faces challenges of import competition, limited markets and unstable currency and exchange rate. Therefore, the services sectors remain the pillar of overall economic growth in South Africa. Given this economic background which is much lightweight in comparison to the other BRIC members, South Africa's joining of the group has raised many eyebrows.

However, for the BRICS members, South Africa represents the economic and political link to the African continent, and an increased access to African markets. According to the South African government, the grouping through joint ventures and cooperation has helped in boosting South Africa's trade and investment, both locally and globally. Among all the BRICS countries, its partnership with China has been very beneficial for the region, and the cooperation between the two is steadily growing over the last few years. It is currently India's second largest trading partner in Africa and bilateral trade between the two countries rose to $15 billion in 2015. The South African government has also emphasized the importance of BRICS in its foreign policy priorities, which enables it to forge deeper trade ties with the BRIC members.

Thus, consistent with the diversity of the group with respect to history, size, economic profile, and political systems, each country continues to bring a particular set of national preferences to the ongoing creation of BRICS process and the various forms of cooperation that preceded it.

Setting up a Different Kitchen

The subtitle of this volume is "setting up a different kitchen" [另起炉灶]. This broad policy was suggested by China's leader Mao Zedong at the origins of the People's Republic of China (PRC) in 1949. The contributors to this volume, who are all China focused, believe that this phrase is appropriate and relevant to varying degrees to the subject under consideration. China's leaders, officials, scholars and media speak about this extensively, even in relation to the BRICS phenomenon.

Since the founding of the PRC, the concept of "setting up a different kitchen" has been applied by the Chinese leadership in its diplomatic practice. The concept had been utilized in different and innovative ways for the past more than six decades. In the Chinese literature, many a time the concept connoted to a complete break from the past diplomatic practices and reinventing the diplomatic wheel once again or simply making a fresh start in the diplomatic work.

As the following graph from the China National Knowledge Initiative (CNKI) data base indicates a number of articles and reports were published by Chinese scholars at the universities and think tanks on the concept and dynamics of "setting up a different kitchen" in 1958-2015 period. This suggests to the enduring influence of this concept in China. It also indicates that this concept has been attracting more attention since the early 1990s – coinciding with China joining several multilateral institutions during the reform period – reaching its peak in 2006 (30 articles), 2013 (42 articles) and 2015 (43 articles). This suggests that indeed the concept has been in high circulation in the last one decade as compared to the previous period.

Fig. I.17: CNKI Database on Academic Trends

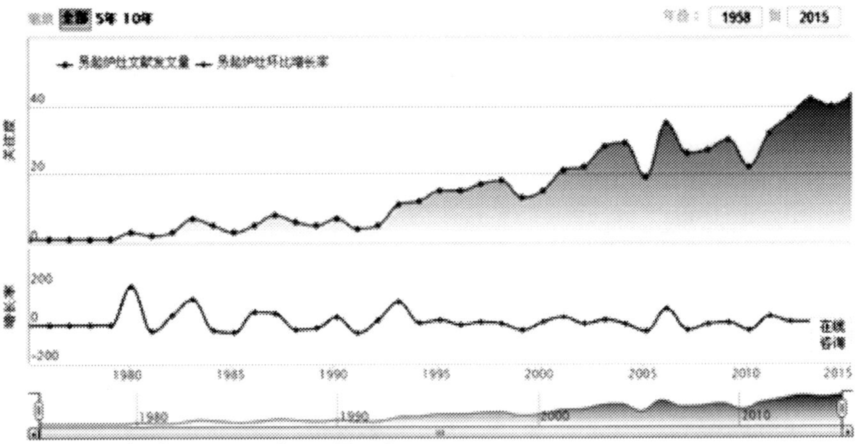

Source: CNKI database on Academic Trends.

The concept has been traced to Mao Zedong in the 1940s. Mao recalled in a speech to communist party secretaries in early 1957 of his conversation with a writer of *Dagong Bao* which carried an editorial "don't set up a separate kitchen" in August 1944 about the Chongqing negotiations between the communists and the nationalists. Mao here suggested that his party was not looking at a stop gap arrangement of reconstruction but a comprehensive plan. Mao defending this policy by suggesting that

> It is [a policy of] mobilizing all positive forces in order to build socialism. This is a strategic guideline. It is better that we carry out this kind of policy; there will be fewer [chances for] trouble. We must explain to the public this idea of comprehensive planning with due consideration to all sectors [so that they may understand] clearly.[19]

Subsequently, this concept became one of the three main principles of China's foreign polices at its inception in 1949[20]. Apart from the "setting up a different kitchen" [另起炉灶], Mao also mentioned "clean up the house and invite the guests" [打扫干净屋子再请客] and "leaning to one side" [一边倒] that of the Soviet Union in 1949. Former US official Henry Kissinger suggested that the "aloof challenge" policy of China is carefully designed by Mao to "manipulat[e]...the barbarians, with great attention paid to meticulous planning and the psychological domination of the other side".[21]

Shu Jianguo and Zhou Yongdong argued that Mao's policy guidelines in 1949 were influenced by the tussle between the communists and the Kuomintang ensuring the leading role of the communists and to safeguard national unity through the "one China" principle. By negating all diplomatic features of the KMT, the communist party secured national interests of China[22]. They cite Zhou Enlai's reasoning in this regard. As the late Qing dynasty's Empress Dowager, Yuan Shihkai and Chiang Kaishek did not follow an independent spirit, they allowed the interference of the international forces in China resulting in several reverses. A complete change in foreign principles and policies will ensure that China's interests could be protected and pursued. Secondly, at the 2nd plenum of the 7th communist party congress in early 1949, Mao declared that as a revolutionary party, it will do away with the old, traditional policies of inheriting national humiliation. Thirdly, as the KMT still exercised influence in several parts of China, in addition o Taiwan and relations with foreign powers, the best policy for the communist party is to cut off such linkages that could usher in "two China's" and assert its independence[23]. Another scholar Men Jing suggested that the revolutionary ideology of Mao had a larger role in the "setting up a different kitchen" for the Chinese diplomacy in the coming years. By refusing to acknowledge and pursue the diplomatic policies of the previous KMT government, Mao was clearly distancing from the past practices and thereby ushering in new perspectives.[24] While this was KMT specific policy, it had implications to the foreign policy of China and in several avatars influence the current thinking of the leadership in China[25].

Nevertheless, while "setting up a different kitchen" has had a huge impact on China's foreign policy practices, the leadership is also careful in downplaying it many a time given the potentially disruptive influence it could have in China's arrangements with other international partners, specifically in the globalisation period. China's diplomatic credibility in the eyes of the international community would also be at stake and impact negatively on the long-term diplomatic partnerships if China is seen always "setting up a different kitchen". Hence in China's diplomatic practice, "setting up a different kitchen" has a dualistic political flavor.

In the background of the BRICS phenomenon China's position is significant given its important role in this global initiative. This is related either to a "status quo" position or a "revisionist" gradualist change in the international order if not a "revolutionary" way of re-ordering the global institutions as Premier Zhou Enlai once mentioned about setting up a "revolutionary" United Nations. While the revolutionary path has been jettisoned by the reformist China since Deng Xiaoping, the other two positions have come under global and regional scanner. While during much of the reform period, China's leaders are contended with their position in the UN and that they are not willing to radically change the system, in the recent times, however, there are increasing calls for the powers that be to accommodate to China's rise, specifically the rules and norms that governed the human kind for all these decades.[26]

The following statements from top Chinese leaders and officials suggest to a uniformed position, albeit with subtle differences. After becoming the new leader of China at the 18th party congress, President Xi Jinping's first visit abroad was to Russia and then to attend the BRICS meeting at Durban in March 2013 – thus highlighting his external priorities. This was viewed widely in China as a "setting up a different kitchen" in the international domain[27]. In a speech at Seattle on September 24, 2015, President Xi Jinping stated:

> As far as the existing international system is concerned, China has been a participant, builder and contributor. We stand firmly for the international order and system that is based on the purposes and principles of the UN Charter. A great number of countries, especially developing countries, want to see a more just and equitable international system, but it doesn't mean they want to unravel the entire system or start all over again. Rather, what they want is to reform and improve the system to keep up with the times.[28]

In another significant speech at the 4th national foreign affairs work conference, that ushered in a new policy of actively involving abroad, Xi Jinping addressed the political and diplomatic corps of the country as:

> While being keenly aware of the protracted nature of contest over the international order, we need to recognize that the direction of reform of the international system will remain unchanged. While fully recognizing the uncertainty in China's neighboring environment, we should realize that the general trend of prosperity and stability in the Asia-Pacific region will not change....China should develop a distinctive diplomatic approach befitting its role of a major country. ... We should ...always base ourselves on our own strength in pursuing the development of the country and the nation, and follow our own path unswervingly.[29]

Premier Li Keqiang addressing the Organization for Economic Cooperation and Development meeting on July 1, 2015 assured the audience that China will:

> ... firmly safeguard the purposes and principles of the UN Charter as well as the post-war international order and system with the UN as the core. Chinese culture has been advocating harmony and virtues since ancient times. China was, is and will be a firm defender and promoter of world peace and international order.[30]

China' State Councilor Yang Jiechi in a speech in 2013 mentioned that "China will honor its due international obligations and work in close cooperation with relevant international organizations in maintaining world peace and security, promoting human development and progress and addressing global issues and challenges".[31] China's foreign minister Wang Yi at a speech at Qinghua University's 2nd World Peace Forum on June 27, 2013 stated:

> China will continue to maintain the present international order and the universally recognized international norms and more actively participate in the reform and improvement of the international system. The post-war international order, built by the peace-loving people across the world with their life and blood, has not come easily and the norms governing international relations represented by the UN Charter is truly precious.[32]

Further, at the National People's Congress session Wang Yi stated to a question from the Xinhua news agency correspondent that China wants reform of the international order but does not intend to set up a different kitchen.[33] Replying to a question from a *Lianhe Zaobao* correspondent at the NPC annual session in March 2016 Wang suggested that the fact that his country's currency renminbi has been accepted as a reserve currency and that China's voting shares in the IMF has been raised suggest that China is not setting up a different kitchen but cooperating with the existing international order. Interestingly he had also suggested that as China's power increases in the international system, it is natural that correspondingly it will look for more space in the international system.[34]

However, Ambassador Fu Ying, Chairperson, Foreign Affairs Committee, National People's Congress distinguishes between the "world order" under the US to the "international order" under the United Nations, thus:

> What you hear from the Chinese leaders is that, China is part of the international order. One need to note that the term used here is "international order" and what it refers to is the UN and its institutions,

> including the principles of international law. This may overlap with the aforementioned "world order" but is not exactly the same. China has a strong sense of belonging to this UN led order system, as China is one of its founders and a beneficiary, a contributor, as well as part of its reform efforts.[35]

The above views by leaders and officials are also reflected in the scholarship. For instance, according to Ye Zicheng, Director for Chinese Strategic Studies at Beijing University, "The biggest difference between the now ascendant China on the one hand, and Germany during World War I and Japan during World War II on the other, is that China has no intent to challenge the existing international system through military expansion. Nor does it seek to create another international system outside the existing system to engage in confrontation." [36]

Nevertheless, in practice and in relation to specific institutions and inherited rules and regulations, increasingly we witness a revisionist streak in the Chinese thinking recently. China is suggesting that it be consulted on the "rule making". Pang Sen, a deputy director-general at China's Foreign Ministry replying to President Obama's statement at APEC on every country abiding by rules, said."If the rules are made collectively through agreement and China is a part of it, then China will abide by them. If rules are decided by one or even several countries, China does not have the obligation to abide by that."[37] If this official position is a carefully thought out policy, then it will have long term implications for the existing order.

Another interesting feature recently is China's position on South China Sea and international arbitration. After the Filipino request to look into the sovereignty dispute over the South China Sea islands was accepted by the international Arbitration Tribunal on October 29, 2015, China's foreign ministry issued a statement saying that this is "null and void, and has no binding effect on China", despite being a signatory to the UNCLOS provisions. China in December 2014 refused to accept the legality of this Tribunal to look into the dispute[38] and finally once the ruling was made on July 12, 2016, China termed it as "illegal". [39] This suggests that even though the Permanent Court of Arbitration ruling is non-enforceable, but a fact on the ground with implications to diplomatic conduct, China had taken recourse to a *realpolitik* position. On the other hand, in a similar case when Bangladesh went to the international court for arbitration on disputed islands, India accepted the verdict on islands off between the two countries.

Agenda Next

BRICS, thus can be situated within the emerging power alliances and multilateral frameworks, with a wider scope of policy areas, that provide opportunities for debate, communication and deliberation, reflecting the features of relations-oriented multilateralism. However, despite the growing influence of BRICS, it is often dismissed especially in view of their limited institutionalization, the lack of binding commitments and the often substantial divergences among participating countries. The organization does not have a secretariat, except the proposal for a "virtual secretariat"[40] being considered by the BRICS members. The 'virtual secretariat' which is an e-facility, will maintain communication between the principal agencies in BRICS nations and ease the drafting of documents for BRICS. There have been additional proposals to formalise and bureaucratise the grouping. The Chairman of the China Association of International Trade, in 2013, suggested that BRICS should consider proposing a free trade agreement, to enhance the power and voice of the emerging economies in the world economy[41]. However, the proposal of FTA has not been taken seriously by the other BRICS members. Their apprehensions about the plan include the fear that it could lead to a surge in imports of Chinese goods into their territory — in turn, hurting local manufacturing and further increasing trade imbalances in favour of China.

India along with South Africa has also pressed for multiple-entry business visas[42] for entrepreneurs from the five nations, to enable easier travel, thereby removing obstacles to greater trade transactions. However, the security concerns expressed vis-à-vis the Chinese by the Indian side have at present foiled plans to issue multiple entry visas to the business persons from BRICS. The first BRICS parliamentarian forum in Moscow on 8 June, 2015, has proposed a BRICS parliamentary assembly[43], which aims to ratify documents and adopt the laws needed for integrating the BRICS countries. To this effect, delegates from BRICS countries attended a two-day meeting of BRICS Women Parliamentarian Forum in India, ahead of the 8th BRICS Summit. In May 2009, the Indian government hosted the first BRIC Academic Forum as a preparatory event to produce ideas for first BRICS Leaders Summit. Since the 2010 summit, the yearly Academic Forum takes place in the same country that hosts the Leaders Summit. However, it has failed to include new ideas about the grouping from the scholars and researchers[44].

The proposal for an alternative rating agency has its origins in the global financial crisis. Although the BRICS nations chose not to be critical of the leading western credit agencies, they suggested an alternative with new methodology of evaluations along with new indictors[45], which will take into consideration the modus operandi of BRICS and developing countries.

There is a suggestion for expanding BRICS further to include other emerging countries such as Indonesia, Egypt and Turkey[46], although some suggest that strict membership criteria should be placed by the BRICS so as to admit only those who have regional and global influence and that they are non-OECD countries.[47] However, BRICS leaders have maintained a cautious approach to the issue of expanding the group's membership. In their view, any hasty decision on the issue would not only jeopardize the very structure of the organization but also affect its goals. Also, the idea for a BRICS military alliance has gained little resonance among the BRICS countries, except Russia[48]. Owing to the mutual distrust among the members and their close ties with the West, especially India, Brazil and South Africa, the proposal of turning BRICS into a military alliance, will remain a distant reality.

Through its substantive essays, this volume offers a range of perspectives about China's interactions with BRICS and the implications for the global order. The book is a collection of twelve chapters, which addresses many key aspects of the multilateral initiative, with the focus being directed to analysing the prospects and challenges for the group in the coming years. The volume is divided into two sections- the first is thematic, which deals with the broad issues of global governance and its debates; the second section focuses on the intra-BRICS relationships. Beginning with China's multilateral diplomacy, the book explores key debates in global governance that involves the rise of emerging powers, especially India and China, the issue of perception and reality, and the roles played by media, think tanks in institutionalizing the initiative as an effective representative of 'south-south' cooperation. It also discusses some of the key issues pertaining to global governance such as the energy factor and the issue of cyber-security that gained much currency following Edward Snowden's revelations to the emergence of smart phone botnets and the Cryptolocker ransomware. In its second part, the volume has dealt with bilateral relations, where the individual relations between China and the other BRICS countries are being analysed.

Obviously, in any collection such as this, some key issues are left unaddressed. It is hoped that those issues and the ones discussed in this book will generate further debates and scholarly examination. This volume is therefore, an attempt to stimulate discussion about China's policies, multilateralism, global governance, of which BRICS form an important part.

Academic and policy studies like this would not have been possible without cooperation from all the contributors and to the vibrant debates, excellent institutional infrastructure and library facilities at Jawaharlal Nehru University. The editors express their gratitude to Ms Piyalee Pandit for making attractive charts and figures for this volume. For bringing out this volume meticulously, the editors would like to thank the publisher Mr Rajan Arya of the Pentagon Press and the copy editor Vibha.

END NOTES

1. Press Release (2010), "Trade to expand by 9.5% in 2010 after a dismal 2009, WTO reports", 26 March [Online: Web] Accessed 5 March 2013, URL: http://www.wto.org/english/news_e/pres10_e/pr598_e.htm
2. The WTO Ministerial Conference of September 2003 witnessed unified position of several developing countries (specifically the Group of 20) such as Brazil, South Africa, India and China on a number of economic issues. Some trace the coordination between these countries for the origins of the BRICS phenomenon later. See Dao Shulin cited in Lin Limin, "BRICs 现象"剖析" [BRICs Phenomenon] 现代国际关系 No. 9 (2004) pp. 44-54 (p.48).
3. Refer to the Joint Statement of the BRIC Countries' Leaders Yekaterinburg, Russia, June 16, 2009, accessed at http://www.brics.utoronto.ca/docs/090616-leaders.html
4. II BRIC Summit - Joint Statement , accessed at http://brics2016.gov.in/upload/files/document/5763e23d75e512nd.pdf
5. Inclusion of South Africa in the BRICS format is mainly for geopolitical rather than economic prowess, according to Guo Yan. Guo Yan, "BRICS – A new Model", *China's Foreign Trade,* May 8, 2011 pp. 32-33. Even though South Africa has smaller economy, population and territory, according to Yu Ping, Vice Chairman of the China Council for the Promotion of International Trade, "South Africa has advantages in economic management, natural resource reserves and good relations with many countries and regions." For Zhang Zhongxiang, Deputy Director of the Department of West Asian and African Studies of the Shanghai Institutes for International Studies, South Africa's joining the BRICS would facilitate opportunities for the other BRICS states to enter the African continent. Cited by Ni Yanshuo, "Adding South Africa to The BRICS Mix" *Beijing Review,* April 28, 2011 p. 16 accessed at http://www.bjreview.com. For Xing Guangcheng, research fellow at Chinese Academy of Social Sciences, BRICS represents not a political and military entity but "global economic hub". In the light of the global financial crisis, this grouping will be able to enhance its economic clout in the future. Xing Guangcheng, "Becoming BRICS", *Beijing Review,* April 14, 2011 p. 14 accessed at http://www.bjreview.com and Ni Yanshuo, "Adding South Africa to The BRICS Mix", *Beijing Review,* April 28, 2011 p.16.
6. BRICS III Summit, Sanya Declaration. See http://brics2016.gov.in/upload/files/document/57566e28a911e3rd.pdf
7. Fourth BRICS Summit-Delhi Declaration, see http://mea.gov.in/bilateral-documents.htm?dtl/19158/Fourth+BRICS+Summit++Delhi+Declaration
8. For an interesting study see *Noshua Watson*, "What's a BRICS bank supposed to do?" September 28, 2012 accessed at http://www.globalisationanddevelopment.com/2012/09/whats-brics-bank-supposed-to-do.html. Watson argued that the proposed Development Bank could look after the following areas: Infrastructure development; Increasing domestic resources, developing local financial markets and SMEs; Focusing financing on underfunded sectors and developing country enterprises rather than multinationals; Investigating policies for financial stability, including a financial transaction tax; Managing trade barriers, including product standards

that come from private sector regulatory schemes; Evaluating energy, water and agriculture subsidies; Researching best practices for negotiating with extractive industries; and evaluating the effect of development policies on women and youth.

9. Differences exist on the nature of the bank, its capital, shares and votes and the location. The seed capital for the bank is supposed to be raised from each BRICS state at $10 billion each – instead of the IMF practice of the share based on the size of the economy (which is proportional to the share of the votes). While India appeared to have suggested that all the BRICS states should have equal shares, China appears to have asked for more- given its comfortable position in foreign exchanges and trade surpluses. There is also a proposal to offer nearly 45 percent stake in the bank for the United States and the United Kingdom so that the credit ratings of the bank could be higher. See Prasanta Sahu, "Brics Likely to Offer Stake in Bank to Non-Members", March 7, 2013 at http://online.wsj.com/article/SB10001424127887323628804578345763055538772.html and John Fraser, "New Development Bank to be Key BRICS Building Block" at http://www.ipsnews.net/2013/02/new-development-bank-to-be-key-brics-building-block/. While China eyeds Shanghai to be the headquarters, Russia had suggested that the headquarters of the bank should be based in Moscow, with a permanent secretariat as well. $50 billion in capital was suggested for the Bank, in addition to $240 billion as special anti-crisis fund. See Tamara Zamyatina, "BRICS should turn into 21st century global forum" *ITAR-TASS,* March 19, 2013 accessed at http://indrus.in/politics/2013/03/19/brics_should_turn_into_21st_century_ global_ forum_ 23045.html. The South African foreign minister Maite Nkoana-Mashabane also suggested that the proposed bank should be based in South Africa and could benefit the whole continent. See "South Africa optimistic for basing proposed BRICS development bank: official" *Xinhua,* March 11, 2013 accessed at http://news.xinhuanet.com/english/africa/2013-03/11/c_132225826.htm. However, according to Jaswant Singh, the proposal "fails to address the discrepancies between the BRICS' interests, or to define the bank's role in reconciling and advancing them" See "Crumbling BRICS" March 19, 2013 at http://www.project-syndicate.org/commentary/the-brics-s-separate-paths-to-development-by-jaswant-singh. See also Anita Powell, "BRICS Development Bank May Take Years" March 18, 2013 at http://www.voanews.com/content/brics-development-bank-may-take-years/1623700.html and Pramit Pal Chaudhuri, "China, the first among equals in BRICS" *Hindustan Times,* March 30, 2012 accessed at http://www.hindustantimes.com/India-news/NewDelhi/China-the-first-among-equals-in-BRICS/Article1-832772.aspx

10. Nevertheless, China had been indicating that such fund should be used appropriately. Li Daokui, an economic strategist and member of the CPPCC stated: "Currency intervention would not be a good use of money... China will only act together with the International Monetary Fund, which has the ability to impose strict conditions.... It would not be appropriate to use money without conditions, and some of the money would be used in the form of Chinese renminbi so that businesses in India and other countries can buy Chinese products.... Emerging markets have split into two groups. There are those that lack good foreign exchange buffers, or have trade and budget deficits. India, Brazil and Turkey will all run into some kind of trouble". Li cited by Ambrose Evans-Pritchard, "China to dictate tough terms on BRICS rescue fund", *The Telegraph*, September 6, 2013 at http://www.telegraph.co.uk/finance/china-business/10292595/China-to-dictate-tough-terms-on-BRICS-rescue-fund.html# disqus_thread

11. Scott Rose, "China Agrees to Give 41% of $100 Billion BRICS Reserve Pool" Bloomberg September 6, 2013 accessed at http://www.bloomberg.com/news/2013-09-05/china-agrees-to-give-lion-s-share-of-100-billion-brics-pool-1-.html. Several Chinese see this idea as conducive towards internationalizing the Yuan (*renminbi*) and exporting capital for more

productive and lucrative investments abroad. Direct renminbi clearing arrangements by China exist with Hong Kong and Macao. In January 2013, China further strengthened the internationalisation of its currency by a similar arrangement with Taiwan. The Bank of China and Central Bank of the Republic of China have concluded this agreement for direct settlement of renminbi payments after an initial framework agreement was signed in August 2012. See Aries Pool and Lorraine Luk, "China, Taiwan Sign Yuan-Clearing Deal", *Wall Street Journal*, January 25, 2013 accessed at http://online.barrons.com/article/SB10001424127887323539804578263451199261528.html?mod=BOL_article_full_more. According to Yi Gang, a vice governor of China's central bank, "It is the basic policy of the People's Bank of China (PBOC) to let the renminbi compete with U.S. dollar or euro fairly in the international market. ...I would be actually pleased to see people have more confidence in the renminbi and choose it over other currencies thanks to a more sophisticated market, better implementation of China's monetary policy, China's macroeconomic stability and social stability, and stronger rule of law". Yi interviewed at "China to pursue renminbi internationalization on market-oriented basis", *Xinhua,* January 27, 2013 accessed at http://english.news.cn/. According to Song Hong, a research fellow with the Chinese Academy of Social Sciences (CASS), "By extending loans in local currencies and establishing a currency exchange system, the BRICS members can reduce their over-reliance on the U.S. dollar and lower trade risks while pushing forward the currency internationalization of the BRICS states". See Song cited at Ding Ying, "Banking on other options", *China Report*, May 2012, pp. 18-19, accessed at www.chinafrica.cn. According to Li Zhongmin, a researcher on BRICS studies with the CASS, the BRICS states need to expand infrastructure financing, currency internationalization, financial credit, mutual investment and trade facilitation so that these states could overcome the ill-effects of global financial crisis. There are also concerns among the Chinese (like Qu Xing, President of the China Institute of International Studies) that such a Bank initiative could be politicized by the western countries and complicates relations with the IMF and the World Bank. For Yue Fubin of CASS, the BRICS will also sow seeds for a new international economic order in the future. Yue Fubin, "China and the BRICs - golden years ahead" November 27, 2011 at http://www.bbc.co.uk/news/business-15911603

12. 5th BRICS Summit- eThekwini Declaration and Action Plan. See http://www.mea.gov.in/bilateral documents.htm?dtl/21482/5th+BRICS+Summit++ eThekwini+Declaration+and+Action+Plan
13. Sixth BRICS Summit – Fortaleza Declaration. Accessed at http://www.mea.gov.in/bilateral documents.htm?dtl/23635/Sixth+BRICS+Summit++Fortaleza+Declaration
14. VII BRICS Summit Ufa Declaration. Accessed at http://brics2016.gov.in/upload/files/document/5763c20a72f2d7thDeclarationeng.pdf
15. See Wang Yan, "金融危机下金砖四国能否冲击世界经济格局?" 经营管理者 [Fiscal & Financial Managers] August 20, 2009, p. 58.
16. See D.A. Mahapatra, "UN HDI Report: BRICS Ahead of West by 2020" March 18, 2013 accessed at http://indrus.in/world/2013/03/18/un_hdi_report_brics_ ahead_of_west_by_2020_23009.html
17. Much of the intra-BRICS trade is in favour of China—leaving huge trade imbalances. To reduce the trade imbalances, the other BRICS states have been insisting on market economy status of China, non-discrimination principle and tariff reductions. See Troye Lund, "SA in BRICS—Are we making the most of it?" March 14, 2013 at http://www.fm.co.za/economy/2013/03/14/sa-in-brics--are-we-making-the-most-of-it
18. Leontyev suggests that the current international system is heavily dependent on the US dollar and that if the BRICS countries trade among themselves in local currencies, then it would be revolutionary. However, this is not going to happen as the BRICS states – specifically

China which invested nearly $1.2 trillion in the US treasury securities - are themselves investing heavily in the US dollar. See Mikhail Leontyev, "BRIC Countries are heavily dependent on the US dollar system" *New Eastern Outlook* at http://orientalreview.org/2010/05/01/bric-countries-are-heavily-dependent-on-the-us-dollar-system/

19. Michael Y.M. Kau, John K. Leung, ed. *The Writings of Mao Zedong, 1949-1976: January 1956-December 1957*, vol 2 (Armonk, New York: ME Sharpe, 1992) p.248.
20. Tang Jiaxuan ed. 中国外交词典 [Dictionary of China's Diplomacy] (Beijing: World Knowledge Publishers, 1999) p.182
21. Henry Kissinger, *On China* (New York: Allen Lane, 2011) pp.100-101.
22. Shu Jianguo and Zhou Yongdong, "论新中国"另起炉灶"的外交方略及其积极效应" [On New China's diplomatic strategy of 'setting up a separate kitchen' and its positive effects] 南昌大学学报, Vol. 44, No. 6 (November 2013) pp. 54-58.
23. Li Jiulin, "毛泽东与"另起炉灶"的外交战略理论和实践" [Mao Zedong and the diplomatic strategic theory and practice of "starting all over again"] 北京工业大学学报(社会科学版) [Journal of Beijing Polytechnic University Social Sciences Edition], No. 1 (2004), pp.50-54.
24. Men Jing in Guo Sujian and Hua Shiping ed *New Dimensions of Chinese Foreign Policy* (Lanham: Lexington Books, 2007) p. 11. See also Zhang Baijia, "Perspective shifts during the development to fin Chinese Diplomacy" in Shao Binhong, ed. The World in 2020 according to China (Leiden: Brill, 2014) p.17.
25. For instance, in the climate change proposals at Copenhagen, a Chinese writer suggested that the developed countries themselves were "setting up a different kitchen" by denying the developing countries of their fair share in developmental experience. Bao Hong argued that "For China, a larger challenge regarding climate negotiations comes from the attempt of the developed countries to "start all over again" by changing international mechanisms and rules on dealing with climate change". See "The West Plotted to "Start All Over Again" During the Climate Negotiations" *International Understanding*, No. 1 (2010) pp. 22-25 (p.25).
26. Liang Xiaojun of China Foreign Affairs University suggested that China is not ready to shoulder great power responsibilities due to lack of domestic consensus, no alternative international order, inability to provide public goods, lacks "great power mentality", etc See "China is destined to lead, but not ready" *East Asia Forum*, September 13, 2016 accessed at http://www.eastasiaforum.org/2016/09/13/china-is-destined-to-lead-but-not-ready/
27. See the commentaries at Xie Huanchi, "评：习近平访俄非 透露另起炉灶主导国际的风格" [Comment: Xi Jinping's visit to Russia and Africa reveal fresh start style of leading internationally] *Xinhua,* March 28, 2013 accessed at http://news.qq.com/a/20130328/000521_all.htm. Some see the BRICS NDB as an alternative to the US dollar itself. See Liang Xiaoyi, "金砖峰会或将重塑国际金融体系" [BRICS Summit or reshaping international financial system] 中国新时代, August 2014, Issue 198 p.27. The Director of Institute of World Economic and Politics of Chinese Academy of Social Sciences Gao Haihong suggested that the NDB will be "setting up a different kitchen" compared to the existing financial institutions. See Gao Haihong interviewed by Zhou Hongda, "金砖金融合作站上新起点- 访 中国 社科院 世界经济 与 政治 研究所 国际金融研究室主任高海红" [BRICS financial cooperation on a new starting point — Interview with Chinese Academy of Social Sciences Institute of World Economics and Politics International Finance Research Office Director Gao Haihong] 中国金融家 [China Finanacialyst] (August 2014) pp. 24-26.
28. "President Xi's speech on China-US ties" *China Daily*, September 24, 2015 accessed at http://www.chinadaily.com.cn/world/2015xivisitus/2015-09/24/content_ 21964069.htm
29. Xi Jinping, "The Central Conference on Work Relating to Foreign Affairs was Held in Beijing" November 29, 2015 accessed at http://www.fmprc.gov.cn/mfa_eng/zxxx_662805/t1215680.shtml

30. Li Keqiang, "Li Keqiang Delivers Speech at OECD, Stressing the Focus on Development for Common Prosperity and Promotion of Mutual Benefits and Multi-win Results Through International Cooperation in Production Capacity" July 2, 2015 accessed at http://www.fmprc.gov.cn/mfa_eng/topics_665678/lkqcxdsqczgomld rhwbsfblsdfgjxzsfwbfwjjh zyfzzzzb/t1278727.shtml
31. Yang Jiechi, "Innovations in China's Diplomatic Theory and Practice Under New Conditions" on August 16, 2013 accessed at http://www.fmprc.gov.cn/mfa_eng/wjdt_665385/zyjh_665391/t1066869.shtml
32. Wang Yi "Exploring the Path of Major-Country Diplomacy with Chinese Characteristics", accessed at http://www.fmprc.gov.cn/mfa_eng/wjb_663304/wjbz_663308/2461_663310/t1053908.shtml
33. "王毅：中国主张改革国际秩序体系 但非另起炉灶" [Wang Yi- China advocates reform of the international system but not reinventing the wheel] 中国新闻网, March 8, 2015 accessed at http://politics.people.com.cn/n/2015/0308/c70731-26656226.html
34. "王毅谈国际秩序：中国并没有另起炉灶 另搞一套" [Wang Yi on the international order – China does not set up a different kitchen all over again] *Xinhua,* March 8, 2016 accessed at http://news.qq.com/a/20160308/037246.htm
35. Fu Ying, "China and the Future of International Order", *Chatham House,* July 6, 2016 accessed at https://www.chathamhouse.org/sites/files/chathamhouse/events/special/2016-07-08-China-International-Order_0.pdf
36. Ye cited in Susan L. Craig, "Chinese Perceptions of Traditional and Nontraditional Security Threats" US Army War College, Strategic Studies Institute, March 2007 accessed at http://www.dtic.mil/dtic/tr/fulltext/u2/a464893.pdf, p. 11.
37. Peng cited by Brad Nelson, "Is China a Status Quo or Revisionist Power?" November 22, 2011 accessed at http://centerforworldconflictandpeace.blogspot.in/2011/11/is-china-status-quo-or-revisionist.html
38. "Statement of the Ministry of Foreign Affairs of the People's Republic of China on the Award on Jurisdiction and Admissibility of the South China Sea Arbitration by the Arbitral Tribunal Established at the Request of the Republic of the Philippines" October 30, 2015 at http://www.fmprc.gov.cn/mfa_eng/zxxx_662805/t1310474.shtml. The Permanent Court of Arbitration Award is available at "PCA Case Nº 2013-19 in the Matter of the South China Sea Arbitration" accessed at http://www.pcacases.com/pcadocs/PH-CN%20-%2020160712%20-%20Award.pdf
39. Ulrich Speck argued that while China and Russia benefit out of the current liberal international order, in terms of trade, investments and free markets, they have a revisionist agenda for the longer term. See "Restoring Liberalism; The Crisis of Liberal Order", *The American Interest,* September 12, 2016 accessed at http://www.the-american-interest.com/2016/09/12/the-crisis-of-liberal-order/. On the other hand Patrick Porter found that there are wide discrepancies in the UNSC members in relation to the implementation of the rule of law in international relations. See *Patrick Porter,* "Sorry, Folks. There Is No Rules-Based World Order," *National Interest,* August 28, 2016 accessed at http://nationalinterest.org/blog/the-skeptics/sorry-folks-there-no-rules-based-world-order-17497
40. The BRICS Post (2015), "Russia announces BRICS 'virtual secretariat", July 3 accessed at http://thebricspost.com/russia-announces-brics-virtual-secretariat/#.V-IXEdJ97Mw & Official Website of Russian Presidency in BRICS (2015), "BRICS Website goes Online", July 9, accessed at http://en.brics2015.ru/news/20150709/418316.html
41. Li, Jiabao, (2013), "Experts call for BRICS free trade pact", March 27, accessed at http://www.china.org.cn/opinion/2013-03/27/content_28372164.htm & Arun, S. (2016), "China's BRICS trade Pact finds no takers", *The Hindu,* September 10, accessed at http://

www.thehindu.com/business/Industry/chinas-brics-trade-pact-idea-finds-no-takers/article9094805.ece

42. Chaudhary, Roy Dipanjan. (2015), "India to press for multiple-entry business visa for Brics entrepreneurs", *Economic Times*, July 2, accessed at http://articles.economictimes.indiatimes.com/2015-07-02/news/64039115_1_brics-summit-brics-countries-brics-nations
43. Surkov, Nikolay. (2015), "BRICS moving towards own parliamentary forum", Russia and India Report, June 19, accessed at https://in.rbth.com/world/2015/06/19/brics_moving_towards_own_parliamentary_forum_43777
44. Steunkel, Oliver (2015), "Connecting the Global South: Why the BRICS Academic Forum matters", May 23, accessed at http://www.postwesternworld.com/2015/05/23/connecting-academic-matters/
45. Beniwal, V. (2016), "Brics bloc keen to set up alternative credit rating agency", June 28, accessed at http://www.bdlive.co.za/world/asia/2016/06/28/brics-bloc-keen-to-set-up-alternative-credit-rating-agency
46. Sara Schonhardta, "BRIC ambitions for Indonesia" September 2, 2010 accessed at http://www.atimes.com/atimes/South_Asia/LI02Df05.html; Marwa Yahia, "Egypt in BRICS bid, obstacles linger on", *Xinhua,* May 10, 2013 at http://news.xinhuanet.com/english/world/2013-05/10/c_124689491.htm and John Fraser, "Building BRICS: Will group grow to include Turkey, Indonesia?" December 1, 2012 at http://www.theeastafrican.co.ke/news/Will-group-grow-to-include-Turkey-Indonesia/-/2558/1634442/-/wbut48z/-/index.html
47. Li Wei, "金砖机制与国际金融治理改革" [BRICS mechanism and reform of international financial governance] 国际观察 [International Observer] No. 1 (2013) pp. 33-40 (p.39)
48. Simha, R.K. (2015), "Why a BRICS military bloc won't happen in a hurry", May 18, accessed at http://in.rbth.com/blogs/2015/05/18/why_a_brics_military_bloc_wont_ happen_in_a_hurry_43163

PART I
THEMES

1

Multilateralism with Chinese Characteristics

Srikanth Kondapalli

We will actively participate in multilateral affairs; support the United Nations, G20, the Shanghai Cooperation Organisation, BRICS and other multilateral organisations in playing an active role in international affairs, and work to make the international order and system more just and equitable.

—Hu Jintao's Work Report to the 18th Communist Party Congress on November 17, 2012[1]

Introduction

Of all the constituents of the BRICS, the role of China has been highlighted globally, partly due to the economic heft that it was able to muster in the last two decades. The rise of the People's Republic of China (PRC) and its endorsement of the multilateral process, as reflected in the above quote, have been the subject matter of a number of debates in recent times. China's role in the multilateral institutions, including in the BRICS (besides providing cushions for its rise), has been impacting gradually on the regional and international orders. Indeed, these two elements—efforts to make a conducive international and regional environment for the enhancement in China's profile and reshaping the global and regional orders for China's "rejuvenation"—

have become the cornerstones in the country's foreign policies. Here, apart from the bilateral efforts, participation in the multilateral institutions and processes provides enormous scope for China's rise in the international system. This chapter situates the BRICS phenomenon in the global context, reflects on the rise of China as the context for new demands to reform the international order, traces the innumerable triggers for the Chinese interest in the BRICS phenomenon, and then evaluates the perceptions of the leadership and scholars on the BRICS. It is argued in this chapter that while multilateralism evolved by a group of states to resolve some overarching issues globally—without bringing in sovereignty issues and State intervention—China's multilateral practices, though rich in content and productive in addressing many issues, are constrained by the specificities of China's diplomatic practices.

The Global Context

After the World War II and the fall of Germany and Japan, the United States and the then Soviet Union established a new bipolar world order in the mid-1940s. The international power system, henceforth, was composed of Bretton Woods Institutions (like the International Monetary Fund and the World Bank) and the United Nations—with its Security Council and different bodies. In addition to these international regimes, a set of rules and norms were suggested and implemented. The world witnessed conventional and strategic military competition, alliances and proxy wars between the then two superpowers in the form of higher defence outlays, expansion of military industrial complexes, NATO vs. Warsaw Pact, etc. For much of the 20th century, this bipolarity provided for strategic stability despite over 300 proxy wars between the then superpowers. After the disintegration of the Soviet Union, the United States became a "lonely superpower"[2]; although soon with the onset of the Kosovo, Iraq and Afghanistan conflicts, the US needed support from its allies in Europe, and made frantic calls for multilateral initiatives to curb terrorism or on other regional security issues.

In recent times, the global situation is undergoing major transformations with the rise of several countries, such as China, India, Brazil, Turkey, Indonesia and South Africa—in addition to others such as Japan and Russia—in what was broadly termed by Fareed Zakaria as the "Rise of the Rest".[3] They have been increasingly participating in the international institutions and in some cases, also changing the norms that govern these structures.[4] For instance, by the mid-2000s, China had joined nearly 66 international organisations, as compared to 92 by France, 77 by the US and the UK, 71 by Russia and 67 by India.[5] Yet, despite being major beneficiaries of these institutions, the emerging economies have not been able to put forward a cohesive, comprehensive and universally acceptable international and regional order of the kind we witnessed in the 20th century, when global commons such as the maritime, cyber, space and other domains have been defined and accepted willy-nilly by the international community. Instead, so far they have suggested to gradual and incremental changes to the received order from the late 1940s. This is the contest for the new demands for revamping the received international order, as some countries have emerged in their local geographical settings and begun knocking at international gates. Among these are the BRICS States, prominently including China. Their emergence coincided with the cataclysmic economic structural fault line of the global financial crisis in 2008[6].

The China Context

As China entered into the process of globalisation nearly two decades ago—reflected in her joining the World Trade Organisation in late 2001—this process coincided with its rise in the international system in a comprehensive manner. China had become the largest exporting country displacing Germany, and had become the largest trading partner to 128 countries in the world[7]. In 2012, China's trade volume surpassed that of the US and stood at $3.87 trillion. In 2010, China became the 2nd largest economy with over $11 trillion in GDP, and with the largest foreign exchange reserves in the world (of more than $3.2 trillion by 2015)[8] China's trade with the United States and European Union is more than $500 billion each, while with that of Japan, South Korea, Taiwan and ASEAN countries is cumulatively more than a trillion dollars. Thus, the developed markets are crucial for the rise of China. However, in the process of this rise, China had also become one of the largest consumers of resources—raw materials like iron and steel, cement, copper, tungsten and others mainly from the developing countries—on the one hand, while its energy imports from West Asia and Africa have also become considerable.

Yet, for a balanced and sustainable growth, China also had to diversify and explore markets and trading partners elsewhere. China's trade constitutes more than half of its GDP, while domestic consumption is less than 40 per cent. This implies that China is more dependent on external markets. Hence, global trade protectionist trends hurt China more than the other states. This complex relationship dependence on both, the developed and developing markets, resulted in a hierarchy of diplomatic choices by China in the recent decades. China's foreign policy objectives then became closely inter-twined by the imperatives of reform and opening up and creating favourable conditions for further rise of the country in the international system[9]. This is partly reflected in the 16th national Communist Party Congress (2002) report which emphasised on "three pillar" strategy (i.e, China's relations major powers, neighbours and developing countries in that order)[10]. Subsequently, the 17th Party Congress (2007) added two more pillars, viz., multilateralism and soft power to the previous three pillars[11]. The 18th Party Congress in 2012 reiterated all the above five pillars as the foreign policy posture of China for the next five years[12]. The party congress thereafter witnessed strategic preparations by the new leadership for the "two centennials" [两个一百] viz., 100th anniversary of the foundation of the communist party in 2021 and that of the People's Republic in 2049[13]. These are of long-term preparations, and suggest that China's diplomatic initiatives and practices would come under increasing pressure in the coming decades.

China also initiated the policy at the 16th Party Congress of "going out" (走出去) in terms of investments abroad, which in the recent period had picked up in terms of mergers and acquisitions. While China needed major powers (like the United States, Russia, European Union, Japan and others) for investments, technologies and markets, developing countries have also become indispensable for markets and resources at the economic level and at the diplomatic level in terms of multilateralism. Former trade minister Wu Yi's trade diversification policies from the developed to the developing markets, although not successful, were intended to relieve China from excessive dependence on the West. Among these developing countries are the newly emerging economies like Brazil, India and South Africa. These countries offer additional benefits for China—not only in the economic sphere but also in political and diplomatic support in shaping the international order.

Chinese Triggers

The above suggests to the interests coinciding between China and the emerging nations. China had, in the recent period, emphasised on its relations with the emerging economies for a number of reasons. Firstly, as a rising country itself, China would like to broad-base its rise with the other countries, as this would provide for cushions in the unchartered course of international power transition; specifically after the Soviet Union's disintegration, and due to increasing differences between the US and China—both at the international and regional levels. And despite cooperation between the two on the Korean

Peninsula nuclear issues, Iranian nuclear issues, economic, trade and investment issues, a subtle contest has emerged between the two. Thus, the US "re-balance" towards the Asia-Pacific since 2010 is being contested with the Chinese idea of One-Belt One-Road of enhancing China's influence in Asia, Africa and Europe. Besides, the maritime commons are also coming under strain with China's forays in the South China Sea, in which many a country is dependent for freedom of navigation. China's territorial sea concept and its intransigence to comply or even opposition to the Permanent Court of Arbitration ruling on the issue had resulted in suspicions on China's intentions. China's leaders have proposed that the rise of China will be peaceful, and that it would avoid the experience of Japan and Germany of the 1930s. However, suspicions linger. In order to avoid being the next Soviet Union, clubbing up with the emerging countries could deflect the US ire and provide space for further expansion in the influence of China.

Secondly, China quickly learnt from the entry into different institutions as it hardly had any experience during the diplomatic isolation period of the past. As indicated by Marc Lanteigne, such experience was rewarding for China, as it provided important lessons in enhancing "structural power" and influence the norms and rules in the international system.[14] Such experience provided expanding China's 'learning curve' on global governance issues as well, besides enhancing the bargaining capacity of the country in various international arrangements.

Thirdly, China's linkages with the other emerging economies represent an ideological trend in the international relations thinking that argues that China needs to identify with the developing countries. This is in line with the multipolarity debate within China and has been a dominant thinking process, given the Chinese government's close connections to the "Third World" countries in the 1960s. However, the current positions appear to be devoid of the left ideological moorings of the past and emphasise on the power element in such relations.[15]

Fourthly, the power element suggests that China's diplomacy, in conjunction with the rise of the country in comprehensive national power indicators, began taking interest in the multipolarity debate. While a number of countries recently have expressed interest for some time in this concept such as the French, Russia, India, Brazilian and others, China found it useful to protect its national interests and expand its appeal in the international domain. This coincided with the United States' wars in Kosovo, Iraq, Afghanistan, and to the coloured revolutions in the Eurasian and other regions.

This also provided a chance for China to cobble up with the like-minded powers in the world. Multipolarity has been given space in the party documents in China as well as in diplomatic practice.[16] There was also the consensus building on this issue at the policy-oriented research institutions and universities across the country. For instance, major points that emerged as a result of the October 1999 discussions by international politics scholars at the Zhejiang University on changing international patterns include: the current world order is complex and in transition from bipolarity towards multipolarity, and in this multi-polar pattern [多极格局] instability characterises the current international pattern for a longer period. While China is neither the defender of this international order [现存秩序的维护者] nor a challenger [秩序的挑战者], its foreign policy, according to some scholars at this symposium should be realistic, responsible and cooperative.[17] In another conference of scholars organised by Tongji University in Shanghai on November 26, 2003, while it was argued that China should continue to embrace economic globalisation, it should also simultaneously promote regional political multipolarity and guard against hegemonism by utilising the economic card.[18] In addition, a survey of Chinese journals between 2008 and 2011 indicated to Nele Noesselt that while post-Mao period diversified the IR subjects in China, they are also characterised by new emerging themes such as "non-unipolar future world order" in the place of the official terms like multipolarity, etc.[19] Ye Jiang had argued that while there has been a forward momentum in China's participation in the international and regional economic and security institutions in the recent period, it is not a threat to the international community as it is focused on the domestic issues.[20] According to Yu Zhengliang multipolarisation is the global trend recently with the US decline due to the costly wars in Iraq and Afghanistan.[21] The following figures from the CNKI database suggest to the widespread appeal of multipolarity debate in the academic circles in China in the recent period.

Fifthly, the Chinese concept of "seeking common ground" [求同存异] is useful in understanding Beijing's posture on the BRICS. As a socialist country, the PRC faced innumerable problems in being recognised by the rest of the world. In the early 1950s, the PRC was recognised by only the Soviet Union and its East European allies, in addition to India, Pakistan and Burma. China's new leaders pronouncements on the export of revolution abroad and rigid policies of "leaning to one side", "setting up a different kitchen" and "clean-up the house and invite the guests" have all had a heavy toll on the diplomatic recognition with other countries. Zhou Enlai, the first premier and concurrently the foreign minister, coined the word "求同存异"

Figure 1.1: China Academic Trends on Mulitpolarity

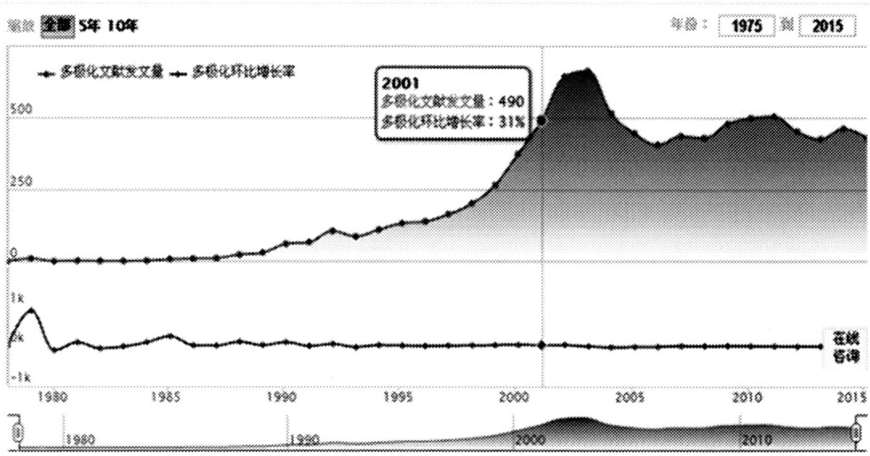

Source: CNKI Academic Trends from the website http://epub.cnki.net

Figure 1.2: Academic Trends on Multipolarity

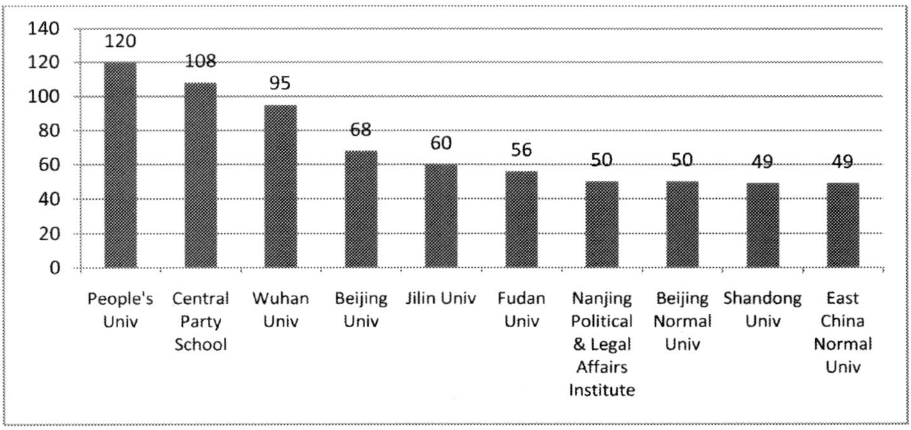

Source: CNKI Academic Trends, 1975-2015 from the website http://epub.cnki.net

[seeking common ground] to reconcile differences with the outside world and enter into some kind of understanding with other countries[22]. With the help of India, Burma and Indonesia, China was able to participate at the 1955 Bandung conference and enter the wider audience in the Afro-Asian community. In the supplementary remarks at the Bandung Conference, Zhou elaborated:

> The Chinese delegation has come here to seek common ground, not to create division. Is there any reason to believe there is common ground

among us? Yes, there is....if we seek common ground along the lines of eliminating sufferings and calamities caused by colonialism, mutual understanding and respect, mutual sympathy and support will easily replace mutual suspicion and fear, mutual exclusion and antagonism[23].

Subsequently, this concept provided rich dividends to China's foreign policy.[24] Several Asia and African countries began recognising China, and even catapulting the PRC into the United Nations Security Council by 1971 despite diplomatic breakaway with Indonesia on charges of fomenting trouble domestically. China, nevertheless, was to utilise the "common ground" subsequently with the United States when President Nixon visited China in 1972. Premier Zhou suggested to the US, on the occasion, on "seeking common ground" while reserving differences[25]. The Soviet Union became a target for both to disintegrate henceforth. Jiang Zemin, who ascended to power soon after the 1989 Tiananmen Square incident, is considered to have resurrected this concept of "common ground" further in order to overcome the diplomatic isolation of China.[26] As the academic trends from the CNKI data base suggests, the number of articles (226) published in China by various think tanks and universities on this concept increased in circulation since the 2000s, with more interested generated since the BRICS formation came into being in 2009. The then foreign minister Qian Qichen suggested in his work that his primary task during these tumultuous years of Western arms embargos and diplomatic isolation is to implement the policy of seeking common ground with the other countries and restore diplomatic normalcy[27]. In major speeches of the Chinese leaders and foreign ministry officials, "seeking common ground" is repeated *ad nauseam.*[28] This is, then, a useful construct in understanding China's policies vis-à-vis the BRICS countries.

Sixthly, connected to the above is China's renewed interest in the multilateral institutions. Multilateralism includes among the member states equality, mutual trust, reciprocity, non-exclusivity (on membership of the organisation), non-specificity of the enemy, non-discrimination, peaceful resolution of disputes, etc[29]. China is a new entrant into the multilateral institutions, but has become adept at the processes in the recent times.

China initially emphasised on bilateral relations in the 1950s and 1960s. After the reform programme was initiated in 1978, China faced the dilemma of adjusting to the international regimes. Specifically, with the economic institutions, China needed information about trade practices useful for the success of its reform policies—and on which it had hardly any information or experience. Last two decades, specifically after joining the WTO in 2001

China re-adjusted its policies. This is reflected in the mild response of China in the Doha round of talks on economic issues in comparison to the vociferous stance of other developing countries like Brazil, India and South Africa.

China's multilateral diplomatic practice is a product of its national objectives and specific experience with the outside world. Although it had limited experience in the beginning (given China's diplomatic isolation), recent times have witnessed to the flowering of China's multilateral diplomacy. In the initial period, the PRC was conditioned by its own socialist ideological moorings and principles and hence was less "acceptable" [合群] to the international community. Between 1949 to 1971, according to Tang Wei, the impact of the Cold War, attitudes towards communist movements across the world, Mao Zedong's three-pronged approaches of "setting up a different kitchen, clean up the house and invite the guests and leaning to one side (Soviet Union)" and Taiwan's retention in the UN have all contributed to the specific Chinese responses towards the outside world. However, after the restoration of the PRC in the UN in 1971 China's multilateral diplomacy underwent radical changes, specifically since the reform and opening up policies were announced by Deng Xiaoping[30]. Unlike in the Cold War period, which constrained China's multilateral diplomacy, the reform period brought in rich dividends to the country. As the Chinese became more and more dependent on foreign capital and technology, they began understanding the intricacies of multilateral diplomacy, specifically in the economic diplomatic aspects.[31] The 1986 Work Report submitted to the National People's Congress explicitly mentioned that the country needs to "extensively participate in various international organisations, conferences, and conduct active multilateral diplomatic activities and strengthen cooperation in all fields".[32] Apart from joining the United Nations in 1971, China began entering into several multilateral institutions[33]. These include those of economic nature such as World Trade Organisation or the Asia-Pacific Economic Cooperation or political and security institutions such as Shanghai Cooperation Organisation (SCO), Conference on Interaction and Confidence Building Measures in Asia (CICA), East Asian Summit (EAS) and others[34]. As the following figures suggest, multilateral diplomacy gained currency in the academic and policy circles in China in the recent times.

However, as Li Xueqin suggested, China's multilateral diplomacy has a few specific features unlike some of the universal connotations, viz., its priority given to the protection of sovereignty issues of the country, secondly in serving the economic diplomacy of the nation; thirdly for diversifying into non-traditional security aspects and finally protecting the interests of the developing

Figure 1.3: Academic Trends on China's Multilateral Diplomacy

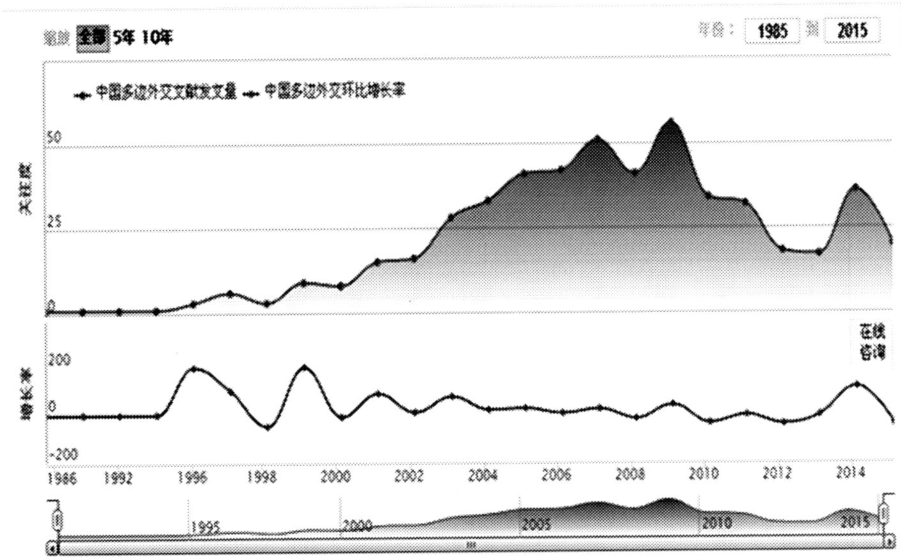

Source: Accessed at the CNKI Database from the website http://epub.cnki.net

Figure 1.4: Institutional Output on Multilateral Diplomacy, 1985-2015

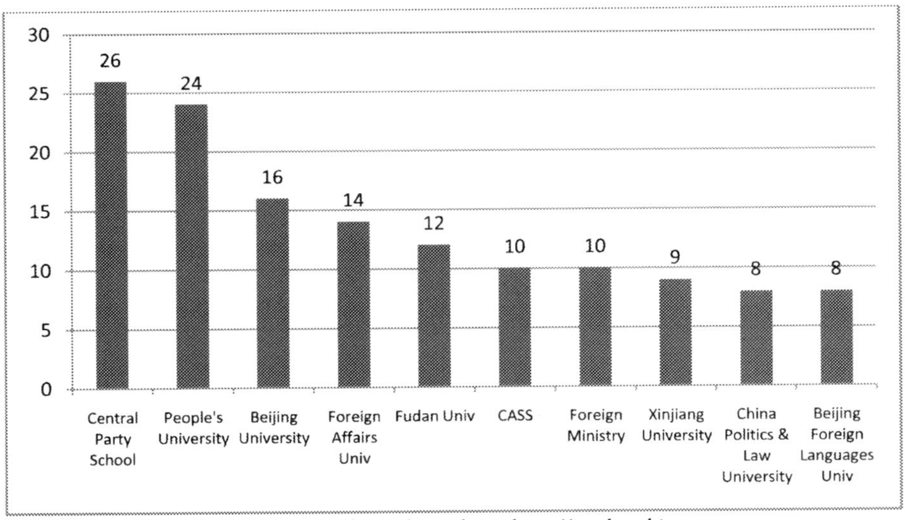

Source: CNKI database 1985-2015 from the website http://epub.cnki.net

countries.[35] Some of these features appear to be at variance with the broader multilateral trends. For instance, universally, it is expected that once a nation joins a multilateral institution with three or more nations, it is expected that the bilateral and sovereignty issues take a back seat with group interests coming to the fore. Specifically on Tibet, Taiwan and recently on South China Sea issues, China's position at times appeared to be hard posing some inconvenience to the multilateral institutions. For instance, the Southeast Asian grouping, which China actively entered into since the early 1990s, today faces the prospect of a summit meeting without a commonly agreed declaration. This is a specificity of China's multilateral behaviour.

China at the BRICS

The predecessors for the BRICS are several initiatives by China, Russia, India and other countries. Russia and China have floated the Shanghai 5 in the 1990s, and then expanded it into SCO in 2001. Russia-India-China have begun the trilateral dialogue mechanism after Russian Premier Primakov gave a call to New Delhi on protecting interests of these countries and opposing unilateral policies. India-Brazil-South Africa (IBSA) has another initiative as democratic and emerging countries to protect the interest of the developing countries during the globalisation drive. The Goldman Sachs report and the global financial crisis and others brought the BRICS countries together recently. China's initiative, participation and interactions in the BRICS have been significant[36]. The following section outlines China's leaders' initiatives and scholarly perceptions about the BRICS.

China's leaders welcomed the formation of the BRICS phenomenon and in general encouraged its activities and outreach. China's President attended all the summit meetings and made speeches for furthering this formation given its emerging status and trans-continental nature[37]. Terming the first formal meeting of the BRIC meeting at Yekaterinburg as a significant event with worldwide attention, a report in the influential magazine Qiushi suggested that the new platform has become an "important force" in the international relations.[38] Citing the first summit declaration at Yekaterinburg, Qin Zhilai of the International Strategic Studies Institute of the Central Party School argued that the BRIC formation is "non-confrontational" [非对抗性的] to the existing institutions.[39] Soon after the first BRIC meeting was held at Yekaterinburg in 2009, Wang Yan of Jilin University Economics Institute suggested that while the new formation is poised to grow in the international domain, differences exist among the member states of this formation. Wang suggested that the BRIC is neither a grouping nor an alliance. To enhance its profile, Wang argued, China should graduate towards a high value end exporter even as it takes countermeasures on inflation and trade protectionism.[40]

Subsequently, South Africa had been admitted as a full-fledged member to form BRICS at Sanya meeting. On this occasion, Zhao Mingwen suggested that the BRICS had shifted from being a dialogue to a cooperative mechanism [41]. According to Li Yang, vice president of Chinese Academy of Social Sciences, the Sanya Declaration of 2011 provided the much needed platform for the producers and consumers of the world, in addition to discussion on reserve currency issues.[42]

At the New Delhi meeting, President Hu Jintao put forward the following suggestions of "common development and promote common prosperity; equal consultation, deepening political mutual trust; adhere to pragmatic cooperation and consolidate the basis for cooperation; and adhering to international cooperation promote world development[43]. As the New Delhi summit meeting of the BRICS indicated in March 2012, quota and governance reforms issues in these institutions need to be amended.[44] The second IMF reforms of 2007 witnessed the growth of new members as a result of the increase in their share—for China up to 6 per cent and in the case of India by 2 per cent. However, while the IMF quota system was reformed in 2010 (agreed to at the G-20 Pittsburg meeting), the BRICS states only have 13 per cent voting rights in this forum, despite producing half of the global economic growth in 2011.[45]

At the Durban meeting in March 2013, President Xi Jinping called upon the BRICS countries to play a bigger role to "uphold international fairness and justice and safeguard world peace and stability; vigorously promote the building of a global development partnership and strive for common prosperity of all countries; and deepen mutually beneficial cooperation and seek win-win results".[46] Attending the Fortaleza meeting, Xi Jinping suggested that the BRICS countries need to keep the spirit of openness, inclusiveness, cooperation and win-win progress, seek new impetus for the long-term development of BRICS countries.[47]

While the political leadership's views are forthcoming and generally bland, China's officials, party intellectuals and scholars are more forthcoming on their country's participation in the BRICS. Many of these views are highly articulate, with global power configurations in mind and exploring how China could further advance its national interests and overall profile through the BRICS mechanism. These perspectives are linked to the subjective understanding of the international system, pattern and the order that the Chinese prefer. They have brought about the differing perceptions, objectives of China in the BRICS, global political and economic governance issues, and power equations with the United States, China's ambitions for power transition at the global and regional levels, invoked China's diplomatic concepts of "seeking common ground", united front tactics and "setting up a different kitchen" and other ideas. Learning lessons from the Soviet disintegration, many of them touched upon the economic issues and influencing global financial structure and institutions. Some are more explicit and imply that as the US power declines; China needs to take the lead in international affairs, while the others wanted China to follow Deng Xiaoping's gradualist "韬光养晦" [keeping a low profile] approach.

Many Chinese scholars argue that despite the increasing levels of interactions between the United States and China in the diplomatic, political, economic, strategic and military fields, on several issues both differ, viz., Taiwan, Tibet, South China Sea, human rights, etc. They suggest that the US hegemony and power politics constrain China's rise in the region. By associating with the multilateral institutions such as BRICS China could stave off pressures from western countries and avoid "easily giving in and compromise" on its policies, besides ushering in "一超多强" [one superpower and many powers][48]. Similarly, Zhang Maorong suggested that while the BRIC countries were increasing their economic profile, the global financial crisis in the United States and Europe had negative consequences for these emerging economies. The global financial institutions were also not able to rescue these countries when in need. Hence, by voicing their concerns through the BRIC formation at the Yekaterinburg meeting in 2009, this group had acquired worldwide attention.[49]

He Yafei, deputy director of Overseas Chinese Affairs Office of the State Council argued that with China's initiative of One Belt and One Road and the establishment of the Asian Infrastructure Investment Bank and BRICS New Development Bank, in addition to the net capital exports by China in 2014-15, it is time for a change from western dominated global governance to the "co-habitation" of East West co-governance model.[50] Echoing similar views, Lu Feng, Li Yuanfeng and Yang Yewei suggested that as an extension of the domestic agenda of intensifying reform and opening up, China's diplomacy should emphasise on building bridges with the BRICS countries further for its effort at reforming the global governance mechanisms. Specifically, Lu et.al. argued that China needs to take further the international financial regulatory reform, reform of international financial institutions, reform of international monetary system, especially the reserve currencies' institutional arrangements and contain the developed countries' spillover of their macro-economic policies.[51] Liu Jianfei agrees that in order to reform the current international order, which he terms as unfair and unjust, China needs to nudge further the AIIB and the BRICS formations.[52]

Yang Jiemian, who served as Shanghai Institute of International Studies head, provided a comprehensive picture of China's purpose, justification and strategies in promoting the BRICS phenomenon. Yang argued that the growth of the BRICS suggest to a "balance of power" in international relations intended to promote "just and rational" order. While the G-20 process serves to overcome the North-South divide, the BRICS bridges the South-South dialogue. The purposes of the BRICS are to promote economic growth quality, establish wide-ranging partnerships, and gradual but "non-confrontational" [非对抗性的] reform and peaceful transition [和平转型中] of the old governance system. He identified optimistic, neutral and pessimistic trends in the BRICS progress although he argued that the grouping remained a "soft mechanism" so far with no secretariat, guidelines or relations with other multilateral institutions. Yang recommends that the grouping articulate its basic guidelines, strengthen and diversify cooperative mechanisms and exchanges.[53]

Yan Xuetong, a leading scholar at Qinghua University and a proponent that China should transit towards "有所作为" [accomplish something], pointed out that while the BRIC as a "third force" after the US and Europe is increasing and to an extent decreasing Japan's influence in the international financial institutions, their impact is mainly in the economic field rather than in the political or security aspects of the globe.[54]

Leading foreign policy expert Jin Canrong of People's University argued that while the BRICS countries are endowed with resources, territory, growth rates and others, they are still new-comers to the rule making mechanisms in the international order. In recent times, due to their aggregate strength and unified voice, the economic decision-making mechanism is undergoing transformation.[55]

Shi Yinhong, another leading international relations expert, argued that even as the US power was depleted due to the counter-terror campaigns, China's rise is creating a positive international environment with the norms governing the international system changing.[56]

Wang Jisi, an American Studies expert was more candid. Wang argued that by associating with the BRICS, China was able to shield itself from the Western pressures, although many of the BRICS nations either have not been able to accept China's positions on Taiwan, Tibet, Xinjiang, human rights, renminbi exchange rates etc. or even have conflicts with China.[57]

According to Zhang Jianxin of Fudan University, the BRICS phenomenon is synonymous to the inexorable transfer of power from the West to the emerging countries. While the western countries had shaped 400 years of international and regional order through four hegemonic orders of Spain, the Dutch, England and the US, the new grouping reflects to non-hegemonic building of a new international order. Zhang suggests that the rise of the BRICS would lead to a balance of power with the G8 so that no one set will be able to dominate the international order.[58]

Wang Youming of a BRICS think tank at the Qinghua University argued that China has become a "facilitator" [推动者] rather than a "challenger" [挑战者] and least of all an "over thrower" [推翻者]—as some Western reports suggest—of the international order. Wang argued that despite differences, the BRICS mechanism should be strengthened for mutual benefit. Instead of challenging the international order, the BRICS mechanism at the most could end the monopoly of the Fund-Bank and other institutions rather than replacing them. In terms of managerial experience, or financial strength or scale of disbursement of loans or influence the BRICS institutions are only of recent origin. Wang suggested that at the moment the BRICS NDB could only complement the existing institutions. However, Wang suggested that the BRICS countries should enhance their pressure on the existing global institutions and participate in the rule making process. Specifically, as a major beneficiary of the existing international order and due to the imperatives of a stable environment for its rise, China should pursue such multilateral engagements.[59]

According to Pu Ping of the People's University, how China handles its relations with the BRICS will have larger implications for its multilateral diplomacy. Although China should pay highest attention to its own national interests, it "should play a leading role by virtue of its economic advantages, it means more responsibility and commitment, rather than acting as the leader in multilateral cooperation."[60] The value of the BRICS mechanism in China's thinking lay mainly in the economic domain—such as warding off the ill effects of the global financial crisis of 2008. However, according to Pu, China also pays attention to shaping a new international political and economic order.[61]

With the growth in the profile of the BRIC countries in terms of GDP indicators, trade expansion, FDI flows, internationalisation of the currencies and others, Liu Shejian argued that other countries may view this phenomenon in an alarming manner and may take stringent measures against these countries. Liu suggested that the BRIC countries need to also sort out their domestic political and economic problems, viz., Brazil with its income inequalities and low growth rates, India's trade restrictions, unemployment rate and skilled labour supply issues, Russian foreign debt and over dependence on energy exports at a time of worldwide decline in commodity prices; and the lopsided economic growth in China, its widening income gap and other problems.[62]

Reflecting on the unique working mechanism of the BRIC formation, Wang Yuhua and Zhao Ping of Shantou University Business School in Guangzhou argued that while differences exist between the member states/ leaders on a number of issues, the forum as such is aimed at strengthening and maintaining common position [共同立场] on a number of issues of interest/concern to the member states.[63] While a number of issues drag the BRICS formation, viz., no specific programme or firmed up procedures, no binding resolutions, and even conflict of interest among member states on a number of issues—often acute differences—Wang and Zhao suggest that in the interests of China's national development, it should actively mould the discourse in this formation.

Zhang Youwen of Institute of World Economy of Shanghai Academy of Social Sciences suggested that the BRIC grouping is an important component in China's foreign and economic policies. While the overall profile of the BRIC countries increased with the globalisation process, enhancing their GDP, foreign exchange reserves and exerted pressure on the international lending agencies and "jointly safeguarded emerging economies", specifically for China the BRIC grouping offers resources and energy supplies and contributes for the economic growth and stability.[64]

According to Dao Shulin, researcher at China Institute of Contemporary International Relations' Afro-Asian Division, the rise of BRIC countries will have a lasting impact on the international strategic situation in breaking the Western countries hold over the international relations, shift from the Atlantic to the Pacific, multipolarisation, sharp correction in the international economic structure, intensification of North-South conflict,[65]

Zhang Xiaojing, head of the Macroeconomic Research Institute of Chinese Academy of Social Sciences argued that the BRICS countries in their drive to catch up with the world powers need to synchronise the hard and soft power and accelerate institutional power; enhance competitive advantages and innovation strategies; strengthen crisis and risk management techniques in the light of sudden and deleterious global trends; emphasise cooperation while overcoming disputes; and usher in division of labour among the BRICS participants. Zhang suggested the BRICS formation need "to set aside disputes, seek common ground, cooperate more while reducing confrontations" [需要搁置争议、求同存异，多合作、少对抗].[66]

Ouyang Xiao argued that the rise of the BRIC formation is a "wonder of the world" [世界奇迹] in recent times. Their assuming greater role is mainly because of the "big power effect" [大国效应] related to economic growth advantages, resources, market potential, economies of scale and product diversity, etc. The BRIC countries are also in the forefront of economic recovery, sustainable development and making efforts at reform of the international economic order. Hence, the BRICS need to assume responsibilities of great powers[67].

According to Zhang Genhai and Wang Yue the development of the BRICS augurs well for the creation of a new international order given the comprehensive plan of the five-nation grouping in politics, economy, culture, science and technology and security issues. However, while the BRICS phenomenon is "inevitable", the authors argued that the differences between them based on competition, trade disputes and mutual distrust could limit the multilateral cooperation.[68]

According to Yang Jun, the long-term goals of China include the creation of multilateral institutions such as the BRICS in order to influence the international financial system, monetary policies and commodity price volatility and have a greater say in the international organisations and the global financial system. Also, the other objective of China, according to Yang, is that the BRICS formation could help in reducing and resolving tensions between China and other countries.[69]

While there has been an enormous enthusiasm among the Chinese scholars and officials for the idea of the BRICS as the above literature survey suggests, not everyone is enamored with the multilateral grouping. Xue Yuning, for instance, suggested that while the Goldman Sachs initial enthusiasm in the rise of the BRICs in four parameters, viz., macroeconomic stability, institutional effectiveness, openness and the education levels of these countries had attracted global attention, nevertheless, due to the on-going global financial crisis many of these parameters themselves are undergoing problems. Inflation, budgetary deficits, decline in investments in human resources etc. recently are putting strains on the BRIC countries.[70]

Assessment

The BRICS has come a long way as an institution in the last three years. As rising economies, the BRICS nations are expected also to move up the political ladder in the international relations. Their voice on the Arab Spring, reform and reorganisation of the UN, norm based approach on use of force in international relations, their coordination in the G-20 on trade, finance and market related issues have been increasing. Instead of merely a "talk-shop" institution, the BRICS also is laying down concrete plans to increase its agenda in the recent period and have succeeded in setting the agenda on a number of issues such as opposing trade protectionism, voting rights at the Fund-Bank, climate change issues and the like.

One of the major outcomes of the BRICS phenomenon is the creation of the New Development Bank (NDB). The idea to form the NDB at the New Delhi Summit meeting in 2012 was welcomed for the structural changes that this new financial institution could bring in the future global governance issues. Subsequently, at the Durban meeting as well as at Fortaleza, the idea took more concrete shape and by 2016 its architecture has been finalized with Shanghai as the headquarters. This bank will be the first international institution since the establishment of European Bank for Reconstruction and Development in 1991 and reflects to the urge of the emerging countries for financing infrastructure projects[71]. In the BRICS development bank—China's contribution will be 41 per cent of the estimated $100 billion.[72] Unlike the Fund-Bank practice hierarchical decision-making structure based on the GDP, the NDB is based on the member countries. Shi Yiqing suggested that this bank will break the traditional monopoly of the US and Europe in global lending practices.[73] The Director of Institute of World Economic and Politics of Chinese Academy of Social Sciences Gao Haihong suggested that the NDB indeed will provide tough competition for the Fund-Bank institutions. While the Chiang Mai Initiative to address the 1997 financial crisis in Asia was unable to provide public services, the NDB, aided by the emerging economies, will be different. She argued that the NDB will be "setting up a different kitchen" compared to the existing financial institutions.[74] The director of Institute of Finance at Chinese Academy of Social Sciences Li Yang argued that given the different economic stages among the BRICS countries, and their dependence on the Chinese economy, it is difficult to usher in the principle of equality in the bank's functioning. Another issue that could provide friction within the BRICS is the choice of currency in the disbursement of loans.[75] According to Sun Yu, a leading foreign exchange dealer, while the BRICS bank will initially trade in the USD gradually it is likely to switch over to the local currencies. Others argued that since the demand for the infrastructure building in these countries is so huge – running into trillions – internal financing is the most likely outcome for the foreseeable future. Liu

Dongliang of the Merchants Bank suggested that in order to create a "*renminbi* zone" China needs to finance NDB projects in the renminbi.[76]

When the former US Secretary of State Hillary Clinton mentioned that the US should learn from the BRICS rise, it is an endorsement of the coordination of the BRICS in the international relations as well as in economic development. Although there are acute differences between the BRICS states on market-economy status, investments, explicit endorsement of the UNSC membership, democracy, limited economic integration with the BRICS with total trade between the five countries accounted for only 4.9 per cent of the total foreign trade of the five countries,[77] no free trade area within BRICS, etc., the grouping is expected to enhance its prestige in the coming years as the globe is witnessing major changes in power re-distribution, financial crisis, etc.

Among the BRICS states, China is a major beneficiary of multilateralism. For, China's foreign policy priority has changed from bilateral equations to that of multilateral interactions coinciding with its rise as the 2nd largest economy. It is trying to enhance "structural power" by influencing global rules, norms and the 'structure' of the relationship patterns within the international system. China needs the BRICS in the current interregnum in the international system and in power transition with the US. China is wary of a direct and violent conflict with the US in this transition at the global level as it would cost its hard earned rise in the international system. While China suggests that it sticks to multilateralism, it is not clear if this is a long-term policy or for a short term co-existence. In the last decade since the formation of this multilateral process, China's statements and actions varied substantially giving scope for speculations on whether China's participation in this initiative transitory or on a long-term basis, whether its enthusiasm for this initiative remains stronger over a longer period or is tempted with proposals such as G-2.

China's relations with the US are factored by Beijing for larger gains in terms of investments, high technology and markets in the West. In the backdrop of the Group 2 (i.e. between US and China) coordination of international and regional security and economic situation as suggested by Brzezinski, China's position in multilateral institutions is quite evident. China had not explicitly opposed the US policies. Instead, Beijing supported Russia, Germany and France in the Second Gulf War in 2003 or on other security and economic issues. Multilateralism then comes in handy for Beijing to shield itself for the time being till its comprehensive national strength surpasses that of the US and power transition at the global levels take place in Beijing's favour.

China and the other BRICS countries have argued that the largest multilateral institution, the United Nations should be reformed and reorganised to serve the interests of all countries—whether big or small, developing or developed, powerful or weak. China also had released a white paper on the subject. The BRICS countries in their joint statements have advocated the basic tenets of the UN—such as its Charter, non-use of force, no regime change, respecting the sovereignty of individual member states, etc. However, when the Group 4 (Brazil, Germany, Japan and India) bidding began and even though this group included two of the BRICS constituents, China's responses are at best vague or even avoiding the issue of reorganisation.

It has been observed that some countries in the BRICS formation are not sensitive to the needs of the other members either in terms of sustainable developmental practices, environmental concerns, trade imbalances and market economy status and transparency and corruption issues. While "rule of law" has been mentioned as a major goal of China by the 4th plenum of the Communist Party, many issues related to its implementation, specifically in relation to the BRICS countries, has been questioned.[78] Some BRICS countries have been making efforts to restrict trade with China through invoking the World Trade Organisation provisions on anti-dumping. China has also not opened its market to the other BRICS countries.[79]

Another critique is to the inconsistencies in the multilateral practices of China. China used to argue that the ASEAN should be in the "driver's seat" in relation to issues of Southeast Asia, ARF, EAS and such multilateral institutions. However, since 2010, there has been a gradual shift in Beijing's position which has become more and more bold since the July 12, 2016 Permanent Court of Arbitration ruling on the South China Sea dispute. The ASEAN is no longer united with schisms becoming more and more apparent since the Hanoi meeting in 2010 but more pronouncedly in the Phnom Penh meeting. Today, the ASEAN is a divided house with Laos, Cambodia and others supporting China on the South China Sea issue.

All the above points raise the question of China's role in the BRICS phenomenon on its motivations, objectives, interests and how far it can go to stick with the BRICS and support other members in the international system.

END NOTES

1 "Full text of Hu Jintao's report at 18th Party Congress," *Xinhua*, November 17, 2012 accessed at http://news.xinhuanet.com/english/special/18cpcnc/2012-11/17/c_131981259_12.htm

2. Samuel P. Huntington, "The Lonely Superpower: The New Dimension of Power," *Foreign Affairs,* March-April 1999. On the other hand, Zbigniew Brzezinski suggested that the United States need to realign its policies towards Russia and China due to the complex geopolitical shifts in regional balances. See "Towards a Global Realignment," *The American Interest*, April 17, 2016 accessed at http://www.the-american-interest.com/2016/04/17/toward-a-global-realignment/. However, Hal Brands argued that despite talk of the decline of the United States power globally, it still retains primacy in the global affairs and that any talk of its retrenchment is counter-productive. See "The Era of American Primacy Is Far from Over," *National Interest*, August 24, 2016 accessed at http://nationalinterest.org/blog/the-skeptics/the-era-american-primacy-far-over-17465
3. "The Rise of the Rest," *Newsweek*, May 12, 2008 accessed at http://fareedzakaria.com/2008/05/12/the-rise-of-the-rest/
4. See WPS Sidhu, PB Mehta and Bruce Jones, eds. *Shaping the Emerging World- India and the Multilateral Order* (Washington, DC: The Brookings Institution, 2013) and Marc Lanteigne, *Chinese Foreign Policy- An Introduction* (London: Routledge, 2009). On how multilateralism itself has become a norm in international relations in the recent times, see Qin Yaqing, "多边主义研究:理论与方法" [Multilateralism—Theory and methods] 世界经济与政治 [World Economics & Politics], No. 10 (2001), pp. 9-14.
5. These figures are from Xu Jia and Cai Wei, "国际制度与中国的选择" [International System and China's choice] 国际政治研究 [International Politics Journal], No. 4 (2007) p. 137. Xu and Cai point out that the emerging countries do not have adequate strength in these institutions in which the traditional dominant countries still play a bigger role and also that if China attempts to change these institutions and create a new order, then vested interests could harm the national interests of the country. (pp.143-44)
6. Chen Dongxiao calls such failure of the multilateral institutions as "competence deficit" that needs to be fixed. See "试论全球政治的新发展和中国多边外交的再思考" [New Developments in Global Politics and Rethinking on China's Multilateral Diplomacy] 国际展望 [Global Outlook], No. 2 (2009) pp. 1-14.
7. Wang Yi, "Exploring the Path of Major-Country Diplomacy With Chinese Characteristics," *China International Studies*, No. 4 (2013) pp. 5-17 (p.5).
8. Hu Angang predicts that China will become an economic superpower in the medium term. See *China in 2020 – A New Type of Superpower* (New Delhi: HarperCollins, 2011).
9. See Yang Jiemian, "China's diplomatic achievements and theoretical breakthrough during three decades of reform and opening up", *China International Studies* (Winter 2008) pp. 20-36
10. See "Full Text of Jiang Zemin's Report at 16th Party Congress" November 18, 2002 accessed at http://www.china.org.cn/english/features/49007.htm#9
11. Hu Jintao, "Hold High the Great Banner of Socialism with Chinese Characteristics and Strive for New Victories in Building a Moderately Prosperous Society in all" October 15, 2007 accessed at http://www.china.org.cn/english/congress/229611.htm
12. Soon after the 18th Party Congress, China's new leadership in June 2013 unveiled a "New Type of Major Power Relations" 新型大国关系 [win-win, non-conflict, non-confrontational] with the United States. See Wang Yi, 2013 pp.11-12
13. Michael Pillsbury argued in a recent work, after extensive surveys, interviews and visits to China, that the intention of China through these centennials is to challenge the United States to become the global hegemon, See *The Hundred-Year Marathon: China's Secret Strategy to Replace America as the Global Superpower* (New York: Henry Holt & Co, 2015). Here Pillsbury suggests that the Chinese leaders "see a multipolar world as merely a strategic way point en route to a new global hierarchy in which China is alone at the top" (p.39).

14. See Marc Lanteigne, *Chinese Foreign Policy: An Introduction* (London: Routledge, 2009), p.57
15. One of the major proponents of this school of thought within China is Yu Xintian – former head of the Shanghai Institute of International Studies – termed by David Shambaugh as belonging to the Global South School of thought in China. See David Shambaugh, *China Goes Global: The Partial Power* (Oxford: Oxford University Press, 2013) pp. 31-32. Others include, according to Shambaugh, nativists, realists, major power adherents, Asia first, selective multilateralists and globalists.
16. See Liu Haijun, "我国多极化思想的演变" [Evolution of China's multipolarity thought] 国际关系学院学报 [Foreign Affairs Institute Journal] No. 2 (2000) pp 3-9; Liu Wei, "浅析 21 世纪初世界多极化趋势的主要表现" [The main manifestations of early 21st century multipolar world trends] 改革与开放 [Reform & Opening] No. 8 (2011) p. 19
17. Zhang Qianming, ""世纪国际格局与中国外交战略"研讨会综述 *21 shiji guoji geju yu Zhongguo waijiao zhanlue' yantao hui zongshu*" [""21st Century International Situation and China's Foreign Strategy" Symposium"] **东南亚研究** [Southeast Asian Studies] Issue 6, 1999 pp. 50-52. Similar views were expressed by Zhang Feng in the Ph.D. thesis "国际体系与中国对外关系：历史演进与当代建构" [International System and China's external relations- Historical evolution and contemporary structure] *Shanghai Foreign Studies University*, May 2009
18. Zhong Zhenming, "国际格局与中国的和平崛起学术研讨会综述" [Symposium on international pattern and China's rise] *Tongji University Journal* (Social Sciences Section), Vol. 15, No. 1 (February 2004).
19. See Nele Noesselt, "Chinese Perspectives on International Power Shifts and Sino-EU Relations (2008–2011)" *GIGA Research Unit* No. 193 April 2012 accessed at http://www.giga-hamburg.de/dl/download.php?d=/content/publikationen/pdf/wp193_noesselt.pdf.
20. Ye Jiang, "Will China be a "Threat" to Its Neighbors and the World in the Twenty First Century?" *Ritsumeikan Annual Review of International Studies*, 2002. Vol. 1, pp. 55-68 accessed at http://www.ritsumei.ac.jp/acd/cg/ir/college/bulletin/e-vol1/1-4jiang.pdf.
21. Yu Zhengliang, "Global Power Structure Shifted and Transitional Multi-polarity Emerged" accessed at http://en.siis.org.cn/index.php?m=content&c=index&a=show&catid=15&id=103
22. Tang Jiaxuan (ed.), 中国外交词典 [Dictionary of China's Diplomacy] (Beijing: World Knowledge Publishers, 1999), p.279.
23. Zhou Enlai, "Speeches at the Plenary Session of the Asia-African Conference" April 19, 1955 in *Selected Works of Zhou Enlai* Volume 2 (Beijing: Foreign Languages Press, 1989), p. 162.
24. For the influence of this concept see Zheng Yiling, "周恩来"求同存异"外交思想的综合效应" [The combined effects of Zhou Enlai's diplomatic thought of "seeking common ground"] 厦门大学学报(哲学社会科学版), [Journal of Xiamen University], No. 2 (1991), pp. 22-28.
25. "尼克松谈周恩来的外交魅力" [Nixon speaks on Zhou Enlai's diplomatic charm] 国际问题资料 [Documents on International Relations], No. 19 (1984), pp. 26-29
26. See Jiang Zemin, *Selected Works of Jiang Zemin* volume 1 (Beijing: Foreign Languages Press, 2010), p.82.
27. Qian Qichen, *Ten Episodes in China's Diplomacy* (New York: HarperCollins, 2005)
28. See "邱耕田：求同识异法视角的马克思主义中国化" **学习时报**, June 1, 2015 accessed at http://theory.people.com.cn/n/2015/0601/c40531-27083929.html
29. John Gerald Ruggie (ed), *Multilateralism Matters :The Theory and Praxis of an International Form* (New York :Columbia University Press, 1993); Robert Keohane, *After Hegemony: Cooperation and Discord in the World Political Economy* (Princeton: Princeton University Press, 1984); Robert Keohane and Joseph Nye, *Power and Interdependence* (New York: Longman,

2001); Stephen D. Krasner (ed), *International Regimes* (Ithaca and London: Cornell University Press, 1983).

30. See Wu Jianmin, "多边外交是构建和谐世界的平台-重新认识多边外交" [Multilateral Diplomacy Provides a Platform for Constructing a Harmonious World – Multilateral diplomacy reconsidered] 外交评论 [Foreign Affairs Review], No. 90 (August 2006), pp. 10-14

31. Tang Wei, "1949-1989 年 中国 多边外 交 的 实践及其 特 点" [China's multilateral diplomatic practice and features in 1949-1989] 国际政治研究 [Studies on International Politics], No. 1 (1998), pp. 15-22. However, Wang Yizhou suggests that unlike in major power diplomacy, in which a good grasp of the global dynamics, policy coordination, skilful use of overseas diplomatic and other assets, etc could be made, China, despite its role and effort at the UN, was unable to participate extensively and realize its multilateral diplomatic objectives. See "中国与多边外交" [China and multilateral diplomacy] 世界经济与政治 [World Economics and Politics] No. 10 (2001) pp. 4- 8

32. The government work report cited by You Hongbo, "中国的多边外交" [China's multilateral diplomacy] 经济与社会发展 [Economic & Social Development] vol. 7 no. 2 (February 2009) pp. 41-44 (p. 42)

33. See Alastair Ian Johnston and Paul Evans, "China's Engagement with Multilateral Security Institutions" in AI Johnston and Robert Ross Ed. *Engaging China: The Management of an Emerging Power* (London: Routledge, 1999) pp. 235-72 and Wu Guoguang and Helene Lansdowne Eds. *China Turns to Multilateralism – Foreign Policy and Regional Security* (London: Routledge, 2008).

34. Qiu Huafei argued that such multilateral efforts have a definite "Chinese" bearing in the sense of retaining the political ideology but merging with globalising trends. See "China's Multilateral Diplomacy" in his Contemporary Chinese Foreign Affairs and International Relations (Beijing: Current Affairs Press, 2013) pp. 336-70.

35. Li Xueqin, "当代中国多边外交的发展" [Development of Contemporary China's multilateral diplomacy] 理论观察 [Theory Observation], No.2 (44) (2007), pp.44-45 (p.45)

36. See Augusto Soto "The extent of China's relations with the BRICS countries," *Catalan International View*, Issue 12 Spring 2012 accessed at http://www.international-view.cat/the-extent-of-china-s-relations-with-the-brics-countries-9; and Pepe Escobar "The BRIC post-Washington consensus," *Asia Times*, April 17, 2010 accessed at http://www.atimes.com/atimes/Central_Asia/LD17Ag01.html

37. Li Wei, "金砖机制与国际金融治理改革" [BRICS mechanism and reform of international financial governance] 国际观察 [International Observer] No. 1 (2013) pp. 33-40 (p.33). Li here argued that one of the reasons why the BRICS were able to create a niche for themselves as emerging economies is that they created a distinct identity globally and began influencing the decisions in the other fora such as G-20, although such identity could be lost if the internal differences between the BRICS countries were to exacerbate. Ibid p.35. Li also suggested that unlike the other initiatives which question the North-South divide, the BRICS in the G-20 has been making efforts to build this gap between the North and the South.

38. "求是杂志" [Origin and status of the BRIC] Bl/fBg×_No. 16 p.61

39. Qin Zhilai, "金砖四国"首次峰会：奏响合作共进的新和弦" [The first summit meeting of the BRIC – Playing a new chord of win-win cooperation] 国际目潦望, No. 5 (2009), pp. 47-48.

40. Wang Yan, "金融危机下金砖四国能否冲击世界经济格局?" [Under the global

financial crisis can the BRIC countries impact the world economy?] 经营管理者 [Managers Journal] No. 16 (2009) p. 58.

41. See Zhao Mingwen, "Rapid Development of the BRICS Cooperation Mechanism " in Qu Xing, Ed. *New International Environment and China' Peaceful Development* (Beijing: World Affairs Press, 2012) pp.233-50.
42. Li cited by Zhu Dong, ""三亚宣言"奏响金砖五国最强音" [Sanya Declaration given the strongest voice during BRICS] 中国金融家 [China Financialist] No. 6 (2011) pp. 57-58 (p.57).
43. See Ruan Zongze, "China's Diplomacy in 2012: Dissolving Challenges and Creating Opportunities" in China Institute of International Studies Ed. *The CIIS Blue Book on International Situation and China's Foreign Affairs* (Beijing: World Affairs Press, 2013) pp. 253-54.
44. See "Fourth BRICS Summit Delhi Declaration" accessed at http://mea.gov.in/mystart.php?id=190019162
45. "*Zhongguo duncu IMF jiakuai gaige zengjia fazhan zhong guojia fayan quan*" [China urges the IMF to speed up reforms to increase the voice of developing countries] April 25, 2010 accessed at http://www.chinanews.com/cj/cj-gncj/news/2010/04-25/2245797.shtml. This report cites the governor of People's Bank of China Zhou Xiaochuan in this regard.
46. Xi cited at Ministry of Foreign Affairs Ed. *China's Foreign Affairs 2014* (Beijing: World Affairs Press, 2014) p.62
47. Xi cited at Ministry of Foreign Affairs Ed. *China's Foreign Affairs 2015* (Beijing: World Affairs Press, 2015) p.61
48. Xiao Mingshu in her MA dissertation argued that in its drive to become a powerful country, China has been guarding against the US. See ""金砖四国" 的崛起与世界格局的转换" [The Rise of the "BRIC" and transformation in the world order] *Jilin University*, December 5, 2008 MA Dissertation pp.20 and 26. For a neo-realist perspective that the regional powers pose challenges to unipolarity see Chun Kwang Ho, *The BRICs Superpower Challenge: Foreign and Security Policy Analysis* (Farnham, Surrey, UK : Routledge. 2013)
49. Zhang Maorong, "金砖四国：合力有多强" [BRIC: How strong a force] 世界知识 November 13, 2011 accessed at http://study.ccln.gov.cn/fenke/zhengzhixue/zzjpwz/zzgjzz/129318.shtml
50. "何亚非：从"西方治理"到"东西方共治"" [From "West governance" to East-West co-governance] 红旗文摘, No. 13 August 4, 2015 accessed at http://theory.people.com.cn/n/2015/0804/c40531-27407793.html
51. Lu Feng, Li Yuanfeng and Yang Yewei, ""金砖五国"的合作背景和前景" [Background and Prospects for BRICS cooperation] 国际政治研究, No. 2 (2011) pp.1-22
52. Liu Jianfei, "全球治理中的国际秩序变革" [Global governance under international order reform] 学习时报 [Study Times] July 4, 2016 accessed at http://theory.people.com.cn/n1/2016/0704/c376186-28520208.html
53. Yang Jiemian, "金砖国家合作的宗旨、精神和机制建设" [The purpose, spirit of cooperation and mechanism building of the BRICS] 人民网-理论频道, April 12, 2011 accessed at http://theory.people.com.cn/GB/14366894.html
54. Yan Xuetong interviewed by Sun Yan and Dong Ling, ""金砖四国" 国带来什么? 合作将给中 专访清华大学国际问题研究所" [What will BRIC cooperation bring about? Interview with Yan Xuetong of Qinghua University International Relations Institute] 中国报道, No. 6 (2009), pp. 60-61. In another article, Yan pointed out that for the "一超多强" [one superpower and many powers] to become the reality, the emerging countries

need to rise and then the US continues to make strategic mistakes. See Yan Xuetong, "世界格局走向及中国的机遇" [Trends in the global patters and opportunities for China] 当代亚太 [Journal of Contemporary Asia-Pacific], No. 5 (2008), pp. 7-13

55. Jin Canrong, "金砖国家崛起的战略影响和前景展望" [Strategic impact and outlook of the Emerging BRICS] interview to Chen Yechun of *People's Daily*, April 11, 2011 accessed at http://theory.people.com.cn/GB/14353525.html
56. Shi Yinhong, "U.S. Power, China's Rise, and World Order," October 2009 accessed at http://www.iaen.edu.ec/wordpress/wp-content/uploads/2009/12/US-Power-Chinas-Rise-and-World-Order3.pdf
57. Wang Jisi, "Foreword" in *China International Strategy Review 2012* (Beijing: Foreign Languages Press, 2012), p. viii;
58. Zhang Jianxin, "后西方国际体系与东方的兴起" [Post-Western International System and the Rise of the East] 世界经济与政治 [World Politics and Economics] No. 5 (2012), pp. 4-20 (pp.17 and 14)
59. Wang Youming, "金砖机制建设的角色定位与利益融合宰" [Role positioning and interest fusion of constructing the BRICS mechanism] 国际问题研究, No. 5 (2015) pp. 116-28
60. Pu Ping, "金砖国家机制在中国多边外交中的定位" [The position of BRICS mechanism in China's multilateral diplomacy] 教学与研究 [Teaching & Research] No. 10 (2014), pp. 52-59 (p.58).
61. Ibid p. 53
62. See Liu Shejian, "BRIC's - 重构全球财富版图?" ["BRICs' - reconstructing global wealth?"] 理财视点 [Financial Viewpoint] (May 2006) pp. 13-15 (p.13)
63. Wang Yuhua and Zhao Ping, ""金砖国家"合作机制的特点、问题及我国的对策 [Features of BRICS cooperative mechanism, problems and China's counter-measures] 当代经济管理, vol. 33, no. 11 (2011) pp. 24-28 (p.25)
64. Zhang Youwen, ""金砖四国"的由来及其国际经济合作" [Origins of the BRIC and international economic cooperation] 求是, April 16, 2010 accessed at http://www.qstheory.cn/zxdk/2010/201008/201004/t20100413_26703.htm
65. Dao Shulin cited in Lin Limin, "BRICs 现象"剖析" [BRICs Phenomenon] 现代国际关系, No. 9 (2004), pp. 44-54 (p.46).
66. Zhang Xiaojing, "金砖四国的赶超之路" [Catching up on the BRIC road] 中国教育报 May 15, 2010 accessed at http://www.qstheory.cn/gj/zgwj/201005/t20100515_29872.htm
67. Ouyang Xiao, ""金砖四国"崛起的大国效应" [BRIC rise is having a big power effect] 光明日 •, February 2, 2010 accessed at http://www.gmw.cn/01gmrb/2010-02/02/content_1048339.htm
68. Zhang Genhai and Wang Yue, ""金砖五国"合作模式：历程、结构与展望" [BRICS model of cooperation – history, structure and outlook] 学术论坛, No. 278 (March 10, 2014) pp.88-91
69. Yang Jun, "金砖国家的崛起" [Rise of BRICS countries] 南风窗 [South Reviews] No. 9 (2011) p.18
70. Xue Yuning, "金融危机下重新审视金砖四国" [Re-examining BRICS under the financial crisis] 世界经济情况 [World Economic Outlook] No. 11 (2009) pp. 12-15
71. Liang Xiaoyi, "金砖峰会或将重塑国际金融体系" [BRICS Summit or reshaping international financial system] 中国新时代, August 2014, Issue 198 p.27. By finding an alternate arrangement to the US $ dominated global and regional trade, the NDB could

provide scope for international financial transactions. It was also pointed out that while the NDB may not be able to challenge the IMF/WB, it could provide some competition and reduce dependency in the short to medium term. However, the World bank President Kim Jim Yong and the IMF suggested that both could supplement the NDB's work.

72. Scott Rose, "China Agrees to Give 41% of $100 Billion BRICS Reserve Pool," *Bloomberg*, September 6, 2013 accessed at http://www.bloomberg.com/news/2013-09-05/china-agrees-to-give-lion-s-share-of-100-billion-brics-pool-1-.html
73. Shi Yiqing, ""金砖银行"：新概念冲击旧秩序" [BRICS Bank- When the new concept meets old order] 国际金融 [Global Finance], May 2012, pp 138-39 (p. 139)
74. Gao Haihong interviewed by Zhou Hongda, "金砖金融合作站上新起点—访中国社科院世界经济与政治研究所国际金融研究室主任高海红" [BRICS financial cooperation on a new starting point—Interview with Chinese Academy of Social Sciences Institute of World Economics and Politics International Finance Research Office Director Gao Haihong] 中国金融家 [China Financialyst] (August 2014) pp. 24-26
75. Li Yang cited by Chen Xilin and Su Hongyu, "金砖银行 搭起 BRICS 桥梁" [NDB puts up a BRICs bridge] 经济 [Economics] No. 1 (2015), pp. 48-49. On the other hand Li Wei argued that the BRICS need to question the US$ hegemony worldwide and diversify the monetary system. See Li Wei, "金砖机制与国际金融治理改革" [BRICS mechanism and reform of international financial governance] 国际观察 [International Observer] No. 1 (2013) pp. 33-40 (p.37).
76. See the excerpts at "金砖银行 离我们的生活并不远" [BRICS bank is not far away from our lives], *Xinhua*, July 18, 2014 at http://news.xinhuanet.com/fortune/2014-07/18/c_1111687837.htm
77. See Ouyang Xiao, Zhang Yabin and Yi Xianzhong, "中国与金砖国家外贸的"共享式"增长" [China and BRICs foreign trade "share" growth] accessed at http://doc.qkzz.net/article/be8fd02c-5ab9-4c00-8af0-fe690c5f548d.htm
78. Mwangi S. Kimenyi & Zenia Lewis, "The BRICS and the new Scramble for Africa" in Foresight Africa the Continent's Greatest Challenges and Opportunities for 2011, *The Brookings Institution*, January 2011 accessed at https://www.brookings.edu/wp-content/uploads/2016/06/01_africa_economy_agi.pdf
79. Yao Shumei and Yao Jingru suggest that the anti-dumping duties of India and Brazil have increased substantially on China in the recent times. See "金砖国家的崛起及其发展前景" [Rise of the BRICS and development prospects] 宏观经济管理 [Macro-economic Management] No. 8 (2012) pp. 84-86 (p.86). For instance India imposed 149 anti-dumping cases on China till 2011, while Brazil had also made several investigations in addition to raising currency exchange issues with China. Here the authors also suggest to the subtle competition between the BRICS countries in Africa in the energy, construction and infrastructure projects.

2

The Changing Economic Order: Linkages and Disconnects

Priyanka Pandit

Introduction

The financial crisis that hit the world economy towards the end of last decade triggered a significant transformation in the global capitalist system. The crisis accelerated major changes in the parameters of global political economy, which was long dominated by the United States through Washington and Washington Consensus plus policies. The emerging economic powers—led by China, India and Brazil—began acquiring a prominent place in the global supply chain and production networks in the aftermath of global financial breakdown, and have become far more integrated into the global economy, including international institutions that have traditionally been dominated by the established powers. Joining the club is the energy-rich and ambitious Russia, who amid domestic vulnerabilities, continue to exert preponderant influence across a large swath of former Soviet member states. The new economic context, thus, characterised by a new cast of actors and an expanding playing field, has generated both widespread expectations and anxieties. This has stimulated an intense debate about the potential transformations of world economic order, preferences for global economic governance and the future trajectories of the rising players within the emerging international system. There are divergent views on the subject—mostly varying between deep pessimism and couched in 'power transition' frameworks—, that suggest greater risk of conflict to those arguing that these powers will follow an emulative strategy, and reinforce the status quo on global economic governance.

For those who support the 'power shift' narrative, argue that uneven patterns of growth will lead to subsequent challenges to the dominant state's global leadership by rising powers, that may be dissatisfied with the status-quo and will, therefore, seek to upset the existing economic order[1]. On the other hand, liberals and neo-liberal institutionalists argue that state preferences vary and one cannot take them by assumption[2]. They suggest that increased economic contacts between states create possibilities of cooperation between the established actors and new players through webs of interdependence which reduces the risk of conflict and violence. In this sense, the contemporary shift in global political economy is towards multipolarity, where there are more than one poles of power to play influential roles in the international economic system[3]. This is indeed an attempt to reduce the North-South divide, which is largely a legacy of the industrial and territorial expansion of Western nations in the 19th and early 20th centuries. These asymmetrical arrangements within the international economic system can be better understood within the classic center-periphery model[4], whereby countries in the center, the core manufacturing states control and influence the peripheral and semi-peripheral states, which operate as suppliers of raw materials to the core. The model, originating in Dependency Theory[5] and World-System Analysis has gone a far way over five decades of theoretical discussion and its empirical application. It is argued that in the post-World War II years, the US controlled the exports of the fast-growing economies of Western Europe and Japan, through an asymmetric trade relation with these countries. Nevertheless, the shift in the locus of hegemony from Britain to the USA after the WW II amounted to a major transformation in the structure of the world-economy itself. Arguing in this line, some scholars view that the recent shift represents the reorganisation of the center-periphery model, where the emerging economies that previously played the role of peripheries, seeks to overcome the peripheral status of low end manufacture and become leading centers of the world economy. However, the complexity of today's global economy cannot be captured either through center-periphery formulations or power transition frameworks; in fact, various conceptualisations of multipolarity can suitably explain the changes in the world economy.

Approaching the rise of the contemporary BRICS (Brazil, Russia, India, China and South Africa) states through this framework, it is argued that the BRICS' rising powers poses a challenge within the global economic governance; they challenge its most liberal content, while becoming dependent on and engaging with its existing institutional structures. The chapter, therefore, contends three conceptual presumptions associated with roles of rising powers in global economic governance. First, global economic governance is not limited to Formal Intergovernmental Organisations (IGOs) like the International Monetary Fund (IMF) or World Trade Organisation (WTO), even though these institutions often serve as the prime arena for negotiations between the emerging and incumbent powers. The world economy, today, has numerous poles in the form of groupings such as the BRICS, IBSA and BASIC, in which relations among the states are coordinated in accordance with certain principles. Second, the study disagree with the approach that emphasise revisionist aspirations of the emerging powers, who are inherently opposed to the institutional orders fostered by dominant states[6]. It instead argues that despite the asymmetrical nature of the global economy and pervasiveness of the conflict of interest and discord, states, nevertheless cooperate even under conditions of anarchy. Third, it differs from the argument that the liberal principles of the international economic order have benefitted the emerging economies of Brazil, China and India and therefore, these powers seek its 'ultimate ascendance' and 'have deep interests in preserving the system'[7]. Although it is true that the BRICS member states have incentives to preserve existing arrangement of transnational processes and regulate the global economy, their domestic structures and policies act as constraint in pursuing the liberal ideas of western-sponsored economic institutions.

The chapter, therefore, presents a critical account of the BRICS within the context of ongoing debates of transformation in the global economy, probing into its key political economy fundamentals. It traces the evolution of BRICS from an international investment strategy to an influential grouping in global governance institutions and also discusses its policy initiatives towards stabilising the world economy in the post-crisis period. It then analyses China's engagement with the group as well as investigates the extent to which China creates an alternative outside the US-dominated international institutions through the newly-created BRICS alliance. The study assesses the inter-regional and intra-regional differences within BRICS, and finally concludes with an analysis of their preferences for global governance and the roles they would play in the global economic system.

BRICS and the Global Economic Governance: An Evolutionary Perspective

The recent financial meltdown and the resulting global recession have rekindled debates regarding the nature of contemporary capitalism. 'Global

Neo-liberalism' can best describe the essence of contemporary capitalism. Neo-liberal ideology and economic theory, which later formed the basis of global institutional structure, acquired vibrancy in the developed world, particularly in the US and the UK in mid-1970s. It became one of the crucial conditions determining the types of inter-state conflicts and in shaping the nature of rising power behaviour in international economic institutions. One of its characteristics is the significant expansion of trans-boundary exchange of goods, capital, including its geographical extent and integration, as compared to the previous phases of capitalism. This also defines the intensive processes of contemporary globalisation, which resulted in the creation of transnational institutions to govern these economic relations. These transnational institutions are multilayered, overlapping, without a notion of sovereignty over particular territory. Nevertheless, they end up being dominated by a hegemon or a group of states, either through their advantageous position in the markets or by exercising control through ideological hegemony. It is within this historical context, BRICS have risen and expanded its transnational integration.

There have been several attempts to conceptualise the distinctive feature of the BRICS economies[8]. It is true that when the US bank Goldman Sachs, following a careful economic study of the global situation, launched the idea of 'BRIC' comprising Brazil, Russia, India and China in 2001, only economists took it seriously. But over the period, as economic data began flowing in, it drew considerable attention of both the academics and the policy makers. The author of the original notion of BRIC, Jim O'Neill, developed the idea as an alternate economic order based on the primacy of the BRIC countries and less dominated by the West and its ideals. This idea was reinforced by the famous columnist, Fareed Zakaria in 2008[9], as the 'Rise of the Rest' and a 'post-American world order'. A few years on, several other influential international relations experts, made similar arguments, indicating that a transformation in the global political economy is underway. While these authors differed in their specifics, they acknowledge the non-liberal, non-Western content of BRIC, in which a greater role is assigned to states in the control and coordination of economic activities. To put it simply, BRICs' is an institutional variant of multilateralism, substantially less liberal than that of the Western core. The rationale of its emergence remains a caucus formation within larger settings of global governance, to pilot and test new ideas, and to reform the contemporary regime of capitalism. Some of the distinctive features of BRICS which distinguish it from the liberal West are: i) prominent role of the state in managing markets; ii) use of industrial policy tools and state directed finance; iii) a combination of state-owned enterprises and private firms to create highly flexible production networks. Additionally, the BRICS countries are endowed in terms of massive natural reserves as both volume and diversity, competitiveness mostly visible in the industrial sector and their agriculture and consumer markets are robust.

The reform of Bretton Woods Institutions constitutes an important aspect of the BRICS' agenda. In fact, it is the increasing disillusionment with the institutions of global economic governance that explains the timely emergence of BRICS. The emerging economies that constitute BRICS have had their deep-seated resentment and frustration with the developed nation's effort towards the current reform of the global financial system and their inability to address concerns of developing and least developing countries in the global trade regime. During the 1990s, the IMF and the US had pressed fora strengthening of international rules to promote capital account liberalisation, a measure that failed after a succession of financial crises in emerging markets[10]. Some hopes grew, when the year 2010 was adopted as the year of IMF reform, and three major changes had been proposed in agreement with the members. First, the fast-growing emerging market countries would have a bigger say in how the institution is run and how it interacts with its membership; second, to improve the Fund's ability to avert financial crises and to respond more flexibly to borrowers' needs; third, the general financial resources of the IMF, which usually have been quite scarce in relation to member countries' financing needs, were to be doubled. However, the failure to implement 2010 reforms by the IMF member states disappointed the BRICS countries further. This had been reflected through numerous statements made at various BRICS and G-20 summits coupled with representations before the IMF/World Bank annual meetings. At the Seoul summit of the G20 in 2010, China opposed a US proposal for using current account surpluses and deficits as indicators of the need to adjust. In 2012, the BRICS expressed reservations towards making further contributions to the IMF to promote global financial stability and expressed that any future contribution would be subject to the BRICS having confidence that the entire membership is truly committed to implement the 2010 reform'. In this regard, BRICS nations began looking for alternatives to make use of its surplus reserves. In March 2013 at the 5th BRICS Summit in Durban, the BRICS went a step further in not only demanding reforms of global governance, but also discussed the possibility of widening their scope of cooperation through a policy initiative. The Summit Declaration[11] stated: "As the global economy is being reshaped, we are committed to exploring new models and approaches towards more equitable development and inclusive global growth by emphasising complementarities and building on our respective economic strengths". Thus, the success of more participatory, informal governance platforms (such as the G-20 instead of the restrictive G-8) in the aftermath of the global economic crisis can be attributed to the growing pressures from the BRICS countries and other emerging economic powers for a more inclusive and participative global governance framework.

When the IMF and IBRD were created at the Bretton Woods Conference in 1944, the governance and voting structures of these institutions were largely dominated by the US and Europe. As years passed, the developing world economies have risen significantly, but the IMF and World Bank's governance structures continue to remain hierarchical and have hardly evolved since 1944. Despite continuous efforts of developing countries to urge reforms of Bretton Woods and to bring about changes in the distribution of voting rights and to democratise the decision making process, it has been very slow and not much has been achieved in this direction[12]. For example, in 2014, before the voting share reforms were approved by the US congress, US controlled 16.75 percent of voting rights in the IMF, whereas the share of IMF voting rights of the BRICS as a whole currently totaled 11.04 percent, despite their share of world GDP being 21.2 percent. However, as per the reform package, which came into effect on January 26, 2016, the 2.6 per cent points in voting rights gained by the BRICS economies is a far from the 20 per cent points gain in the economic gains over the past decade. Equally frustrating for the developing nations is the understanding that the US and European countries have about the selection of the Managing Director (MD) of IMF. As per this agreement, the MD will be a European, a reciprocal measure by the US as it enjoys a veto power in the IMF. Also, countries like US and West European nations have nearly 47 percent of the votes in the IMF, which makes it easy for them to select an MD of their choice. Thus, it can be convincingly argued that the increase in influence of the BRICS nations within the Bretton Woods, does not match their increased contributions to the world economy.

Table 2.1: BRICS Voting Rights in the IMF as Compared to GDP
(GDP share measured in nominal US dollar terms; IMF voting rights as of February 2016)

BRICS countries	*% Share of IMF Voting Rights*	*% Share of World GDP*
China	6.11	15.49
India	2.64	2.97
Russia	2.60	1.68
Brazil	2.23	2.45
South Africa	0.43	0.64

Source: IMF Quota & IMF World Economic Outlook, 2016.

One of the most significant changes in the WTO system has been its expansion in membership. The addition of the new members, especially admission of developing and least developing nations to the WTO is important[13]. It has led to significant changes in the character of the regime. Once dominated by the rich members, this trade organisation is gradually turning inclusive to the needs of the developing countries. The inclusion of China in 2001 and Russian accession in 2011, the WTO community now represents major nations of the world (see figure 2.1). As the WTO increases its scope, with an expanded membership, the hegemonic model dominated by US, EU, Japan and Canada, has been receiving greater challenges. In this context, Brazil, India and China have played an important role in the Doha round negotiations. Although Doha round has stalled from time to time, a compromise could be reached between both the developed and developing countries on key trade issues, with exemptions being granted to the developing and least developing nations.

Figure 2.1: Expansion of WTO membership

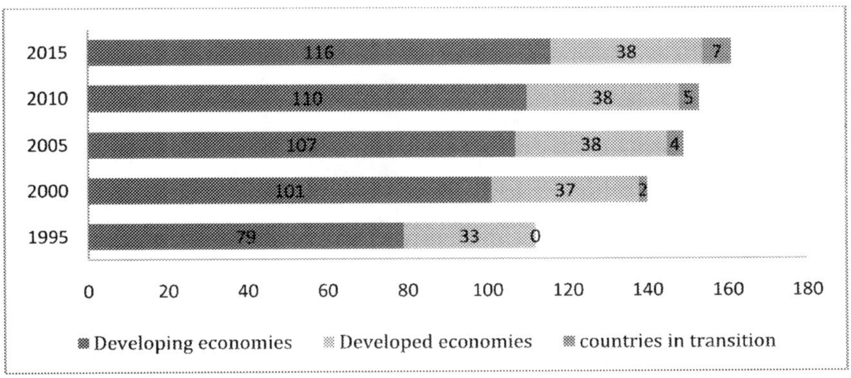

Source: WTO trade Statistics 2015.

Also assessing voting behavior of BRICS nations in the United Nations General Assembly (UNGA), BRICS nations except Russia, have a stronger record of voting in favour of resolutions than the average for the General Assembly (GA) as a whole (see table & figure 2.2).[14] The only state in this group with a lower rate of voting positively than the GA average is the USSR/ Russia. However, within BRICS, there is greater divergence in terms of responses to issues that arise in the UNGA. From the summit declarations, it can be understood that BRICS have an idealistic vision of the international system, which should be based upon international law, supremacy of the UN, democracy in international relations, multilateral diplomacy, collective decision making, fair and just development. While they express similar positions on international security, they differ in their support to the candidature of other BRICS nations to become permanent members of the UN Security Council. For instance, while Brazil, India and South Africa harbour ambitions to become UNSC members, China and Russia, openly refrain from supporting their candidatures.

Table 2.2: Voting Records of BRICS in UNGA 1946–2014 (% of Voting Choices)

	China	*India*	*Russia*	*Brazil*	*South Africa*	*BRICS*
Yes	78.77	78.85	69.58	80.33	87.59	76.91
No	3.25	7.21	14.26	6.69	0.73	8.04
Abstention	8.31	13.15	15.41	11.96	9.49	12.41
Absent	9.67	0.78	0.75	1.03	2.19	2.65

Fig. 2.2: Voting Records of BRICS in UNGA (% of voting choices)

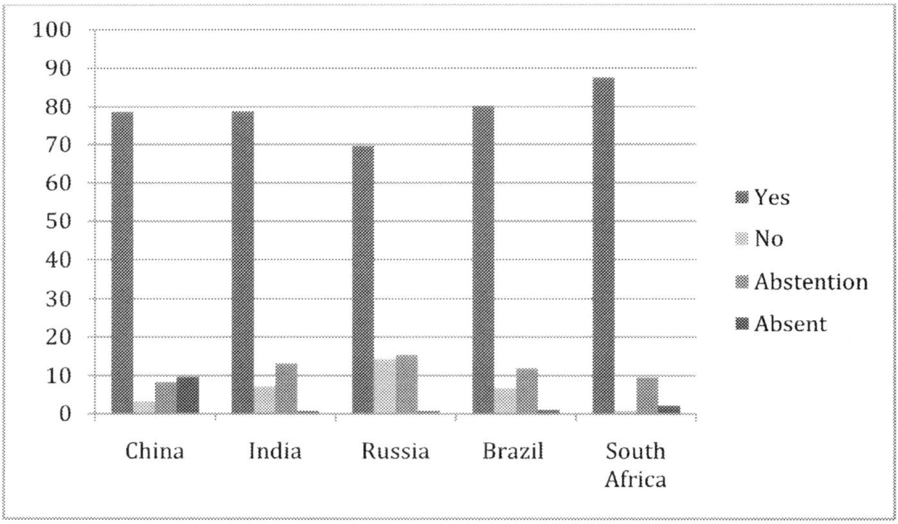

Source: Developed from Laura Peitz[15]

Talking about the empirical significance of BRICS, within the span of two decades, BRIC have consolidated and even further expanded their strong position in the world economy. After the years following the global financial crisis of 2008-2009, when many of the developed countries had lost their economic dynamism, the BRICs' weight in nominal GDP continued to grow and reached 20.5 percent of global GDP (an increase of four percentage points). While the share of the BRICS countries collectively in world trade stood at 3.6 per cent in 1990, it rose to over 25 per cent in 2010. Similarly, the share in global GDP, which recorded 10 per cent in 1990, crossed 30 per cent in 2015. Moreover, increased market size of products and services with infrastructural developments has made the BRICS an attractive destination for foreign direct investment. Yet, at the same time, they are regarded as developing countries in international comparisons, due to their substantial developmental needs, regional income disparities, informal economic sectors and poverty alleviation necessities.

Policy Initiatives

The 5th and 6th BRICS Summits in 2013 and 2014 marked a watershed in the evolution of the BRICS group as one of the key governing bodies with the establishment of the first BRICS institutions. These included the BRICS New Development Bank, the CRA, the BRICS Business Council and the Think Tanks Council. As an effort to reshape Bretton Woods governance structure and also an initiative to strengthen the legitimacy of BRICS, the BRIC countries established their own developed bank. The discussion amongst the BRIC countries was underway since 2012, and the detailed planning was subsequently undertaken in the lead-up to the 6th BRICS Summit in Fortaleza[16] in July 2014. It was then, the decision to set up the New Development Bank (NDB) was formalised along with a Contingent Reserve Arrangement (CRA) with capital of US$ 100 billion. The goals behind their creation were: 1) to finance infrastructure and sustainable development projects; and 2) to be an external account support facility to help developing countries manage balance of payments crises. The official statement signed by the leaders of the BRICS nations at the Summit in 2014, stated that "international governance structures designed within a different power configuration show increasingly evident signs of losing legitimacy and effectiveness. We believe the BRICS are an important force for incremental change and reform of current institutions toward more representative and equitable governance." The Fortaleza Declaration claimed that the NDB will strengthen co-operation among the BRICS, and also supplement the work of multilateral and regional financial institutions in global development.

At the time of the NDB's launch in 2014, the BRICS countries announced that each of the five member countries would initially have equal capital shares and equal governance votes and that the total initial capital of the NDB would be $50 billion, of which 20 per cent would be paid-in capital. Thus, the scale of initial capital of the NDB was limited by the fiscal/reserve capacity of the smallest member state of BRICS, which is South Africa. The BRICS New

Development Bank recently announced its first lending commitment of $811 million to the four countries of the south bloc on April 17, 2016. In its first phase of lending, the NDB agrees to provide $300 million to Brazil, $250 million to India, $180 million to South Africa and $81 million to China to fund renewable energy projects in these countries. Established at the 7th BRICS Summit 2015[17], this multi-billion dollar bank is considered as an alternative funding initiative to complement the existing international banking system. Current financing and investment patterns are inadequate in meeting the investment needs of developing economies. In this regard, the BRICS bank is expected to play a pivotal role in mitigating the challenges of funding faced by developing countries in the field of infrastructure and sustainable forms of development. Additionally, the new bank is significant since it signals an assertion of the global South vis-à-vis the North in the international economic order.

The BRICS countries especially, China and India have been quite vocal in advocating reforms of the international economic institutions like World Trade Organisation (WTO), International Monetary Fund (IMF) and World Bank which would make them more representative and fair to the needs of the developing countries. As per the lending policy of the IMF, loans are generally given on the implementation of certain economic policies by the borrowing countries. These conditions tend to involve in reducing government borrowing- higher taxes and lower spending; ii) higher interest rates to stabilise the currency; iii) allow failing firms to go bankrupt; and iv) structural adjustment like privatisation, deregulation, reducing corruption and bureaucracy. As a result, these policies of structural adjustment which are often imposed with little or no consultation with the affected countries worsen the situation leading to a greater economic chaos.

During the Asian crisis of 1997, many countries such as Indonesia, Malaysia and Thailand were required by IMF to pursue tight monetary policy (higher interest rates) and tight fiscal policy to reduce the budget deficit and strengthen exchange rates[18]. However, these policies caused a minor slowdown to turn into a serious recession with mass unemployment. Similarly, in 2001, Argentina was forced into a similar policy of fiscal restraint. This led to a decline in investment in public services which arguably damaged the economy. IMF, however, claims in the recent years, that it has drawn lessons from the crises and streamlined the demand it attaches to a loan. Contrary to its claims, the report by the European Network on Debt and Development (Eurodad)[19] reveals that conditions have become more intrusive on domestic policy, with an increase from an average of 14 in 2007 to almost 20 attached to each loan today.

The scope of sectorial and country-specific lending of the BRICS bank has been defined by the BRICS leaders in the 2013 Durban Summit Declaration. The NDB is set up as an alternative with the necessary savings and foreign exchange reserves of the BRICS countries. Its primary objective is to financially assist the developing countries in their infrastructure projects. The modalities of each loan would differ based on borrower's preferences. Among the key features of the new bank include equal voting rights of the five founding members, and the ability of the non-BRICS countries (emerging and developing as well as developed ones) to contribute capital provided the BRICS countries always have a minimum of 55 per cent of the total capital share. These features implies an important shift in the international financial architecture with NDB as the new platform of BRICS to advance reforms that favour developing and emerging countries, in general. Nevertheless, significant challenges remain. One of the strengths of the World Bank is its credit rating, and its sound financial position as well as the strength and diversity of its government shareholders. The World Bank's strong credit ratings from international rating agencies, combined with its extremely sound financial management and liquidity position, gives it an excellent access to international capital markets for its programs[20]. In comparison, the NDB has a less favourable financial profile in the view of international capital markets, due to the smaller number of government shareholders and their lower sovereign credit ratings contrary to the major shareholders of the World Bank. Owing to the lack of regulatory and systematic financial analyses, NDB will not have an established track record to begin with, which will be less favourable in international financial markets, making the cost of borrowing higher. There are also issues related to governance and expansion of the bank's membership which alongside lack of clear leadership of the NDB (with five equal founding shareholders) may hinder effective implementation. Additionally, presenting a viable domestic environment for investment, most of which are plagued by inefficient governance and the poor ability of repayment even with a concessional interest rate in smaller developing countries, will be a challenge for the NDB to avoid defaulters. Thus, it remains to be seen the extent to which the scale of lending by the BRICS bank will make meaningful impacts given the huge level of un-met needs indentified in the developing and emerging economies.

An alternate model to the Western hegemony, the BRICS bank has increasingly become a useful tool for China to exert influence in the developing world. Although, its capital contribution remains same as the other BRICS nations, China's economic performance continues to surpass its BRICS counterparts regularly. Most succinctly, China's GDP is over 1.5 trillion dollars larger than the combined economic output of the other BRICS members. Given the power disparity between them and China, the non-Chinese BRICS members, therefore, are unable to resist the new financial institution from becoming a Chinese-dominated one. Beijing, on the other hand, has long term plans vis-à-vis the new bank. Alongside the Asian Infrastructure Investment Bank (AIIB), the BRICS bank will finance China's "One Belt, One Road" program that involves constructing a chain of infrastructure projects across the world. This in turn, would further boost the Chinese domestic economy by obtaining contracts for Chinese companies in BRICS bank-funded projects.

One of the impacts of financial crises has been sudden surges in liquidity. As a result of this abundance of financial assets, the emerging economies are often compelled to absorb increasing level of short term capital, making it vulnerable to volatile capital inflows and outflows. In this context, there has been considerable discontent with the main multilateral institutions such as the IMF and World Bank. The growing frustration of the developing countries including poor nations of Africa, for failing to get a greater voice in decision-making in the Bretton Woods Institutions, has led to the creation of this alternate fund which would help them during times of capital flight. In the form of financial packages during the crisis, these established institutions have unfairly imposed inappropriate structural adjustment programmes on developing countries, which the developed countries themselves would refuse to implement in their own economies in return for funding. Brazilian President Dilma Rouseff said at the launch: "It will help contain the volatility faced by diverse economies as a result of the tapering of the United States' policy of monetary expansion"[21]. The launch statement declared the Contingency Reserve Arrangement would help BRICS countries to deal with 'short-term liquidity pressures, promote further BRICS co-operation, strengthen the global financial safety net and complement existing international arrangements'.

In order to prevent such economic instability, one of the proposals of the 5th BRICS Summit policies has been that members should combine their estimated $240bn in foreign exchange reserves to protect individual members from short-term liquidity volatility. The idea would be that the funds would be accessible to individual members as an emergency fund when faced with balance of payment problems. The BRICS members have set up a $100bn contingency reserves pool, called the Contingent Reserve Arrangement (CRA) denominated in US dollars, with China's initial commitment of US$41 billion, Russia, Brazil and India US$18 billion each and South Africa US$5 billion.

The primary objective behind its creation is to provide support to the BRICS members through liquidity and precautionary instruments in response to actual or potential short-term balance of payments pressures. This new contingency reserve fund is also seen as an alternative to the International Monetary Fund (IMF). Although the contingency reserve fund is based on the Chiang Mai Initiative, it is modest in size. The CMIM has a reserve pool of US$240 billion and the IMF resources of US$780 billion. The emergency fund was established in May 2000 at the ASEAN+3 Finance Ministers' Meeting, as a liquidity support mechanism for the region, gradually recovering from the Asian financial crises. The CMI, however, ultimately relied on the IMF as an enforcer, with release of 80 percent of the funds conditional on the negotiation of an IMF programme[22]. A key feature of the arrangement, explained in Article 5 of the CRA treaty, is "30 percent of the maximum access for each Party, shall be available subject only to the agreement of the Providing Parties, which shall be granted whenever the Requesting Party meets the conditions stipulated in Article 14 of this Treaty", whereas in the 'IMF-linked portion' the access to the remaining 70 per cent would depend on a conditionality-based agreement with the IMF is concluded. Thus, while all parties will have access to the fund, there are limits to the amount of resources each participant is entitled to. This has led to criticism of the CRA, that IMF interference to it would lend the instrument ineffective to a greater extent[23].

As per the treaty, the governance of newly created BRICS CRA will occur at two levels; by a Council of CRA Governors (the "Governing Council") and a Standing Committee. The decision making will be with the governing council, and through consensus among its members. The Governing Council includes two representatives from each party at the level of finance minister or central bank governor. The responsibilities of the council include review and modify the size of the committed resources of the CRA as well as approve changes in the size of individual commitments; approve new countries as Parties to the CRA; modify the CRA's instruments, number of renewals, interest rates, spreads, and fees and the percentage of access de-linked from IMF arrangements and also decides upon the creation of a permanent secretariat or the establishment of a dedicated surveillance unit. At the second level of governance of the CRA, the Standing Committee comprises two representatives from each party, ordinarily central bank officials, and is primarily tasked with providing and facilitating requests for assistance from participating parties. Some decision will be made by weighted voting of providing parties whereas the others will be taken by consensus.

Thus, BRICS Development Bank and the contingency reserve fund largely represent the ongoing attempts of the developing countries to create an alternative monetary, finance system, free from the dictates of the Western world. Infact the upcoming 8th BRICS summit in Goa, India is focused more on the instituionalisation of the BRICS[24]. There is a proposal of creating of four new institutions and institutional arrangements with varying degrees of formalisation. These initiatives include: i) New Development Bank Institute (NDBI), where issues of economy, currency, credit rating, political risk, industrial models and development options will be discussed; ii) a second arrangement to facilitate free trade agreements; iii) a third institutional framework for digital economy where BRICS members are already key stakeholders; and iv) finally, BRICS must formalise institutional collaborations to promote the BRICS development agenda. However, doubts have been expressed regarding the efficacy of these bodies and to what extent. It can shield itself from the influence of the Western regime. It is argued that these alternate initiatives, perceived as a form of insurance and assurance, it is unlikely to replace the IMF and World Bank in the near future as the latter will still remain powerful players in the global economic system. Also, the creation of alternative associations by no means indicates that the BRICS members will necessarily quit the World Bank or the IMF. On the contrary, a BRICS bank is expected to be a valuable addition to the existing network of multilateral, regional and national development banks. However, much still depends on China's long term intentions vis-à-vis the bank and the extent to which it can maintain balance between its own influence on the bank and other members' impact.

China Factor

In the early 21st century, China was still a growing nation, trying to enter the club of major powers in the world. Most of the debates in the United States and elsewhere till the middle of the 20th century, focused on whether China should be a part of the international community and more specifically, of the global trading regime[25]. However, after getting further integrated into the global economy facilitated by its entry into the WTO, its economic power grew rapidly along with military and diplomatic capabilities[26] (James 2011). The global financial downturn of 2008 proved to be crucial when the fissures and fault lines of the American economy were revealed, giving China a more prominent place in the global architecture of multilateral economic coordination[27]. This has sparked a lot of academic and policy debates about the impact of 'China Rise' on the international economic system. A careful reading of these debates clearly reveals that most of the realist writings on China's rise are couched in the power transition theory framework, identifying China as the major challenger to the existing global economic configuration of power. This body of thought places emphasis on the structural conditions to explain and analyse China's rising stature within the economic system. International material structures or power configuration is their primary focus. The theory is centered on two key explanatory variables: relative power and degree of satisfaction with the international order[28]. Scholars arguing within this framework predict that China is growing belligerent as it accumulates material capabilities and it will no longer follow the rules of global economic governance, instead create its own rules and pose a threat to US hegemony. Power Transition theorists (Organski 1958; Organski and Kugler 1980; Gilpin 1981; Modelski 1987; Kugler and Lemke 1996; Thompson 2000; Lemke 2002)[29] argue that uneven patterns of growth may lead to subsequent challenges to the dominant state's global leadership by a rising power that may be dissatisfied with the status-quo and wish to challenge the existing international order. Thus, the stream of writings inspired by realism, particularly offensive realism entails a skeptical attitude towards China's behaviour in the international economic system. Majority of the debates have its origins in the West itself. The scholarship primarily argues that China is increasingly using its financial power to gain political and diplomatic influence, most importantly as a hedge against the excess US hegemony. However, consensus is yet to be reached among the scholars of this school on whether China will completely revamp the economic order in its own favour or amend certain rules and norms aimed at unsettling the hegemonic domination of the Western-led economic order.

Nevertheless, in the 'shift of power' narrative, the 'China story' has been extended, in an intuitive rather than analytical way. In these debates, potential plays a much bigger role than reality. In other words, current strong economic performance, coupled with population size, issued as a basis from which to extrapolate future economic and political trends. On the basis of the latter, power and influence are inferred. Not many Chinese scholars have couched their assessments about China's behaviour in WTO through realist lens. Yan Xuetong (2006:2011)[30] argues that China's power status is undergoing a characteristic change. Although US supports China's participation in WTO and G-20, but their core interests are in conflict with each other. During this transition, China is adjusting its foreign policy in order to best safeguard national interests. However, China's power is already large enough to disturb international political stability by shifting its strategic stance. Therefore, Yan, in a very much realist manner undermines the aspect of economic cooperation to the high politics of security issues and suggests that China's rising power status is going to be a major threat to the existing international order.

Contrary to the pessimists, there are enthusiasts and also pragmatists who view China's rise Wei Lang (2007)[31] argues that the market-driven dictates of the globalised economy have been the principal drivers of China's currently very high level of international economic integration. In turn, the pragmatic imperative to continue rapid economic growth and the benefits of globalisation has gradually led China to participate more actively and cooperatively in the global economic regimes. He suggests that it is best to understand China today as both a willing and a capable partner in the mostly liberal international economic order, so long as China's leaders continue to see such participation as consistent with China's national interest. Liang Jianwu (2006)[32] talking about the failure of Doha Round negotiations argue that every government, including China wants to safeguard their national interest during negotiations on multilateral trade issues and therefore, takes rigid positions to prevent the business community as well as the general population from losing out in the global competition. He argues that the failure of Doha Round has not caused any harm to Chinese economic interests, because it has attached lot of importance to bilateral trade parleys. According to Jane Golley and Ligang Song (2011)[33], there is a pressing need for structural adjustments in the institutions that govern the international political and economic system, as it is the only effective way to limit the behaviour of rising powers, while those of incumbent powers become more accommodating and cooperative. In their opinion, as China is increasingly expected to play a leadership role, this multilateral framework this multilateral framework will provide an important institutional basis to carry out global exchanges a positive-sum rather than a zero-sum game.

When the tsunami of financial chaos engulfed the world, what everybody asked each other was "could China save the global capitalism?" Even before the crisis broke out, China had already established itself an economic power, and received much-deserved attention and respect in almost every international summits. In 2004, Joshua Cooper Ramo in his paper, published by the Foreign Policy Centre, Great Britain had first suggested of the term 'Beijing Consensus' or a Chinese model of development to capture the essence of global transformations taking place and believed that China, 'the new economic power-centre' would soon replace the hegemonic 'Washington Consensus' by its own. The term Beijing Consensus has been used to collectively refer to different aspects of China's economic development based on principles of political principles of non-interference and self-determination. It was during the peak phase of the meltdown, when the term started gaining currency as the Chinese stretched their helping hand by increasing overseas investment along with consumer demand as a possible way out of the crisis. Along with admiration, there were simultaneous concerns and worries about China's role and rising influence in the global economic system. Concerns grew more with the decline of the dollar and also with the failure of the "Wall-Street model". Some economists and think tank experts from China, believed that as the world economy staggered into recession, China's exports which had fuelled the Chinese economy for years would fall significantly first from bleak international demand and on the other hand from insufficient domestic demand. This would undoubtedly affect numerous export oriented firms, small businesses particular and bring down the growth rates. At a December Press Conference for the launch of CASS annual comprehensive report on Chinese society, Li Peilin, head of the Institute of Sociology at CASS said that the financial crisis had affected the Chinese economy in a different way than that of the US. He told Shanghai based China Business News that in the US, financial crisis spread from virtual economy to real economy while in China, it first appeared in real economy, featuring the financial difficulties or even bankruptcies of many export oriented small and medium sized companies and then spread to the virtual economy, consumption and other sectors. Contrary to the negative views, some leading institutions like China Centre for International Economic Exchange (CCIEE) remained highly optimistic about China's economy. In their view, the global recession would not hamper China's growth and they expected China to achieve the 8 percent target growth rate proposed at the Central Economic Work Conference and also believed that the economic correction offered an opportunity for China to accelerate its pace of industrialisation. The Chinese Government on the other hand, maintained a 'cautious optimistic' tone about the global financial crisis. It agreed to the rippling effects of the global financial storm on China's economy especially in its drastic decline in exports but was hopeful about its market potentials and stable banking sector.

China, with its international reserves at $2 trillion and rising, had been leading in the face of recession stuck years. Globally, it was trying to gain greater access to resources by strengthening its economic diplomacy in Latin America, Africa and Middle East. China continued to rise as an exporting power since 2007 and also managed to withstand the recessionary effects of the global meltdown as compared to other developing economies as well as United States. In 2008, exports accounted for 37.8 percent of China's GDP whereas exports in the United States accounted for 12.7 percent of its GDP in that same year[34]. China's holdings of foreign exchange reserves increased rapidly from 2003 to 2010 both in dollar terms and as a percent of total foreign holdings. In September 2008, China overtook Japan to become the largest foreign holder of US Treasury securities.[35]

Table 2.3: Top Three Foreign Holders of US Securities During the Global Financial Crisis, as of June 2011

Type of Security	*Total*	*Long Term (LT) Treasury*	*LT Agency*	*LT Corporate*	*Equities*	*Short Term Debt*
China	1,727	1,302	245	16	159	5
Japan	1,585	818	258	140	302	67
United Kingdom	982	118	12	394	441	16
Total	12,440	4,049	1,031	2,651	3830	878

Source: U.S. Department of the Treasury, Report on Foreign Portfolio Holdings of U.S. Securities as of June 30, 2011.

Crisis proves to be good testing ground for any economic model. As the 'neoliberal model' of Washington consensus flounders in the face of 'credit crunch' and sluggish economy, experts, practitioners and academics turn their attention towards the Chinese model of development also called 'Beijing Consensus', lauding the 'responsible role' played by China in tackling the crisis. These discussions mainly revolve around the question of whether China's 'statist' political economy can be an alternative to the neoliberal market fundamentalism, in the context of China's rise and decline of the dollar hegemony. With particular reference to 'Beijing Consensus', concerns are expressed about the viability and wisdom of the model, its capacity to succeed and also its very existence in the global economy. With full recognition to the fact that China plays an important role in the global economy, Arif Dirlik (2007)[36] raises some pertinent questions about the very idea of Beijing Consensus becoming the distinct historical possibility. He argues that the term lacks coherent economic or political position and only stands as a loose expression of its deep dissatisfaction with the neo-liberal globalisation project. Moreover, if carefully studied the successes of the Chinese economy resonates capitalist characteristics and is also attributed to manipulation of a neo-liberal global economy.

China's growing interest in global multilateralism started roughly around the same time when the opening up and reform programme[37] was launched in the late 1970's. The 1980s witnessed a continuous process of integration into the international system with China's accession to numerous international institutions and regimes. The accession to WTO marked a new phase of multilateral activism for China. It provided China with a larger platform to economically engage with almost all nations of the world. Thus, many scholars rightly note that China's economic rise would have been an empty slogan without its active economic multilateralism. For example, from Shanghai Cooperation Organisation (SCO) and Association for South East Asian nations (ASEAN), to G8 and BRICS, China today is the key player with a greater number of followers as compared to Washington. Unlike the reform era when China's multilateral engagements were borne out of economic necessities, today they are mostly directed by political and strategic motives in the international political economy[38]. At the economic front, not only does it depend on its engagement with international economic institutions but also on the length and breadth of bilateral and regional economic ties and arrangements[39]. Compared to the earlier period, China is now vigorously promoting different levels of diplomacy, from bilateral to regional and multilateral levels. One of the examples is BRICS. The unprecedented level of emphasis the Chinese leadership attaches to the BRICS nations reflects the profound changes in China's perceptions of itself and of the outside world. In Beijing's view, the 2008 financial crisis has dramatically changed the mapping of the world economy, deeply damaging the strength of the traditional developed countries. The economic recovery of the US and Japan has been sluggish, while the Euro-zone crisis has lingered on for years. The relatively impressive momentum for growth now comes from emerging economies, especially the BRICS nations. On the basis of current economic indicators, India, Brazil and Russia, along with China, are the most dynamic elements of the world's economy. Due to the growth and convergence, the BRICS countries contribute to the global growth more than 30 percent. Rising economic standing of the BRICS is supported by favorable external conditions. Among them are: free trade, free capital flow and easy financial conditions, and commodity prices growth. The BRICS countries succeeded in improving internal framework. In three years, flexibility in exchange rate has dramatically increased. External and public debt declined, and reserves have significantly capitalized. Developed countries' relative importance as suppliers in international markets is also declining. The share of world trade of goods and services attributed to BRICS has grown over time. In 2014, BRICS traded more than US$ 3 trillion in goods and imported over US$ 700 billion in services whilst exporting around US$ 500 billion which is in part due to the increase of trade with China. (See figures 2.3 & 2.4). In the recent years, the trans-national corporations from BRICS (TNCs) have expanded their investments broadly and deeply (see Table 2.4).

These countries, and in particular China and Russia, control a large pool of surplus capital, a factor that capital deficit countries such as the United States have to take into account. Altogether these countries hold almost half of the world's foreign exchange reserves. China holds by far the largest proportion of this, followed by Russia, India and Brazil in that order. Also, large enterprises from the BRICS have grown speedily and their influence on the world economy has grown during the past ten years. Although large enterprises from developed countries occupy dominant position, the enterprises from BRICS countries are better in terms of performance (see tables 2.5).

Table 2.4: Top 500 World Enterprises (2010)

BRIC countries	*No. of enterprises*	*Income (In hundred million US$)*	*Profit (In hundred million US$)*	*Total Assets*	*Total Stock holder equity*	*No. of Employees*
China	54	21548.37	1297.22	95235.16	12120.10	12188471
India	8	2365.93	130.17	5142.29	950.91	425133
Russia	6	2720.33	458.68	7426.22	3284.51	1080282
Brazil	7	3079.94	321.99	13836.86	2193.94	507788
Total	75	29714.57	2206.06	121640.53	18549.46	14201674

Note: data for South Africa is not available.
Source: Developed from Zhang, Guo[40] (2009)

Table 2.5: Comparative Study of Top 500 World Enterprises (2010)

Country	*No. of employers*	*Average Income (In hundred million US$)*	*Profit (In hundred Average million US$)*
BRICS Countries	75	396.19	29.41
Developed Countries	276	483.88	16.54
Average in Percentage (%)	27.1	76.29	177.81

Source: Developed from Zhang, Guo (2009).

Fig. 2.3: Export of Goods and Services

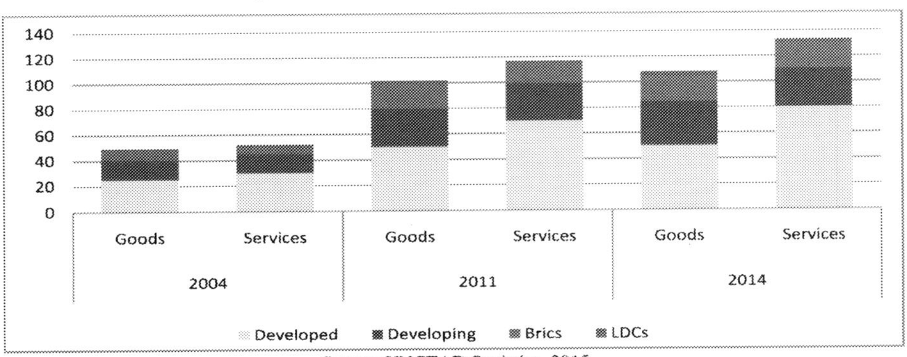

Source: UNCTAD Statistics, 2015

Source: UNCTAD Statistics, 2015.

Fig, 2.4: Import of Goods and Services

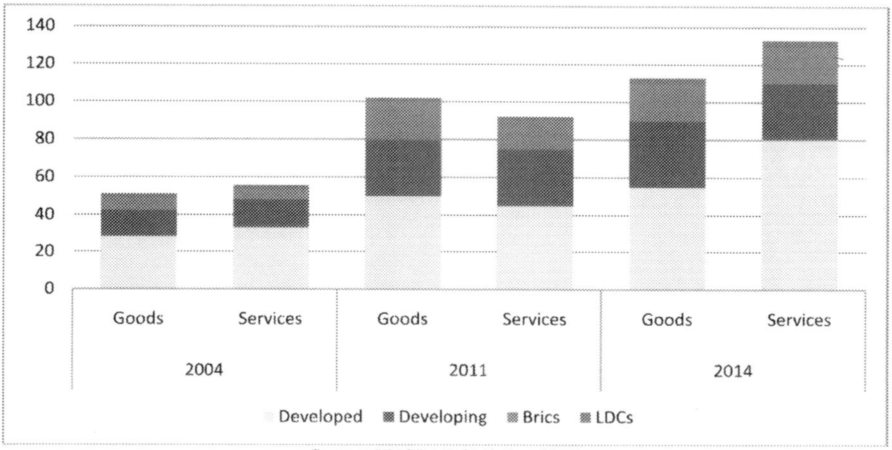

Source: UNCTAD Statistics, 2015.

The reason why China has acquired a significant influence in the international economic system is not just because of its growing economic weight, but also because of its ability to influence international relations. In contrast to traditional middle powers, China's modus operandi is embedded in the market economy rather than in traditional politics. Through these institutional innovations in the form of New Development Bank, BRICS fund, Asian Infrastructure Investment Bank and Silk Road Fund, it is true that China seeks to bring about changes in the global economic governance, long dominated by Western powers. Chinese intentions nevertheless are part of its strategy to expand influence the region and thus, serve directly to further China's interests, be they political or economic. However, these projects supported by China, often create pressures on the resources along with an increasing likelihood of competition and conflicts both with the established powers and the other rising powers.

Inter-regional and Intra-regional Differences

For any institutional grouping, inter-regional coalitions are the order of the day. However, these coalitions are never without leadership, who represent the concerns of the coalition, take initiatives and negotiate its interests in the larger forum. In BRICS, China remains the undeclared leader, despite the group's opposition to hegemony and unipolarity. Additionally, there are issues related to both intra-regional and inter-regional differences which challenge the cohesiveness of the grouping. First, the BRICS are geographically, politically and economically a diverse group with little commonality in terms of values and interests. China and Russia are authoritarian and practice variants of state capitalism, while India, Brazil and South Africa are large, fractious democracies. These political differences often form the basis of their differing positions on various other forums of global governance, thus, revealing the inherent fractures within the BRICS community. Second, with regard to economy, China and India are commodities importers, China specialises in manufactures and India in services. By comparison, Russia and Brazil are commodities exporters, Russia specialises in natural resources and Brazil in agriculture. Since the drivers of economic growth differ in these countries, they take different approach with respect to key issues in the WTO. For instance, the major countries of BRICS did not side with India at the 9th WTO Ministerial meeting in Bali in 2013 on the issue of food security. While India and South Africa opposed the Bali Package, the rest of the BRICS countries agreed to the subsidy cuts.

Third, there are also great mistrust and tensions in the bilateral relations within the BRICS, which limit the scope of full-fledged cooperation within the grouping. For instance, the Sino-Indian relations have significant differences over contentious issues such as unresolved border disputes, China's political and military support for Pakistan, and China's perception of India's support for Tibet. India, on the other hand, feels threatened by China's improved relations in the Asian region over its closeness to Junta regime in Myanmar, proximity to Pakistan, assistance to Bangladesh and Nepal and growing closeness with Sri Lanka, which could possibly curtail India's influence on its neighbours and as well as in the region. China too is insecure about India's partnership with Japan, Singapore and the Indo-China. They compete with each other over the control of the Indian Ocean and China strongly opposes India's interference in the South China Sea. Right from the beginning, India has not been comfortable with the idea of using Yuan as a currency of trade between the BRICS countries. At the Ufa Summit in 2015, there were suggestions that almost 50 per cent of intra-BRICS trading could be invoiced in Yuan, the leading currency in the group. However, India's apprehension arises from Beijing's policy of keeping its currency weak which would put India in an unfavourable situation since in a swapping arrangement, the country with the weaker currency, gains. The Sino-Russian relations have areas of tensions as well, although their relations have improved after the fall of the USSR. With the military reform launched in 2008, there was an increase in defense orders from the developing countries and their major dependence on Chinese orders has reduced gradually. Moreover, the increasing concern related to the expansion of Chinese military industry, have issued a note of caution among the Russian authorities. They are careful when negotiating deals with China to manufacture military equipment under licence, as this enables the Chinese to acquire the expertise to produce their own high-grade arms[41]. Besides, difficult negotiations over Chinese imports of weapons from Russia, there is considerable mistrust that exists at the level of energy cooperation. Russia feels threatened by the economic and military growth of China and dreads of being reduced to only an energy supplier to the rapidly growing China. The relationship also suffers owing to the duo's interest in Central Asia as well as in the Russian Far East, where, Russia sees China as a potential threat. Although China and Brazil share a strong bilateral relation, there also exists some underlying tension which is slowly complicating the relationship. For instance, there is concern and discontent among the Brazilian manufacturers, whose products are getting killed by cheap Chinese imports that make Brazil's industry uncompetitive in the global marketplace and at home. Also, the importance of the relations with the United States, the European Union or even Japan for each of the BRICS member states, deepens the mistrust factor and prevents deeper cooperation on trade, investment and technology related issues among them.

Lastly, the intra-regional differences which arise out of the growing economic disparities, social tensions along with the concern of being dominated by these countries in the region, raises doubt over the cohesiveness of the group and the seriousness of its institutionalisation. For example, the number of protests, especially by indigenous people, against Brazilian resource grabs and its over increasing role in the internal affairs of neighbouring countries, as a financer to major controversial projects is mounting. This includes hydroelectric dams and roads in countries such as Bolivia, Peru and Paraguay[42]. The Bolivian road was being funded with a $332m loan from Brazil's development bank, the BNDES, and built by OAS, one of several Brazilian construction firms that operate across Latin America. These projects would have benefitted Brazil in terms of easy transportation of export products from Pacific ports in Chile and Peru. Similarly, Russia faces resistance in its bid to be a regional hegemon due to its strained relation with Georgia, disputes in Ukraine over resources, prices and supplies, and refusal to extend preferential energy rates to Belarus. Although China's low-end-manufacture have benefited the North Asian economies over the past decade, Southeast Asian economies, more closely resembling China and offering similar comparative advantages, have often found themselves outmuscled more recently by their much larger neighbour. South Africa's popularity as a leader in the African continent is slowly fading away, due to its aggressive commercial expansion across the continent. South African dominance over the continent is often portrayed as 'imperialist' and its friction with Nigeria has come to symbolize the trade obstacles that have hobbled Africa's growth[43].

Thus, as the status of the BRICS countries grow, concerns about their hegemony in the region rises. Besides, these institutional arrangements are rife with insecurities. The factors, discussed above, act as major barriers to the emerging market powers as they seek adjustments in their course of reforming the global order. Therefore, BRICS responses to the tensions of continuity and discontinuity, contested neoliberal norms, and regional differences will bear greatly on the evolution of global order in the coming decades.

Conclusion

The developmental multipolar discourse, since the mid-2000s, created the conditions for the emergence of BRICS. It is China and India who initiated the discourse through actively promoting South-south cooperation. As the two countries have begun playing key roles in the international institutions through forming coalitions of developing countries, differences of interests on key issues of global governance between the developed and developing bloc, are on the rise. They have also become the major proponents, emphasising the need to transform the existing structures of economic governance. In this context, China has identified itself as 'the major developing country' that would promote the interest of other developing countries in an international system marked by the transition to multipolarity. In this process of transition from a liberal–unilateral to a developmental–multipolar world order, the emergence of China as an important economic power dragged the developing countries like Brazil, Russia and South Africa into its sphere of influence, with the recent financial crisis further denting confidence in the US financial system and in the stability of dollar. Indeed, development and multipolarity are the cornerstones of the BRICS initiative. However, the politics of this new forum called BRICS have led to the unequal distribution of power, turning them into vehicles for pacts among elites in their efforts to promote global value chains. They are well ahead of most other developing countries on several measures. Thus, their agendas of reform remain more symbolic than policy significant and their pursuits are considered as' minilateralism'[44], through which they suggest reforms with a bit of caution, in order to avoid disruption of multilateral statecraft and legal rules. Thus, the transition in global order has features of both continuities and discontinuities. The shift is more towards a hybrid system of global governance, where the provision of collective goods is no longer confined to the hands of the superpower but has become a matter of collective goodwill.

END NOTES

1. Paul Dicken, *Global Shift: The Internationalization of Economic Activity* (London: Paul Chapman, 1992); Paul Dicken, "A New Geo-Economy," David Held and Andrew McGrew (eds.) *The Global Transformations Reader* (Cambridge: Polity, 2002), pp. 249-251. Also see John Mearshimer, 'Why We Will Soon Miss the Cold War', *Atlantic Monthly*, August 1990. pp.35-50. A.F. Organski, *World Politics* (New York: Knopf, 1958) for the classic statement on power transitions in history and why all power transitions are bound to lead to intensified competition, heightened insecurity and possibly war.
2. Keohane RO (1984) The world political economy and the crisis of embedded liberalism. In: Goldthorpe JH (ed.) *Order and Conflict in Contemporary Capitalism*. Oxford: Clarendon Press, 1–30. Also refer to Keohane RO (2002) *Power and Governance in a Partially Globalized World*. London: Routledge. Keohane RO and Nye JS (2001) *Power and Interdependence*, 3rd edn. New York: Longman.
3. Unay, Sadik (2013), "Reality or Mirage?: BRICS and the Making of Multipolarity in the Global Political Economy", Insight Turkey, 15(3): pp 77-94. Also see Mittelman, James H. (2013), "Global Bricolage: Emerging Market Powers and Polycentric Governance", *Third World Quarterly*, 34(1): 23-37.
4. Simon, Wilson (2011), "Centre-periphery Relationship in the Understanding of Development of Internal Colonies", International Journal of Economic Development Research and Investment, 2 (1): pp.147-156. Also see Wallerstein, I. (1974). *The Modern World-System*, New York: Vintage Books.
5. Michael Bordo and Marc Flandreau, "Core, Periphery, Exchange Rate Regimes and Globalization," *Working Paper 8584* (Cambridge: National Bureau of Economic Research, 2001), p. 45.
6. Gilpin R (1981) *War and Change in World Politics*. Cambridge: Cambridge University Press. Also see Schweller RL (1999) Managing the rise of great powers. In: Johnston AI and Ross RS (eds) *Engaging China: The Management of an Emerging Power*. London: Routledge, 1–31. Van der Pijl K (1984) *The Making of an Atlantic Ruling Class*. London: Verso & Van der Pijl K (1998) *Transnational Classes and International Relations*. London: Routledge.
7. Ikenberry GJ (2011a) The future of the liberal world order. *Foreign Affairs* 90: 56–62. Ikenberry GJ (2011b) *Liberal Leviathan: The Origins, Crisis, and Transformation of the American World Order*. Princeton, NJ: Princeton University Press. Ikenberry GJ and Wright T (2008) *Rising Powers and Global Institutions*. New York: The Century Foundation.
8. Becker U (2013) Measuring change of capitalist varieties: Reflections on method, illustrations from the BRICs. *New Political Economy* 18(4): 503–532. Nölke A (2012) The rise of the 'B(R)IC variety of capitalism': Towards a new phase of organized capitalism? In: Overbeek H and Apeldoorn BV (eds) *Neoliberalism in Crisis*. Houndmills: Palgrave Macmillan, 117–137. Nölke A and Vliegenthart A (2009) Enlarging the varieties of capitalism: The emergence of dependent market economies in East Central Europe. *World Politics* 61(4): 670. Ten Brink T (2011) *Institutional Change in Market-Liberal State Capitalism: An Integrative Perspective on the Development of the Private Business Sector in China*. Max-Planck-InstitutFürGesellschaftsforschung Discussion Paper, 11(2). Cologne: Max Planck Institute for the Study of Societies.

9. Fareed Zakaria, *Post-American World* (New York: W.W. Norton, 2008).
10. Michael P. Dooley, David Folkerts-Landau and Peter Garber, 'An essay on the revised Bretton Woods system', working paper 9971 (Cambridge, MA: National Bureau of Economic Research, 2003).
11. Ministry of External Affairs (2013), "5th BRICS Summit - eThekwini Declaration and Action Plan", [Online Web] http://www.mea.gov.in/bilateraldocuments.htm?dtl/21482/5th+BRICS+Summit++eThekwini+Declaration+and+Action+Plan, Accessed on September 1, 2016.
12. Biswas, Rajiv (2015). "Reshaping the Financial Architecture for Development Finance: -e new development banks", Working Paper no. 2, [Online Web] http://www.lse.ac.uk/internationalRelations/centresandunits/globalsouth/documents/LSE-GSU-Working-Papers/working%20papers/LSE_Working_Paper_02_15.pdf Accessed on September 4, 2016.
13. Barton, Goldstein, Joslin & Steinberg (2006), The Evolution of the Trade Regime: Politics, Law, and Economics of the GATT and the WTO, Oxford & Princeton, Princeton University Press.
14. Ferdinand, Peter (2014). "Rising powers at the UN: an analysis of the voting behaviour of brics in the General Assembly", Third World Quarterly, 35(3): 376-391. Also refer to Thakur, Ramesh (2014), "How representative are BRICS?", *Third World Quarterly*: 35(10), pp. 1791-1808.
15. Peitz, Laura (2015), "The BRICS: Rhetoric or Reality" [Online Web] http://www.e-ir.info/2015/12/22/the-brics-rhetoric-or-reality/ Accessed on September 4, 2016.
16. Ministry of External Affairs (2014). "Sixth BRICS Summit – Fortaleza Declaration", [Online Web]http://www.mea.gov.in/bilateral-documents.htm?dtl/23635/Sixth+BRICS+Summit++Fortaleza+DeclarationAccessed on September 1, 2016.
17. BRICS Information Centre (2015), "Ufa Declaration", University of Toronto [Online Web] http://www.brics.utoronto.ca/docs/150709-ufa-declaration_en.html Accessed on September 2, 2016.
18. Corsetti, Presenti & Roubini (1998), "What caused the Asian currency and financial crisis", [Online Web] http://pages.stern.nyu.edu/~nroubini/papers/asiacri2.pdf Accessed on September 3, 2016.
19. Eurodad Report (2014), "Harmful conditions increasingly attached to IMF loans, according to new research", [Online Web] http://eurodad.org/Entries/view/1546183/2014/04/02/Harmful-conditions-increasingly-attached-to-IMF-loans-according-to-new-research Accessed on September 3, 2016.
20. Liu & Tang (2009), "Subnational Credit Ratings: A Comparative Review", 5013 Policy Research Working Paper, [Online Web] http://siteresources.worldbank.org/INTDSRE/Resources/389451-1250785355895/WPS5013.pdf. Accessed on September 2, 2016.
21. Ibid.
22. Singh K, 'Strengthening Financial Stability? The Promise and Pitfalls of BRICS' 100 Billion Dollar "Contingency Reserve Arrangement" (CRA)', Global Research, 5 July 2014; Stuenkel O, 'Towards Institutionalization: The BRICS Contingency Reserve Arrangement (CRA)', Post-Western World, 12 May 2013, http://www.postwesternworld.com/2013/05/12/the-politics-of-the -brics-contingency-reserve-arrangement-cra/
23. Eichengreen B, 'Will the new BRICS institutions work?', World Economic Forum, Agenda, 15 August 2014, [Online Web] https://agenda.weforum.org/2014/08/brics-newdevelopment-bank-contingent-reserve-agreement/, accessed 8 September 2015.
24. Saran, Samir & Rej, Abhijnan (2016), "Brics Summit in Goa: Ahead of 8th conference, the bloc must focus on institution-building", Firstpost, [online web] http://www.firstpost.com/

world/brics-summit-ahead-of-8th-conference-the-bloc-must-focus-on-institution-building-3010578.html Accessed on September 20, 2016.

25. Li, Lanqing. (2009). *The birth of China's opening up policy* (Trans. Ling Y. & Zhang S.). Oxford: Oxford University Press.
26. James, Harold. (2011). "International Order after the Financial Crisis", *International Affairs*, 87(3): 525-537.
27. Buzan, Barry. (2010), "China in International Society: Is 'Peaceful Rise' Possible?", *The Chinese Journal of International Politics,* 3: 5–36.
28. Ibid.
29. Efird, B., Kugler, J., & Genna, G. (2003). From War to Integration: Generalizing Power Transition Theory. International Interactions, *29*(4), 293–313. See Art, R. (2008). The United States and the rise of China. In R. Ross & Z. Feng (Eds), *China's ascent* (pp. 260–290). Ithaca: Cornell University Press. Bergsten, F.C. (2008). A partnership of equals: How Washington should respond to China's economic challenge. *Foreign Affairs, 97*(4), 57–69. Kugler, J. (2006). The Asian ascent: Opportunity for peace or precondition for war? *International Studies Perspectives, 7*(1), 36–42. Kugler, J., & Lemke, D. (Eds). (1996). *Parity and war: Evaluations and extensions of the war ledger.* Ann Arbor: University of Michigan Press. Rapkin, D., & Thompson, W.R. (2003). Power transition, challenge and the (re) emergence of China. *International Interactions, 29*(4), 315–342 (2006). Will economic interdependence encourage China and India's peaceful ascent? In A.J. Tellis & M. Willis (Eds), *Strategic Asia 2006–07: Trade, interdependence, and security* (pp. 65–103). Seattle, WA: National Bureau of Asian Research.
30. Yan, Xuetong (2006), "The Rise of China and its Power Status", Chinese Journal of International Politics, pp. 5-33. Read Xuetong's How China Can Defeat America (New York Times, 2011). Also see Feng Huiyun (2009), "Is China a Revisionist Power?", Chinese Journal of International Politics, 2, pp. 313–334.
31. Liang, Wei (2007), "China: Globalization and the Emergence of a New Status Quo Power?" *Asian Perspective,* 31(4): 125-149.
32. Liang, Jianwu (2006), Why the Doha Round Came to a Disappointing Conclusion", [Online Web] http://www.cicir.ac.cn/chinese/Article_782.html Accessed on September 3, 2016.
33. Jane Golley and Ligang Song (2011), "Rising China: Global challenges and opportunities", East Asia Forum, [Online Web]http://www.eastasiaforum.org/2011/07/13/rising-china-global-challenges-and-opportunities/ Accessed on September 5, 2016.
34. Chow, Daniel (2010), "China's Response to the Global Financial Crisis: Implications for US-China Economic Relations", *Global Business Law Review,* 1: 47-81.
35. U.S. Treasury securities such as bills, notes and bonds are debt obligations of the U.S. government, which are used to finance the federal budget deficit. They constitute the largest category of U.S. securities held by China.
36. Dirlik, Arif (2007), "Global South: Predicament and Promise", The Global South, 1(1): pp. 12-23.
37. Wei, Pan (2015), Behind China's Economic Miracle: The Coalition of Rural Collective Industries & Grassroots Authorities (Trans. By Maya X. Guo), Beijing: Foreign Language Press.
38. Hoadley and Yang (2007), "China's Cross-Regional FTA Initiatives: Towards Comprehensive National power", *Pacific Affairs,* 80(2): 327-48.
39. Department of Policy Planning (2011), China's Foreign Affairs, Ministry of Foreign Affairs, People's Republic of China. Also see China's Foreign Affairs 2012, 2013 & 2014.
40. Zhang, Guo (2010), "#金砖四国$与#金柱四国$间大公司势力状态比较", translated, A

comparative research of large enterprises between in BRICS and FGPCs, Guanghua School of Management, 32(12), pp. 49-55

41. Carlsson, Oxenstierna and Weissmann (2015), "China and Russia – A Study on Cooperation, Competition and Distrust", [Online Web] file:///C:/Users/user/Downloads/foir4087%20(2).pdf Accessed on September 5, 2016.
42. Philips & Cabitza (2011), "Bolivian president Evo Morales suspends Amazon road project", [Online Web] https://www.theguardian.com/world/2011/sep/27/bolivian-president-suspends-amazon-road Accessed September 6, 2016.
43. York, Geoffrey (2016), "Economic dispute between Nigeria, South Africa still unresolved", [Online Web] http://www.theglobeandmail.com/report-on-business/international-business/african-and-mideast-business/economic-dispute-between-nigeria-south-africa-still-unresolved/article29088247/ Accessed on September 6, 2016.
44. Brummer, Chris (2014), *Minilateralism: How Trade Alliances, Soft Law and Financial Engineering are redefining economic statecraft,* New York: Cambridge University Press.

3

Perception and Reality in the Changing International Order

Amrita Jash

Introduction

Since the late 20th century, one of the major developments in international politics has been the formation and development of multilateral processes, wherein China has been closely associated with most of them. With its role as an initiator as well as an active participant, China's recent turn to multilateralism in its foreign policy has been both apparent and demonstrated—given its active involvement in global and regional multilateral institutions and signifying its ambitions to reshape the international order. Beijing's aspirations lie in the drive to lead the reform of global governance, as witnessed primarily in China's greater involvement in the economic arena which is gradually diversifying into security areas too. In this process, BRICS (Brazil, Russia, India, China, and South Africa) forms an important platform where China is proactively trying to consolidate its own leadership as well as strengthen relations with each member in the grouping. Accordingly, this platform is boosting China's great power ambitions in the changing international environment, where she has had a limited role in shaping.

In the 30 years since Deng Xiaoping's "reform and opening-up" (*gaige kaifang*), China has seen great change. The Third Plenary Session of the 11th Central Committee of Communist Party of China held on December 18-22,

1978 represented a great turning point. It was a landmark in the history of 'New China' as the country shifted from "class struggle-oriented" to "economic construction-oriented", from "semi-rigid/rigid" to "comprehensive reform" and from "semi-closed/closed" to "opening up".[1] With its reform agenda, "China is, step by step, establishing a road with Chinese characteristics—a road that will lead to socialist modernisation".[2] What is noteworthy is that China's own impact on international issues has grown considerably with its development. Although Beijing pursued a low profile foreign policy under Deng Xiaoping's dictum of "Keeping a low profile and biding its time" (*tao guang yang hui*), China's international influence has been expanding with its economic rise. That is, China has increasingly become a part of a larger world environment that provides opportunities and constraints on its policy options. This has caused China to become more sensitive to its own position in the changing international environment.

With its robust economic rise, China has developed into the world's second-largest economy, thereby becoming the world's largest exporter and importer of goods, mainly driven by its greater integration with the global economy. In addition, its penetration into multilateral institutions such as World Trade Organisation (WTO), the Group of Twenty (G-20), and the Asia-Pacific Economic Cooperation (APEC) further substantiates its expanded role in the present international order. This Chinese behaviour reflects Beijing's attachment of great importance to its multilateral policy in acting within the current international system. That is, for China, multilateralism has become a tool of convenience in fostering relationships as well as increasing its influence in the international system—especially after its accession to WTO in 2001 and moreover, after the global financial crisis in 2008. In its act of greater integration with the global order, the most significant attempt has been China's attempt to modify the existing West-dominated economic order by integrating with other major and emerging countries; most important to note is China's association with BRICS. This does not suggest that China is changing the existing international system; rather China is changing its own behaviour for a greater global multipolarisation.

In this context, the present chapter aims to understand China's perceptions of the international order and how she perceives herself in that order. In doing so, the case in point is China's association with BRICS—how it perceives BRICS in general, and Beijing's own role in BRICS in particular.

China's Perceptions of the International Order

In international relations, 'perception' is understood in terms of how actors understand and interpret their environment, including the behaviour of others and situations they find themselves in. As Robert Jervis posits that "[in order] to understand international behaviour, we need to look inside the 'black box' of the state, and indeed to study the goals, beliefs and perceptions of the decision-makers".[3] From this view of Jervis, it appears that in an international relations setting, the attribution of the context or situation does play an important role in channelising the action-reaction mechanism of international politics. That is, the behaviour of actors depends heavily upon how they construe the situation they face.[4] The key factor is '"definition of the situation"[5] where the crux of the matters lie in "perception, choice and expectation"—the crucial components that construct the "definition of the situation"—which is built around the projected action as well as the reasons for the action.[6] It is the perceptions of reality that are representative of the problems they (states) encounter in international politics.[7] Therefore, perceptions play a crucial role in defining any state's international behaviour, based on how they perceive and make sense of the world. In view of this, it becomes imperative to understand: how does China perceive the "International Order"? How does it perceive herself on the world stage? What role does she want to play in that international order as an emerging actor?

In making sense of how the Chinese perceive international order, there are two different perspectives that seek to understand the Chinese perceptions: sinicised view and Chinese view of the world order.[8] The sinicised approach entails that the Chinese perception of the world order is driven from China's experience of being a latecomer to the modern international order. It is mainly argued that prior to being colonised by the imperial forces, China existed in an East Asian hierarchical order, centered around the ideas of *tianxia* (all under heaven) and *chaogong tixi* (tribute system). The notion of *tianxia* constitutes the core of the Chinese traditional concept of political order. As Edward Wang points out, "Zhongguo [the Middle Kingdom, China, N.G.] indicated the center of the world, hence the "central state" or "middle kingdom", while Tianxia referred to the extended Chinese world, despite its ecumenical claim."[9] From a Chinese perspective, *tianxia* comprises the whole known geographic space. It was the relation to and acceptance of the sinocentric civilisation that determined the position of people and countries within the order.

In 1960, John King Fairbank, in his edited volume entitled *The Chinese World Order: Traditional China's Foreign Relations*, notes that "*Zhongguo*, the

Middle Kingdom, China, implies an awareness of the country as both a political and geographical unit of the Chinese Empire. *Tianxia*, all under heaven, which was ruled over by *Tianzi*, the son of Heaven [...] the Emperor of China [...] was used to embrace the whole world. These 'sinocentric' ideas originated from the fact that China's superior size, power, history and resources—all made her the natural center of the East Asian world. This made China's relations with non-Chinese peoples to be coloured by the concept of 'Sinocentrism and an assumption of Chinese superiority'".[10] However, with the Opium Wars[11] and facing the imperialist aggression in the hands of western powers and Japan, China's world view witnessed a crisis, resulting in the breakdown of such a China-centric perception.

Therefore, from the sinicised perspective, it is clear that the Chinese view of the world order was based on a system of interstate relations based on a set of organising principles, different from those of the Westphalia nation-state system that governs international relations today. Wherein, unlike the Westphalia system founded on the principles of sovereignty, equality, treaty and diplomacy, the Chinese world order operated on a system of hierarchy, inequality and tributary relations.[12]

The second approach reflects on the Chinese view of the world order which exhibits a transition from the sinicised viewpoint. This approach reflects China's changed view of the world from a modern and pluralist perspective. According to this perspective, Chinese view of the world order in the post-1949 phase has been subjected to considerable changes, wherein the three sustaining themes that shaped China's perception of the international order are[13]: first, China views the post-war international order as full of injustice and inequalities. The old political order, according to Deng Xiaoping, was "based on colonialism, imperialism and hegemonism". The old international economic order was, on the other hand "imperialist exploitation and plunder" of developing countries. Second, the existing hierarchical structure of the international system and its dominance by the two superpowers lay at the very root of the unjust and irrational international order of the contemporary world. In this regard, China's pledge to never be a superpower underlined not only China's opposition to, but also its determination to change such an order. And third, China follows that sweeping reforms, either radical or gradual, of the international system were not only necessary but also desirable. Thereby, New China's view of the world order was "more decisively oriented toward change than toward order".[14]

This Chinese view has further undergone significant changes in the post-Cold War dynamics, wherein the complexity of the international situation has been coupled with three powerful factors that mark profound changes in the international affairs. According to Wang Yusheng, the former director of the Information Department of the Chinese Foreign Ministry, the Chinese perception of the present international order is as follows[15]: first, to a great extent, the emergence of developing countries has turned the wheel of history. Their resurgence has changed the world's political map as a new force, making it hard for America to maintain hegemony. Although the United States (US) is still the most powerful nation in the world, it will be impossible for it to maintain this lead through the next five decades. Secondly, the central preoccupation for developing countries in the new era has shifted from battling against capitalism to pursuing peaceful development. In doing so, what the developing countries need to do now is to step up the development of a multipolar world, advocate democracy in international relationships and diversity of development approaches, urge greater political autonomy and bring change to the unfair and unreasonable global economic order. And thirdly, China has become a significant factor in changing the trend of international relationships and issues. Wherein America maintains a watching brief on China that is expected to be a defining feature of a number of its strategies, and still looks for opportunities to out-manoeuvre China.[16]

Given this Chinese view of the international order, the changing perceptions of the international order have significantly shaped China's self perception in the international order. That is, the two forces—an old identity formed from 1949 to 1979 and new identity formed since the 1980s—have shaped and formed China's current international identity.[17] China views itself as a "developing country" and feels obligated to promote the interest of the developing world; and at the same time, China is a major regional and even global power, and works closely with the developed countries. In this respect, Chinese perceive that the current international order has many problems, wherein the central issue is the severe disparities in the global order that are unfavourable to developing countries' economies.[18] In view of these disparities, China has constantly affirmed its position on the establishment of a "new world order" that will "ensure a long-term stable and peaceful international environment", as stated by Chinese Foreign Ministry spokeswoman Zhang Qiyue in Beijing on June10, 1999.[19] In concurrence, in 2002, the 16th National Congress of the Communist Party of China (CPC) noted:

> "...the old international political and economic order, which is unfair and irrational, has yet to be changed fundamentally. [...] We [China] stand for establishing a new international political and economic order that is fair and rational."[20]

This statement reflects China's present perception of the international order which is predominantly seen to be "unfair and irrational", and that China's ambition lies in establishing a "new world order". Given these Chinese perceptions of the international order, it is the dual identities of China—"a developing country and a major power, a *status quo* power and a reformer, a non-western country and a modernising country"[21]—which defines China's international behaviour in the changing international system.

In this context, with the identified changes in Chinese perceptions of the international order, it becomes important to explain China's policy response to the international system. This is significant not just because it is necessary, but also because it provides an important alternative to the understanding of China's international behaviour.

Multilateralism as China's International Strategy

With the unequivocal rise of China's national power, the dominant perception is that China will continue to grow and will not be content with the current distribution of status and influence. To which, many realists argue that China's current attitude and behaviour are perfectly predictable as China is merely acting the way that any major power would, such as the US.[22] However, Chinese scholars recommend that in assessing China's increasing global profile, it deems necessary to note that China's actions and words may have not been fundamentally different from the past. In other words, "perception is not the reality", and if perception is reality then there are domestic and international causes that justify it.[23] As Zhao Qizheng, spokesperson of the Chinese People's Political Consultative Conference (CPPCC) National Committee, said:

> "When a country is weak, not many listen carefully to everything you say. But as the nation gets stronger, even the same words will have a very different impact. That's why some foreigners feel China's attitude is different."[24]

With Beijing's changing perceptions of as well as behaviour in the international order, one of the key elements of China's contemporary diplomacy is noted to be its gradual acceptance and adoption of multilateralism, defined as a "practice of coordinating national policies in groups of three or more states, through ad hoc arrangements or by means of institutions."[25] China is increasingly practicing multilateralism, which can be traced back to the 1980s when she opened her doors through economic liberalisation reforms. To note, although not familiar with multilateralism at the beginning of reform, China has gradually accepted multilateralism. Having joined more and more multilateral organisations established by the Western countries, China has not only followed the rules of the games in these institutions but has also become an increasingly active participant in these multilateral organisations. China's accession to WTO in 2001 marked a new phase in her participation in global multilateralism and henceforth, the country has become more active in championing for multilateralism. Most important to note is that Beijing's support for multilateral organisations has expanded beyond active participation in existing institutions to that of initiating new institutions and promoting multilateralism more generally. Here, the central query lies in understanding whether China, in its international aspirations, aims to act as a status quo power accepting the rules of the international order or if it will act revisionist by creating its own institutions, and thus, set new rules of a new order.

This change in attitude of Beijing in practicing multilateral diplomacy in international politics is much debated. To this, some commentators suggest that China is being socialised into the prevailing norms of the international system. While others conclude that China is not only heeding calls to become a responsible global power, but that Beijing's strategic objectives have been modified such that they accord more closely with maintaining the international status quo.[26] However, with the changing nature of global politics as a result of a shift in the global balance of power, the dominant criticism is that China is growing "assertive". Of which, one of the visible areas is China's serious involvement in interest-based multilateral institutions. The most significant queries lie in understanding why China pursues multilateralism? Does this signify that China seeks to influence, shape or preserve the status quo in global affairs?

Beijing's attitude towards multilateralism is well reflected in the policy pronouncements of Chinese decision-makers. In 2005, Chinese President Hu Jintao, in his speech titled Build Towards a Harmonious World of Lasting Peace and Common Prosperity, delivered at the United Nations (UN) Summit on September 15, made a suggestion to "uphold multilateralism to realise common security", as he emphasised that in order to build a "harmonious world", multilateralism needs to be observed and that the role of UN has to be strengthened.[27] In strengthening the multilateral vision, Hu Jintao in his speech entitled "Unite as One and Work for a Bright Future" at the 64th United Nations General Assembly (UNGA) on September 23, 2009, further called for "greater multilateralism and cooperation in international relations". Hu stated:

> "The world today is undergoing major development, major changes and major adjustments. The trend towards peace, development and cooperation, which represent the call of our times, has grown stronger than ever. As the world moves further towards multi-polarity and economic globalisation, multilateralism and democracy in international relations have won greater popular support, while opening up, cooperation for mutual benefit and win-win progress have become the shared aspirations of the international community. Countries have become more interdependent."[28]

Given this significant shift in China's international behaviour, Wang Jianwei notes, "Beijing's attitude towards multilateralism evolved from passive response to active participation and even initiation; multilateral diplomacy has become an integral part of Chinese foreign policy."[29] While Wang Hongying argues that China has not only become a member of multilateral groups, but that it has also expressed support of the major principles of multilateralism.[30] As the Chinese government has repeatedly stated that it advocates "equality among members, open and free trade and investment and non-discriminatory treatment."[31] This shift in China's international policy exhibits the departure in China's longstanding refusal to join the multilateral organisations which Beijing viewed as instruments of Western imperialism. What is interesting to note is that China's multilateralism is further centered on specific interests of developing countries; wherein the three related corollaries, as Wang notes are: first, trade and investment liberalisation has to be considered in the context of its consequences for developing countries. If such liberalisation benefits developed countries at the expense of developing ones, then it should be delayed or abandoned because it would be unfair and would undermine the development of the latter countries, and thus, the common prosperity of the region. Second, given the vastly different levels of economic development among the countries, it becomes important to tolerate different paces of liberalisation and avoid subjecting all nations to a unified set of rules. And finally, procedurally, multilateral arrangements must operate on the basis of informal consultation and consensus-building as formal institutions in Chinese view, tend to engender the imposition of the preferences of some countries on others.[32] These components are well reflected in Hu Jintao's speech at the UN in 2005, wherein he stated:

> "We should work actively to establish and improve a multilateral trading system that is open, fair and non-discriminatory, and further improve the international financial regime with a view to putting in place a healthy and orderly trading environment and a stable and efficient financial environment which is conducive to global economic growth."[33]

From the above statements, it is clear that China's official position on multilateralism is embedded in the aspiration of establishing a just world order with a goal of maintaining world peace and fostering greater involvement of the developing world. This can be said so, as Chinese vice foreign minister Wang Yi, in 2004 at the 14th Ministerial Conference of the 116-member Non-Aligned Movement (NAM) held in Durban, stated:

> "China maintains that the establishment of a new international order which is fair and rational, the realisation of democracy and rule of law in international relations and the promotion of multi-polarisation represents the only way to facilitate the development of multilateralism. [...] And that "without extensive participation and equal status of the vast majority of the developing countries, we can by no means realise democracy in international relations or a fair and rational international order, let alone stronger multilateralism."[34]

It is to note that Chinese policymakers and analysts view multilateralism with a profound sense of pragmatism. In view of this, Li Mingjiang contends that Beijing's aspiration to obtain more decision-making power in various multilateral settings is driven by three pragmatic objectives. At the foremost, China believes that multilateral diplomacy is a powerful instrument for coping with uni-polarity and opposing hegemonism.[35] Multilateralism is useful in checking the unilateral impulses of the US; and will also help to facilitate the formation of a multi-polar world in which China is expected to play a more prominent role, together with other major powers. Second, Beijing believes that its participation in multilateralism could help diminish the "China threat" thesis and build a "responsible power" image for China. China has repeatedly stated that one of the purposes of building global multilateralism is to achieve the goal of *hexie shijie* (a harmonious world). Official statements constantly advocate *he er bu tong* (harmonious but different) and *he wei gui* (peace as the ultimate objective) as noted above in the speeches of Chinese leadership. Third, China believes that multilateral diplomacy can provide new platforms for international cooperation. China is aware that many of the newly-emerged transnational externalities such as climate change, global financial instability, resource depletion, international terrorism, environmental degradation and pandemics cannot be tackled effectively by any single country, but must to be dealt with through multilateral cooperation with other states.[36]

In this perspective, it is important to note that in the multilateral arena, China is acting on two fronts[37]: first is within the international organisations that include both the United States and China, which were previously viewed by Beijing with suspicion as the US dominated institutions. For example, UNGA, United Nations Security Council (UNSC), World Health Organisation (WHO), WTO and others. And second pertains to new multilateral organisations where China has sought to expand its influence since the turn of the millennium with clubs that don't invite the United States to join. These include institutions such as BRICS, East Asia Summit, Shanghai Cooperation Organisation (SCO), Forum on China-Africa Cooperation (FOCAC) and others.

From the above understanding of Beijing's multilateral behaviour, liberal thinkers might argue that the question of whether Chinese policy is informed by liberal internationalism or realist internationalism is "much less important" than the fact that "China has become more active multilaterally".[38] While according to the Chinese perspective, China's "assertiveness" implies China's willingness to play a constructive role in world affairs without compromising its core interests. As Fang Lexian argues that the "assertiveness" reflects only the confidence in its position in the international community, and is based on a more rational perception of its place in the world.[39] Similarly, Su Changhe contends that China's track record of participation and credible pledges in the WTO demonstrates China's commitment to maintaining the "status quo", and that its active engagement in summit meetings such as SCO, Six-Party Talks, BRICS and others reveal that China is "actively embracing multilateral institutions".[40] Further reflecting on "China's embrace of multilateral institutions", Li Hongmei notes in *People's Daily Online:*

> "[T]he deteriorating international political and economic conditions have repeatedly compel[led] China to decide whether it would remain silent on the world stage or make a distinct utterance letting its voice be heard. [...] In order to get rid of the destructive effects, China has to, again, join in the chorus combating the dollar hegemony along with other emerging economies. [...] The increasing popularity of multilateral institutions, and the fact that Beijing is growing up to be a visible player in multilateral cooperation on various occasions, might have prompted China to reset its diplomatic strategies, as a new phenomenon seen currently in many of the international events indicates China is now prepared to play a more active and substantial role and in a departure from its stereotyped international image, seeking to voice its opinions."[41]

With multilateral engagement, China intends to strengthen its cooperation with all countries, especially developing ones. Wherein, significantly China's perception of its role in world affairs is becoming more and more comprehensive.[42] That is, China is using its new found international strength to forge new relationships in the developing world and thereby, will change the nature of international affairs. Therefore, given China's perception of the international order as 'unfair and unequal', multilateralism acts as an efficient international strategy for Beijing in fulfilling its objectives in the changing international environment.

BRICS in China's International Calculus

With an ambition to create a 'just world order' against the existing unfair international system, China regards participation in multilateralism through cooperation and coordination with other emerging powers as a useful means; wherein the desire is to achieve tangible goals in terms of pushing for a more equitable and fairer international political and economic order, striving for a larger share of decision-making power in various international institutions—especially in the economic and financial institutions, such as the World Bank and International Monetary Fund (IMF), and boost its international influence. To fulfil these ambitions, as Li Mingjiang argues, Beijing feels that it will be too difficult for China alone to wrestle power from the Western developed countries, but it would be more possible if China collaborates with other like-minded emerging powers as a joint venture.[43] In view of this, among the emerging new multilateral regimes, the BRICS[44] grouping is largely perceived positively by China.

The 18th National Congress of the CPC in 2012 identified BRICS as one of the most important multilateral platforms for China, via which Beijing wants to play "an active role in international affairs, and work to make the international order and system more just and equitable".[45] China attaches great importance to BRICS in view of expanding its multilateral interests.

What makes Beijing perceive BRICS with such positivity in the changing dynamics of the international order? What prompted China to support the BRICS grouping as an emerging world order against the existing international order? In view of this, Wang Yusheng points at "five common glittering features of the BRICS"[46] which brings the group together are: first, they are all big emerging countries or relatively big countries, with fast development, great potential and varying degrees of sustainability. Their combined foreign exchange reserve exceeds USD 3 trillion—equivalent to over 40 per cent of the world's total, making them important players in the international financial arena, and that the countries took a lead in the recovery from the financial crisis. Second, they have independently chosen their own models of development in line with their national traditions and characteristics rather than simply accept the "Washington Consensus"[47] or any other consensus. Third, they all hope and call for the establishment of a more equitable, just and reasonable international economic and political order. Fourth, they all want a peaceful international environment, advocate democratisation and equality in international relations and disagree with the outdated Cold War mentality and confrontational policies. And fifth, despite their different social systems and ideologies, they share a strategic goal of building a more democratic and just multi-polar world with the UN playing the central role.

Some scholars link China's proactive multilateral diplomacy towards an emerging order to the notion of "Beijing Consensus".[48] For instance, Arif Dirlik, in recognising the importance of Beijing Consensus, posits:

> "[For] PRC, the search for autonomy and self-determination has taken the form not only of maintaining controls over the economy internally, but also by taking a multilateralist approach to global relationships—which contrasts sharply with the increasingly unilateralist direction US policy has taken over the last two decades. The most important aspect of the Beijing Consensus may be an approach to global relationships that seeks, in multinational relationships, a new global order founded on economic relationships, but which also recognises political and cultural difference as well as differences in regional and national practices within a common global framework. This global order would also be founded, not upon homogenising universalisms that inevitably lead to hegemonism, but on a simultaneous recognition of commonality and difference. Deng Xiaoping's reforms beginning in the 1980s gave priority to economic intercourse over political correctness. [...] A century of revolutionary socialist search for autonomy, bolstered by recent economic success, qualifies the PRC eminently to provide leadership in the formation of an alternative global order."[49]

However, the consensus on "Beijing Consensus" is highly ambiguous and uncertain, as there is no common understanding of what it means and whether it implies uniqueness or not.

Given these characteristics of BRICS, Beijing's positive attitude towards BRICS can be assessed from China's three major considerations. Li Mingjiang notes: first, BRICS countries boast strong economic power. This is one of the strong points of BRICS. As even before the addition of South Africa to the grouping in 2011, Chinese analysts frequently perceived that the BRIC[50] countries boasted 42 per cent of the global population, 14.6 per cent of the global GDP, and 12.8 per cent of the global trade—and also held a huge amount of international foreign reserves. Second, China believes that this joint venture among BRICS countries is possible because they have many common positions and interests in international relations, particularly in the economic arena. Third, for China, the BRICS as a new institution is not only significant in and of itself, but more importantly, it could serve as a powerful proxy to push for reforms of other major existing international institutions.[51] With this perspective, Chinese analysts believe that the BRICS countries should get united to negotiate with the developed world to promote their common interests in world politics. This Chinese viewpoint is well reflected in Wang Yusheng's words as he notes:

> "The BRICS countries are united in seeking a more just and reasonable international economic and political order. They all want a peaceful international environment, democratic and equitable international relations and international cooperation based on win-win solutions. They all support the central role of the United Nations (UN) and hope to establish a "democratic and just multi-polar world"."[52]

Similarly, on the importance of BRICS in reforming the international system, Wang Lijiu argues that the BRICS countries need to coordinate positions to advance promised reform in the World Bank and IMF based on "increasing the representation of emerging economies and developing countries, and establishing more scientific and reasonable international financial and economic management mechanisms and patterns."[53]

China's Expectations of BRICS in the Changing International Order

It is clear that BRICS is an important policy option in China's international calculus, wherein with a goal towards building a new equitable international order, China's expectations from BRICS are mainly centered on reforming the existing order by increasing the say and representation of emerging economies and developing countries—given China's own self-identity as a "developing country". It is to say that China represents itself as a force for responsible but fair change to the global distribution of power which should result in a greater voice and role for developing states. In this regard, with the strategic shifts in the international order, the importance of BRICS in China's eyes can be assessed from the Chinese leadership's vision with regard to BRICS. To say, the key components of China's perception towards multilateralism in general, and BRICS in particular, can be traced from the Chinese leadership's speeches at various BRICS Summits since 2009.

In the backdrop of the global financial crisis, on June 16, 2009 (at the First BRIC Summit in Yekaterinburg, Russia), Chinese President Hu Jintao presented a "four-point proposal" for dealing with the financial crisis. The four-point proposal entailed BRIC countries commitment towards: (i) an early recovery of the world economy; (ii) pushing forward the reform of international financial system; (iii) implementing the UN Millennium Development Goals (MDGs) and (iv) ensuring the security of food, energy resource and public health.[54] In view of this, Hu noted: "We [BRIC countries] should seize the historic opportunity to strengthen unity and cooperation, and jointly safeguard the overall interests of developing countries."[55]

Similarly, on April 15, 2010 at the Second BRIC Summit in Brasilia, Hu in his speech titled Cooperation, Openness, Mutual Benefit and Win-Win Strategy stressed:

> "The current international situation is complex and the international landscape is undergoing profound adjustments. However, no matter how the international situation changes and how the international system changes, the goal of mutual benefit and win-win results cannot change. The principle of democracy and fairness cannot change, the direction of mutual respect cannot change and the spirit of sharing mutual concerns of people in the same boat cannot change."[56]

At the Third BRICS Summit held on April 14, 2011 in Sanya on Hainan Island, China, Hu Jintao, in his speech titled Broad Vision, Shared Prosperity, reflected on the key question: how to bring about a peaceful and tranquil 21st century in which humanity can enjoy common prosperity. In answering this query, Hu offered four pointers for the BRIC grouping to endeavour towards: (i) maintaining world peace and stability; (ii) promoting common development of all countries; (iii) bolstering international exchanges and cooperation and; (iv) strengthening the BRICS partnership for common development.[57] Specifically to the common interests of BRICS, Hu called for:

> "Step[ping] up coordination in the international economic, financial and development fields and strengthen the standing and role of emerging markets and developing countries in global economic governance. [...] so as to further strengthen the economic and social foundation for BRICS cooperation."[58]

At the Fourth BRICS Summit held on March 29, 2012 in New Delhi, India, Hu, in his speech titled Strengthening Mutually Beneficial Cooperation for a Better Future, put forward four proposals on strengthening the BRICS cooperation, which entailed commitment to:

(i) common development and promoting common prosperity;

(ii) consultation on an equal footing, deepen political trust, take into full account each other's major interests and concerns, build the model of mutual respect and consultation on an equal footing in the international community and be good friends and partners forever;

(iii) pragmatic cooperation, cement the basis for cooperation, promote cooperation in all fields, consolidate the economic and social foundation of and people's will for cooperation, step up the fiscal and financial departments' consultations and cooperation and develop projects with brand effect and;

(iv) international cooperation, promote the development of the whole world, push for the reform of global economic governance, raise the representation and voice of emerging markets and developing countries, boost South-South cooperation and South-North dialogue, reinforce coordination and communications in the international economic, financial, trade and development fields, enhance coordination within such multilateral mechanisms as the G20 and the UN and show commitment to and support for multilateralism.[59]

From the above speeches by Hu Jintao at each BRICS Summit, it is clear that China's multilateral vision with regard to BRICS aims at building an equitable order. There is a marked emphasis (most importantly) on: common interests among BRICS countries, common development, reforming the international order, win-win cooperation, bridging the North-South gap, building the South-South cooperation and others. This thereby, reflects that China's initiation of BRICS is mainly aimed at creation of a new mechanism which strengthens the role of the developing nations in the international system, by making their voices more prominent and strong in the international order. Here, the goal is to transform and make the existing international order into a just and fair one.

China's viewpoint has not undergone any significant shifts with its leaderhship change in 2013. For instance, China's new President Xi Jinping on March 27, 2013 at the Fifth BRICS Summit held in Durban, South Africa, in his speech titled Work Together for Common Development (besides reiterating Hu's points) pointed out that the BRICS members should work vigorously to promote the establishment of global development partnership and promote common prosperity of all countries.[60] With special mention to China, Xi emphasised:

> "[Beijing] would continue to strengthen its cooperation with other BRICS members for stronger economic growth, improved cooperation framework and more fruitful cooperation with all BRICS members. By doing that, China would bring about tangible benefits to peoples of all BRICS members, thus contributing more to world peace and development."[61]

While on July 15, 2014 at the Sixth BRICS Summit held in Fortaleza, Brazil, Xi Jinping in his speech summed up the BRICS countries' cooperation experiences and charted out the direction for future cooperation. Taking stock of the past progress and plan for the future, Xi stressed:

> "BRICS countries should carry forward the spirit of openness, inclusiveness and win-win cooperation, and develop a closer, more comprehensive and more solid partnership". He further 'proposed for boost[ing] BRICS countries' moral appeal to others, adding that BRICS countries should jointly provide solutions in international affairs, seek justice and practice equality". In this regard, Xi emphasised that China should particularly treasure the cooperation between BRICS countries and put it as a diplomatic priority."[62]

At the Seventh BRICS Summit on July 9, 2015 held in Ufa, Russia, Chinese President Xi Jinping delivered a keynote speech titled Jointly Build Partnership for Bright Future, wherein he stressed that BRICS nations should "build a new type of state-to-state relations with win-win cooperation at the core".[63] Xi very categorically stated:

> "The BRICS countries should resort to a peaceful development, never impose their own wills on others, uphold a philosophy of mutual respect, mutual trust and win-win cooperation, firmly adhere to the multilateralism, cherish the victorious outcome of World War II, safeguard the purposes and principles of the UN Charter, reform and improve global economic governance and promote more countries to support initiatives such as New Development Bank of BRICS nations, Contingent Reserve Arrangement, the "Belt and Road", Asian Infrastructure Investment Bank (AIIB) as well as the Silk Road Fund, so as to inject impetus into world economic growth and reform of the international system of financial currency."[64]

From the above statements by Xi Jinping, some assessments can be drawn regarding Beijing's perceptions of BRICS. However, it is important to note that this only implicitly hints at the Chinese desire of building a 'new global order' based on the aforementioned principles, which in its means to do so exhibits a departure from the present 'West-led global order'. Also to note, the statements further reflect on China's departure from Deng Xiaoping's old dictum to "keep a low profile" (*tao guang yang hui*), which officially has not been given up by Beijing, but to say that China's aspirations have become more global in nature.

From these perspectives, it is clear that although China and BRICS are not trying to overthrow the existing international order but are seriously attempting to reform the shortcomings in the present order by working within the existing system in order to make it more inclusive and non-discriminatory in approach. That is, in order to bridge the existing gaps, China perceives cooperation mechanisms among emerging economies represented by BRICS countries as a new model of global economic cooperation and an important way of pursuing multilateralism.

Challenges for China within BRICS: Perception versus Reality

It is noted that China in BRICS endorses the logic of working together and creating a new world order with the emerging economies. However, this perception is faced with intractable challenges that heavily constraints the effectiveness of BRICS as a close-knit group. Most importantly, it raises doubts over the effectiveness of China's role in BRICS as a 'leader' or 'team player'. This can be examined in three ways:

First, on the economic front, the effectiveness of China to act as a team player rather than a leader is faced with constraints. To say so, a deeper look into the economic configuration in BRICS reveals significant unevenness between China's economic profile and the other four countries. China's economic clout surpasses the other members in BRICS. Thereby, it is being perceived as the *de facto* economic leader of the BRICS group. At the foremost, China is the second largest world economy, which sets it apart from the other emerging economies. Thereby, within the BRICS grouping, it is the largest economy with a GDP that is double of each of the other four economies. China also tops the BRICS in terms of its growth momentum—given its high savings rate, rapid pace of urbanisation and strong investment in infrastructure. China also leads the other BRICS countries in terms of contribution to global commodity trade, as the country itself accounts for almost three-fourths of the BRICS collective global trade. In terms of dependence on intra-trade within the BRICS, China needs the BRICS much less than the other four countries. With respect to trade openness, China is the most highly integrated economy with the rest of the world among the BRICS. Adding further, collectively, the BRICS own nearly half of global foreign exchange reserves—the bulk of which is held by China. And most importantly, China was one of the first economies to rebound from the economic downturn.[65]

Secondly, on the political front, China's role as a team player is again a query of interest given the challenges of the strategic rivalries and different aspirations within BRICS. At the foremost are China's strategic rivalries with Russia and India. The problem lies in the fact that China, Russia and India consider themselves as "big countries" with strong regional clout and similar aspirations of becoming major powers in the international arena.[66] With respect to Russia, China and Russia clashed over a border dispute in the late 1960s, and there is a discomfort in the changing power equations between China and Russia, given Russia's erstwhile superpower status to that of China's emerging global clout. The discord lies in disagreements over arms sales and energy security issues. Most notably, although the two countries are members of SCO, they hold different views over where the SCO should be heading as Russia prefers security cooperation while China attaches priority to economic cooperation as SCO's primary focus.[67]

With respect to India, the discord is much deeper. China and India had fought the 1962 border war, which had resulted into a significant mistrust in the relationship. The prominent bilateral issues between the two are: unresolved border disputes, the Tibet issue, China's support of Pakistan and China's building of ports in countries nearby to India (which severely constrains their equation). In addition to this, they have contradictory global institutional perspectives and multilateral differences with respect to UNSC reform, the global non-proliferation system and others. To say so, as ignoring the "developing country" status, Beijing has never exclusively supported India's candidature openly; while it has openly backed greater representation of African countries, and has openly backed South Africa's candidature for a permanent seat in the UNSC.[68]

Thirdly, Beijing's vision of creating a new type of 'non-western' world order is constrained by the interest of other four countries to associate with multilateral regimes—mostly led by the United States. For instance, Russia is a member of the G8; India, "the largest democracy", is strongly interested in forging cooperation with the "most powerful democracy"—the United States; Brazil is a member of the Organisation of American States (OAS), in which the United States serves as the leader.[69] These factors do constrain China's perception of an emerging order of developing countries.

These crucial factors suggest that there is a significant gap that exists between China's perceptions and the reality of the equation within the BRICS grouping. The divide ranges from economic and political to that of preferences for international integration. Of which, China's economic, political and global clout appears to be a stark contrast to that of the other four economies. There is a dilemma between China's global role as an emerging superpower to that of China's self perception of being a "developing and emerging power" within the BRICS. Hence, there remains an important challenge for China as to whether it should act as a leader or a team player within the BRICS.

Conclusion

The above assessments provide evidence on China's role in the international system, given its perceptions of the changing international order. The chapter suggests that China exhibits no revisionist ambition so far in terms of toppling the existing international order. Although China aspires for a more equitable world order, it seeks to make it so by being a part of the existing order. That is, by greater engagement, active participation and initiation of new institutions in order to play a greater role in the existing system. In this regard, BRICS for China is a platform that brings about reform in the present order by its inclusiveness and non-discriminatory approach, unlike the West-led multilateral institutions. BRICS for China is an international strategy to practice its multilateralism with other emerging economies. However, China's role as a team player over a leader acts as a significant constraint, wherein the perception of an equal order is challenged by the realities of strategic rivalries within the BRICS grouping. Therefore, China's perception of making BRICS a 'close knit and influential grouping' remains uncertain.

END NOTES

1. "Third Plenary Session of 11th Central Committee of CPC held in 1978", *People's Daily Online*, 09 October 2008, URL: http://en.people.cn/90002/95589/6512371.html (Accessed 18 August 2016).
2. "90th anniversary of Communist Party of China 1921-2011", http://www.chinadaily.com.cn/china/cpc2011/2011-05/10/content_12480513.htm
3. Robert Jervis (2002), "Signaling and Perception: Drawing Inferences and Projecting Images", in Kristen Renwick Monroe (ed.) *Political Psychology*, Mahwah, NJ: Lawrence Erlbaum Associates, Publishers, p. 294.
4. David A. Welch Welch, David A. (2005), *Painful Choices: A Theory of Foreign Policy Change*, Princeton, NJ: Princeton University Press, p. 20.
5. Richard C. Snyder, H.W. Bruck and Burton Sapin (1954), *Decision-Making as an Approach to the Study of International Politics*, Princeton, NJ: Princeton University Press.
6. Richard C. Snyder, H.W. Bruck and Burton Sapin (eds.) (1962), *Foreign Policy Decision Making: An Approach to the Study of International Politics*, New York: Free Press, p. 66.
7. Robert Jervis (1976), *Perception and Misperception in International Politics*, Princeton, NJ: Princeton University Press.

8. Wang Jisi and Zhu Feng (2015), "Conclusion: The US, China and World Order" in G. John Ikenberry, Zhu Feng and Wang Jisi (eds.) *America, China, and the Struggle for World Order: Ideas, Traditions, Historical Legacies and Global Visions*, New York: Palgrave Macmillan.
9. Nadine Godehardt (2016), "No End of History: A Chinese Alternative Concept of International Order?", SWP Research Paper, No. 2, January 2016.
10. John King Fairbank and Kwang-Ching Liu (eds.) (1980), *The Cambridge History of China*, Volume II, Cambridge: Cambridge University Press, p. 143.
11. Opium Wars, two armed conflicts in China in the mid-19th century between the forces of Western countries and of the Qing dynasty, which ruled China from 1644 to 1911/12. The first Opium War (1839–42) was fought between China and Britain, and the second Opium War (1856–60), also known as the Arrow War or the Anglo-French War in China, was fought by Britain and France against China. In each case the foreign powers were victorious and gained commercial privileges and legal and territorial concessions in China.
12. Huang Xiaoming (2009), *Politics in Pacific Asia: An Introduction*, New York: Palgrave Macmillan, p. 235.
13. Yongjin Zhang (1998), *China in International Society Since 1949: Alienation and Beyond*, New York: Palgrave, p. 104
14. Ibid.
15. Wang Yusheng (2008), "A path for developing nations", China.org.cn, 10 December 2008, URL: http://china.org.cn/china/reform-opening-up/2008-12/10/content_16927875.htm (Accessed 18 August 2016).
16. Ibid.
17. Da Wei, "A Partnership for Collective Emergence: BRICS in China's International Strategy" in Francis A. Kornegay, Jr. and Narnia Bohler-Muller (eds.) *Laying the BRICS of a New Global Order: From Yekaterinburg 2009 to eThekwini 2013*, Pretoria: Africa Institute of South Africa, p. 38.
18. Ibid. p. 39.
19. Embassy of the People's Republic of China in the United States of America, "China Wants New World Order", URL: http://www.china-embassy.org/eng/zmgx/zgwjzc/t35080.htm (Accessed 18 August 2016).
20. 16th National Congress of the Communist Party of China (2002), "Full Text of Jiang Zemin's Report at 16th Party Congress", URL: http://www.china.org.cn/english/features/49007.htm#9 (Accessed 18 August 2016).
21. Ibid.
22. Chen Dingding and Wang Jianwei (2011), "Lying Low No More?: China's New Thinking on the Tao Guang Yang Hui Strategy", *China: An International Journal*, Vol. 9, no. 2, p. 210.
23. Ibid. p. 207.
24. Ibid. pp. 207-208.
25. Quoted in Li Mingjiang (2011), "Rising from Within: China's Search for a Multilateral World and Its Implications for Sino-U.S. Relations", RSIS Working Paper, No. 225, 25 March 2011.
26. Anna Samson (2012), "A 'Friendly Elephant' in the Room? The Strategic Foundations of China's Multilateral Engagement in Asia", *Security Challenges*, Vol. 8, no. 3, p. 59.
27. "Build Towards a Harmonious World of Lasting Peace and Common Prosperity", Statement by H.E. Hu Jintao President of the People's Republic of China at the United Nations Summit, 15 September 2005, New York, URL: http://www.un.org/webcast/summit2005/statements15/china050915eng.pdf (Accessed 18 August 2016).
28. People's Republic of China Mission to the United Nations, "Unite as One and Work for a

Bright Future", Statement by Hu Jintao at the General Debate of the 64th Session of the UN General Assembly, 23 September 2009, New York, URL: http://www.un.org/ga/64/generaldebate/pdf/CN_en.pdf (Accessed 18 August 2016).

29. Quoted in Yongnian Zheng and Chi Zhang (2012), "'Soft power' and Chinese soft power" in Hongyi Lai and Yiyu Lu (eds.) *China's Soft Power and International Relations*, Oxon: Routledge, p. 31.
30. Wang Hongying (2000), "Multilateralism in Chinese Foreign Policy: The Limits of Socialization", *Asian Survey*, Vol. 40, no. 3, p. 481.
31. Ibid.
32. Ibid., pp. 481-482.
33. "Build Towards a Harmonious World of Lasting Peace and Common Prosperity", 15 September 2005.
34. Ministry of Foreign Affairs of the People's Republic of China, "China urges multilateralism in maintain world peace", 18 October 2004, URL: http://www.fmprc.gov.cn/ce/ceza/eng/zghfz/t165284.htm (Accessed 18 August 2016).
35. Hegemonism here mainly refers to the predominance of United States in the global affairs.
36. Li Mingjiang (2011), "Rising from Within", pp. 9-11.
37. Stefan Halper (2010), *The Beijing Consensus: Legitimizing Authoritarianism in our Time*, New York: Basic Books.
38. Thomas G. Moore (2008), "Racing to integrate, or cooperating to compete? Liberal and realist interpretations of China's new multilateralism" in Guoguang Wu and Helen Lansdowne (eds.) *China Turns to Multilateralism: Foreign Policy and Regional Security*, Oxon: Routledge, p. 47.
39. Fang Lexian (2010), "Peaceful rise still way forward", *China Daily*, 07 June 2010, URL: http://www.chinadaily.com.cn/cndy/2010-06/07/content_9940498.htm (Accessed Online 15 August 2016).
40. Cited by Joseph Yu-shek Cheng (2016), *China's Foreign Policy: Challenges and Prospects*, New Jersey: World Scientific, pp. 547-548.
41. Li Hongmei (2009), "China's embrace of multilateral institutions: from a have-to to an active diplomacy", *People's Daily Online*, 23 June 2009 (Accessed Online 15 August 2016).
42. Fang (2010), "Peaceful rise".
43. Li Mingjiang (2012), "Rising from Within: China's Search for a Multilateral World and Its Implications for Sino-U.S. Relations" in Li Mingjiang (ed.) *China Joins Global Governance: Cooperation and Contentions*, Lanham: Lexington Books, p. 38.
44. The original BRIC acronym representing Brazil, Russia, India and China originates from a 2001 paper titled "Building Better Global Economic BRICs" which analysed the emergence of these economies as powerhouses. In this paper by Goldman Sachs, the economist Jim O'Neill coined the collective description of these economies as BRICs. The study had forecasted that these economies would be among the six largest economies by 2050. In 2003, Goldman Sachs published a follow up paper "Dreaming with BRICs: The Path to 2050", which predicted that by 2040, GDP for BRICs' economies collectively would be larger than the Group of Six (G6). The G6 is made up of United States, United Kingdom, France, Germany, Italy and Japan. By 2025, it is predicted that BRICs economies will account for over half the size of the G6.
45. The 18th National Congress of the Communist Party of China (CPC), "Report of Hu Jintao to the 18th CPC National Congress", 16 November 2012, URL: http://www.china.org.cn/china/18th_cpc_congress/2012-11/16/content_27137540_11.htm (Accessed 18 August 2016).

46. Wang Yusheng (2010), "The BRICs: Rhythm of the Era", *Chinese People's Institute of Foreign Affairs*, The 96th Issue, URL: http://cpifa.org/en/q/listQuarterlyArticle.do; jsessionid= 034489E401F67668 CDA8C0B81687E865? pageNum=5&articleId=165&quarterlyPage Num=16 (Accessed 19 August 2016).
47. Washington Consensus was first conceived by economist John Williamson in 1989. This Consensus became generally accepted as the most effective model by which developing nations could spur growth. Embracing ideals of free-market capitalism, which included open trade policies, privatisation, and deregulation, it provided a prescription for development in the Third World. The ten propositions of the "Washington Consensus" are: Fiscal discipline, reordering public expenditure priorities away from non-merit subsidies and toward public goods (e.g. health and education), tax reform that combines broad tax base with moderate marginal rates, liberalized interest rates, a competitive exchange rate, trade liberalization, liberalization of inward foreign direct investment, privatization, deregulation to ease barriers of firms for entry and exit of sectors and strong protection of property rights.
48. Beijing Consensus is a model of development based on China's model for economic growth and political principles of non-interference and self-determination. The term "Beijing Consensus" for the first time appeared in the international lexicon in 2004, coined by Joshua Cooper Ramo in his influential position paper titled "The Beijing Consensus" where he defined it as the "new physics of Chinese power." The essential elements of the "Beijing Consensus" are- financial support for state sector, restrictions on private sector development and tight political controls- which form the core of China's development.
49. Arif Dirlik (2006), "Beijing Consensus: Beijing 'Gongshi': Who recognizes whom and to what end," *Position Paper, Globalization and Autonomy Online Compendium*, p. 5, URL: http://www.globalautonomy.ca. (accessed 20 August 2009).
50. Originally "BRIC"- Brazil, Russia, India and China, which got extended to "BRICS" after the addition of South Africa to the Bloc in 2011.
51. Li Mingjiang (2012), "Rising from Within", pp. 38-39.
52. Wang Yusheng (2011), "Sun to shine on BRICS in Sanya", China.org.cn, 14 April 2011, URL: http://www.china.org.cn/opinion/2011-04/14/content_22356470.htm (Accessed 18 August 2016).
53. Wang Lijiu (2011), "BRICS sets sail for a better future", China.org.cn, 15 April 2011, URL: http://www.china.org.cn/opinion/2011-04/15/content_22365561.htm (Accessed 18 August 2016).
54. "Chinese president makes proposal for tackling global financial crisis at BRIC summit", *Xinhuanet (English)*, 17 June 2009, URL: http://news.xinhuanet.com/english/2009-06/17/content_11553352.htm (Accessed 20 August 2016).
55. Ministry of Foreign Affairs of the People's Republic of China (2009), "The Meeting of BRIC Leaders Is Held in Yekaterinburg and President Hu Jintao Attends the Meeting and Delivers an Important Speech", 17 June 2009, URL: http://www.fmprc.gov.cn/mfa_eng/wjdt_665385/zyjh_665391/t568489.shtml (Accessed 20 August 2016).
56. Consulate-General of the People's Republic of China in Melbourne (2010), "President Hu Jintao Delivers an Important Speech at the Second Summit Meeting of BRIC Leaders", 16 April 2010, URL: http://melbourne.china-consulate.org/eng/zyxw/t682910.htm (Accessed 20 August 2016).
57. Ministry of Foreign Affairs of the People's Republic of China (2011), "Hu Jintao Presides over and Delivers an Important Speech at the Third BRICS Leaders Meeting in Sanya, Hainan Province", 14 April 2011, URL: http://www.fmprc.gov.cn/mfa_eng/topics_665678/jinzhuanguojia2011_665762/t816047.shtml (Accessed 20 August 2016).

58. Ibid.
59. Ministry of Foreign Affairs of the People's Republic of China (2012), "The Fourth BRICS Summit Kicks off Hu Jintao Delivers an Important Speech", 29 March 2012, URL: http://www.fmprc.gov.cn/mfa_eng/topics_665678/hjtatnsnss_665720/t919321.shtml (Accessed 20 August 2016).
60. Ministry of Foreign Affairs of the People's Republic of China (2013), "Chinese President Xi Jinping Attends 5th BRICS Summit in Durban and Delivers an Important Speech", 27 March 2013, URL: http://www.fmprc.gov.cn/mfa_eng/topics_665678/xjpcf1_665694/t1026742.shtml (Accessed 20 August 2016).
61. Ibid.
62. "Xi proposes closer, more solid BRICS partnership", *China Daily*, 16 July 2014, URL: http://www.chinadaily.com.cn/world/2014xibricssummit/2014-07/16/content_17802884.htm (Accessed 20 August 2016).
63. Ministry of Foreign Affairs of the People's Republic of China, "Xi Jinping Attends 7th BRICS Summit and Delivers Important Speech", 09 July 2015, URL: http://www.fmprc.gov.cn/mfa_eng/topics_665678/xjpcxjzgjldrdqchwhshhzzzcygyslshdswchy/t1280846.shtml (Accessed Online 15 August 2016).
64. Ibid.
65. Lye Liang Fook and Zhang Yang (2010), "China in the BRICS: Pursuing Closer Cooperation Not Hegemony", *East Asian Policy*, Vol. 2, no. 4, pp. 62-67.
66. Ibid., p. 68.
67. Ibid., p. 69.
68. Jagannath P. Panda (2012), "A 'BRICS" Wall? The Complexity of China-India Multilateral Politics", *Indian Foreign Affairs Journal*, Vo. 7, no. 2, p. 189.
69. Li Mingjiang (2011), "Rising from Within", p. 13.

4

The Role and Representations of Media

Tilak Jha

Introduction

Despite this being the best time for Western-based large media corporations, this is also the time when the media industry is going through a serious crisis-—not only as an industry but the way journalism has been—courtesy internet, among others. Few of the players which are thriving today are without pure commercial considerations. From *Times of India* group in India and Globo in Brazil to Murdochs in the United States, in terms of this particular fact, there is little difference between the East and the West. Cross ownership and multi-national conglomerates further appear to have wiped away the distinction of culture or regional identities (read North-South differences). In effect, this is more so because the biggest of media monopoly MNCs are North-based, and the South still has a long way to cover. Indeed, silver linings like the idea of net neutrality (i.e. of unimpeded access on internet and open source to name a few) hold big promises to limit the monopoly of big corporations.

There is another aspect to this (largely) West-led centralisation. It is West-led because the US is the biggest producer and exporter of cultural products, and all the biggest news agencies (AFP, AP and Reuters) are also run by them. They also own major stakes in the media sector in the developing world through cross ownerships and share markets. Curiously, despite that, the very rise of the developing world in general and BRICS countries—especially India and China, which home nearly 38 per cent of world population, in particular—is having a decentralisation effect on the world media. The same economics that is causing monopoly in favour of NewsCorps and Time Warners have become responsible for ending their domination. For example, if the case of Hollywood is taken (despite it still being the world's biggest film industry), it is now increasingly dependent on Eastern, particularly Chinese, market. This has not only compelled them to accommodate Chinese government's concerns, but is also making them work with the Chinese movie industry and accommodate their world view. Bollywood's own genre of song-and-dance kind of movies has audience across the world going well beyond the Indian diaspora. This has happened in spite of the fact that the Western media giants from NewsCorp and Disney to Viacom and Sony Pictures have increased stakes in the Bollywood since it got industry status in 2001. The purse strings have their role in making the film industry one with a global appeal. And if the increasing popularity of Bollywood be read as a pointer, the industry has gotten a lot bigger, better and decentralised today, and it is influencing a greater number of people across the world. The same applies for Chinese film industry, and for many others media industries—from advertisements and animation to online news and TV industry. The economics of these transitions across the media industry is playing a key role in influencing and shaping the media agenda.

However, there is another side to this: world's largest selling English newspaper is India's *Times of India*; world's biggest selling newspapers are in China and world's fastest growing media groups are all based in the developing world. It would not be surprising if developing world's, particularly Chinese media groups, become tomorrow's NewsCorp—the way Chinese oil giants have been acquiring their Western counterparts. Beyond this possible undercurrent ownership shift, the global North's agenda is also under pressure from the spread of online journalism and increasing viewership/readership of Western media platforms in BRICS countries is shaping the way they always saw the world. Add to this the multiplicity of viewpoints in the global news industry as brought by China and Russia through their global media initiatives CCTV and Russia Today respectively, and the world definitely has one more opinion to listen to. Once the rest of BRICS join the forces and unite, they could pose a formidable competition to the flow of information currently under near complete monopoly of the big US and Europe-based MNCs. The ownership of media industry across the world has diversified and multiple stakeholders with various vested interests—primarily profit—join hands. This sort of dilutes the very agenda for which the industry exists. Indeed, not all is simply about economics as the Edward Snowden and Julian Assange incidents showed us. Had it not been for the global South countries like China, Ecuador and Russia—who for whatever political purposes made sure he stayed away from the reach of the US spy agencies—they would have not even been news for long. Also, the rise of technology platforms has given enough power even in the hands of individuals and small groups to somehow decisively influence what even complete ownership cannot do. So, if NewsCorp-owned newspapers in Britain indulged in malafide practices of, say phone tapping, the newspaper had to be shut down. The developing world also has such examples of its own—pointing towards the limits of ownership, a diversified stakeholders from South and North and in turn, the pressure to bring greater transparency and accountability to this industry controlled by the very few and the very powerful.

The Concept

> "*Generating information is the most important source of power today. When you generate information, you generate perception.*"
>
> —Brazil's ambassador to China at the first BRCIS Media Summit in Beijing on December 1, 2015

That information is a source of power had been realised long ago by the people in power in all forms of political system. Secret services have existed since empires were formed and edicts followed to propagate the state's writ. In recent history, Orson Welles tasted the power of information when his 1938 War of the Worlds broadcast saw listeners going into panic. Willi Boelcke accounted in his 1970 book, The Secret Conferences of Dr. Goebbels: The Nazi Propaganda War, how Goebbel's persuasive rhetoric at the height of Nazi power in Hitler's Germany had shown the world one extreme of what a relentless motivated media propaganda could do. Communist Russia institutionalised it for the ends of communism. However, it was Mao's China which used rhetoric on a scale never seen before to mobilise the world's largest population in one of the only two continuing civlisations. Mao, Hitler and Welles proved in many ways Marshal McLuhan's iconic saying: Medium is the message.

Things have changed over the past century. The study of media paradigm during this period quantified the limitations of dominant paradigm, and the oversimplifications argued by limited effects paradigm in favour of cumulative effects that media facilitates coming over a long period. Today's media despite much more sophisticated technology at its disposal has to deal with multiplicity of information coming from a host of dependent and independent stakeholders. However, what has come as a real holder of information dissemination levers is the ownership of global media networks. It is this lever which, in the contemporary economic world, has come to be of critical linkage if media rhetoric is to be the perception or the public opinion.

Nearly four decades since the MacBride Report in 1980 argued for a New World Information and Communication Order (NWICO) can the coming together of BRICS symbolise a South South information order? It is a difficult question to answer—nonetheless a possibility. At what cost is something we would explore in this paper. However, as Thussu notes, with the rise of digital medium, Media Transnational Corporations (TNCs) like NewsCorp have effectively shifted the ideology of "media culture from public service to profit-oriented programming".[1] Not only has the idea of equity in communication gone, in most cases, it is becoming worse. In such a context, whether or not the BRICS media going to fundamentally provide a more inclusive and fair alternative media model is the real question. Or if not an entirely different model, will it at least follow a different reporting model which can be considered fairer than the one we have currently? This paper deals with whether BRICS as a group, with China in the lead, can offer an acceptable alternative, and whether the Chinese media and the respective media of other BRICS countries can come together.

Political-Economy of BRICS Media

Samir Saran, Senior Fellow and Vice President at the Observer Research Foundation, a non-governmental think tank and a member of BRICS Think Tank Council, gives an interesting analogy of how BRICS matters to the member countries. His analysis, although expressed with reference to India, applies equally to South Africa, and even Brazil. It is them gaining "far greater bargaining power in negotiating its (their) place within the global political and economic governance institutions—currently dominated by the West". Beyond that, it will gain importance, but not necessarily a fundamental shift.[2] His arguments basically boil down to a proposition that there are certain limits to the cooperation among BRICS despite the rise of BRICS economies—spurring an economic shift of the global center from the Western to Eastern shores.

Simultaneously, as the graphs below show, the shift is a defining one from demographic (43 per cent of the world's population lives in BRICS countries)

point to the fact that BRICS constitutes of countries that are growing way faster compared to the developed West.

Fig. 4.1: BRICS Countries Average Estimated Expenditure on Consumer Electronics in 2013

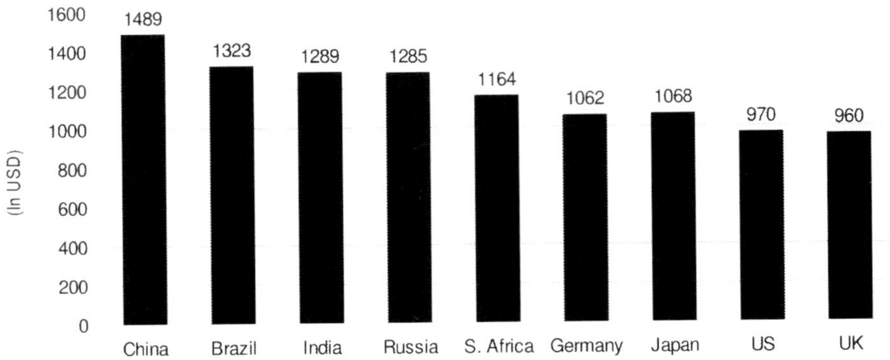

Source: Accenture cited in Statista.[3]

This includes India and China—two fastest growing major economies expected to contribute most to global growth over the coming years. These factors have brought phenomenal growth in expenditure on advertisement, which is the bread and butter of media, and in turn media sector.

Table 4.1: Total Advertising Expenditure of BRICS (In USD million, current prices)

Country	*2009*	*2010*	*2011*	*2012*	*2013*
Brazil	11.216	13.248	14.397	15.293	16.38
Russian Federation	5.678	6.665	8.107	9.208	10.217
India	4.043	4.579	5.028	5.429	5.860
China	22.679	28.422	33.540	37.202	40.951
S. Africa	2.945	3.484	3.874	4.186	4.499

Source: Based on WAN-INFRA (2015), *World Press Trends Report 2014,* pp. 52-53.[4]

Economically, all five have largely capitalist set-up but politically, they are quite different with very different media systems on the face of it—even though their ownership patterns have similarities. In their case, the differences in their political systems have impacted their media and its workings.

While Russian and Chinese media systems are largely state-controlled, the rest three have commercial media systems. In the Chinese political economy of media, politics has a clear upper hand. South Africa is the only country among the five with strong public-service alongside community media. Brazil also has abundant community media. But the community media in India, China and Russia is very weak. India is the second biggest in terms of total number of dailies and lowest in Internet penetration (hardly 20 per cent in 2011).

Table 4.2: Total Paid for and free dailies, total average circulation (000)

Country/Year	*2009*	*2010*	*2011*	*2012*	*2013*	*Adult Population*	*Average circulation/ add populations (copies per 000)*
Brazil	8920	8358	8651	8806	8480	152775	557
Russian Fed.	12341	9545	9059	9059	–	120540	-
India	109937	109937	109937	112892	112892	889018	1270
China	107850	109902	108111	120061	120061	1113052	1079
S. Africa	1733	1733	1683	1436	1346	37617	358

Source: Based on WAN-INFRA (2015), *World Press Trends Report 2014,* pp. 40-41[5]

Table 4.3: Internet Users (000)

	2009	*2010*	*2011*	*2012*	*2013*	*Adult Population in (000)*
Brazil	75.791,32	79.245,74	88.49476	98.02859	103.38675	152275
Russian Fed	41.13650	60.95250	69.54570	75.61292	88.10891	120540
India	59.15380	87.82035	125.01824	156.18045	189.07308	889019
China	384.76882	459.03673	514.80179	568.56857	621.68004	1113052
S. Africa	4.93202	8.99843	10.62322	-	25.90819	37617

Source: Adapted from WAN-INFRA (2015), *World Press Trends Report 2014,* pp. 52-53.[6]

As the chart above shows, India and China are not only countries with significant adult population, but also ones with significant average circulation. Although complete data is not available, India is arguably the one with highest copies of circulation.

Table 4.4: Newspaper Reach in BRICS (In per cent)

	2010	*2011*	*2012*	*2013*	*2014*
Brazil	27	27	26	24	21
Russian Fed	7	6.1	8.5	10.4	9.1
India	41.8	41.8	–	–	—
China	66.8	63.1	–	39.8	39.8
S. Africa	29	31	30.9	29.8	–

Source: "World Press Trends Report 2015" in Carro, Rodrigo (2016), "Brazilian Newspapers: The Risk of Becoming Irrelevant," Reuters Institute for the Study of Journalism, p. 22[7]

The same report also finds that among BRICS countries, India and China have the highest reach of newspapers to people. Again, figures for all the years are not available, but that is the broad trend. South Africa is also not far behind. India's major media platforms are either family-owned—many of them with deep association with one or the other political party. The media in the 'managed' democracy of Russia faces a different kind of threat to its credibility—both inside and outside Russia. But Internet penetration in Russia is the highest among BRICS countries at 61 per cent, and its media is sufficiently multilingual like India or South Africa. Socially, inequality is deep in Brazil, India and South Africa, and relatively better in China and Russia.[8]

Coming to the media coverage, all these states fall irrelevant and are guided by different, sometimes unrelated factors. For example, the coverage of BRICS countries in each other's media is not always in the context of BRICS alignment. China is given most prominence among the BRICS countries in Russian, Brazilian and South African media. China does get prominence in Indian media as well, but mostly for the wrong reasons—courtesy the long-standing border dispute and emerging contest in the Indian Ocean, among others. In Russian and South African media, India is the second and Brazil, the third most important BRICS country. Mostly, their discussion in each other's media is independent of their BRICS identity, and they do not see each other as part of a community.[9]

When it comes to BRICS countries' coverage of BRICS in their media, it is almost always for political-economic reasons and not socio-cultural aspects. China gets great coverage in Russia, Brazil and South Africa, but mostly as the world's second biggest economy or trade partner. Chinese are most influential in South African media, but here, either coverage is mostly about political-economic aspects. Russian media talks of China mostly in economic and IR domain; important cultural exchanges are also taking place amid the two giant neighbours in the historical domain though. Russian coverage of BRICS often presents it in contrast to G7, and considers Russia as the most developed of BRICS countries. India's coverage of China is political-economic, but dwells often on the unsettled issues of their border and supremacy rather than BRICS. Part of the reason behind this kind of coverage is rooted in the kind of media products that come out of these countries and the identities that they have built for themselves—yet again something unrelated to BRICS. For example, Brazil usually gets political economic coverage for its important position in South America and its huge natural resources, but it also gets socio-cultural coverage far beyond BRICS. Brazilian *tele-novelas* (TV serial dramas which are shorter than soap operas) impressed Soviet and Chinese audience in late 1980s. Russian TV later also broadcast famous Brazilian carnivals. But there was little reverse flow—either through programmes or investments. Rather, in Brazil, after a 2002 amendment that allowed foreign investment in media companies, most investors came from the US and Europe—keeping the levers of ownership firmly away from anything distinctly South.[10] To be precise, ownership of Brazilian media lays in the hands of four families, which together control nearly 500 outlets and domestic conglomerates across radio, TV, print and online media.[11]

India is another BRICS country that has generated significant appeal for its film industry across the world. As an independent industry, Indian movies are driven by commercial consideration, with little involvement from BRICS countries. In general, apart from movies, India's coverage in South Africa is mostly about the 1.3 million-strong South Asian diaspora around Durban and Johannesburg. Many Indian TV channels are available via DSTV in South Africa. In Russian and Brazilian media, India gets less but largely positive coverage. However, in Chinese media, India's coverage is usually not that positive, despite bilateral trade standing at an impressive USD 70 billion. Despite that, there is an organic cooperation emerging in the field of movies. India and China signed an audio-visual co-production agreement in September 2014. Three Chinese films have been filmed in India in the recent past: Lost in India, Kung Fu Yoga and Xuan Zang. Of these, Xuan Zang was a co-production between Chinese Film Company Ltd. and Eros (India) International.

South Africa usually comes at last among the BRICS countries. South African media coverage maintains balanced approach to all BRICS countries. But in terms of investments, South Africa has investments in all the BRICS countries. Naspers, a South African media company, is 80 per cent owned by Tencent in terms of market cap, and its subsidiary MIH has a 9.9 per cent stake in Beijing Media Corp—publishers of Beijing Youth Daily. Naspers also has 30 per cent of Mail.ru—Russia's leading Internet service and Internet portal, and two of the largest Russian-language social networks—Odnoklassniki.ru ('Classmate') and Moi Mir ('My World')—among others. Naspers also owns 30 per cent stake in Brazil's leading media company called Abril, and a 91 per cent interest in Buscape group—Brazil's largest e-commerce company. Naspers also has stakes in India's Flipkart.com, Ibibo, TravelBoutiqueOnline and Internet company called ACL Wireless.[12]

Globally, the Russian media outlets are far less aggressive and have small stakes in Indian companies like Flipkart. The Chinese are the most aggressive in trying to promote their media interests. China has been making big investments in its 'Go Global' project by launching multi-lingual TV channels and websites, and sponsoring a host of cultural activities. Indeed, all of this is coming from the state media. Today, the CCTV claims covering 98 per cent of earth. CCTV reports more on developing countries compared to Western media channels. Nonetheless, Chinese media's sensitivity about certain issues leads to questions about its impartiality.[13]

Other Constraints

Victoria Panova observes a certain level of overestimation of BRICS potentials to the need for what she calls "realistic and down-to-earth directions and options for cooperation".[14] The group benefits from the earlier precedents and has attained what took earlier organisations years to achieve. However, media cooperation at such a diverse level is quite an uncharted territory. There are few examples of media coverage playing decisive roles in policy making and bilateral and multilateral relations. It is a relatively new challenge which the BRICS is trying to get a hold on. Media plays particularly important role in bilateral relations of these countries—an important case being that of India-China relations. Unlike many countries, where media usually follows the government line, in India, media is on its own. Not to deny the lack of strategic trust, border differences and the questions of accommodating each other's expectations, the media in India or China often behave like share markets when it comes to covering each other.

The BRICS countries have, since the beginning, maintained that while South-South cooperation is important, their relation with the West remains equally important. Therefore, the BRICS cooperation mechanism still continues to be loose. The equal importance of BRICS member countries is not a privilege of the powerful members but a necessary condition that they must agree with. This is primarily because of the developed countries' reluctance to consider the concerns of developing economies in their agenda. In the BRICS grouping, China has two primary power contestants: Russia and India. However, Russia's confrontational ties with the West compounded after its economic, military and other geopolitical troubles left it with little option but accommodating China. India, on the other hand, is yet to catch up economically. China's willingness to maintain a strategic silence on Pakistan's anti-Indian agenda also constitutes the biggest threat to India-China media cooperation.

Adding to the difference in the way journalism is perceived among BRICS countries, and China again stands out in this regard. As shown in the figure below, while Brazil, India and South Africa fall in the close league, Russia and China are far from being a free place to pursue journalism. This, therefore, makes working together more difficult.

Fig. 4.2: Rough Measures of Media Freedom[15]

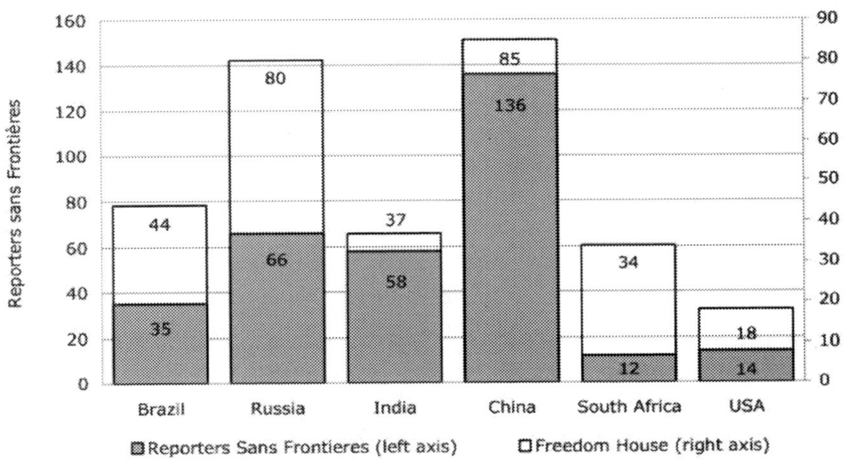

Source: Transparency International Corruption Perceptions Index 2011, Developed from Collins (2014).

BRICS Media and China

China's eagerness to embrace global capitalism and attain an elevated status in the new world order is a well-documented fact. It is that similar urge that has led China to actively explore the possibility of BRICS media. However, China's media system is way different from other BRICS countries despite having similar ownership patterns. It caters to the Communist Party of China's propaganda goals, which happen to be one of the strong pillars of the single party Chinese state. It is the Chinese nationalism which shapes their position on South China Sea and other key foreign policy issues. Back home, China moulds the rhetoric to suit their official policy. For example, anti-WTO voices were suppressed and media outlets were required to support official policy on WTO, despite concerns expressed by the farmers and small industries.

In the field of media, as in others as well, we are less likely to see an open clash being waged with the West for now. For that matter, CCTV, China's most influential global platform, is in effect not a rebellion against the Western media domination when it comes to the way it covers day-to-day stories. On that count, what it essentially provides is more coverage of China and its interests. They are more in line with what Jacques calls "sponsoring a new China-centric international system which will exist alongside the present system and probably slowly begin to usurp it".[16] Nonetheless, post-WTO and Beijing Olympics, mass media and TV markets have largely remained tightly shut in China, except when allowed. The Chinese leadership has mostly followed a policy in which it has balanced harnessing new media technology and economic growth with those of protecting their own ideological power. Even when allowing foreign capital to invest in media advertising and management, the Party-state never gives up on being the ultimate editorial authority. Will China be willing to share this for BRICS? If not, how far will the rest of BRICS be willing to agree on it?[17]

Of no small importance is the fact that news media and TV are the last frontiers of propaganda for the Party-state. China sheltered this sector from four decades of foreign competition—indeed small sacrifices were made here and there. In the film industry, China allows all but nearly three dozen Hollywood films in a year, other than following a policy that strongly favours the domestic industry. Will it render this sector open to unrestrained flow from India or Brazil which have strong TV and film industries? By all count, China will not allow a new Buddhism from India to enter and set its foot. Will the 'dominant structure' of Communist ideology controlling media in China and its ventures beyond China allow the 'emerging structure' of media professionalism to flourish? Precedents suggest the opposite. Lastly, it might be very difficult for the BRICS media to adopt a common stand on issues of bilateral disputes. The most difficult nut to crack could be India-China relations indeed. Zhou He says that Chinese media has transformed itself from a propaganda apparatus to what he calls 'Party Publicity Inc' to promote a positive image of the Party-state.[18] This capitalist system with a socialist agenda works inside China. It can even work abroad as long as it is Chinese media's fully-owned and controlled operation. However, as a group agenda of BRICS media, it will have little or no chance.

Chinese Media on BRICS

Chinese media has played a largely supportive and appreciative role when it comes to covering the BRICS. During the summits prior to 2012, when BRICS was still BRIC, the still-in-the-offing grouping attracted less attention of the Chinese press. It largely stuck to the official releases—reporting speeches delivered and statements made by the government. Opinionated pieces that appeared were few and far in between. The media in the other BRIC countries was also still testing waters as to how the BRIC work out. The very headline of a '2009 Interfax' news as reported by BBC Monitoring says it all. It said: "Russian summit to show if potential BRIC organisation has a future — Kremlin". The 2010 BRICS summit was cut to one day because of the earthquake in China. Indeed, the Chinese media did give calls to come together. In 2011, the first time when South Africa participated in the then BRIC, a *China Daily* report quoted an official's statement: "The BRICS countries have similar concerns or stances on important issues such as the global economy, international finance and development."[19]

Beginning in 2012, the Chinese media coverage expanded beyond official speeches and notes in its stand that BRICS is not a counter to the West. In 2012, in a report, China's official news agency Xinhua dismissed concerns about BRICS emerging as West's rival bloc. It said that BRICS countries have become "indispensable engine for the world economic growth", and that the developed countries "have benefited much from the growth of BRICS countries". Allaying fears about BRICS, it wrote:[20] "It would be a misinterpretation to call BRICS a political bloc rivaling industrialised economies. In fact, the BRICS countries, including China, have viewed major developed economies as strategic partners for development and always aimed to build a constructive relationship with them. For the world to quickly pull out of the on-going crisis, a stronger tie should be cemented between developed countries and emerging economies to pool their resources together in order to address pressing global challenges."

In recent years, Chinese media has become even more active. *People's Daily* in its overseas edition wrote, commenting on the on the fifth BRICS summit, that Goldman Sachs 2003 prediction of BRIC leading the world economic trend by 2050 was rather conservative. It said that BRIC countries grew over the first decade of the 21st century at a GDP growth rate of above 8 per cent, compared to around 2.6 per cent in developed countries and global average of 4.1 per cent. It identified BRIC becoming a force to be reckoned with and working for the creation of a fair and reasonable new international political and economic order. It observed that while China was world's factory, Russia was the gas station, and that India was the world's office and Brazil, a raw material giant. South Africa also neatly complemented the grouping due to its position in Africa.[21]

Beijing Youth Daily wrote, reporting about the sixth summit in 2014, that the BRICS summit had entered the middle stage of institutionalisation in a short span of time. It said that post-2008 financial crisis, with the existing system of international economic governance, the world could do precious little as it hardly reflected the changed global economic hierarchy. It said that the West got together in practising "合作霸权" (*hézuò bàquán*) or cooperative hegemony at the cost of "包容性增长" (*bāoróng xìng zēngzhǎng*) or inclusive growth. It did recognise that the economic cooperation among the BRIC countries was not to reset the global economic governance, but to supplement for its inefficiencies, incompetencies and unwillingness. In this regard, BRIC—the transcontinental grouping—symbolised a new model of cooperation, it claimed. It asserted that BRIC would bring new and more equitable global economic governance.[22]

Who will Own the BRICS Media?

Thussu says that BRICS has raised theoretical questions about its contribution to global political, cultural and economic discourse, and broadly, their impact on global communication.[23] Internationalisation of media and communication is a long-delayed project since the MacBride days and yet, the US domination remains overwhelming through ownership of all forms of dominant media platforms. BRICS, on the face of it, is arguably the most viable of the groupings which could influence and even change the Western stranglehold over media.

Ironies will have their way in any case, as is the fact that Western domination of the media world today increasingly survives on money generated in the Eastern world. In entertainment, Hollywood rules the world, even though Hollywood movies draw a significant share of their revenue from China. ESPN and MTV draw upon global telecast rights often beyond the US shores as well. In the financial media, Bloomburg, Wall Street Journal, The Economist—all have their growth and revenue increasingly coming from BRICS and other emerging economies. Similarly, in the domain of social media, the domination of Google, YouTube, Facebook, Twitter et al is near complete, except in China and some other countries. It would be important how the new formation maintains its separate and impartial existence. Besides its clash of interests with the West, there could be serious issues inside BRICS regarding such a platform as well. Given the diversities in terms of the individual nations' priorities, it will be a difficult task. The reason why either of the BRICS countries would be reluctant to play a secondary role is because all of its members are rising economies, wielding considerable regional influence.

Credibility Issues

Qatar's Al Jazeera emerged as a strong voice in the Middle East and inspired by its success, many countries have tried repeating the experiment. Russians opened a multi-lingual network in the name of Russia Today in 2005. Although it claims a global reach of 550 million viewers, its anti-US perspective gets described as the 'Voice of Kremlin'. RT's coverage of BRICS is limited. The BRICS countries are yet to reach even the level of Al Jazeera English, which prioritises coverage of Global South.

In India, English journalism has a long tradition and significant advertising revenue. However, Indian global television news has not even been tried, either by the government or the private sector—both of which remain focused on the domestic ground. The absence of state broadcaster in this domain is surprising, given the fact that countries like Japan and China—with hardly any base of English speakers—have been in this domain for years. According to observers, "Indian journalism and news media in general is losing interest in the wider world —particularly in other BRICS nations—at a time when Indian industry is increasingly globalising and international engagement with India is growing across the globe."[24]

Among BRICS countries, the most serious effort on the international scale has come from China's CCTV and *Xinhua*. With nearly USD 7 billion external communication programme to back them up; together, they have invested billions and spread across the world to promote China's official discourse against Western propaganda. CCTV, in 2012, had broadcasts in six languages and claimed 200 million viewers outside China. *Xinhua* is one of the largest news agencies in the world, with bureaus in more than 100 countries. In Africa, *Xinhua* has more than 28 offices, which is continuously shaping and reshaping China's image as one of a benefactor in the region. South African University of Witswatersand is also running a journalism school that has a China-Africa reporting project to improve the quality of reporting around China-Africa issues. There is also a Research Unit for Media in the Global South (RUMIGS) at Rhodes University, and in the digital domain, a blog hosts podcasts and updates from Facebook.

There is another specialisation to the coverage of the BRICS by Chinese media—which use a lot of words and phrases that hold meaning in the Chinese context but sometimes carry different connotations for rest of the BRICS. For example, Chinese press regularly use words like 'vow', 'hegemony' and 'harmonious development'. The rest of BRICS, however, largely cater to the global media's terminologies for various reasons. It would therefore be interesting to see that such terminologies with Chinese communist identities of their own would echo with the wider BRICS audience. In terms of reporting an incident as well, the Chinese media reporting on political issues in general, including BRICS, rarely follows a genuinely balanced and analytical approach. The kind of criticality and impartiality that generates trust and faith in a media institution is greatly missing. The Chinese media—least among the BRICS countries—continues to be in some form of propaganda mode, and is yet to establish its style of writing and reporting as per global standards. However, there are signs of change. Reports on the recently-held first BRICS Media Summit have tended towards maintaining a balance.[25] *Xinhua*, in its story, limited to reporting without using Chinese style and turning analytical and critical. It still falls far short of setting a different and credible standard, but it does point towards change. Even if Chinese media adopts relatively different standards in their reporting of international news—both domestically and in its global editions—it will take some major reporting leadership demonstration by them to be contesting the global public opinion maker's chair. For now, Chinese media's perception is largely that of a spokesperson, which contradicts the basic goals it cherishes.

How the Chinese Media Coverage Differs?

In terms of coverage, the Chinese media is possibly the least political—compared to Indian standards at the least. On an average day, most that a mainstream Chinese newspaper would tend to cover would mostly be positive developmental stories, avoiding sensationalisation—especially of news which could turn politically sensitive and most such negative developments—and stick to covering politics in the most official manner imaginable. The rest of the coverage is again somehow influenced by this political coverage standard. Breakthroughs and investigative stories are rare, and news in China is usually a celebration of good events rather than a critical chronicle. *The Hindu*—the Indian newspaper which partnered with Xinhua in hosting the first-ever BRICS Media Summit—is considered very restrained compared to general Indian media's reporting standards. However, *The Hindu* would possibly be the boldest newspaper in all spheres of reporting—including political—compared to mainland Chinese standards.

A glance at the *Russia Today* website—except the common strain of anti-Western reporting—would make it clear that it follows the traditional definition of news and sensationalisation. On BRICS and other international issues, its coverage adheres to the line of Kremlin's anti-West agenda. Thus, in a way, *Russia Today* adopts a more open anti-Western propaganda. Nonetheless, when it comes to domestic affairs—political included—the Russian media platforms like *The Moscow Times* do take critical stand, which is something quite rare in mainland China. The South African, Brazilian and Indian media are more or less on the same page—with all shades of journalism being able to survive. By all shades, here it means anti-establishment, pro-establishment, neutral and market-oriented. Of course, there are constraints to them... but there is a fair level of diversity, unlike the Chinese media.

News versus Entertainment

In today's world, it is entertainment networks that primarily impact the global media flows, not news. In entertainment, the US dominates globally. Among the BRICS countries, the Russians and the Chinese are struggling to go global in this domain. Russians produce movies in double digits, and the best known Chinese movies come mostly from Hong Kong and Taiwan. Brazil's TV industry, centered on the *telenovela* format, has registered much more success than CCTV. Its programmes have got dubbed and adapted in most of Latin America and beyond, in around 100 countries. South Africa's media market is less developed among BRICS nations, even though its film production has multiplied from five in 2005 to 60 in 2012.

That leaves India, whose USD 30 billion entertainment and media (E&M) industry in general and the USD 3.5 billion Bollywood in particular, as the most visible BRICS media product globally. Bollywood produces most number of films than any other single film industry in the world, including Hollywood. In the international arena since 1930s, Bollywood movies are seen today in more than 70 countries—including in BRICS nations. India's "escapist musical melodramas" were a huge draw in Soviet Russia and China. In recent years, Aamir Khan has become a household name in China. In Brazil as well, the 2009 Bollywoodised soap opera titled India—A Love Story became hugely successful.[26]

Entertainment is not only leading in developing economies. Almost all the world's largest media companies have their news biz trailing behind entertainment. "Serious journalism has increasingly been McDonaldised and trivialised, whereas infotainment, gossip and scandals have taken over to pander to the instant gratification of mass consumers. In such a time of profit seeking, there are few takers of journalistic ideals—Rupert Murdoch's censoring of programs and canceling books to please Chinese leaders being a case in point."[27]

Towards a BRICS Media

For the BRICS, attaining media cooperation remains one of the major challenges. As a first step in this direction, on *Xinhua's* initiative, the first BRICS Media Summit was held in Beijing last December. The 25 participating media organisations hoped to create new institutional frameworks to benefit their media with deep global South linkages. Held under the theme 'Innovation, Development, Cooperation and Trust', the Summit participants deliberated on media's role in improving, and improving closer ties among BRICS countries. The Summit underlined the important and critical role media plays in promoting cooperation between nations, and proposed coming together to tell stories that reflect BRICS' cooperation—a pointer towards the domination of Western media in agenda-setting. One of the initial moves in this direction was regarding developing consensus among BRICS media on "coverage of G-20 Summits in tune with the priorities of the emerging economies."[28]

The Summit ended with a declaration to "strengthen ties among our five countries, whether in the economic, social or political sphere, with objective, impartial, comprehensive and timely media reports". It said that cooperation between the BRICS in the media realm will serve two functions; the first as a means of enhancing globally the idea of a new multipolar world and the second, as a means of facilitating mutual understanding between the BRICS nations themselves—to "learn more about each other" and to "find a way of receiving news directly rather than from outside sources".[29] The initiators included China's *Xinhua*, India's *The Hindu*, Brazil's *Empresa Brasil de Comunicacao*, *S/A* and *EBC*, Russia's International Information Agency *Rossiya Segodnya* and South Africa's *Independent Media.*[30] Since then, at least one more get-together of media heads took place at FICCI Frames in March 2016. This saw coming together of public broadcasters of the BRICS countries who exchanged ideas on TV and film cooperation, among others.

In any case, achieving the goals underlined during the first BRICS media meet is a long process. For now, the BRICS is not fully together—even on BRICS Bank or the New Development Bank, and the coverage reflects that. While Chinese media was constantly and thoroughly for the Bank, India had its reservations. Indian media had more—something that was not unknown to the Chinese media.[31] On the part of Chinese media, it was clearly visible that they realised China's greater role and the benefit it will draw from the Bank. As *Beijing News* noted, the new bank would provide not only economic but strategic benefits to China.[32] Another Chinese newspaper called *Chinese*

Enterprise News clearly wrote that Beijing had a bigger say in the BRICS grouping.[33] On the contrary, the caution in Indian media on this count was more than pronounced. Such differences not only weaken the ability of BRICS media to be an agenda setter, but also provide others a scope to influence it. It would be difficult to imagine a fully coordinated BRICS media without each of the five countries in the BRICS accommodating each other's core concerns.

Recommendations

The trend of the media summits held across the 'liberal' world (read West) in recent years has been industry based—mostly organised by it and primarily involving professionals and practitioners. For that matter, organising media summits itself has not been happening for long. Media summits on the lines of government being a party to it to shape the agenda have been few and far in between in contemporary times. Even the Arab Media Summit or the Nordic Summit—arguably regional summits with focus on countries in the region—are not far from it. Partially, it is also because the media platforms are mostly privately controlled. China is the only major exception to this, where even the private media is rather bound to exercise restraints on issues flagged by the government. Nevertheless, the significant weight of Chinese media in terms of scale and reach—due to generous government support as part of its objective to counter what it calls the Western propaganda—gives it an influential say in the BRICS media scheme. This somehow provides this grouping with an identity and agenda of a unique kind. Given this context, it has the opportunity to learn from the existing media cooperation forums and improvise.

In this regard, the first and foremost thing is to gain credibility for the BRICS identity. For that to happen, a sufficient and regular flow of media and entertainment products among BRICS countries has to be facilitated. This would require bilateral and multilateral cooperation in producing media products. Second, to facilitate a real BRICS media sense of cooperation among the people, adequate socio-cultural and political activities are required to ensure that the private sector media provides sufficient coverage of the same. This could be done through BRICS study exchange, games, film awards, political and socio-cultural summits and exchanges etc. Third, the world of civil societies today plays an active role. An initiative on the part of civil societies of the BRICS countries are required to hold exchange programmes—which in turn will spur citizen journalism, development journalism and people-to-people interactions. Fourth, a major step could be promoting tourism by giving a BRICS Visa, like EU visa. Tourists are particularly good sources of promoting citizen journalism. A special feature in this regard could be a visit to the BRICS countries every year on a multilateral basis. For instance, BRICS countries may have a 'Visit Brazil Year in 2017'—with provisions for special packages. Fourth, to give the BRICS media cooperation a real professional punch, an advisory/regulatory body constituting of journalists and media professionals has to be put in place. It could act as a body that addresses coverage inconsistencies and issues guidelines and admonitions if required, while simultaneously staying clear of getting termed 'biased'. Indeed, journalism awards, citizen journalism awards, best BRICS blogger awards or best BRICS travel blog award could be constituted to facilitate more interactions. Fifth, an award ceremony could be organised in the field of literature like, the Jaipur Literature Festival, that celebrates the best of each other's conformist and dissident literatures. There could also be BRICS Quiz organised at multiple levels to encourage people to learn and know more about the BRICS countries.

Finally, this could go to the next level if BRICS countries come together on instituting and supporting research related to global South's role in history, and the implications it will hold for the future. These steps could be multiplied by instituting a multiple entry visa regime for professionals, including journalists. The key to any such media forum has to be a bottom-to-top movement rather than the other way around. For example, a yearly conference of few media heads and famous people is not going to influence the nature of coverage in terms of promoting BRICS. These countries should engage in learning the best from each other. So while rest of BRICS could learn from China about how the governments could facilitate merger of media platforms to improve the financial health of a media group, India and Brazil could take the lead in film and TV serial making respectively. None of the above could attain scale if serious political mistrusts continue to haunt the concerned countries in this grouping though. Hence, it would be highly beneficial if the above steps could be accompanied to ensure strategic assurance on bilateral issues of dispute.

Conclusion

In a world where limits of hard power have been put to test over the last decade, soft power could hold the key. Media can be a powerful tool for soft diplomacy, and the Chinese are not alone in trying to wield it. Nonetheless, in an increasingly multilateral world, the diverse geo-political groups hold the key to an alternative form of agenda setting through media. It is here that BRICS comes into play. The earlier initiatives in the developing world to institute such *media multilateralism* as the discussion around NWICO suggests were more about countering the well-organised and financially and technologically dominant global North's media hegemony, couched under the "development" rhetoric. That did question the monotony of media monopoly from North, but fell far short of generating a sustainable momentum. The BRICS initiative comes at a time when the economics of the media industry is decisively shifting towards the global South's shores for good. Somehow, there is a credible doubt that it is leading towards another round of media imperialism to serve the handful of media oligarchs in the global South. If the direct and indirect influence of the Chinese media model—both within and outside the BRICS—is a pointer, the political-economy of Chinese media remains the central model around which BRICS media is set to evolve. To be precise, it canonises media coverage of issues in a way that prioritises stability over freedom, order above law and the collective above the individual. This model could effectively mean a different kind of agenda-setting and media prioritisation, where the concept of 'media for greater good' takes precedence over the current standard of it being the watchdog.

On the negative side, it could lead to untested kinds of domination with little way out for dissidents and non-conformists. Overall, this could be a better model for societies and nations, where multilateral cooperation would be easier to work out, unlike the current case of media and the government relations in most of the developing and developed countries. Nevertheless, it remains to be tested. For now, in BRICS, the real test would be in addressing the potentially difficult issues as and when they come. For instance, it is yet to be seen how it will handle the report of a corruption in China or the report of a political protest in Brazil, South Africa or Russia—that would hold the key to winning trust and credibility. However, the bilateral disputes often take over multilateral interests. For example, the coverage of a terror attack by Pakistan on Indian territory by BRICS media, particularly Chinese media, would face more scrutiny than other issues. Therefore, bilateral disputes remain crucial, and a continuing lack of trust among the BRICS nations could prove BRICS media to remain an ephemeral idea.

END NOTES

1. Thussu, Daya Kisha and Kaarle Nordenstreng (2015), "Contextualising the BRICS media," in Nordenstreng, Kaarle and Daya Kisha Thussu (eds), *Mapping BRICS media*, Routledge pp. 57-59.

2. Saran, Samir (2015), "From Cold War to Hot Peace: Why BRICS matters," *Lowy Interpreter*, 13 July, [Online: Web] http://www.lowyinterpreter.org/post/2015/07/13/Cold-War-to-Hot-Peace-The-Russian-Presidency-and-BRICS.aspx#, accessed on 29 August 2016.
3. Richter, Felix (2016), "BRIC Consumers Plan to Spend Big on Consumer Electronics," Statista.com, 14 January, [Online: Web] https://www.statista.com/chart/824/consumer-electronics-purchase-plans-for-2013/, accessed on 4 September 2016.
4. WAN-INFRA (2015), *World Press Trends Report 2014,* pp. 52-53, [Online: Web]http://www.arpp.ru/images/123/51253_WAN-IFRA_WPT_2014.pdf, accessed on 8 September 2016.
5. WAN-INFRA (2015), *World Press Trends Report 2014,* pp. 40-41, [Online: Web]http://www.arpp.ru/images/123/51253_WAN-IFRA_WPT_2014.pdf, accessed on 8 September 2016.
6. WAN-INFRA (2015), *World Press Trends Report 2014,* pp. 56-57, [Online: Web]http://www.arpp.ru/images/123/51253_WAN-IFRA_WPT_2014.pdf, accessed on 8 September 2016.
7. "World Press Trends Report 2015" in Carro, Rodrigo (2016), "Brazillian Newspapers: The Risk of Becoming Irrelevant," Reuters Institute for the Study of Journalism, p. 22.
8. Thussu, Daya Kisha and Kaarle Nordenstreng (2015), "Contextualising the BRICS media," in Nordenstreng, Kaarle and Daya Kisha Thussu (eds), *Mapping BRICS media*, Routledge pp. 1-11.
9. Wasserman, Herman, Fernando Oliveira Paulino, Dmitry Strovsky, and Jukka Pietiläinen (2015), "Intra-BRICS media exchange," in Nordenstreng, Kaarle, and Daya Kishan Thussu (eds.), *Mapping BRICS media*, Routledge, pp. 228-242.
10. Wasserman, Herman, Fernando Oliveira Paulino, Dmitry Strovsky, and Jukka Pietiläinen (2015), "Intra-BRICS media exchange," in Nordenstreng, Kaarle, and Daya Kishan Thussu (eds.), *Mapping BRICS media*, Routledge, pp. 228-242.
11. Barranco, Veronica (2012), "What Do You Know About the Media in Brazil? Part I," *Edelman*, November 29, [Online: Web] http://www.edelman.com/post/what-do-you-know-about-the-media-in-brazil-part-i/, accessed 14 August 2016.
12. Wasserman, Herman, Fernando Oliveira Paulino, Dmitry Strovsky, and Jukka Pietiläinen (2015), "Intra-BRICS media exchange," in Nordenstreng, Kaarle, and Daya Kishan Thussu (eds.), *Mapping BRICS media*, Routledge, pp. 228-242.
13. Zhang Xiaoling (2010), "Chinese state media goes global," *East Asian Policy*, pp. 42-50, [Online: Web] http://www.eai.nus.edu.sg/publications/files/Vol2No1_ZhangXiaoling.pdf, accessed 15 August 2016.
14. Panova, Victoria (2016), "Who makes BRICS more alive than BRICSers themselves," *Russian International Affairs Council*, 19 May, [Online: Web] http://russiancouncil.ru/en/inner/?id_4=7699#top-content, accessed on 19 August 2016.
15. Sparks, Collins (2014), "Deconstructing the BRICS," *International Journal of Communication*, Vol. 8, p. 406.
16. Jacques, Martin (2012), *When China rules the world: The rise of the middle kingdom and the end of the western world,* Penguin UK, pp. 362-385.
17. Lee, Chin-Chuan (2003), "The global and the national of the Chinese media," in Lee, Chin-Chuan (ed), *Chinese Media, Global Contexts*, Routledge, pp. 1-29.
18. He, Zhou (2000), "Chinese Communist Party press in a tug of war: a policial economy analysis of the Shenzhen Speical Zone Daily," in Chinn-Chuan Lee (ed.), *Power, Money, and Media: Communication Patterns and Bureaucratic Control in Cultural China*, Evanstron IL: Northwestern University Press, pp. 112-151.

19. *China Daily* (2011), "BRICS urged to deepen ties," 14 April, [Online: Web]http://www.china.org.cn/business/2011-04/14/content_22357452.htm, accessed on 20 August 2016.

20. BBC Monitoring (2012), "Chinese article dismisses fears of BRICS as West's rival bloc," *Xinhua* report, 28 March.

21. Qin Wang (2013), "金砖"未来成色更好" [Jīnzhuān" wèiláichéngsègènghǎo],, People's Daily Overseas Edition, 27 March, [Online: Web] http://paper.people.com.cn/rmrbhwb/html/2013-03/27/content_1216530.htm, accessed on 26 August 2016.

22. Bo Yongguan (2014), "金 • 国家第六届峰会 新 • 大国合作的新 • 段" [Jīn zhuān guójiā dì liù jiè fēnghuì xīnxīng dàguó hézuò de xīn jiēduàn], *Beijing Youth Daily*, 14 July, [Online: Web]http://epaper.ynet.com/html/2014-07/14/content_72863.htm?div=-1, accessed on 24 August 2016.

23. Thussu, Daya Kisha and Kaarle Nordenstreng (2015), "Contextualising the BRICS media," in Nordenstreng, Kaarle and Daya Kisha Thussu (eds), *Mapping BRICS media*, Routledge p. 2.

24. Thussu, Daya Kisha and Kaarle Nordenstreng (2015), "Contextualising the BRICS media," in Nordenstreng, Kaarle and Daya Kisha Thussu (eds), *Mapping BRICS media*, Routledge p. 7.

25. Zhang Qiao Su (2015), ""让金砖国家发出更大声音"——外国媒体代表和驻华使节谈首届金砖国家媒体峰会," ["Ràngjīnzhuānguójiāfāchūgèngdàshēngyīn"——wàiguóméitǐdàibiǎohézhùhuáshǐjiétánshǒujièjīnzhuānguójiāméitǐfēnghuì], *Xinhua*, 1 December, [Online: Web]http://news.xinhuanet.com/world/2015-12/01/c_1117322733.htm, accessed on 23 August 2016.

26. Lee, Chin-Chuan (2003), "The global and the national of the Chinese media," in Lee, Chin-Chuan (ed), *Chinese Media, Global Contexts*, Routledge, pp. 1-29.

27. Gunther, Richard and Anthony Mughan (eds) (2000), *Democracy and the Media: A comparative perspective*, New York: Cambridge University Press.

28. Aneja, Atul (2015), "China hosts first BRICS media summit," *The Hindu*, Nov. 30, [Online: Web]http://www.thehindu.com/news/international/china-hosts-first-brics-media-summit/article7933793.ece, accessed on 20 August 2016.

29. Ryan, Danielle (2015), "BRICS not content to leave West with mass media monopoly," *RT.com* Dec. 24, [Online: Web] https://www.rt.com/op-edge/326967-brics-media-west-mainstream/, accessed on 19 August 2016.

30. *Xinhua* (2015), "Full text: Beijing Declaration of the BRICS Media Summit," December 1, [Online: Web]http://www.chinadaily.com.cn/china/2015-12/01/content_22597943.htm, accessed on 20 August 2016.

31. *Sina.com* (2014), ""印度与中国争夺金砖银行总部世行IMF高调迎新 [Yìndùyǔzhōngguó zhēngduójīnzhuānyínhángzǒngbùshìháng IMF gāodiàoyíngxīn], 16 July, [Online: Web] http://finance.sina.com.cn/world/20140716/025519714862.shtml, accessed on 18 August 2016.

32. Chu Xin Yan (2014), ""巴西峰会有望成立"金砖开发银行 [Bāxīfēnghuìyǒuwàngchénglì "jīnzhuānkāifāyínháng"]."*Beijing News*, 15 June, [Online: Web] http://epaper.bjnews.com.cn/html/2014-07/15/content_523891.htm?div=-1, accessed on 18 August 2016.

33. Wang Ying (2014), 盟友+对手金砖银行背后的较量 [Méngyǒujiāduìshǒujīnzhuānyínhángbèihòu de jiàoliàng], *Chinese Enterprise News*, 14 July, [Online: Web] http://news.hexun.com/2014-07-14/166614490.html, accessed on August 20, 2016.

5

The Role of Think Tanks

Hu Xiaowen

When the concept of BRICS was created in 2001 by Jim O'Neill, chief economist of Goldman Sachs, it initially endowed BRICS with sub-governmental characteristics. BRICS, then an official mechanism for economic cooperation, has expanded its functions from an economic-centric dialogue to a pragmatic and comprehensive mechanism. Accordingly, its participants have gradually expanded from government officials and entrepreneurs to think tank experts. It can be expected that the sub-government activities and involvements will increase further, contributing to the development of BRICS as well as global governance. Among all the BRICS Summits; the Durban Summit in 2013 is still regarded as the turning point of BRICS cooperation. The Durban Declaration states: "We aim at progressively developing BRICS into a full-fledged mechanism of current and long-term coordination on a wide range of key issues of world economics and politics."[1] This indicates that the cooperation is "transforming from a 'dialogue' to a 'full-fledged mechanism', and 'political cooperation' and 'pragmatic cooperation' have been stressed and added for further consideration".[2] Subjects like politics, science and technology, climate change, energy, terrorism, culture etc. have been included under the framework of BRICS. Besides economic concerns, BRICS countries can seek more common interests under this transitioning mechanism. In this context, the BRICS cooperation operates on a multi-level mode: summit level meetings for leaders—Ministers' meeting—meetings for officials and entrepreneurs and think tanks. Think tanks, therefore, are playing a significant role in linking the government and the public, and contributing to the objective of BRICS.

Think Tanks in BRICS: An Evolutionary Study

Early in the 2008, a year before the first summit, the BRIC Think Tanks Meeting was held in Russia. In the following years, a numbers of academic or think tanks dialogues and meetings were organised (See table 1). All of these meetings paved the way for the official establishment of BRICS Think Tanks Council in 2013 (BTTC).

Table 5.1: Academic/Think Tanks Activities

Year	*Events*
2008	BRIC Think Tanks Meeting in Russia
2009	BRIC Track 2 Meeting 2009 in India
2010	BRICS Think Tanks Seminar in Brasilia
2011	BRICS Think Tanks Symposium in Beijing
2012	The 4th BRICS Academic Forum: Stability, Security and Prosperity in India
2013	The 5th BRICS Academic Forum and Think Tanks Workshop in South Africa
2014	The 6th BRICS Academic Forum in Brazil
2015	The 7th BRICS Academic Forum in Russia
2016	The 8th BRICS Academic Forum in India

Besides, there is another important forum called BRIC Academic Forum, which was launched in 2009. As a preparatory event, this forum was initially convened to produce ideas that would feed into the first BRICS Leaders Summit in Yekaterinburg (Russia) a month later. Since the BRIC's Brasília Summit in 2010, the yearly academic forum has been taking place in the same country that hosts the Leaders' Summit. Stuenkel (2015) from International Relations at the Getulio Vargas Foundation made a comment on these events:

> "In fact, a far more important result of the yearly encounter is the establishment of ties between research institutions that previously barely knew about each other's existence. As a result of the meetings, a growing number of scholars have begun travelling to other BRICS countries, where they are usually hosted by institutions that were represented at the BRICS Forum. This is particularly the case for Russia and Brazil, whose academic communities are not yet as internationalised as those of South Africa and India."[3]

Think tanks officially appeared in the BRICS in 2013, when the fifth summit was convened. In the Durban Declaration, it read:

> "We welcome the establishment of the BRICS Think Tanks Council and the BRICS Business Council, and take note of the following meetings which were held in preparation for this Summit: Fifth Academic Forum; Fourth Business Forum; Third Financial Forum."[4]

For the first time, think tanks were clearly stated in the Declaration, indicating a growing demand on think tanks' participation in BRICS cooperation. After the Durban Summit, the BRICS Think Tanks Council (BTTC) was established. Every country designated a think tank to join the Council, the members of the BTTC are: Observer Research Foundation (India), China Centre for Contemporary World Studies (China), National Committee for BRICS Research (Russia), Institute for Applied Economic Research (Brazil) and Human Sciences Research Council (South Africa). The Declaration says that the BTTC will form the platform for exchange of ideas among researchers, academia and think tanks, and it will be responsible for convening the BRICS Academic Forum.

From then on, every Summit has mentioned think tanks in their Declarations. In the Sixth BRICS Summit—Fortaleza Declaration, it read:

> "We welcome the BTTC Study "Towards a Long-Term Strategy for BRICS: Recommendations by the BTTC". We acknowledge the decision taken by the BTTC —taken at its Rio de Janeiro meeting in March 2014—to focus its work on the five pillars, upon which the BRICS long-term strategy for cooperation will rest. The BTTC is encouraged to develop strategic pathways and action plans that will lead to the realisation of this long-term strategy."[5]

In the seventh summit —the Ufa Declaration of 2015, it stated:

> "We welcome activities of BRICS Think Tanks Council (BTTC) and the Long-Term Strategy for BRICS Report as well as the 7th Academic Forum in Moscow for expanding BRICS cooperation. We value this permanent platform for in-depth expert opinion and look forward to further consolidate high quality research, analysis as well as effective think-tank discussions on issues of mutual interest. The BTTC should further strive to enhance cooperation in future-oriented research, knowledge sharing, capacity-building and policy advice between think tanks in BRICS countries."[6]

In this context, the BTTC carried out a numbers of meetings and activities since 2013

Table 5.2: BTTC Activities

Year and Chair	*Events*
2013: South Africa	The first meeting The second meeting
2014: Brazil	The third meeting: the Report by BTTC and Approved by the 6th BRICS summit: *Towards a Long-Term Strategy for BRICS—recommendations by the BRICS Think Tanks Council*
2015: Russia	The roadmap report by BTTC and approved by 6th BRICS Summit: *Towards a Long-Term Strategy for BRICS—A Proposal by the BRICS Think Tanks Council*
2016: India	The 8th BRICS Academic Forum in India and BTTC meeting (forthcoming)

Furthermore, the BRICS Trade and Economic Research Network (BRICS-TERN) was proposed by two think tanks from India and China respectively—CUTS International and Shanghai WTO Affairs Consultation Centre. With the joining of think tanks from the other three counties of BRICS, BRICS-TERN was launched in Shanghai in November 2011 by Fundação Getúlio Vargas (Brazil), Eco-Accord (Russia), CUTS International (India), Shanghai WTO Affairs Consultation Centre (China) and South African Institute of International Affairs (South Africa). The aim of BRICS-TERN is to form a think tank network where they would work together on issues of trade and economic issues, and jointly produce outputs which can assist policy making of BRICS. It focuses on objectives related to trade and economics, promotion of fair markets, inclusive growth and sustainable development. The reason for setting up such think tank forums, according to experts, is that BRICS need platforms to explore their common interests, because "BRICS countries have big differences among their political and cultural values, the composition of their economic structures and outreach and, above all, the lack of a common history (with exception of some bilateral relations)"[7]. The theme for the 5th BRICS-TERN organised by Brazil was the "The Impact of Mega Agreements on BRICS", which focuses on the impact of TPP, TTIP and RCEP on BRICS countries.

From the above, it can be seen that the gradual institutionalisation of think tanks has happened, and that think tanks today are playing a bigger role in BRICS; one of the examples being the establishment of New Development Bank. The 4th BRICS Academic Forum meeting, hosted by the Observer Research Foundation of India in 2011, had made a host of recommendations for the 5th BRICS Summit Leaders meet which was held in New Delhi. One of the main recommendations they proposed was studying the establishment of financial institutions such as a 'Development Bank' and an 'Investment Fund'/'Contingency Reserve Arrangement' that would assist in the development of BRICS and other developing countries. The concept note was drafted by the officials in Indian Ministry of Finance, and the idea of BRICS bank was formally discussed and mentioned in the New Delhi Summit in March 2012. The 'New Delhi Declaration' (2012) stated: "We have considered the possibility of setting up a new Development Bank for mobilising resources for infrastructure and sustainable development projects in BRICS and other emerging economies and developing countries to supplement the existing efforts of multilateral and regional financial institutions for global growth and development."[8] Consequently, 'BRICS Think Tanks Forum' was hosted by China Centre for Contemporary World Studies in September 2012 in Chongqing, under the theme of feasibility of new BRIC Bank.

With the several years of bargain, the New Development Bank (NDB) was officially created by BRICS in 2015, and the first loan of 811 million has been approved in April 2016 for green energy project. The realisation of NDB shows the importance of think tanks, both for idea creation and also realising them in the form of policies and initiatives.

Think Tanks from BRICS Countries

While analysing the development of think tanks in BRICS, it is important to know the organisations involved, and the think tanks doing research on BRICS from BRICS countries. In Brazil, there are three think tanks actively involved in BRICS-related research, and two of them are university-affiliated institutes. Institute for Applied Economic Research (IPEA) is a federal public foundation linked to the Strategic Affairs Secretariat of the Brazilian Presidency and "it provides technical and institutional support to government actions—enabling the formulation and reformulation of public policies and Brazilian development programs". It is also the official member of BRICS Think Tank Council. So far, IPEA has organised two BRICS Think Tank Council meetings since 2011.

BRICS Policy Centre (BPC) is a joint initiative of the City of Rio de Janeiro and the Pontifical Catholic University of Rio de Janeiro (PUC-Rio), established in 2011. It is ranked among the top 10 think tanks associated with universities and among the "best trans-disciplinary research programs in a think tank" by *Global Go To Think Tank Index Report*, and it is the only one in Latin America. Its research covers areas such as politics, security, economics, trade and environmental issues. The subjects to be studied include BRICS and South-South cooperation. Fundação Getulio Vargas (FGV) is an institute of higher education which also functions as a think tank. In 2015, FGV was listed by *Global Go To Think Tanks Index,* and is ranked the top think tank in Latin America for the 7th consecutive year. There are several professors pursuing BRICS-related research in the institute. They are mainly from the economics and international relations background. With regard to Russia, there are no specific think tanks designated for BRICS studies. However, Russia has established the Russian National Committee on BRICS Research which is chaired by Vyacheslav Nikonov, chairman of the State Duma Committee on Education to coordinate the BRICS studies. The members of National Committee belong to the Institute of Far Eastern Studies and Institute of Economy in the Russian Academy of Science. In India, Observer Research Foundation (ORF) is a non-governmental think tank and a member of BRICS Think Tank Council. ORF has a research initiative on BRICS, and several fellows in ORF focus on BRICS studies. Some researchers from Delhi University and Jawaharlal Nehru University has also undertaken studies on BRICS.

In China, the Centre for Contemporary World Studies (CCCWS) is a government-affiliated think tank and official member of BRICS Think Tank Council. It is supported by the International Department of the CPC Central Committee, which is a ministry level government agency for party diplomacy in China. CCCWS has limited manpower to conduct research, but it has strong ability to coordinate research on BRICS studies by nationwide research institutes. Shanghai WTO Affairs Consultation Centre is a member of BRICS Trade and Economic Research Network. It is supported by the Shanghai government, and is designated to provide consultation on legal, economic and trade issue on WTO and other related issues. As one of the initiators of BRICS Trade and Economic Research Network, it aims to provide policy recommendations for trade facilitation among BRICS countries. Some top public university in China has also set up BRICS research centres—including BRICS Economic Think Tank, initiated by Tsinghua University. It is supposed to host BRICS Economic Think Tanks Forum annually, and think tanks from other BRICS countries have been invited to join the Forum. Fudan University in Shanghai also established BRICS Research Centre in 2012, and its director Fan Yongming is an expert consultant with the Ministry of Commerce, China.

The think tanks actively involved in BRICS studies in South Africa include three agencies: BRICS Research Centre, the National Institute for the

Humanities and Social Sciences and The South African Institute of International Affairs; the former two are supported by the government and the third one is a non-governmental think tank. Their research mainly focuses on the economic aspect of BRICS and the bilateral relations between BRICS and Africa. Human Sciences Research Council is a "preeminent BRICS multi-disciplinary think tank in line with the HSRC's legislated mandate to serve as an advisor to government on policy based research" in South Africa. To further enhance its research on BRICS, BRICS Research Centre (BRC) was established in August 2014 "to coordinate, facilitate and undertake BRICS research" in South Africa and aboard. The National Institute for Humanities and Social Sciences (NIHSS) supported by the South African Ministry of Higher Education and Training was designated as permanent host of the South African BRICS Think tank, including Academic Forum. One of their main objectives is to "provide a platform for researchers and academics to exchange ideas and to generate evidence-based policy recommendations". The South African Institute of International Affairs, the premier research institute on international issues and a non-governmental think tank, has also set up a program called "Emerging Powers, BRICS and Africa", which does research on BRICS, specifically on economic issues. It publishes papers and articles occasionally.

Apart from think tanks, universities are also an important platform for delivering academic ideas and policy advice, and the level of universities' engagement also indicates a country's soft power. According to the QS University Rankings: BRICS 2016 (a ranking of the 250 top universities in the five BRICS countries: Brazil, Russia, India, China and South Africa), 86 Chinese universities find positions in the list, whereas the number of universities listed from Russia, Brazil, India and South Africa are 55, 54, 44 and 11 respectively. It can be noticed that Chinese universities occupy the first five places in the ranking list. Under the index of "academic reputation", seven Chinese Universities are listed in the top 10 list. All of these indicate that China enjoys strong academic resources and advanced intellectual strength in BRICS countries. Although universities differ from think tanks, they have overlapping functions in terms of studying BRICS, and their perspectives are more or less similar. This is due to the following:

1) Most Chinese think tanks on BRICS study are virtual bodies, where most of their researchers are from universities.
2) BRICS cooperation and their policies are overall a top-down decision process; and think tanks as a track II initiative have limited influence on policy making, with the exception of few elites from think tanks or universities playing the effective role.

Therefore, to understand Chinese universities' role in BRICS, it is imperative to understand Chinese think tanks' view on BRICS.

Chinese Think Tanks and BRICS

Think tanks in China nowadays are booming. In 2004, China released 'Guidelines on Further Prosperity and Development of Philosophy and Social Sciences'. It stated for the first time that "academics of social science need to work as think tanks for the government" (2004). The guidelines, which were issued by top echelons of CCP, offered a perspective for understanding the basic characteristics and developmental direction of Chinese think tanks. In 2014, Chinese President Xi Jinping called for setting up of a new think tank, which would cater to Chinese needs as the country seeks to modernise its governance. "Building a new type of think tank with Chinese characteristics is an important and pressing mission. It should be targeted on promoting scientific and democratic decision making, promoting modernisation of the country's governing system and ability as well as strengthening China's soft power,"[9] Xi said at the meeting. Following this, think tanks have been put into national-level designing in China.

Although think tanks have limited influence on BRICS issues, their participation is increasing in China. For instance, some elite experts can influence the policy maker through their own personal network, and think tanks' view on BRICS can impact the public view. The figures below show academic trends, media attentions and academic influence on BRICS, which will help in analysing the impact of BRICS study in Chinese academic circle and the media.

Fig. 5.1: Academic Trends on BRICS: 2004-2014

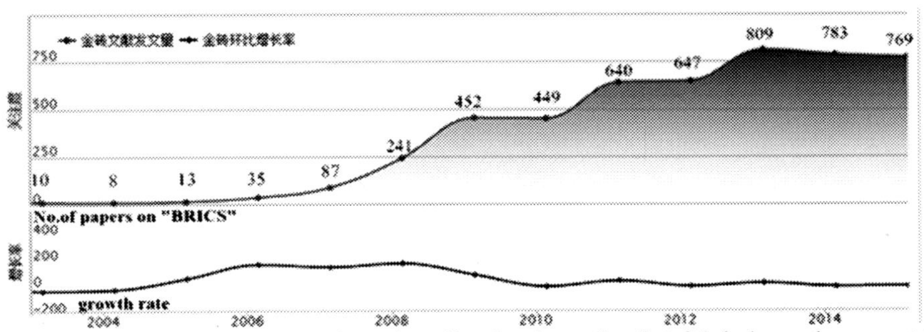

Note: Produced by CNKI Database, http://epub.cnki.net/kns/brief/default_result.aspx, with inputting the key word as "金砖"(BRICS).

Fig. 5.2: The Media's Focus on BRICS: 2004-2014

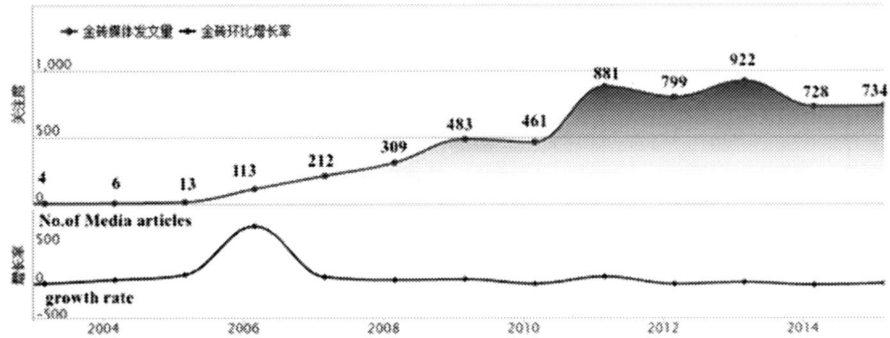

Note: Produced by CNKI Database, http://epub.cnki.net/kns/brief/default_result.aspx, with inputting the key word as "金砖" (BRICS).

Fig. 5.3: Academic Influence on BRICS: 2004-2014

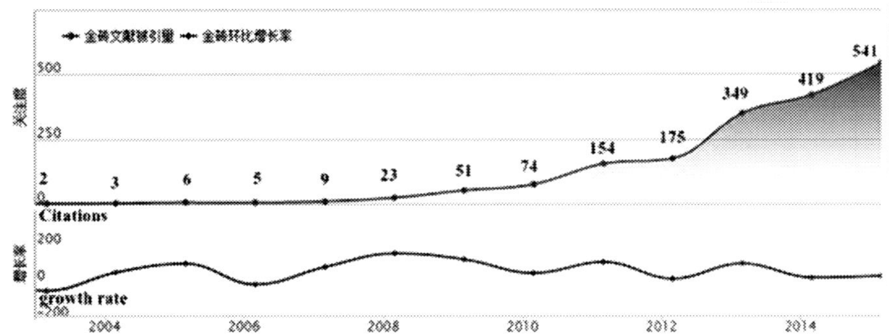

Note: Produced by CNKI Database, http://epub.cnki.net/kns/brief/default_result.aspx, with inputting the key word as "金砖" (BRICS).

Fig. 5.4: Academic Trends on BRICS Economy: 2006-2015

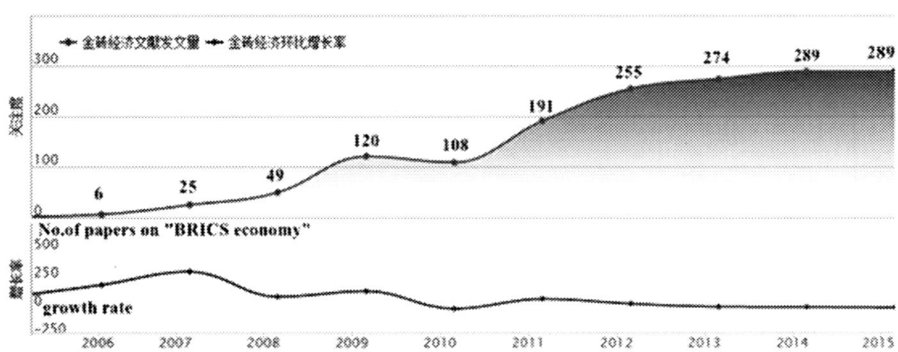

Note: Produced by CNKI Database, http://epub.cnki.net/kns/brief/default_result.aspx, with inputting the key word as "金砖经济" (BRICS Economy).

Fig. 5.5: The Media's Focus on BRICS Economy: 2006-2015

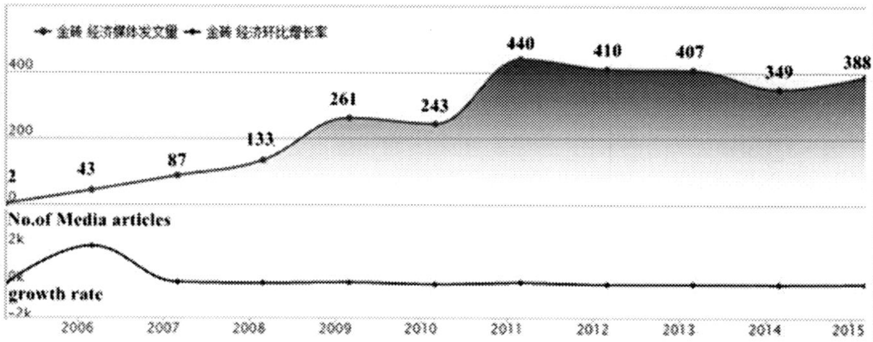

Note: Produced by CNKI Database, http://epub.cnki.net/kns/brief/default_result.aspx, with inputting the key word as "金砖经济" (BRICS Economy).

The main concerns of the Chinese think tanks vis-à-vis BRICS are summed up as the following:

Emerging Economies: Chinese experts prefer to use the term "Emerging Economies" to describe BRICS countries. BRICS has become the driving force of the world economy.[10] It was highlighted that from 2001 to 2010, the import and export of goods sustained a rapid growth in BRICS countries, and the speed with which they grew is much higher than the global average. However, BRICS economic development still depends on the markets of developed countries, and the trade volume among BRICS is very small.[11] Although the capabilities of BRICS on attracting FDI are increasing, its foreign investment is relatively low.

International Order: With the power transition underway and the development of multi-polarisation, the economic gravity is inclined to emerging economies. There are three groups competing in the world; one is "the old power vs. the new power", which refers to the competition between US, EU and Japan and the emerging powers; the second group is G7 versus BRICS; the last one is competition among North America, Europe and Asia. The raising of the BRICS will push the change of international order.[12] With the development of the emerging economies, the developed countries, especially G8, confront the problems of "rationality" and "effectiveness". However, it is also difficult for them to manage the world economy effectively without the participation of BRICS.[13] Hence, BRICS, along with G20, plays an important role in reshaping the world economic order and reforming its economic regimes.[14]

Intra-BRICS Economic Relations: It is widely argued by the Chinese scholars that BRICS countries have strong economic complementarities and commonalities. The countries of the group aim to expand foreign trade, intra-BRICS trade, promote trade liberalisation, reform the international monetary system and also acquire positions of influence on the globe. BRICS countries, except Russia, face the problem of increasing foreign capital inflows which may lead to inflation and asset bubble. However, the competition among the BRICS nations cannot be denied. Firstly, trading dispute and contention related to commodity pricing is intense, especially in the manufacturing goods industry and resources industry such as oil, natural gas and iron ore. Secondly, argument on RMB exchange rate has never reached a consensus after India and Brazil demanded appreciation of the RMB. To this, the Chinese experts argue that instead of blaming China, it will prove more useful for BRICS members to work together and set restrictive fiscal and monetary policies towards maintaining economic stability.[15] Thirdly, the economic growth impetus in BRICS countries differs from country to country. In BRICS, all the countries, expect Brazil, have high investment rate; and the economic development of China and India appears to be highly dependent on foreign investment.[16] Also, the four BRICS nations, except Brazil, have problem of under-consumption in terms of the world's average consumption rate. India is 15 per cent lower, Russia is 12 per cent lower and China remains 30 per cent lower than the global average.[17]

Fig. 5.6: The Academic Trends on New Normal

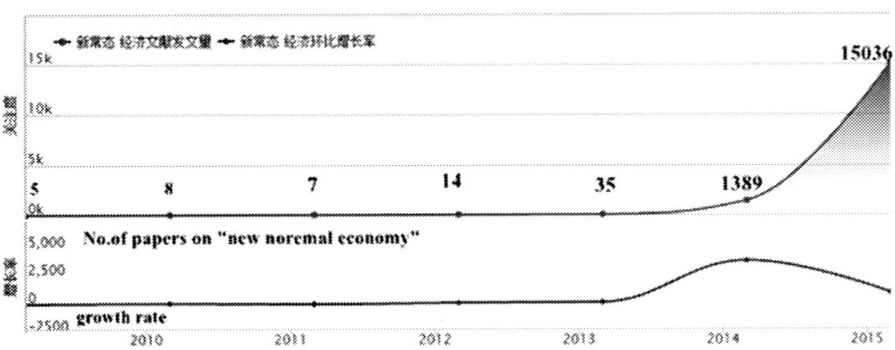

Note: Produced by CNKI Database, http://epub.cnki.net/kns/brief/default_result.aspx, with inputting the key word as "新常态经济" (New Normal Economy).

"New Normal" and BRICS: Since Chinese President Xi coined the conception of "New Normal", writings on this subject have quadrupled (see figure below). According to CNKI data base, the academic trends of the articles on New Normal have significantly increased. Between 2010 and 2013, the number of writings on were less than 30, which jumped to 1389 in 2014; and in 2015, this number rose to 15035. Think tanks are increasingly involved in explaining the New Normal statues of the Chinese Economy.

Experts point out that China's New Normal represents the feature of China's current economic development. "New" indicates present, which is different from the past development features. "Normal" means China's economic development has entered a stable stage, which is different from the fast economic growth period over the last three decades.[18] Similar to the Chinese, New Normal state has happened in Europe, US, Japan and South Korea successively as well. Under New Normal, the Chinese economic structure has adjusted to the structural and global realities with an increasing focus on boosting domestic demand, regional inequalities and in loosening the state control on macroeconomic features.[19]

Not only China, the entire BRICS are facing the issue of New Normal. The economic developments in all BRICS countries are declining. India, for example, has proposed a new round of economic reform, South Africa and Brazil face the problem of distortions of economic structure such as excessive reliance on natural resources, weak infrastructure etc. It is, therefore, argued that China should play the key role in bringing together other BRICS countries in order to reform the international economic architecture.[20]

China is a major advocate of IMF re-organisation. In January 2016, the IMF 2010 quota reform finally went into effect. China's voting rights has risen to 6 per cent from 3.8 per cent, and IMF resources will double to about $660 billion. China became the third-largest member in IMF—with Brazil, India and Russia entering into the list of top-10 members. China's Central Bank commented that the reform "will improve the representation and voice of emerging markets and developing countries in the IMF, and is conducive to protecting IMF's credibility, legitimacy and effectiveness".

For a long period of time, the IMF 2010 Reform had not been passed by the US Congress. From the perspective of Chinese think tank experts, the previous IMF quota formula did not reflect the growth of economic power in developing countries, and inversely exaggerated the relative economic positions of developed countries[21]. After China successfully established the Asian Infrastructure Investment Bank (AIIB), the IMF received major criticism leading to its announcement of 2010 reforms[22]. The reform began by giving an increasing share of voting rights among the developing countries. A research report by China International Economic and Exchange Centre (CCIEE) suggests that China should recognise its role in the reform of the international monetary system. They further argue that China cannot create a new system or pursue its interests within the system; rather, it should aim for stabilising the IMF by including RMB in the SDR and also through internationalisation of RMB[23]. Chinese President Xi Jinping, in the press conference after the 2016 G20 summit, has mentioned that China agrees to continue with further reforms of IMF, and supports a complete realisation of the 2010 reform package. China aims to achieve equality in terms of voting rights, and increase the representation and participation of developing countries.

Features and Roles of Chinese Think Tanks

From the above, it can be seen that think tanks in BRICS are increasingly playing a bigger role. This section summarises the main functions and characteristics of Chinese think tanks, which also explains its significance in the multilateral mechanism of BRICS. The functions are as follows:

Firstly, to provide the rationale for the establishment and growing of BRICS, so that it fits itself within the status-quo and is acknowledged by the developed countries. As far as the function of BRICS is concerned, the core issue in the eyes of Chinese think tanks is the relations between the BRICS—the representative of emerging powers—and the current global financial institutions, which is a reflection of the post-Second World-War power structure. They provide a somehow contradictory but realist mission for BRICS: an evolutionary but not a revolutionist system; that is to say, it will make amendments and reforms to the current system rather than revise the system and build a new one. Due to the increase in the share of BRICS in the world economy, the objective is currently viewed as legitimate and useful for the world.

It is widely understood in Chinese think tanks circle that until today, BRICS has formed the initial institutional cooperation framework which includes foreign minister, finance ministers, central bank governors, coordinators and resident envoys as the basis and think tanks forms the supplement.[24] Under this framework, the BRICS should emphasise on comprehensive cooperation in various fields and establish a new partnership among the BRICS countries. It is important to strengthen the inclusive relationship between BRICS countries and other developing as well as developed countries. It is repeatedly claimed and suggested by the Chinese think tanks that the BRICS countries do not aim to challenge the current international regime; instead, its objective is to adjust the international system in a non-confrontational way. BRICS is, therefore, seeking to reform the governance system gradually in the context of accepting the existing rules. Furthermore, BRICS aims to forge a bigger global voice on economic issues for the group[25]. It is necessary for BRICS to build up an institutional framework based on mutual cooperation, and urge the existing international institutions to make changes in the favour of emerging economies. Thus, it can be understood that BRICS cooperation mechanism is a useful supplement to the existing international regime.[26]

(i) To actively promote the growing significance of BRICS in the international system and provide explanation for the slowing world economy in recent years. From Chinese think tanks' view, the Western countries have complex feelings on transformation of the international system. On one hand, they worry about the potential challenges from BRICS countries and on the other hand, they feel complacent about dominating the international order for several decades. Therefore, they are often pessimistic about the BRICS cooperation, and tend to exaggerate the negative aspects of it. They belittle the burgeoning entity of BRICS, and describe it as a challenger to current international order. The Western writings about BRICS, too, are couched in negative connotation, predicting a heightened risk of conflict in the international system.[27]

Being an easy target of Western media and critics, think tanks in China are cautious to criticise and downplay BRICS, and therefore, try to defend the importance of BRICS from the perspective of long-term development. The decrease of growth rate for BRICS countries after 2008 economic crisis does not prevent BRICS to be more vibrant, it actually provides an opportunity for BRICS to increase cooperation and institutional building for the sake of faster economic development. Experts from Chinese think tanks point out that the economies of BRICS countries have grown fast over the years. However, the depth of structural reforms has been neglected, which may adversely influence the long-term economic development. Nevertheless, their cooperation on finance and economics are getting deeper and more pragmatic, and has expanded to the security domain. The establishment of BRICS Development Bank and the Contingent Reserve Arrangement with around $100 billion as start-up fund conveys a very strong signal to the world: that the institutionalisation and maturity of BRICS cooperation is growing. The "contingency arrangements" is helpful to resist the potential instability caused by the United States' gradual withdrawal from Monetary Easing Policy; at the same time, it can prevent the negative impacts of New Normal policy adopted by the developing countries. Thus, the above perspectives about think tanks in China provide an alternative perception of BRICS, which justifies its formation as a vehicle to promote international cooperation on key issues.

(ii) To provide roadmap for the future of BRICS. There are various levels of economic complementarities among BRICS countries. It is described as the getting together of "World Factory" (China), the "World Raw Material Base" (Brazil), "World Gas Station" (Russia) and "World Office" (India); and their strengths in terms of industry, resource and marketing.[28] Some experts suggest developing the "BRICS Spirit" in the form of the following; open development, collaborative development, inclusive development and innovation development. The most important factor which decides BRICS' influence is its strategic coordination among the countries rather than on economic factors. Thus, the strategic influence of BRICS as a group depends upon the extent to which the BRICS Spirit can effectively be used for coordinating various positions among BRICS countries on the key issues of governance.[29]

(iii) To provide suggestions on think tank cooperation in BRICS. For the development of BRICS in the long run, experts point to the fact that it is necessary to strengthen non-government communications—especially people-to-people communication—and that the function of think tanks and experts should be emphasised. It is suggested that an experts group should be established, which will be in charge of doing research on BRCIS, setting agenda for the annual cooperation and evaluating the cooperation results. Furthermore, BRICS can take the experience from PECC and CSCAP and set up national committees of officials, enterprises and scholars, before it is officially established.[30] The BRICS cooperation should be developed in an inclusive manner to intensify institutional innovation and make full use of the institutional advantages, and also integrate the local government, enterprises, media, universities and think tanks, and make them the effective pillars of BRICS cooperation.[31]

The characteristics of Chinese think tanks on BRICS can be understood as the following: Firstly, most think tanks on BRICS in China are "virtual" bodies. They do not have resident researcher and most of their researchers have positions in other institutes, and they work for BRICS think tanks as honorary research fellows. In this regard, think tanks play the role of assembling experts who conduct research on BRICS. Such as in the BRICS study centre in Fudan University, all its researchers have permanent positions in other centres and universities (such as Peking University, Sichuan University or CASS). Usually, there are also think tanks; and even though they are not named as BRICS think tank, yet they pursue studies on BRICS, and it is included in their research agenda. Their influence on BRICS depends on the personal clout and networks of the minority elite experts—such as Yang Jiemian in Shanghai Institutes for International Studies, Yan Xuetong in Tsinghua University.

Secondly, the main function of current think tanks is to describe and explain the BRICS work rather than doing systematic and deep analysis. Especially in Chinese think tanks, the themes which occupy utmost importance are: "economic complementarities among BRICS", "opportunities, challenges and perspective of BRICS cooperation", "exploration of cooperation mechanism", "BRICS and the world" etc.[32] All these topics try to explain the BRICS working mechanism, explain its rationale and provide impetus for further research work in the area.

Thirdly, it can be noticed that Chinese think tanks are very sensitive to comments from the Western countries, and are in a process of refuting them constantly. With the growing skepticism from Western countries, Chinese think tanks have responded to them in various ways. They emphasise inclusive development, and BRICS as a new category of relation, which do not intend to challenge the current international order. In this context, Chinese think tanks play a defensive role on dealing with the Western world on BRICS issues.

Fourthly, the study on BRICS in China lacks substantive research. Most of the research focuses on the importance of BRICS to international system, and hardly any research projects have been conducted on new aspects of their cooperation. Some commentators remarked that Chinese think tanks are doing research based on pragmatism and experimentalism, and that they take the matter on its merits. Chinese scholars prefer "procedure" instead of "process", which requires the analysis of cause and effect—and that is missing in the way research is conducted in the Chinese think tanks. This shortcoming also gets reflected in the study on BRICS. Since think tanks in China have increased, there are huge spaces for them to deepen the BRICS study and increase their influence on policy making.

In this backdrop, it can be concluded that Chinese think tanks play two roles with respect to BRICS cooperation. Firstly, they play the role as an advocate. Advocate is the one that argues for a cause—as a supporter or as a defender. Advocacy think tanks are often seen as one of the following: think tanks which argue for specific position-based results as opposed to open-ended analysis; the ones which uses scientific methodology primarily to influence policy in ideologically-preferred directions or the ones who focus on marketing ideas rather than just the research aspect.[33] Therefore, in the strict sense, advocate does not participate in the policy process; its main job is to explain, elaborate the policy and to convert the policy language into public awareness and educate the public. In bilateral relations, it explains policy intentions to other countries, and defends its nation's policy interest. Although think tanks work as an advocate, the studies conducted by them are somewhat less relevant to policy-making in China.

In China, the BRICS affairs are mainly conducted in the track one level; it is a top down decision making process, and Chinese think tanks basically cannot have deep impact on BRICS policy, thereby limiting Chinese think tanks' role in policy making process. Chinese think tanks play the role of an advocate. The mainstream voices of Chinese think tanks on BRICS are mostly trying to explain the rationale of BRICS cooperation. By using economic complementarities theory, the think tanks in China mainly try to prove the sustainability of BRICS economies. In face of Western challenges, Chinese think tanks defend BRICS cooperation, emphasising its inclusive development concept. They also try to use the concept of "new type of relations" to explain the BRICS cooperation. Although this concept is a governmental initiative, Chinese think tanks' scholars use this concept in their research projects to explore ways of furthering the cooperation among BRICS countries.

In contrast to pursuing a much more serious research on BRICS, Chinese think tanks are more active on convening conferences where they get the scholars from BRICS countries and also other countries to share their views. They provide the necessary platforms for communicating and explaining Chinese understanding of BRICS.

Secondly, they play the role as an initiator. Initiator is someone who initiates in making something happen. The role of an initiator is one of taking the responsibility of raising a subject, creating a policy concept, or introducing some new ideas so that some policies are formed, or at least discussed at the level of the government. In this regard, think tanks play a bigger role in the early stages of policy making process, and therein lies the problem of definition/

perception. Chinese think tanks do not appear to be initiators most of the time, but still displays this characteristic on some occasions. The case is to raise the concept of 'BRICS Spirit'. The director of Shanghai Institute for International Studies raised the concept of BRICS Spirit in his article published in 2011, where he concluded the BRICS Spirit as "development", "partnership", "inclusion" and "contribution". In 2014, Chinese President Xi put forward the ideas of BRICS Spirit in the Sixth BRICS Summit as "opening", "inclusion", "cooperation and "win-win solution", which is similar to Yang's initiative. It is through these ways that the Chinese think tanks can play the role of an initiator.

Conclusion

It doesn't matter whether it is in China or in other BRICS countries, most think tanks are just "virtual" bodies which have not done enough for the increasing demand to come up with a perspective on the issues related to BRICS, its operation and governance. Most think tanks are working on explaining and theorising the current status of BRICS and lack of research on the operating mechanism. Joint studies by the think tanks of BRICS countries are very few; until now, only two reports have been jointly put together. One is the a report by BTTC and approved by the 6th BRICS Summit titled *Towards a Long-Term Strategy for BRICS—Recommendations by the BRICS Think Tanks Council*; and the other one remains the roadmap report by BTTC which was approved by 6th BRICS Summit titled *Towards a Long-Term Strategy for BRICS—A Proposal by the BRICS Think Tanks Council.* Apart from these, no other substantive cooperation has been found. The other important areas which have not been studied by the think tanks yet are BRICS position on oil and gas resources cooperation, climate change etc. In addition, the independence of the BRICS think tanks needs to be strengthened. Most think tanks, except ORF in India, are government-affiliated or semi-government bodies, which sometimes restrict the diverse concerns to be expressed on BRICS. The requirement of independent think tanks is increasing, and mostly because they are expected to play a significant role in promoting and further institutionalising the idea of BRICS. It requires greater cooperation and networking among the think tanks of the BRICS countries as well as an increasing research on various aspects of BRICS to make this happen. Thus, the track-II level cooperation needs to be taken seriously by the BRICS countries, where think tanks can play the central role.

END NOTES

1. Fifth BRICS Summit (2013), "eThekwini Declaration", 27 March, [Online: Web] http://brics2016.gov.in/upload/files/document/5763be1c4da6e5th1.pdf, accessed on 12 August 2016.
2. Zhu, Jiejin (2014), "金砖国家合作机制的转型" [Jin zhuanguojia he zuojizhi de zhuanxin], International Review, issue 3, pp. 59-73.
3. Stuenkel, Oliver (2015), "Connecting the Global South: Why the BRICS Academic Forum matters", 23 May [Online: Web] http://www.postwesternworld.com/2015/05/23/connecting-academic-matters/, accessed on 13 August 2016.
4. Fifth BRICS Summit (2013), "eThekwini Declaration", 27 March, [Online: Web] http://brics2016.gov.in/upload/files/document/5763be1c4da6e5th1.pdf, accessed on 13 August 2016.
5. Sixth BRICS Summit (2014), "Fortaleza Declaration", 15 July [Online: Web] http://brics2016.gov.in/upload/files/document/57566d35a13456declaration.pdf, accessed on 13 August 2016.
6. Seventh BRICS Summit (2015), "Ufa Declaration", 9 July, [Online: Web]http://brics2016.gov.in/upload/files/document/5763c20a72f2d7thDeclarationeng.pdf, accessed on 13 August.
7. Lauer, Adrian (2012), "A new BRICS think tank network", 28 June[Online: Web] https://onthinktanks.org/articles/a-new-brics-think-tank-network/, accessed on 13 August 2016.
8. Fourth BRICS Summit (2012), "Delhi Declaration", 29 March [Online: Web]http://brics2016.gov.in/upload/files/document/57566ddcc42a94th.pdf, accessed on 13 August 2016.
9. *Xinhua News* (2014), "做强新型智库提升国家软实力," [Zuoqiangxinxingzhiku, Ti sheng guojiaruanshi li] 14 October [Online: Web] http://news.xinhuanet.com/newmedia/2014-10/14/c_127095048.htm, accessed on 13 August 2016.
10. Gao, Zugui, Wei, Zonglei, Liuyu (2009), "新兴经济体的崛起及其影响" [Xinxingjingjiti de jue qi ji qi yingxiang], International Data Information, issue 8, pp. 1-19. (GaoZugui is deputy director of Institute for International Strategic Studies of the Central Party School of the Communist Party of China.)
11. Lv Bo (2012), "'金砖国家'间的贸易和投资" [Jin zhuanguojiajian de maoyi he touzi], *Journal of International Economic Cooperation*, issue 10, pp. 27-30. (Lv Bo is a research fellow in Chinese Academy of International Trade and Economic Cooperation (CAITEC) under the Ministry of Commerce.)
12. Chen, Fengying (2011), "新兴经济体与 21 世纪国际经济秩序变迁", [Xinxingjingjitiyuershiyishijiguojijingjizhixubianqian], *Foreign Affairs Review*, issue 3, pp. 1-15 (Chen Fengying is Director of Institute of World Economy of China institute of contemporary international relations.)
13. Huang, Renwei (2011), "金砖国家崛起与全球治理体系", [Jin zhuanguojiajue qi yuquanqiuzhi li ti xi], *Contemporary World*, issue 5, pp. 24-27. (Huang Renwei is the president of Shanghai Academy of Social Sciences.)
14. Chen, Fengying (2011), "新兴经济体与 21 世纪国际经济秩序变迁", [Xinxing jingji ti yu ershiyishiji guojijingjizhixubianqian], *Foreign Affairs Review*, issue 3, pp. 1-15
15. Wang Yongzhong, Yao zhizhong (2011), "金砖国家峰会的经济议题、各方立场与中国对策", [Jin zhuanguojiafenghui de jingjiyiti, ge fang li changyuzhongguo dui ce], *International Economic Review*, issue 3, pp. 74-83. (Wang Yongzhong is a research fellow from Institute of World Economics and Politics, China Academy of Social Sciences.)
16. Yang, Shengming (2011), "世界经济结构调整和优化问题研究", [shijiejingjijiegoutiaozheng

he you hua wen tiyanjiu], *Economic Review*, Issue 11, pp. 24-38. (Yang Shengming is a senior research fellow and member of academic committee in Chinese Academy of Social Sciences.)

17. Lin, Yueqin (2010), "金砖四国:经济转型与持续增长", [Jin zhuansiguo: jingjizhuanxinyu chi xuzengzhang], *World Economy Studies*, Issue 10, pp. 127-131. (Lin Yueqin is research fellow in from Institute of World Economics and Politics, China Academy of Social Sciences.)
18. Li, Zuojun (2015), "引领经济新常态走向好的新常态", [yin ling jingjixinchang tai, zouxianghao de xinchang tai], *Journal of Chinese Academy of Governance*, Issue 1, pp. 21-25. (Li Zuojun is a senior research fellow in Development Research Centre of the State Council.)
19. Li, Zhi (2014), "新常态下中国经济发展态势和结构动向研究", [xinchang tai xiazhongguojingjifazhan tai shi he jiegou dong xiangyanjiu], *Price: Theory & Practice*, Issue 11, pp. 7-12. (Li Zhi is a research fellow from Peoples University.)
20. Li, Daokui (2014), "金砖国家进入新常态或渐进式改变国际格局", [jinzhuanguojiajinruxinchang tai, huojianjinshigaibianguojigeju], 14 October [Online: Web] http://news.xinhuanet.com/newmedia/2014-10/14/c_127095048.htm, accessed on 19 August 2016. (Li Daokui is the Director of Centre for China in the World Economy, Tsinghua University.)
21. Si, Wen (2016), "G20 就继续推进国际金融机构份额和投票权改革达成共识", [G20 Jiu xi xutuijinguojijinrongjigou fen e he toupiaoquangaige da cheng gong shi], 6 September [Online: Web] http://finance.sina.com.cn/roll/2016-09-06/doc-ifxvpxua7964724.shtml, accessed on 19 August 2016. (Si wen is a research fellow in China institute of contemporary international relations.)
22. Lu, Feng (2016), "G20 就继续推进国际金融机构份额和投票权改革达成共识", [G20 Jiu xi xutuijinguojijinrongjigou fen e he toupiaoquangaige da cheng gong shi], 6 September [Online: Web] http://finance.sina.com.cn/roll/2016-09-06/doc-ifxvpxua7964724.shtml, accessed on 19 August 2016. (Lu Feng is professor and director of Macro-economic research centre in Peking University.)
23. China Center For International Economic Exchanges (CCIEE) Research Group (2013), "中国在国际货币体系改革中的定位与策略选择", [zhongguozaiguojihuo bi ti xi gaigezhong de ding weiyucelue xuanze], *Globalization*, Issue 1, pp.16-26.
24. Zhao, Kejin (2014), "中国国际战略中的金砖国家合作", [zhongguoguojizhanluezhong de jizhuanguojia he zuo], *International Review*, Issue 3, pp. 44-58. (Zhao Kejin is an associate professor in International studies centre of Tsinghua University), *International Review*, Issue 3, pp. 44-58.
25. Yang, Jiemian (2011), "金砖国家合作的宗旨、精神和机制建设", [jinzhuanguojia he zuo de zongzhi, jingshen he jizhijian she], *Contemporary World*, Issue 5, pp. 22-23. (Yang Jiemian is the President of Shanghai Institutes for International Studies.)
26. Xu, Xiujun (2013), "金砖国家开发银行：借鉴与创新," [Jin zhuanguojiakaifa yin hang: jiejianyuchuangxin], *China Forex*, 1 April, pp. 19-21. (Xu Xiujun is a research from Institute of World Economics and Politics, China Academy of Social Sciences.)
27. Niu, Haibing (2014), "如何看待金砖国家经济增长放缓," [ru he kandaijinzhuanguojiajingjizengzhang fang huan], *Contemporary World*, Issue 3, pp. 9-12. (Niu Haibing is anassociate professor and the deputy director of American Studies Centre of Shanghai Institutes for International Studies.)
28. Niu, Haibing (2014), "如何看待金砖国家经济增长放缓," [ru he kandaijinzhuanguojiajingjizengzhang fang huan], *Contemporary World*, Issue 3, pp. 9-12.
29. Zhao, Kejin (2014), "中国国际战略中的金砖国家合作", [zhongguoguojizhanluezhong de jizhuanguojia he zuo], *International Review*, Issue 3, pp. 44-58.

30. Yang, Jiemian (2011), "金砖国家合作的宗旨、精神和机制建设", [jinzhuanguojia he zuo de zongzhi, jingshen he jizhijian she], *Contemporary World*, Issue 5, pp. 22-23.
31. Zhao, Kejin (2014), "中国国际战略中的金砖国家合作", [zhongguoguojizhanluezhong de jizhuanguojia he zuo], *International Review*, Issue 3, pp. 44-58.
32. McGan, James G. (2007), Think Tanks and Policy Advice in the United States, London: Routledge, 2007. pp. 124-126.

6

The Energy Factor

Prachi Aggarwal

Introduction

The concept of BRICS has gained much currency in discussions about institutional reforms and global governance. However, not much attention has been paid to the evolution of BRICS' role in strategic aspects like the global energy governance. Energy, in general, is an understudied phenomenon, both among the scholars and policy makers. The research on energy issues have mostly been looked at from a competition-conflict point of view, in which one country's pursuit of energy puts it in competition with the other. This constitutes a narrow geopolitical focus on energy, which remains inadequate to explain the changes in the global energy architecture as well as in analysing the role played by the emerging economies. In that backdrop, this chapter is an attempt to understand the role played by the BRICS countries in bringing about reforms in the global energy governance. The international energy structure is fraught with several challenges—ranging from issue of fossil fuel scarcity and swing in energy prices to the problem of environmental deterioration due to rising consumption along with the challenge involved in shift from a fossil fuel mix to a clean energy structure. Many scholars also argue that international energy governance has not kept pace with the emergence of major developing nations, with the changing relations between oil producers and consumers, with the emergence of climate mitigation as a central energy policy issue and with the technology revolution that is required. Therefore, the rise of BRICS raises an important question as to what extent the countries of the group can act as a coalition to effect global governance reforms on energy.

Energy Share: An Analysis

While analysing the major 'energy' characteristics of each member countries within the BRICS, it has been found that except India and China, the rest of the three nations comprise the energy suppliers to the world. Russia has its rich oil and gas heritage, Brazil produces ethanol and is a world leader in bio-fuel technology and South Africa, too, is 'leading by example' in the clean coal technology segment. China also has rich coal reserves and is leading the world in acquiring stakes in various oil blocs of the world. This leaves India as the most vulnerable member of the group with declining coal reserves and negligible oil and gas deposits, and greater dependence on external energy supply. A panel discussion on the Fourth BRIC Summit, which was held in New Delhi, India, had pointed out that "BRICS provide a perfect division of labour in the energy sector as Russia and Brazil pump it up while India and China provide the receipts"[1]. Hence, the discussion strongly advocated for cooperation by the BRICS partners in the energy sector, where the bilateral rivalries for strategic scrambling of resources takes a back seat and 'status quo politics' and cooperation as a forum emerges. The panelists on the discussion argued that this cooperation would lead to BRICS' active engagement in the global energy management, and that it could even establish an alternative order to the Western style global energy governance[2]. However, in order to achieve this, a lot needs to be done by the two 'consummate consumers'—India and China, whose bilateral competition at the global energy market challenges the optimism of the forum.

In 2015, Russia and China signed their breakthrough deal on energy; and China, at the same time, is heavily investing in Petrobras (USD10 billion), the Brazilian state energy company. It is, therefore, quite clear to China that its partners in the BRICS forum are not under-developed nations who would be gratified by its abundant dose of capital and toe the lines of accepting the notion of its superiority, but are self-respecting developing economies that are themselves in the race of development, albeit a little farther from China. Hence, while China basks in all the attention that is showered upon it by the 'Look East' policy of various nations, it should also generously reciprocate and give equal footing to its partners at the international forums like BRICS—so that a collective voice can be raised on key issues of the world, like energy.

Martynov identifies 12 different areas of cooperation between the BRICS members, namely; constitutional, economy, energy, science and technology, natural resources, ecology, agriculture and food stuffs, information security, social security, military security, civilisational and cultural security, humanitarian security and regional and global security[3]. It should be noted that Martynov placed energy cooperation at a higher pedestal than cooperation in military security, at the third spot, right after the economy. This proves the fact that more and more thinkers are considering international threats to be non-military in nature, and hence, advocate cooperation in the same fields. In Martynov's view, "closest attention must be paid to new directions of security strategy. We mean the natural resources and ecological and energy security, which is directly connected with the problems of climate change[4]. He cites two national documents of Brazil and Russia: Document on National Defense Policy of Brazil (2005), which reveals that "future disputes of the world will be energy resources". The Strategy of the National Security of Russian Federation until 2020 argues "the pivotal point of the world policy for the long-term period will be concentrated around the possession of the world sources of energy"[5]. China's Energy White Paper (2012) also argues on the similar lines in its section on strengthening international cooperation in energy.

China is an active and responsible participant in international energy cooperation, and it has established bilateral dialogue and cooperative mechanisms in the field of energy with the US, the EU, Japan, Russia, Kazakhstan, Turkmenistan, Uzbekistan, Brazil, Argentina, Venezuela and many other countries and regions, and has strengthened dialogues, exchanges and cooperation with these countries regarding oil, natural gas, coal, electric power, renewable energy, technology, equipment and energy policy. China is also a member of or important participant in many multilateral organisations and mechanisms.[6]

One of the major tasks among the various functions, which India has also enlisted under the power and energy division of its planning commission, is:

> Evaluate strategies and policies for promotion of emerging issues in all energy sub-sectors such as for Clean Coal Technologies, In-situ Coal Gasification, extraction of Coal Bed Methane, Coal Liquefaction, Carbon Capture and Sequestration, Low Carbon Growth, LNG import, transmission pipelines, New Exploration Licensing Policy (NELP) etc.[7]

Since all members have their priorities defined, Martynov writes that BRICS members have a major task to prevent the nurturing of these "seeds of war", especially energy issues that could bring an unprecedented scourge if left untamed. Shiv Shankar Menon, at the BRICS conference in 2009, had exhorted the idea that BRICS members should not only "look outwards at the world, but also look inwards among ourselves at the complementarities between our economies"[8]. He hints towards the world being at the "cusp of a new type of multipolarity"[9]. Since BRICS was established largely to cater to financial crunches of the member states, the concept of a New Development Bank (NDB) was envisaged in 2014. This bank, which is headquartered in Shanghai, issued 4 billion Yuan bonds in China for clean energy projects. It was noted that BRICS bank, despite having different rules and regulations as compared to other international financial institutions, shall be working in close tandem with other financial institutions—especially those based in Asia, like Asia Infrastructure Investment Bank (AIIB), China Development Bank or the Silk Road Fund etc.[10] It is to be noted that NDB, despite having a democratic approach in its administrative structure, shall be collaborating mainly with those centres which are China-led or where China has the biggest say—either as a shareholder or as a political and economical influencer. Needless to say that given the fact that NDB has its headquarters based in Shanghai, China would have a dominating effect on the functioning of NDB, as and when it requires.

Undoubtedly, NDB—which is currently struggling to get an international ranking despite having gained the support and membership of five major countries of the world—has smoothly obtained triple A rankings from China's 'domestic agencies'[11]. Perhaps 20 per cent of equal voting rights may be understood as eyewash, and like the UN—which is obliquely dominated by the US—BRICS may have to tow the line of its un-appointed leader, China, too. However, Wu and Xin (2016) argue that it is naive to predict a 'straight arrow' future for BRICS which is pointing towards China, as India—which was considered as the weakest member of the group—is slowly transforming her 'image from being the 'sick man' to being the 'bright spot' of the group, especially at a time when China's economy is over-heating, South African economy is stagnant and Brazilian and Russian economies are going in 'reverse direction'[12]. Maybe, just like when China flourished when the world remained over-awed by the US, India is undergoing the same phase and abiding by Deng's policy of '*dao guang yang hui*' i.e. keeping a low profile and biding time—and is giving China space to hog the limelight while it takes baby but steady steps towards development. Stanford University historian Ian Morris said: "institutions such as the NDB could help new economic powers such as China and India rise"[13]. He also points that these countries, at micro-level, should find ways to build up 'new opportunities' by taking up initiatives in searching for establishing 'new institutional frameworks'; yet, at the same time, at the macro-level should limit their working to within the ambit of international order. Loddgaard prefers to call it as the interconnectivity in the world without the West"[14].

J. Panda has defined BRICS as a "multilateral forum belonging to rapidly emerging economies, with its core members (except Russia) being well-known members of the developing world; and a group which is based on North-South divide, and aims to bring reforms to the global financial institutions in favour of the developing world"[15]. Analysed within this framework, BRICS is seen as the champion of the cause of the developing world, where her members not only have the potential but also the power of acceptance to be positioned as an alternative to the G8 or such organisations of the developed world. Melchoir (2012) has also argued that the emergence of BRICS nations, both individually and collectively, has led to changes in the 'hub and spoke model' of the world order in which North America and Western Europe had once been the core of the group[16]. Panda credits China for the success of BRICS as an institution by citing examples of non-China institutions like IBSA (India, Brazil and South Africa) or even BASIC (Brazil, South Africa, India and China; where China played a marginal role) that could not take off into doing some actual groundwork and now remains hidden as 'obscure, redundant tasks' in official files.

Zhang et al are also in favour of a China-led BRICS—especially in the energy sector. They mention in their study that by observing the policies related to renewable energy, it is seen that China is the only country whose renewable energy policies are thriving and are geared to complete their target. This is reflected in the fact that China has become a lead producer of wind and solar energy. The paper also argues that Russian policies are 'not working' and Brazilian and Indian policies have not yet reached the desired outcome. Hence, the solution lies in the fact that "China should mandate the promotion of renewable energy, develop biomass energy on the base of comparative advantage and enhance renewable energy industry chain integration"[17]. Thus, the extant literature seems to promote a China-led BRICS, not only because China is the most powerful member of the group but also because China has made things happen—in her own country as well as in the international or regional institutions. Yet, centralisation of power steals the autonomy of other members. For instance, BRICS is a geo-politically diverse group, with members who have more or less the same prowess and potential to develop. Perhaps, this is one of the reasons when NDB was envisaged, the members voted in favour of a currency reserve pool rather than a Yuan-based model. Also, the presiding powers are of rotating nature to preserve the 'democratic ethos'. The 2014 BRICS Summit had also led to the establishment of a BRICS Energy Association (upon the suggestion of Russian President Vladimir Putin) which would actually be a "reserve fuel bank and an institute for energy safety", as described by President Putin[18].

Fig. 6.1: BRICS Energy Consumption Collectively in 2008

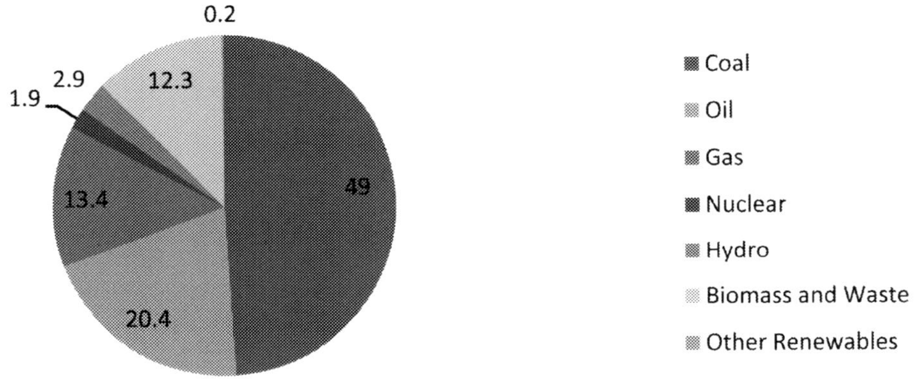

Unit percent
Source: NUPI Report 2012.[19]

The figure above shows that the BRICS are still heavily dependent on fossil fuels, despite all rhetoric about renewable energy policies. Also, it can be discerned that coal is the natural preferred choice for countries like China and India, while Russia opts for oil and gas. Thus, BRICS countries are still heavily dependent on their domestically available resources. Criticising BRICS, Loddgard argues that the rising consumers have not given energy its due consideration, and have just paid lip service to it at various summits. He also says that although the joint statement from 2009 Summit cited lofty goals of 'diversification of energy resources and supply (including renewable energy, the security of energy transit routes, the creation of new energy investments and of new energy infrastructure and international cooperation in the field of energy efficiency), these objectives have not seen any concrete future and have been merely relegated to 'consensual objectives'. It was only in the 2012 Summit in India that Delhi action plan was launched and a commitment was made to initiate action for 'multilateral energy cooperation within BRICS framework'[20]. Given below is the total energy consumption of BRICS nations from 2000 to 2013:

Table 6.1: Total Energy Consumption of BRICS Nations from 2000 to 2013

Year	*Brazil*	*China*	*India*	*Russia**	*South Africa*
2000	190	1019		1616	91
2001		1053			
2002		1116			
2003		1287			
2004		1494			
2005	218	1652	362	1700	
2006	226	1811	392	1754	86
2007	238	1964	418	1770	85
2008	253	2040	441	1800	92
2009	244	2187	507	1738	83
2010	269	2275	523	1822	
2011	272	2436	535	1868	
2012	284	2532	571	1893	
2013	296	2625	575	1869	

Unit million tonnes oil equivalent *million tonnes of conventional (equivalent) fuel
Source: National Statistics Offices of the BRICS.[21]

Table 6.2: Total Primary Energy Production of BRICS Nations from 2000 to 2013

Year	*Brazil*	*China*	*India*	*Russia**	*South Africa*
2000	153	945	204	2726	153
2001		1006			
2002		1045			
2003		1203			
2004		1376			
2005	201	1514	239	2480	
2006	212	1626	253	2553	154
2007	223	1731	265	2579	154
2008	237	1824	278	2616	157
2009	241	1922	306	2509	157
2010	253	2078	318	2661	
2011	257	2226	320	2693	
2012	257	2333	320	2713	
2013	258	2380	332	2734	

Unit million tonnes oil equivalent *million tonnes of conventional (equivalent) fuel
Source: National Statistics Offices of the BRICS.[22]

The above two tables reveal that India and Russia are in deep deficit of their energy accounts while China seems to be almost at a breakeven point.

Brazil is the only country which is producing in excess of its consumption. The data related to South Africa is insufficient to provide any concrete analysis.

Loddgard (2012) has attempted to find reasons for lack of commitment between the BRICS nations towards achieving their energy goals, and he had singled out Russia as a reason—the country does not want to become a 'raw material appendage' and has 'price issues with China'[23]. Yet, given the billion dollar deal signed between the two countries just three years later shows that nothing in politics is permanent—including worries and anxieties, and China and Russia seemed to have melted their differences at least at the bilateral level. This leaves room for development of energy trade even at the regional level if the largest producer and largest consumer of the BRICS nations join hands for the same. Another reason pointed out by him was Brazil and South Africa, who have been beneficiaries of Western investment and do not want their involvement in BRICS to hamper their individual relation with the Western nations. However, if the recent reports are to be believed, then both Africa and Latin America (especially Brazil) have seen a shift in the trend of energy investment; and China is now becoming a more dominating face in their state energy companies rather than Western (especially American) investments. Hence, the analysis that 'in some ways, Brazil and South Africa are both buffers between the Asian giants and the Western world' can be tapered down to believe that both countries can find investors within the BRICS group (read China and India), and do not need to balance between their regional and international loyalties. Perhaps the reason that binds BRICS together is the lack of dictatorship. None of the BRICS countries have been allowing unceremonial powers, and there are always two or more nations to counter a nation if it tries to up its ante. Another reason pointed out by Loddegard is the non- binding nature in the functioning of BRICS, especially the policy of non-interference in the internal affairs of any state. This allows the BRICS nations to not only engage with other energy-rich nations but also among themselves, without being under the pressure of West-determined rules and regulations. Hence, Erikson et al. point out that "when defined as an issue of governance rather than geopolitics, energy emerges as a commodity for which governance mechanisms can be established to correct market failures and ensure predictability and transparency"[24]. So a regional or multilateral organisation, unlike bilateral relations, ensures greater transparency and a fairer share for both sides.

Valizadeh and Houshialsadat share an Iranian perspective of an energy-rich nation towards BRICS. In their words, "one of the central issues for the future of the BRICS, as a new alliance by economic emerging countries, is energy security that anybody's failure to work towards energy security will have massive impact on the energy security of their neighbouring nations and the countries surrounding them"[25]. This implies that no matter how much potential the BRICS nations have to develop, they cannot rise until and unless they have a sound backing of energy security, which can only be achieved if these "bigger, developing nations" rely on smaller energy-rich nations of the Middle East and Africa. Given the fact that the world is increasingly getting multi-polar in nature, nations within the regional organisations have to establish consonance and coherence not only in their own energy priorities, but also amongst themselves and with the supplier nations. Arguing within the same framework, Loddgard (2012) also feels that it is essential for the BRICS to maintain support base of the energy delivering nations, and that they should not shift towards the Western-dominated bloc. The Indian Prime Minister's statement at the Sixth BRICS Summit also clearly indicated the need to maintain the sustainability of the development process among the BRICS nations, without compromising on the growth mechanism[26]. A similar emphasis was made by the ex-Prime Minister Manmohan Singh, arguing for a deeper cooperation on energy front amongst the BRICS members (Ministry of External Affairs, Government of India, 2014):

> "We are rich in resources, material and human population. We are strengthened by the complementarities of our resource endowments..... We have the opportunity to give concrete meaning to the concept of sustainable and balanced development, and produce innovative models of development. We can cooperate in clean and alternative sources of energy and technologies. Nuclear safety has emerged as a major source of concern the world over after the tragedy in Japan. We should cooperate in this area, as well as in disaster relief and management."

Thus, it is to be noticed that Indian leaders have continuously stressed on energy cooperation in their statements at the BRICS Summits more than the leaders of any other country.

Intra-BRICS Energy Dimensions

Ebinger and Avasarla rightly remark "the scale of the energy dilemma is not new, nor are the problems and the solutions". Expressing concerns for India, they argue that if India does not alter its speed in implementing reforms, it might become the first "fallen angel" of the BRICS nations. They appreciate Chinese domestic political structure which enabled it to make, break and remake energy policies at blinking speed. Moreover, China's energy reserves are better off than India's because of its coal deposits and investments and stakes undertaken at the bilateral level. They woefully conclude that "India has a government that historically has been incapable of fully executing painful energy reforms. If India is to continue as a vibrant emerging market, it will have to tackle its energy-security weaknesses immediately"[27]. Yet, to discount India because of its fragile energy security could be a conclusion made too soon; for it should be noted that India has taken active steps in developing its solar and wind sector, and also its large sections of population have lived without electricity or petrol, accepting it as a way of life. Krishna Srivastava from the Centre for Studies on Energy and Power mentions that as a means to improve their energy efficiency, BRICS nations should stop importing irrelevant technologies from the West and 'jointly share the technologies for the conversion and utilisation of energy'. He cites the example of making glass buildings which have been emulated by the Indian constructors from the cold climate countries. Glass being a heat trap increases the temperature of the building, due to which air conditioners are used profusely in hot tropical countries like India, thereby leading to increase in energy consumption rather than decreasing it[28].

Apart from Tables 6.1 and 6.2, it can be seen that Li, in his dissertation, also points out the energy consumption of all the BRICS nations in the first decade of the 21st century. The table given below discounts the counting of certain kind of energies which are mentioned below:

Table 6.3: Energy Consumption of all the BRICS nations from 2000 to 2011

Year	*Brazil*	*China*	*India*	*Russia*	*South Africa*
2000	18,862	101,872	27,122	162,500	
2005	21,616	165,198	33,614	172,700	19,902
2006	22,374	181,073	36,344	177,500	20,985
2007	23,602	196,356	38,764	179,100	
2008	24,970	204,014	41,345	182,000	
2009	24,093	214,653	39,700	175,800	
2010	26,480	227,500		270,700	
2011		222,600			

Unit: Ten thousand tonnes of oil equivalent standard.
Source: Li (2013).[29]

In the above table, the total energy consumption includes coal, crude oil and its products— natural gas, electric power (not including the use of low calorie valued fuel), biomass and solar energy. Total energy consumption is divided into three parts: final energy consumption, energy conversion losses and energy losses. Also, it can be seen that China's energy consumption has been the maximum and Russia's energy consumption has escalated since 2010. It has been noticed that over the past 30 years, the consumption of several basic commodities by the BRICS countries has increased in comparison to the global consumption.

Table 6.4: Energy Consumption of China and other BRICS Members from 1980 to 2010

Year	*Oil*	*Steel*	*Copper*	*Aluminium*	*Iron Ore*
China					
1980-1990	14.8	59.0	11.0	8.7	128.7
1990-2000	24.8	53.2	31.5	42.5	87.9
2000-2010	46.6	120.3	138.7	81.9	85.4
Rest of the four countries					
1980-1990	14.5	0.3	-14.4	26.3	148.9
1990-2000	-11.0	-20.5	0.7	-7.6	20.2
2000-2010	20.7	8.2	17.8	10.9	9.3
All the five countries					
1980-1990	29.3	59.3	-3.4	35.0	277.6
1990-2000	13.7	32.6	32.2	34.9	108.1
2000-2010	67.3	128.4	156.5	92.8	94.8

Unit: Per cent.
Source: Lu et al (2011)[30]

From the table above, it is clearly evident that it is China who has consumed more energy than the rest of the four countries put together. The 21st century shows that BRICS have been consuming '$2/3^{rd}$ of the global oil, out of which China has been consuming almost 47 per cent of the total; aluminium and iron ore almost nearing 100 per cent and steel and copper exceeding 100 per cent—out of which China's consumption has been exceptional. Lu et al argue that given the energy consumption patterns and GDP growth rates of China in comparison to the rest of the countries, it can be seen that BRICS growth story is essentially a China growth story. BRICS, without China, loses its relevance of being an organisation which is growing fashionably fast. They further add that 'the direct and indirect influence of China's rapid economic catch-up and its increasing growth are playing a unique and important role during this period of historical transition. The prospect of cooperation between the BRICS depends indirectly but substantially upon how relations among the groups are handled, and on how China understands the relationship between advancing its domestic transition and reform and its participation in global governance'[31].

Hence, it is specified that the "Chinese understanding" of the relationship is extremely important if BRICS aims to grow as an institution. In fact, as shown in the table below, there has been slight variation in patterns of energy consumption as revealed in their latest data:

Table 6.5: Primary Energy Consumption of BRICS Countries in 2014

Country	*Coal*	*Natural gas*	*Oil*	*Nuclear*	*Hydroelectric*	*Non-hydro renewable energy*
Brazil	06	14	39	01	11	29
China	66	05	16	01	01	09
India	46	05	22	01	01	24
Russia	14	54	22	07	02	01
South Africa	66	03	17	03	<01	11

Unit: percentage
Source: Greenpeace (2015)[32]

It also shows that India and China, the two most populous countries of the world, are still heavily dependent on coal consumption. India seems to have diversified better than China by reducing its dependence on fossil fuel consumption and expanding its renewable energy consumption. On the other hand, China despite becoming one of the leading countries in solar and wind production has failed to make an impression on the renewable energy front. Russia leads in natural gas production by a huge margin primarily due to its abundant domestic resources. Although oil still seems to be a favourite among the BRICS nations, most of them are trying to scale down their dependence as well as vulnerability on external resources (read: oil) in particular. Brazil has revealed itself as the beacon of hope amongst the emerging economies by expanding its renewable energy sector.

In another analysis done by Matei and Stamin, an attempt was made to draw a co-relation between GDP and energy consumption of these nations. It was found that during the period 1990 to 2015, India had the lowest escalation of per capita consumption of resources while Russia and China had the highest. During the same period, Brazil recorded the highest GDP per capita while India had the lowest[33]. Hu and Qin attempted to evaluate the total factor energy efficiency of the BRICS nations by adopting the DEA model. He found that the energy efficiency of the BRICS nations as a group was low; however, Brazil has been one of the leading countries in promoting energy efficiency. This is primarily because Brazil, amongst the five, leads in hydro-electricity and renewable energy consumption[34]. Another interesting conclusion that they drew from their findings was that except India and China, the countries of the group are affected by their energy consumption structure, whereas India and China still continue to be governed by their economic structure. Similar findings are supported by Cao, who reiterates the relationship between GDP and carbon emissions of the BRICS nations (note: South Africa is not analysed here). The findings reveal that China's GDP and carbon emissions are negatively related, unlike other nations. Also, rising GDP has led to increase in coal and oil consumption, which in turn has increased China's carbon emissions[35].

In fact, China has been a major importer of energy not only from other nations but also from BRICS nations. It is seen that China imports minerals from Brazil and India, fossil fuels from Russia and precious metals from South Africa. It also imports oil products from Brazil. The given table sums up Chinese imports from the members of the BRICS nations in various categories.

Table 6.6: China's Energy Trade with Other BRICS Members

Year	*Total imports*	*India*	*Brazil*	*Other four members*
Minerals				
2000	31	11.9	14.3	34.4
2001	42	13.1	18.2	38.4
2002	43	14.6	19.1	41.3
2003	72	18.9	19.1	43.3
2004	173	24.9	17.0	48.4
2005	260	21.2	15.6	42.6
2006	322	16.3	17.5	38.9
2007	540	16.3	17.9	39.2
2008	864	16.6	17.8	40.5
2009	696	11.4	18.9	37.7
2010	1086	10.8	16.9	34.3

Year	*Total imports*	*Russia*	*Other four members*
Fossil fuels			
2000	207	3.8	4.2
2001	175	4.6	4.9
2002	193	6.6	6.9
2003	293	7.2	7.3
2004	480	8.7	9.7
2005	641	10.2	11.2
2006	891	10.6	11.9
2007	1049	8.9	10.9
2008	1691	7.1	8.4
2009	1240	7.6	9.0
2010	1887	6.8	9.6

Year	*Total imports*	*South Africa*	*Other four members*
Precious metals			
2000	24.2	19.8	22.6
2001	9.9	13.9	24.6
2002	27.1	19.9	25.0
2003	18.5	20.0	32.0
2004	26.5	27.8	38.3
2005	34.7	27.6	37.6
2006	46.2	25.7	32.8
2007	62.2	21.4	28.4
2008	75.4	22.6	29.3
2009	65.5	26.1	35.9
2010	108.5	21.6	34.2

Year	*Total imports*	*Brazil*	*Other four members*
Oil Products			
2000	31	15.2	15.5
2001	33	18.5	18.7
2002	28	32.6	32.7
2003	57	29.7	30.4
2004	74	28.2	28.8
2005	82	29.2	29.4
2006	81	37.2	37.4
2007	123	31.8	32.1
2008	232	31.4	31.7
2009	210	35.0	35.1
2010	271	30.1	30.3

Unit: hundred million US dollars
Source: Lu et al (2011).

The above table reveals that China is an avid consumer of energy products, and is into heavy trade with other BRICS members. This implies that despite all political rhetoric of BRICS becoming a defunct organisation, China has maintained steady bilateral relations with each of the BRICS members. It is this individual effort, point out the Chinese analysts, which make China an indispensable member of the group not only because of her qualities as an economic powerhouse but because of her ability to bind each member state into a trade relation. As revealed, China's import of minerals from India and Brazil has increased by 30 times in the last decade. With respect to fossil fuels from Russia, China's imports has increased by 8 times; and similarly, with respect to precious metals and oil products, the import by China has seen an unprecedented rise. Lu et al (2011) point out that BRICS organisation as a whole has reflected the collective power of the emerging economies, and given the post financial crisis, this group as a whole is in a better position to bargain for a reformed international structure.

Fig. 6.2: Trend of GDP Indicators from 1971 to 2009 of China vis-à-vis Other Countries

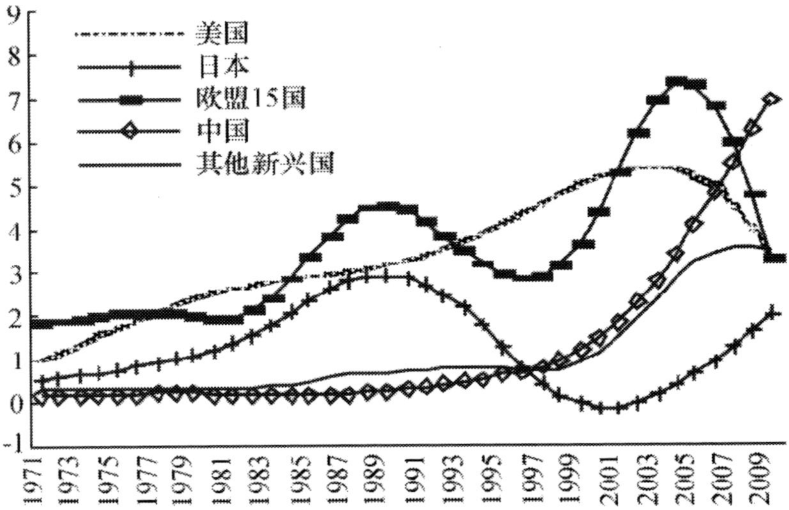

Notes: Unit one hundred billion US Dollars
Source: Lu et al (2011)
(Line 1: United States of America ; Line 2: Japan; Line 3: 15 countries of European Union which include Germany, France, Italy, Spain, England, Ireland, Denmark, Belgium, Switzerland, Greece, Holland, Luxembourg, Portugal, Austria, Finland; Line 4: China; Line 5: emerging economies which include India, Russia, Brazil and South Africa)

The above figure indicates the trend of GDP indicators from 1971 to 2009 and compares China's growth rates to some of the major economies of the world, including the European Union and other emerging economies, which clearly involve other members of the BRICS group. It is seen that the US had a fairly constant rise in its GDP until the turn of the century, while Japan and the EU have both seen fluctuating trends throughout the indicated period. Emerging economies had a stagnating economy until they began to see a trend of gradual rise in their development. The figure above reveals that it is only China which has seen a gradual rise in their GDP. It can be seen that China's GDP has been continuously rising since 1981, when the effects of 'economic reforms' began to become visible. This implies that China has embedded the best of both, domestic policies and international circumstances, and had prepared herself well before she arrived on the international scene. In fact, the above table indicates that by 2009, China's GDP had become the highest in the world, exceeding even traditional economic powerhouses like the US and the EU.

In fact, many Chinese scholars are in favour of cooperation between the BRICS nations, particularly at the financial level, because they feel that emerging economies as a collective group can bring in reforms amongst the international financial institutions. Li[36] is in favour of diversification of international monetary system which, he feels, will provide a broader platform of exchange among developing countries—whose interests in the present scenario are harmed by the 'current internal contradictions' of the international monetary system.

Conclusion

It could be argued that BRICS group is a misnomer to be called a collection of emerging economies. It is, in fact (if viewed holistically), a strategic entity which is 'self sufficient and self reliant' in its own self—and more so in energy terms. It not only has sufficient resources in terms of quality and quantity, but also has a reliant market of producers and consumers of the energy resources. Also, since BRICS incorporates representation from almost all sections of the world, it cannot be doubted that BRICS reflects the aspirations and willingness of the major population of the world. So, a hypothesis can be postulated that BRICS does not need to rely on any Western country; and if the members decide to strengthen the bond between them by opting for preferential treatment of each other, then BRICS could emerge as a single power bloc in this multi-pluralistic world.

However, a fact cannot be discounted that solidarity of BRICS shall face two major issues: first issue is that BRICS nations are a bunch of ambitious nations who aim to restore their lost glory and avenge the wrongs done to them in the historical past. This implies that no member country shall readily accept the domination of another member state, and that solid rivalries shall emerge and be maintained behind all political rhetoric. Case in this point is Sino-Indian rivalry and to some extent Sino-Russian rivalry. On the other hand, most of the BRICS nations have had a long association with the Western countries—whether as colonial rulers or as trade partners of the globalised world. This indicates that member states have stronger bilateral relations with other countries than with each other at bilateral or multilateral level; hence, under any circumstance, it would be hard to obliterate the Western influence and build on an independent BRICS group. Yet, energy issues of BRICS members, both individually and collectively, can influence the future policy course of their foreign policy and determine the course of cooperation for future energy initiatives.

END NOTES

1. This has been taken from Panel Discussion "BRICS and the New Delhi Summit: The Way Ahead" [Online: web] *bricspolicycenter.org/homolog/arquivos/coloquio%20aparajita.ppt* Accessed on 4 August 2016.
2. Ibid.
3. Martynov, Boris (n.a) "BRICs": cooperation perspectives in the international security sphere" [Online: web] http://www.ipea.gov.br/bric/textos/100409_BRICMartynov1.pdf Accessed on 4 August 2016.
4. Ibid.
5. Ibid.
6. *Xinhua News Agency* (2012) "Full Text: China's Energy Policy 2012" [Online: web] http://news.xinhuanet.com/english/china/2012-10/24/c_131927649.htm Accessed on 4 August 2016.
7. *Planning Commission, Government of India* (2014) "Power and Energy" [Online: web] http://planningcommission.nic.in/sectors/index.php?sectors=energy Accessed on 4 August 2016.
8. *Ministry of External Affairs, Government of India* (2009) "Address by Foreign Secretary Shivshankar Menon on BRICs in the New World Order" [Online: web] http://www.mea.gov.in/SpeechesStatements.htm?dtl/1041/Address+by+Foreign+Secretary+Shivshankar+Menon+on+BRICs+in+the+New+World+Order Accessed on 4 August 2016.
9. Ibid.
10. Ibid.
11. Wu, Wendy and Zhou Xin (2016) "BRICS bank readies debut bond issue for clean energy projects" South China Morning Post [Online: web]http://www.scmp.com/news/china/diplomacy-defence/article/1930508/brics-bank-readies-debut-bond-issue-clean-energy Accessed on 4 August 2016.
12. Ibid.
13. Ibid.
14. Eriksen Sundstol Seine et al. (2012) "BRICS, Energy and the New World Order A Study by NUPI for ONS Summit 2012: The Geopolitics of Energy" *Norwegian Institute of International Affairs* 1-36.
15. Panda, Jagannath (2013), "China and IBSA: Possible BRICS Overreach", *Strategic Analysis* 37 (3): 299-304.
16. Eriksen Sundstol Seine et al. (2012), "BRICS, Energy and the New World Order A Study by NUPI for ONS Summit 2012: The Geopolitics of Energy", *Norwegian Institute of International Affairs* 1-36.
17. Zhang, Huiming et. al (2011) "Comparison of Renewable Energy Policy Evolùtion Among the BRICs" *Renewable and Sustainable Energy Reviews* 15 (9): 4904-4909
18. *The Economic Times* (2014) "Five Key Takeways from the BRICS Summit" [Online: web] http://articles.economictimes.indiatimes.com/2014-07-16/news/51600584_1_brics-summit-protectionist-energy-association Accessed on 4 August 2016
19. Eriksen Sundstol Seine et al. (2012) "BRICS, Energy and the New World Order A Study by NUPI for ONS Summit 2012: The Geopolitics of Energy" *Norwegian Institute of International Affairs* 1-36
20. Eriksen Sundstol Seine et al. (2012) "BRICS, Energy and the New World Order A Study by NUPI for ONS Summit 2012: The Geopolitics of Energy" *Norwegian Institute of International Affairs* 1-36

21. **National Statistics Offices of the BRICS* "Energy Statistics" [Online: web] http://www.brics.ibge.gov.br/dados.html?themeID=4&varID=e194ee413805ba5a6aabf4d34db2066149dc0369&theme= Economically%20Active%20Population&variable= Consumption%20of%20energy Accessed on 9 September 2016.
22. Ibid.
23. Eriksen Sundstol Seine et al. (2012) "BRICS, Energy and the New World Order A Study by NUPI for ONS Summit 2012: The Geopolitics of Energy" *Norwegian Institute of International Affairs* 1-36.
24. Ibid.
25. Valizadeh, Akbar and Seyyed Mohammad Houshialsadat (2013) "Iran and the BRICS: The Energy Factor", *Iranian Review of Foreign Affairs* 4(2): 135-164.
26. *Ministry of External Affairs, Government of India* (2014), "Prime Minister's Statement in the 6th BRICS Summit on the Agenda: Sustainable Development and Inclusive Growth" [Online: web] http://pib.nic.in/newsite/PrintRelease.aspx?relid=106696 Date of Access 4 August 2016
27. Ebinger, K. Charles and Govinda Avasarla (2012), "The Energy-Poor BRIC" Op-ed *Brookings* [Online: web] url. https://www.brookings.edu/opinions/the-energy-poor-bric/ Accessed on 4 August 2016
28. Srivastava, Krishna (2014), "Blog Response to Vivek Kumar Singh's "Why is there a need for energy efficiency in BRICS countries?" [Online: web] https://www.researchgate.net/post/Why_is_there_a_need_for_energy_efficiency_in_BRICS_countries Accessed on 4 August 2016
29. Li, Lei (2013), *Jinzhuan Wu Guo Huobi Faxing yu Jingji Fazhan Bijiao yanjiu 金砖五国货币发行与经济发展比较研究 [A Comparative Study of Currency and Economic Development in BRICS Countries]* Master's dissertation Guiyang: Guizhou University of Finance and Economics.
30. Lu, Feng et al (2011) "Jin Zhuan Wu Guo de Hezuo Beijing he Qianjing" "金砖五国"的合作背景和前景 Background and Foreground of Cooperation in BRICS Nations *国际政治研究 International Politics Quarterly* 32 (2):1-21
31. Ibid.
32. Greenpeace (2015), "Laggards and Leaders: the energy transition in BRICS countries" [Online: web]http://www.greenpeace.org/international/Global/international/briefings/climate/COP21/Greenpeace_BRICS_factsheets.pdf Accessed on 27 August 2016
33. Matei Iuliana and Cristina Stamin (2016) "Explaining the Relationship between Energy Consumption and Economic Growth in A Dynamic Panel Model: Are the BRICs Countries Different?" *International Journal of Environment and Agricultural Research* 2(7):183-88
34. Hu, Genhua and Qin Siyi (2012) "Jinzhuan Guojia" Quan Yaosu Nengyuan Xiaolue de Bijiao Yanjiu –Jiyu DEA- Tobit Moxing "金砖国家"全要素能源效率的比较研究——基于 DEA-Tobit 模型 [Comparative Research of Total-Factor Energy Efficiency in BRICS Based on DEA and Tobit Models] *Ziyuan Kexue 资源科学 Resources Science* 34(3):533-40.
35. Cao, Guangxi (2011) "Jinzhuan Si Guo de Tan Paifang, Nengyuan Xiaofei He Jingji Zengzhang "金砖四国"的碳排放、能源消费和经济增长 [Relationship among CO_2 Emissions, Energy Consumption and Economic Growth of BRICS] *Yatai Jingji 亚太经济 Asia-Pacific Economy* 6:18-22.
36. Li, Yonggang (2014) "Jinzhuan Wu Guo Jinrong Hezuo de Xianshi Fenxi ji Celue Xuanze "金砖五国"金融合作的现实分析及策略选择 An analysis of the Situation and Strategies of Financial Cooperation among BRICS" *郑州大学学报 (哲学社会科学版) Journal of Zhengzhou University* 47 (5) 66-70.

7

Cyber Security Issues

Kaushal Kishore

Introduction

Following the footsteps of the United States, North Atlantic Treaty Organisation (NATO), in June 2016, also officially declared cyberspace as the fifth domain of war after land, sea, air and outer space[1]. This has altered the way cyberspace is perceived across the globe, and has also accelerated the cyber arms race. This is the reason why many nations have started investing huge sums of money in this new domain so as to build both offensive as well as defensive capabilities. Apart from this, proper functioning of cyberspace is closely linked to the developments in the field of national economy, society, polity, diplomacy etc. And disruption in the smooth functioning or non-functioning of cyberspace can lead to disruption in the functioning of an entire nation and can also lead to huge loss. It has already been witnessed in Estonia (2007), in Georgia (2008), through 'Stunet' incident in Iran and many other similar incidents.

These incidents have not had a very visible impact on China. China, on the one hand often claims itself as a victim of such cyber-attacks; and on the other hand, she has allegations of being one of the most aggressive nations in cyberspace. China has been blamed time and again for sponsoring cyber-attacks and hacking activities, which was completely denied by the Chinese government. For instance, many terabytes of data related to blueprint of America's most advanced F-35 stealth fighter jet were allegedly stolen by

Chinese hackers[2]. Another revelation came by an American private cyber security firm named Mandiant, which pointed[3] out that Chinese PLA-affiliated unit 61398 located in Shanghai has been responsible for dozens of attacks on foreign companies and governments.

There were many similar allegations against China, which resulted in evident repercussions on the Sino-US relations. For e.g., five PLA officers were indicted on the charge of cyber espionage. Another example is when the US was also ready to impose economic sanctions if China failed to stop carrying out economic cyber espionage against the US. This kind of reaction by the US clearly shows the kind of decisive role cyber issues have started playing in international relations. Hence, China was confronted with the US pressure to discuss the cyber issues in Sunnyland Summit of July 2013; however, nothing substantial was achieved in the Summit due to Snowden's revelations and the US was pushed on the back foot. In September 2015, China signed a 'Sino-US Cyber Deal' with the US. After the 2015 'Cyber Deal', China has been trying to portray itself as a responsible stakeholder in global cyber governance mechanism. These messages were heard loud and clear when in December 2015 at the Second World Internet Conference, Chinese President Xi Jinping expressed[4] that China with its 650 million Internet users should have a say in drawing up the global rules, and that they should include the right to decide what to censor and block. China, being the second largest economy, will play a crucial role in shaping up the global governance mechanism for cyberspace. Therefore, it is imperative to analyse Chinese views and perceptions regarding the same.

Also, many nations have released their National Cyber Security Strategy, which reflects the kind of priorities that are being given to cyber security. According to one study[5], over 20 states had released a National Cyber Security Strategy (NCSS) or National Information Security Strategy (NISS). Another study[6] claims that more than 50 nations have published some form of cyber-strategy defining what security means to their future national and economic security initiatives. According to NATO database[7], around 65 nations and nation groups (like EU, AU etc.) have published their NCSS. Unfortunately, People's Republic of China is not there in the list. However, she has already published a white paper on Internet titled The Internet in China on June 8, 2010, which serves as one of the official policy documents. Also, in 2014, Chinese President Xi Jinping, at first session of Central Network Security and Informatisation Leading Group (CNSILG), emphasised[8], "No informatisation, no modernisation, no cybersecurity and no national security." This statement itself expresses the kind of priority given to cyber security in

China; however, not much is known about the Chinese concept of 'cybersecurity'. What constitutes China's cybersecurity?; is it different from Western perception?; If yes, then how?; are there any commonalities between them or not? This article explores these issues, and also tries to study the position of BRICS nations on this issue: whether they support China's views or not; whether they contest the issue or co-operate et al.

The Chinese Discourse on Security

You Ju, a political expert in a military research institute, said, "Every country has its own security needs, and all of them cannot be separated from cooperation with peripheral countries and the path of peaceful development," (People's Daily Online, May 21). China, according to its own security needs, has come up with few security concepts. One of the concepts was "New Security Concept", which appeared in the China's defence white paper published in 1998 titled China's Defence. In the first section titled International Security Situation, China talked about five principles of peaceful co-existence and equated economic security at par with military security. China's new concept of security focuses on enhancing trust through dialogue and promoting security through cooperation. In China's view[9], the core of such new security concept should include mutual trust, mutual benefit, equality and coordination. This concept does not say anything specific on cyber security; however, China's approach to security was outlined.

On May 21, 2014 at the "Conference on Interactions and Confidence Building in Asia", President Jinping strongly advocated and fostered a new framework of Asian security known as "New Asian Security Concept"[10] that includes four core elements: common security, comprehensive security, cooperative security and sustainable security. Among all these, he explained the comprehensive security means[11], "Upholding security in both traditional and non-traditional fields. The challenges brought on by terrorism, transnational crimes, environmental security, cyber security, energy and resource security and major natural disasters are clearly on the rise. Traditional and non-traditional security threats are interwoven. (Security is a growing issue in both scope and implication.)" Hence, according to this concept, cyber security is considered as an emerging issue. Another concept came in the form of "Overall National Security Outlook", which was put forward by President Jinping on April 15, 2014 at the first meeting of National Security Council. Through this security outlook, he talked about security in 11 vital fields: politics, territory, military, economy, culture, society, science and technology, information, ecology, nuclear and natural resources. It includes security in information domain as a national security issue as well.

Chinese Views on Cyber and Related Terminologies

Although the terms 'Cyberspace' and 'Cyber Security' have their origin in the West, some Chinese scholars have studied and traced the history so as to understand when and how the term cyber got associated with the computer, Internet or both. Most of the Chinese authors (like Meng Fansong, Han Yining, Shi Rong, Li Jian, Huang Pengtao, Li Hao, He Minjue etc.) trace the origin of the term cyberspace in a novel named 'Neuromancer (神经漫游者)' written by William Gibson and published in 1984. However, two Chinese scholars, Ding Jianlin (丁建林) and Zhang Yong (张勇), trace the origin of the term 'cyberspace' three years earlier (i.e. in 1981) in another novel titled Burning Chrome by the same Canadian author, William Gibson. They argue that the term was first used in 1981 but became popular in 1984 with publication of Gibson's second novel, Neuromancer, which seems quite possible. Another discourse by a group of Chinese scholars consisting of Sun Zhixin (孙智信), Zhao Zhao (赵炤), Li Zili (李自力) and Shui Chao (水超), in their work[12] titled Conception Analysis and Thought on the Term Cyberspace (2012), traces the origin of cyberspace in William Gibson's work of 1982. Now, which year is the correct year of origin? Wikipedia says Burning Chrome was published in 1982, but that Gibson first read the story at a science fiction convention in Denver, Colorado, in the autumn of 1981. Hence, 1981 can be considered as the year of origin, but if verbal narration is not considered as authentic proof, then 1982 is the year of origin. Sun, Zhao and group went further ahead and looked into the origin of word 'cyber', and how it started being associated to the world of computers. They argue that the word 'cybernetique' had originated from the Greek word, which according to Britannica Encyclopaedia is '*kybernetikos*' (meaning good at steering). They argue that this word was first used by French physicist Andre Marie Ampere in 1834, which roughly translated into 'Science of Governance', but its meaning changed (even the word changed to cybernetics) in 20th century, and its contemporary meaning comes from 'Macy Conference' of 1940s. It is argued that the term cyber was associated with computer in 1970s, when Control Data Company (控制数据公司 CDC), while promoting its super computer products, proposed 'cyber' as a synonym for computer. In their detailed account, they trace the following path, on which the term 'cyber' travelled after its origin to reach its current position.

Fig. 7.1: The Development Process of Cyberspace

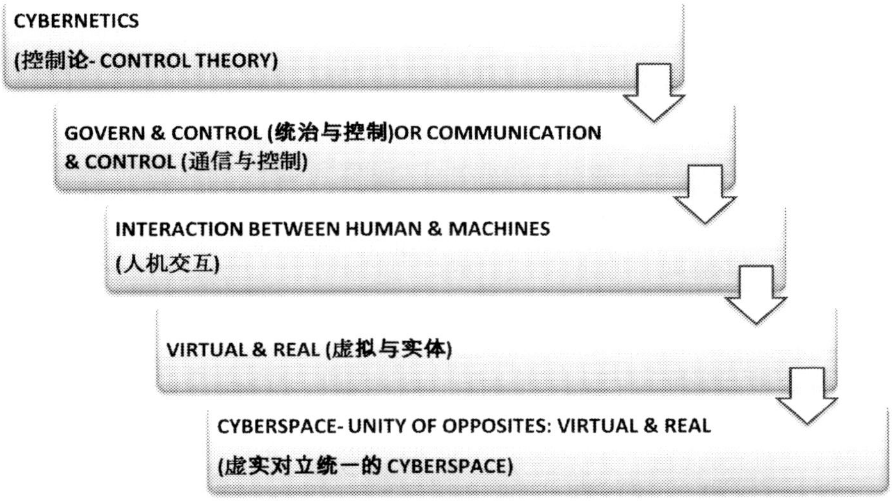

Source: Sun *et al*, Conception Analysis and Thought on the Term Cyberspace (2012, p. 5).

In China's official document, the term 'cyberspace' first appeared in China's Defence White Paper in 2013 under the title of New Situation, New Challenges and New Missions, which acknowledges the changing landscape of conflict and reaffirms the importance being attached to cyberspace. However, it does not talk about cyber security at all. Another Defence White Paper[13] titled China's Military Strategy, published in May 2015, attaches great importance to cyberspace. It says, "Outer space and cyber space have become new commanding heights in strategic competition among all parties."

The form of war is reaching a new stage to informationisation. While talking about making preparation for military struggle, it also emphasises, "In line of evolving war and national security situation, the basic point of preparation for military struggle will be placed on winning informationised local wars. Integrated combat forces will be employed to prevail in system-Vs-system operation featuring information dominance, precision strikes and joint operations." This official discourse does not only recognise cyberspace as a new and critical security domain (other than maritime, outer space and nuclear domain), but also puts forward the strategic task for China "to safeguard China's security and interests in new domains". Under the theme of "Force Development in Critical Security Domains", it mentions:

> Cyberspace has become a new pillar of economic and social development, and a new domain of national security. As international strategic competition in cyberspace has been turning increasingly fiercer, quite a few countries are developing their cyber military forces. Being one of the major victims of hacker attacks, China is confronted with grave security threats to its cyber infrastructure. As cyberspace weighs more in military security, China will expedite the development of a cyber force, and enhance its capabilities of cyberspace situation awareness, cyber defence, support for the country's endeavours in cyberspace and participation in international cyber cooperation so as to stem major cyber crises, ensure national network and information security and maintain national security and social stability.

The White Paper (2015) also does not talk about cyber security directly; however, it clearly shows how cyber security is directly linked to China's military security and national security. None of the White Papers use the term cyber security; however, Chinese versions of the official documents use terms like "Network Security (网络安全)" and "Information Security (信息安全)"; the former is closer to the meaning of cybersecurity. In this regard, Cai, a well-known Chinese scholar from Fudan University working on cyber security, claims, "It is difficult for the word 'cyber security' to achieve complete equivalent in Chinese language, and there is no official definition with respect to the concept of 'cyber security'. Chinese media, policy-makers and researchers are still struggling with conclusive choice of words for cyber security and related terms." Meanwhile, she also asserts that the Chinese term for "Network Security (网络安全)" is often translated as 'cyber security' in English.

In spite of having an equivalent in both languages, the sense that they portray and the area that they focus on are different from each other. This difference is also reflected in the ITU report[14], which while differentiating between information security and cyber security asserts that information security focuses on confidentiality, while cyber security focuses more on integrity and availability. Cai's opinion also accords when she writes, "Network tends to emphasise network hardware and network space, while information is more focused on data information in the network, which is usually referred to as 'content'."

In this context of defining the Chinese equivalents for cyber security, another expert Amy Chang adds, "These definitions support the argument that the Chinese strategy for network security encompasses not only controls and regulation of information and network assets, but also their employment to serve national (i.e., domestic) objectives beyond pure defence or use in warfare." Cai, while differentiating between the Chinese and English version, elaborates, "The term 'Network Security' is mostly a purely technical term. However, 'Cyber Security' now not only includes technology, but also human behaviours as well as relationship between different actors. It not only refers to the security of network hardware, network information and cyber security software, but also indicates the orderliness of human activities in the cyberspace society." Therefore, humans are an inseparable part of cyberspace, which is often ignored whenever composition of cyberspace is perceived or talked about. In recent years, in academic publications, transliterated term of 'Cyber Security' i.e. (赛博安全 saiboanquan) 'Saibo Security' is also used; however; the way they are perceived the two languages are still different not just because different terms having different implications are used, but also due to the fact that both the nations have completely different domestic conditions, including political, social structures etc.

Concerns about Cyberspace

China's perception of cyber security is shaped by factors like China's concerns, interests, threat perception etc. in or through cyberspace. She has her own distinct and unique concerns in cyberspace, both at the domestic as well as at the international level. One of the grave concerns China has is the US behaviour as a hegemon in cyberspace. Chinese President Xi Jinping, in the second World Internet Conference, said[15] that no country should pursue "cyber hegemony" or engage in activities that undermine others' national security. He also emphasised, "There should be no unilateralism, and decisions should not be made with one party calling the shots or only a few parties discussing among themselves."

Fang Binxing, generally credited as the architect of the Great Firewall, argued[16] that American hosting companies currently control the Internet and those companies are in turn controlled by the US government. Severine Arsene, who has studied Chinese authors' opinions, claims that Chinese authors view the current Internet order as an anarchic or disorderly space where global hegemons reproduce their domination over the world in the digital age. The author also concludes that there is, as yet, little belief in the notion of Internet as a global common good among mainstream academic views of the Internet in China. And that is the reason why China always emphasises the crucial role of sovereign nation. Another important concern for China is American control over core cyberspace technologies.

Dong Niao, a well-known Chinese author on cyber issues, writes[17], "In the field of core cyberspace technologies, the US, having best reserve of talents and huge financial support, is far ahead of any other nation." He further elaborates, "Ranging from optical fibre to personal computer, from router to operating system, from core electronic component to basic software, the US controls most of the core technologies." All these core technologies are controlled by American companies; for e.g., Microsoft in the field of operating system; Intel in Central Processing Unit (CPU); Cisco in modem; Seagate in hard disc etc. Also, the US Federal Bureau of Investigation and the Pentagon continue to insist[18] that Silicon Valley's global companies have a first loyalty to American interests, whether in opening their systems to law enforcement or devoting their talents to developing new weapons. These companies have monopoly in their field, and China views it as a threat—especially after the PRISM incident, as the US had used such American companies for its own benefit, can use it again anytime in the future and might not be exposed every time.

In this context, Xi Jinping advocated[19] a global governance system to "curb the abuse of information technology and oppose network surveillance". Another related concern for China, as Dong Niao[20] points out, is the American domination over root servers, Domain Name System (DNS), distribution of IP address through organisations like Internet Corporation for Assigned Names and Numbers (ICANN) etc. Even the location of main root servers and their control is in the hands of the US. He even argues to this extent that most of the top servers are controlled by the US and if the US shuts these servers down once, the Internet will turn into "a pipeline without water". One more Chinese concern pointed out by Dong Niao is the US' development of 'Kill Switch', which will empower the US President to switch off the Internet whenever required. This was proposed by the US Senate in a 55 page law on April 1, 2009 (p. 13).

Another crucial concern, not just for China but also for many other nations, is the weaponisation of cyberspace—especially after the 'Stuxnet' incident. President Jinping, at Second WIC, also emphasised[21] on fighting against cyberspace arms race. Although it is a common concern for many nations; however, instead of fighting against it, each one is busy in developing its own offensive and defensive capabilities as there is no legal restriction on it, and no nation wants to take risk till the legal framework is agreed upon and put into effect. In this regard, China has taken a responsible position by claiming, "No First Use" of "Cyber Weapons" (Li Zhang), which means China might be developing cyber weapons but will use it only if she is attacked.

Apart from these international concerns about cyberspace, there are several domestic concerns for China, which shapes her behaviour and foreign policy posture in the international cyberspace. Amy[22] also agrees that China's foreign policy behaviour, including its cyber activities, is driven primarily by the domestic political imperative. One of the most important is the threat of 'Arab Spring' replicating in China and challenging the Chinese Communist Party (CPC) regime, and thereby undermining the political, social and economic stability. This concern echoed in Chinese media[23]—"Although most developing nations have a pressing need for ICT, they are still not mature enough to keep up with the rate of ICT evolution. So developing countries urge the rights for government to intervene in cyberspace to prevent government failure, economic dependence, social chaos, and even culture erosion". Dong Niao also expresses this concern through a Chinese saying, "The water that carries the boat is the same that swallows it (载舟之水足以覆舟)". What he means is that if the water (i.e. cyberspace) is handled properly, the boat (i.e. the CPC regime) can survive; if not, the water can swallow the boat.

The Communist Party leadership also sees[24] the promotion of Western-style practices, such as multi-party elections or an independent judiciary, as designed to undermine their rule through a creeping peaceful evolution that will inexorably result in turmoil. China was also afraid of 'Colour Revolutions' to such an extent that by the end of 2005, she had decided not to allow foreign newspapers to print their editions in China. It was decided by the head of the General Administration of Press and Publication, who explained[25]: "When I think of the 'Colour Revolutions,' I feel afraid... The Colour Revolutions were a reminder not to let saboteurs into the house." This is also the key reason why Internet in China is kept under censorship. Even President Jinping himself justifies this by stating[26] that there needs to be a proper balance in "freedom" and "order", and that "freedom is the end of order and order the guarantee of freedom". Even Western experts have similar opinion in this regard. Scott Malcomson, a former senior advisor to United Nations and International Crisis Group, argues[27], "The key point is that Internet restrictions in Russia and China were secondary to the primary effort of keeping Chinese and Russian citizens away from foreign funding, foreign ideas and foreign journalism—these were seen as inspiring serious threats to the social order. In China, the Internet story is very much subordinate to the political story."

China is also worried about its dependence on the US for most of the cyberspace technologies and devices for its domestic use. China wishes to reduce its dependence by putting in huge investments in Research and

Development (R&D), and promoting the vision[28] of building China an innovative nation by 2020; an international leader in innovation by 2030; and of making China a world powerhouse of scientific and technological innovations by 2050.

Strategic Interests and Goals

China's interests in cyberspace have not been articulated through official documents; rather, it has to be understood through China's policies, priorities, behaviour etc. in cyberspace both, at national and international levels. Cai[29] points out that pursuit of political stability can be seen as a core interest of China's current cyber strategy. Another expert Amy Chang[30] also agrees, "China's network security strategy is, just as with its overall strategy, primarily driven by the goal of prolonging the power of the Chinese Communist Party, and domestic concerns maintaining internal stability, curbing social and political unrest and promoting economic growth." The political stability being treated as the prime priority for China was visible during the "Umbrella Movement "of Hong Kong in 2014, in which social media and Internet played an important role. According to one report[31], many suspect the Chinese government of launching Distributed Denial of Service (DDoS) attacks that crippled PopVote—a site designed by University of Hong Kong and Hong Kong Polytechnic University—which was readying its systems for an unofficial referendum on how citizens would choose to directly vote for executive. These attacks were unprecedented in scale and sophistication. It was not only the pro-democracy websites that were targeted but also the social media applications like WhatsApp, Wechat etc. on both Android and iOS devices that were bugged. Another newspaper reported[32], "Cross-Platform attacks that target both iOS and Android devices are rare, and indicate that this may be conducted by a very large organisation or nation state." Through the infected viruses, Chinese government was keeping a close eye and had all the information like identity, location, plans (who were they talking to, chatting to, sending messages to, where and whom were they meeting) etc. of the organising body and people involved. Thus, cyberspace also serves as a means of snooping into people's thought processes and action plans, which helps China in staying ahead; and that was probably the reason why the movement could not succeed. And China would probably not allow any future mass movement to succeed either.

Cai Cuihong further states, "China's strategic interests in cyberspace are subject to general economic, social and political security." Amy Chang adds one more field, i.e. military, to Cai's list when he points out, "Beijing's thinking about cybersecurity, and its cybersecurity strategy consists of three main component drivers: economic, political and military." Samson Yuen identifies two domestic priorities for China: 'Content Control' and 'Technological Self Sufficiency'. Samson further elaborates:

> These two strategies are key building blocks in China's conception of cybersecurity, a notion defined by Chinese officials as technologies and processes designed to protect against Internet-based threats to a wide range of domains, including political and ideological integrity, data, technology, applications, businesses and communication channels. These strategies are not only aimed at maintaining regime survival and protecting national security, but are also intended to nurture the domestic economy—particularly the technology industry.

Although it seems these fields are different from each other, they are intertwined in China's case. Economic stability the three decade-long continuous economic development provided legitimacy to the CPC regime, and China will never let this economic stability be disturbed. This is the reason why Yan Xuetong, in his analysis of China's national interest, has identified economic development as the core national interest. If economic stability is disturbed, it will lead to social unrest and people's protest, which finally may threat the stability of CPC regime. And it seems cyber espionage is also one of the Chinese strategic interests as Amy points out, "China attempts to ensure domestic economic growth and maintain domestic firm competitiveness against global rivals in part by conducting cyber economic espionage." However, in September 2015, China signed a "Sino-US Cyber Agreement", according to which China agreed that it will not carry out any cyber economic espionage and intellectual property right (IPR) theft. The deal only includes cyber economic espionage and IPR theft issues; hence, there is absolutely no reason why China would not indulge in other forms of cyber espionage.

Another crucial interest, which is not just a threat to political and social stability but also to China's sovereignty and territorial integrity, is addressing the "Three Forces (三股势力) (Terrorists, Separatists and Extremists)" in cyberspace. On more interest which is also shared by other developing and developed nations is the security of Critical Information Infrastructures (CIIs), which are vital for smooth functioning of any nation. China's new Cyber Security Law, which is expected to pass this year, identifies China's CIIs and lays down the norms for 'Key Information Infrastructure Operators (KIIOs)'[33]. Most of which, these KIIOs are foreign firms as China is highly dependent on foreign technologies. Apart from all these, Cai also categorises what constitutes China's national security threat in cyberspace:

> Any anti-government or anti-social activities through cyberspace, any dissemination of words and deeds destabilising the society, any cyberspace activities inciting ethnic hatred and terrorism, any planning, organisation and implementation of any act of subversion, division or sabotage, any violent separatist terror attacks aimed at China's territorial integrity and political power consolidation through the network, any public opinion attack on information network that could undermine the consolidation of the Chinese regime, the stability of political system as well as unity and harmony of all peoples, along with any other equivalent acts—all fall in the primary category of threats to national security.

On February 27, 2014, President Jinping in his first speech[34] at the Central Network Security and Informatisation Leading Group proposed the goal of becoming a 'Cyberpower' (网络强国). He also emphasised on the need of pulling the human resources and on nurturing world class scientists, military leaders with command over cyber technologies, superior engineers and highly skilled innovations team. He also mentioned that it is easy to find a thousand soldiers, but really difficult to find a good general (千军易得，一将难求). It is quite visible that Jinping's focus for achieving the goal, which has been identified by Cai as strategic goal, was on human factor of the cyberspace. Cai further elaborates that the strategic goal has two aims: one is to hope to become a major power in cyberspace, and another is to improve national power through networks. Cai also outlines what kind of cyber power China wants to become. She says China's alleged 'Cyberpower' does not mean that it will impose its own cyberspace doctrine on others, but that their own cyberspace capabilities should be strong enough to be self-sufficient, without the need to depend on others.

One more component of becoming 'Cyberpower' has been put forward in 2015 White Paper on defence, which emphasises that China must "expedite the development of a cyber-force", and also enhance its capabilities in "cyberspace situation awareness" and cyber defence. China, for the first time, has expressed its intention of building a cyber force and cyber capabilities publicly. This is also echoed in the two lines of work[35] for achieving the goal of 'Cyberpower': Informatisation and Cybersecurity. Jinping also linked this goal with the "Two Centenary Goals" of "China Dream" which he had proposed by the end of 2012. He said that strategic deployment of becoming a Cyberpower should go together with the "Two Centenary Goals", which means it would be completed in two phases: one by the end of 2021 and another by 2049. However, what will be achieved by 2021 and what by 2049 was not specified. Nevertheless, Jinping did put forward a few objectives: strong self-reliant innovative capabilities, overall development of information economy, effective network security assurance et al. For becoming a Cyberpower, Jinping points out that China needs to have its own technology, have rich and overall information services, have prosperously developed network culture, and have highly qualified team for network security and 'informatisation'. President Jinping also stressed on research and development in cyber technologies and having multilateral exchange and cooperation.

Cyber Sovereignty

This term first appeared in the China's White Paper on Internet titled Internet Sovereignty. Chinese President Xi Jinping, in the second World Internet Conference held in Wuzhen, said that the global Internet governance reform needs to be based on a principle of Internet or cyber sovereignty (often used interchangeably). Elaborating the notion of cyber sovereignty, he emphasised[36], "We should respect the rights of individual countries in choosing their own Internet development path, Internet governance and Internet policies, and take part in cyberspace governance on an equal basis; that we must not push cyberspace hegemony or interfere in other countries' internal affairs or engage in or support cyberspace activities that jeopardise the national security of others." China envisions this notion not only as the basis for administering its domestic cyberspace but also as the basis of reforming the global cyberspace governance. China has been attaching great importance to sovereignty in the territorial domain; and for the cyberspace, same principle has been suggested as China considers[37] sovereign equality as one of the basic norms in contemporary international relations enshrined in the Charter of the United Nations, and that is the reason why China wants it to be applicable to cyberspace as well. Shen Yi[38] also pointed out, "It is quite clear that the sovereignty must have a proper position in handling with cybersecurity issues when more and more multi-source attacks have appeared in the cyberspace." Another Chinese scholar Wen Baihua writes[39], "Cyber sovereignty means not only national interests but also national obligation. This makes it possible to cooperate among different countries to deal with common and emerging cyber threats. It is cyber sovereignty that explains why, under logic, China promised to cooperate with the US to fight international cybercrime in 2015." He further elucidates:

> China's principle of cyber sovereignty has caused rising concern in developed countries for fear of absolute cyber sovereignty like state sovereignty. Although cyber sovereignty is rooted in legal aspects of state sovereignty, any single country cannot preserve absolute cyber sovereignty

> alone. The definition of cyber sovereignty is more like a kind of redistribution of interests and power among all stakeholders, including sovereignty states.

Yet another expert Samson Yuen discusses the concept in detail and relates it to China's cybersecurity:

> The concept of "cyber sovereignty" (wangluozhuquan 网络主权) is a principle stipulating that national governments have the right to supervise, regulate and censor online information within their own borders. The concept has become China's foundational policy in promoting the need of national information borders on the diplomatic front, especially in the wake of Edward Snowden's revelations about US cyber espionage on foreign countries, including China. According to government rhetoric, "cyber sovereignty" and "cyber security" are closely-related concepts in China's Internet policy: while "cyber sovereignty" serves as a diplomatic principle on the global arena, "cyber security" concerns the safety of domestic cyberspace. Despite their different orientations, both concepts share the same goal: the need for a state-centric approach to monitoring cyberspace.

Multilateralism and Multi-Stakeholderism

The notion of cyber sovereignty is also reflected in China's vision for global cyber governance. China advocates a 'Multilateral Approach' for governing the international cyberspace, which empowers sovereign nations as the chief governing, law making, and law enforcing and co-ordinating entity. (However the Western approach advocates a 'Multi-Stakeholder' approach which conceptually ensures participation and consultation of each stakeholder.) Lu Wei, the head of Office of the Central Leading Group for Cyberspace Affairs, commonly known as Cyberspace Administration of China (CAC) (wangxinban 网信办), puts forward China's stand[40]:

> With regard to the cyberspace governance, the US advocates "multi-stakeholders" while China believes in "multilateral". "Multi-stakeholder" refers to all Internet participants on an equal footing making the rules, and is considered more "people-centered" while "multilateral" refers to the state making rules based on the idea of the sovereignty of the nation-state representing its citizens.

China's position is often criticised as a 'State-Centric' approach, which does not support the idea of free and open Internet. However, after Snowden's revelations, China got a point to argue that you are no different from us. This difference in approach towards global cyber security and cyber governance always acts as an obstacle in the way of cyber cooperations. However, in recent years, China has softened its position. In an article, Wen Baihua wrote[41], "China advocates (a) cyber sovereignty based on the multi-stakeholder model and (b) cyber governance via the multilateral model. China tries to combine both, the multi-stakeholder model and the multilateral model, not to alternate both models." Even Lu Wei also argues[42], "These two alternatives are not intrinsically contradictory. Without 'multilateral', there would be no 'multi-stakeholders'."

Cooperation and Conflict with BRICS Nations

BRICS nations started attaching importance to cyber security since their 2013 Summit as they collectively, for the first time, mentioned in the Durban declaration (also known as "eThekwini Declaration"), "Wesrecognize the critical positive role the Internet plays globally in promoting economic, social and cultural development. We believe it's important to contribute to and participate in a peaceful, secure and open cyberspace, and we emphasise that security in the use of Information and Communication Technologies (ICTs) through universally accepted norms, standards and practices is of paramount importance." Although the declaration emphasised on the peaceful, secure and open cyberspace; however, it did not talk about how to achieve it. In the next year's Fortaleza Declaration, they reiterated what was said in 2013 Declaration, and it was decided by the National Security Advisors to establish a group of experts of BRICS member states, which will elaborate practical proposals concerning major fields of cooperation and coordinate our positions in international fora. The central role of the United Nations was identified in the cooperation on combating cybercrimes. The Declaration further stated, "We agree it is necessary to preserve ICTs, particularly the Internet, as an instrument of peace and development and to prevent its use as a weapon. Moreover, we commit ourselves to working together in order to identify possibilities of developing joint activities to address common security concerns in the use of ICTs." Thus, prevention from weaponisation of the Internet was agreed upon; however, again, without putting forward any concrete roadmap.

Next Declaration began by reaffirming the general approach set forth in the eThekwini and Fortaleza Declarations on the importance of security in the use of ICTs and the key role of the UN in addressing these issues. This was the most comprehensive declaration from the perspective of cyber security as it addressed many cyber issues, and also put forward some concrete plans to tackle them. One crucial decision was to constitute a BRICS working group on ICT cooperation. Another important agreement was of ensuring human rights and fundamental freedoms, including the right to privacy of the ICT and Internet users. For the governance of international cyberspace, the declaration states:

> We consider that the Internet is a global resource, and that states should participate on an equal footing in its evolution and functioning, taking into account the need to involve relevant stakeholders in their respective roles and responsibilities. We are in favour of an open, non-fragmented and secure Internet. We uphold the roles and responsibilities of national governments in regard to regulation and security of the network. We acknowledge the need to promote, among others, the principles of multilateralism, democracy, transparency and mutual trust, and stand for the development of universally agreed rules of conduct with regard to the network. It is necessary to ensure that the UN plays a facilitating role in setting up international public policies pertaining to the Internet. We support the evolution of the Internet governance ecosystem, which should be based on an open and democratic process, free from the influence of any unilateral considerations.

This agreement talks about both multilateral and multi-stakeholder approaches with an emphasis that nation is also one of the important stakeholders. On the one hand, it supports the Western idea of open, non-fragmented and secure Internet; and on the other hand, it also opposes any unilateral decision referring to the hegemony of the US. Another important consensus of BRICS nations which pointed fingers at the behaviour of the US was the position that we (BRICS nations) reiterate our condemnation of mass electronic surveillance and data collection of individuals all over the world, as well as violation of the sovereignty of states in general, and of human rights in particular, the right to privacy.

They agreed to cooperate on the issue of "cybercrime" and the "use of ICTs for criminal and terrorist purposes" under "the UN auspices". For initiating cooperation, they also identified few areas: "sharing of information and best practices relating to security in the use of ICTs; effective coordination against cybercrime; the establishment of nodal points in member states; intra-BRICS cooperation using the existing Computer Security Incident Response Teams (CSIRT); joint research and development projects; capacity building; and the development of international norms, principles and standards." Cooperation in these areas will be the responsibility of "Working Group of Experts of the BRICS states on security in the use of ICTs". BRICS members have placed high faith in the UN, and they reaffirm the central importance of the principles of international law enshrined in the UN Charter, particularly the political independence, territorial integrity and sovereign equality of states, non-interference in internal affairs of other states and respect for human rights and fundamental freedoms.

BRICS nations are also cooperating on the project of BRICS Cable, an alternative world internet system independent of the US and Britain. The proposed BRICS undersea cable would be a fibre-optic link running from the Brazilian city of Fortaleza, through Africa and Asia, to Vladivostok in Russia (shown in fig. 7.2). The BRICS Cable would span 34,000 km (21,000 miles) and be ready for use by the end of 2015. However, the cable has not been completed, and there no longer appears to be an active discussion about its creation.

Fig. 7.2. BRICS Cable

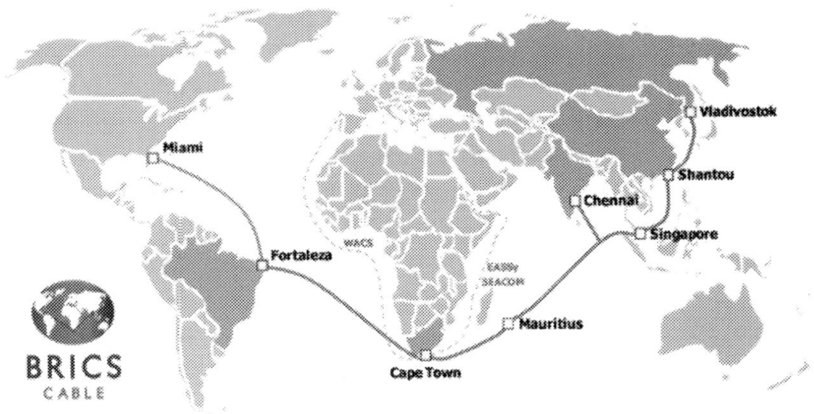

Source: https://jsis.washington.edu/news/reactions-u-s-cybersecurity-policy-bric-undersea-cable/

Apart from all these agreements at this multilateral forum, BRICS nations individually also have their own agreements and disagreements with other member states on cyber issues (and the prime reason behind all these is the US). China has been closely cooperating with Russia on cyber issues, and often comes together to counter the US. Scott Malcomson also argues, "That is what primarily brings China and Russia together is opposition to the US. Russia and China have been making common cause against American hegemony since the 1990s." Hannes and Tim also write[43] that in September 2011, Russia and China mobilised the Shanghai Cooperation Organisation to introduce the 'International Code of Conduct for Information Security' understood as a deliberate attempt to counterbalance US dominance. China and Russia initiated their first cyber agreement[44] in 2009 through the Shanghai Cooperation Organisation, and submitted an updated version of this 'Code of Conduct for Information Security' to the United Nations General Assembly in 2011. By the end of 2014, China and Russia considered signing another agreement[45] which intended to avoid a cyber security incident from getting out-of-hand through measures like creating dedicated hotlines between national authorities. The agreement would enable the two countries to work on joint projects and "conduct joint cyber security operations". However, it was signed in 2015, and had two key features[46]: mutual assurance on non-aggression in cyberspace and language advocating cyber sovereignty.

The emphasis in both 'International Code of Conduct for Information Security' and advocacy of 'Cyber Sovereignty' has been given to empowering of sovereign nations for both, domestic control of cyberspace and for global cyber governance. Apart from countering the US, another reason for close cooperation between China and Russia is the kind of government they have and the domestic concerns they share. However, Western experts are skeptical about their relationship in cyberspace cooperation. Scott writes[47], "Sino-Russian cooperation will result in a shared isolation of both countries' citizens from international civil society, international media and the Internet." He further adds that Sino-Russian initiative tries to portray that the initiative is motivated by a desire to protect against extremism, pornography, drug sales etc., but the essence of it was two major nations getting together to compare notes on how to build walls.

China is also cooperating with South Africa at the bilateral level. In June 2015, both the sides signed[48] 'Cyber Security Pact' as a part of a '5-10 Year Strategic Framework on Cooperation Deal', that was first signed in 2014. The pact will focus on nine key areas identified by the respective governments which includes cyber security, R&D in ICT, technology transfer etc. Other than these bilateral agreements, China also gets the support from other multilateral groups of developing countries. One such group where some of the BRICS member states are present is IBSA. Through the joint statement of 2010, IBSA also expressed concern over ICANN's legal status and the US hegemony in governing cyberspace, which is similar to China's concern:

> A central issue in Internet governance is the management of Critical Internet Resources. Although there is a positive movement towards improving transparency and accountability in the activities of the ICANN, its legal status remains problematic. The fact that only one country, instead of the international community of states, is the provider and guarantor of

> the management of names and numbers of the Internet in all countries contravenes established UN principles and universally accepted tenets of multilateralism.

Hence, nations like Brazil, India and South Africa are also referred to as "Swing States"[49]; as they, on the one hand, support multi-stakeholder approach advocated by the US but on the other hand, come together to counter the US due to their common concerns. They have also been referred as "Moderator States" as Brazil, in 2014-15, while chairing[50] the United Nations Group of Governmental Experts, tried to reconcile the gap between both camps' views on appropriate cyber norms. The same happened at the Internet Corporation for Assigned Names and Numbers and the United Nations General Assembly, where Brazil consistently argued that multilateral and multi-stakeholder approaches to Internet governance are not mutually exclusive, and can coexist. The position of India and Brazil was not well articulated, and has also shifted with time. In India's case, Mahima writes[51]:

> India's stand has varied in language, but the sentiment has indicated that it is not comfortable with the current Western-dominated structure of Internet governance, especially given the fact that the West seeks to encourage commercial interests by keeping the Internet a free trade zone; while developing countries like India are still struggling with baser questions of access and inclusion. Therefore, India is keen to retain a system that is government-led and not market-led.

She also asserts that it would also be fair to say that members of the BRICS grouping are also in the same boat as India—they do not align themselves completely with the multi-stakeholder Internet governance structures the West promotes. However, on June 22, 2015, Indian minister of Communications and Information Technology Ravi Shankar Prasad announced[52] India's support for the "multi-stakeholder model" of Internet governance during the opening ceremony of ICANN's 53rd public meeting in Buenos Aires. In case of Brazil, which was infuriated by Snowden's revelation, Brazilian President Dilma Rousseff also cancelled her state visit to the US, unexpectedly moved closer to the US. Brazil moving away[53] from its former position of 2012, in which the country had joined China and Russia to call for a government-led Internet, squarely putting its weight behind the multi-stakeholder system.

These shifts in position, which also earned them the nickname "Swing State", are also attributed to their domestic political structure—which also seems to be one of diving lines between BRICS nations. The democratic nations, due to pressure from civil societies and other stakeholders, have changed their positions—which is not visible in case of non-democratic governments. Nevertheless, India and Brazil have clearly stated their position that they support 'Multi-Stakeholder' approach. However, in joint statements and agreements with China and Russia, they have also used the term multilateralism for cyberspace governance. In April 2016, Russia, India and China, in their Foreign Ministers' meet, agreed[54] on the need to ensure Internet governance based on multilateralism, democracy and transparency with multi-stakeholders in their respective roles and responsibilities."

Conclusion

It is evident that China started participating in international cyber security mechanism and started taking official stand only after she was confronted with the US pressure in Sunnyland Summit of July 2013. This Summit served as a wake-up call for China, and compelled her to behave responsibly in the field of cyberspace. Before the Summit, China used to take advantage of: the non-existing legal framework for cyberspace; existing loopholes in international laws applicable to cyberspace; and the related ambiguities. China allegedly quite frequently used to indulge in cyber attack and cyber espionage activities. Since spying is not illegal according to the international law, China did nothing illegal when it carried out cyber espionage activities for whatsoever purpose. However, it was only the economic cyber espionage and IPR theft concerns of the US that lead to 2015 'Sino-US Cyber Agreement'. Still, cyber espionage other than IPR theft-related and economic espionage will keep on taking place. The exposure of classified PRISM surveillance programme also gave China the point to argue that the US should not only point fingers at others, but must also watch its own behaviour. All these international incidents along with epoch-changing episode of 'Stuxnet' compelled China to broaden its concept of security in order to accommodate new and emerging threats from cyberspace. They also compelled China to identify her own concerns and threats in cyberspace, and based on that, China outlines its cyber security vision, strategies and goals. Due to its distinct domestic situation, China has its distinct concerns in cyberspace—out of which, political stability remains the most important. That is why Internet content is highly controlled by China and the "Great Firewall" has also been put into use. Owing to these typical concerns, China's perception of cyber security is slightly different from the Western narratives. And hence, China focuses more on authoritative role of sovereign nation as one of the crucial stakeholders. China advocates multi-stakeholder approach for domestic cyber security; however, supports multilateral approach for global cyber governance, which is also visible in the Chinese notion of "Cyber Sovereignty".

China does not seem to and probably will never accept interference of other nations in the domestic cyber governance. However, China's position on global cyber governance seems to have softened recently as talks of multi-stakeholder approach and nonexistence of one without the other have taken place. These two approaches also divide BRICS nations into two blocs, but China has been engaging with other nations including, BRICS member states, at bilateral level so as to garner support and avert international isolation. Softening of China's approach provide an opportunity for BRICS nation to transcend above these approaches and work towards building of an open and robust cyber security framework based on equal participation. However, one factor that BRICS nations really need to work on is the cyberspace technology, which is mainly concentrated in the hands of the US. The BRICS nations' cooperation on the issue of cyber crime has to be expanded; more consensuses on cyber terrorism, Critical Information Infrastructures and other crucial sectors have to be built on. BRICS is also perceived as the only multilateral group which can challenge the domination of the US in cyberspace, and hence, the hope from the upcoming meet in India is quite high. It seems the upcoming BRICS meeting in India would reiterate the earlier agreements, and would also expand cyber agreements both in volume and content.

END NOTES

1. Anna Ferrara, David Inserra, "NATO designate Cyber as Official Domain for Warfare", 29 June 2016, URL -http://dailysignal.com/2016/06/29/nato-designates-cyber-as-official-domain-for-warfare/, accessed on 15 July 2016.
2. Sasha Goldstein, "Chinese Hacker stole F-35 Fighter Jet Blueprint in Pentagon Hack", 20 Jan 2015, URL- http://www.nydailynews.com/news/national/snowden-chinese-hackers-stole-f-35-fighter-jet-blueprints-article-1.2084888, accessed on 30 July 2016.
3. David Cohen, "The Growing Spotlight on China's Cyber Activities", 20 Feb 2013, URL- http://thediplomat.com/2013/02/chinas-cyber-problem/, accessed on 25 July 2016.
4. John Sudworth, "Xi Jinping Calls for Cyber Sovereignty", 16 Dec 2015, URL - http://www.bbc.com/news/world-asia-china-35109453, accessed on 30 July 2016.
5. Eric Luiijf, Kim Besseling, and Patrick De Graaf, 'Nineteen National Cyber Security Strategies,' International Journal of Critical Infrastructures, Alexander Klimburg (Ed.), National Cyber Security Framework Manual, NATO CCD COE Publication, Tallinn 2012.
6. Alexander Klimburg (Ed.), National Cyber Security Framework Manual, NATO CCD COE Publication, Tallinn 2012.
7. https://ccdcoe.org/strategies-policies.html, accessed on 23 July 2016.
8. Xi Jinping's speech at the first meeting of Central Network Security and Informatizaion leading Group, URL- http://www.cac.gov.cn/2014-02/27/c_133148354.htm, accessed on 27 Aug 2016.

9. China's Position on New Security Concept, URL - http://www.china-un.org/eng/xw/t27742.htm, accessed on 13 July 2016.
10. Xi Jinping' Speech "New Asian Security Concept" at Conference on Interaction and Confidence Building Measures in Asia, 21/05/2014, URL - http://www.fmprc.gov.cn/mfa_eng/zxxx_662805/t1159951.shtml#, accessed on 27 July 2016.
11. Xi Jinping' Speech "New Asian Security Concept" at Conference on Interaction and Confidence Building Measures in Asia, 21/05/2014, URL -http://www.fmprc.gov.cn/mfa_eng/zxxx_662805/t1159951.shtml#, accessed on 27 June 2016.
12. Sun *et al*, "Conception Analysis and Thought on the Term Cyberspace", 2012.
13. China's White Paper, "China's Military Strategy" published in May 2015, URL- http://english.gov.cn/archive/white_paper/2015/05/27/content_281475115610833.htm, accessed on 18 July 2016.
14. http://www.itu.int/ITU-D/cyb/cybersecurity/docs/ITUNationalCybersecurityStrategyGuide.pdf, accessed on 20 July 2016.
15. John Sudworth, "Xi Jinping Calls for Cyber Sovereignty", 16 Dec 2015, URL -http://www.bbc.com/news/world-asia-china-35109453, accessed on 31 July 2016.
16. S Scott Malcomson, "How Russia and China are Cooperating to Dismantle America Dominance" URL- http://www.huffingtonpost.com/scott-malcomson/russia-china-internet_b_9841670.html, accessed on 27 June 2016.
17. Dong Niao, "We can't Lose the Cyber War", p. 16, 2010, Hunan People's Publication.
18. Scott Malcomson, "How Russia and China are Cooperating to Dismantle America Dominance" URL- http://www.huffingtonpost.com/scott-malcomson/russia-china-internet_b_9841670.html, accessed on 27 June 2016.
19. http://www.bbc.com/news/world-asia-china-35109453, accessed on 20 June 2016.
20. Dong Niao, "We can't Lose the Cyber War" page -17-18, 2010, Hunan People's Publication.
21. http://www.bbc.com/news/world-asia-china-35109453, accessed on 12 July 2016.
22. Amy Chang, http://www.cnas.org/sites/default/files/publications-pdf/CNAS_WarringState_Chang_report_010615.pdf, accessed on 27 July 2016.
23. http://english.chinamil.com.cn/news-channels/pla-daily-commentary/2016-04/07/content_6996108.htm#, accessed on 19 Aug 2016.
24. http://www.huffingtonpost.com/nathan-gardels/china-color-revolution-west_b_11597202.html, accessed on 04 Aug 2016.
25. http://www.huffingtonpost.com/scott-malcomson/russia-china-internet_b_9841670.html, accessed on 07 July 2016.
26. http://www.ecns.cn/2015/12-17/192751.shtml, accessed on 29 June 2016.
27. http://www.huffingtonpost.com/scott-malcomson/russia-china-internet_b_9841670.html, accessed on 07 July 2016.
28. http://news.xinhuanet.com/english/2016-05/19/c_135372956.htm, accessed on 09 Aug 2016
29. Cai Cuihong, "Cybersecurity in Chinese Context", URL - https://www.swp-berlin.org/fileadmin/contents/projects/BCAS2015_Cai_Cuihong_Web.pdf, accessed on 20 June 2016.
30. Amy Chang, URL- http://www.cnas.org/sites/default/files/publications-pdf/CNAS_WarringState_Chang_report_010615.pdf, accessed on 27 July 2016.
31. http://motherboard.vice.com/read/inside-the-unending-cyber-siege-of-hong-kong, accessed on 06 July 2016.
32. http://thediplomat.com/2014/10/chinas-cyber-war-against-hong-kong-protestors/, accessed on 19 Aug 2016.
33. https://iapp.org/news/a/how-the-cyber-security-law-of-china-is-about-to-change-things/, accessed on 08 July 2016.

34. Xi Jinping's speech at the first meeting of Central Network Security and Informatizaion leading Group, URL- http://www.cac.gov.cn/2014-02/27/c_133148354.htm, accessed on 27 Aug 2016.
35. Cai Cuihong, "Cybersecurity in Chinese Context", URL - https://www.swp-berlin.org/fileadmin/contents/projects/BCAS2015_Cai_Cuihong_Web.pdf, accessed on 20 June 2016.
36. http://www.ecns.cn/2015/12-17/192751.shtml, accessed on 24 Aug 2016.
37. http://www.chinadaily.com.cn/business/tech/2015-12/16/content_22728202.htm, accessed on 28 July 2016.
38. http://link.springer.com/article/10.1007/s41111-016-0002-6, accessed on 07 July 2016.
39. http://english.chinamil.com.cn/news-channels/pla-daily-commentary/2016-04/07/content_6996108.htm#, accessed on 11 July 2016.
40. http://www.huffingtonpost.com/lu-wei/china-cyber-sovereignty_b_6324060.html#, accessed on 07 Aug 2016.
41. http://english.chinamil.com.cn/news-channels/pla-daily-commentary/2016-04/07/content_6996108.htm#, accessed on 24 July 2016.
42. http://www.huffingtonpost.com/lu-wei/china-cyber-sovereignty_b_6324060.html#, accessed on 07 Aug 2016.
43. http://jia.sipa.columbia.edu/online-articles/cyberspace-rise-brics/, accessed on 19 July 2016.
44. http://blogs.cfr.org/cyber/2016/06/30/despite-cyber-agreements-russia-and-china-are-not-as-close-as-you-think/, accessed on 07 July 2016.
45. http://www.computing.co.uk/ctg/news/2377766/russia-and-china-to-sign-cyber-security-treaty-in-november, accessed on 27 Aug 2016.
46. https://jsis.washington.edu/news/china-russia-cybersecurity-cooperation-working-towards-cyber-sovereignty/, accessed on 18 July 2016.
47. http://www.huffingtonpost.com/scott-malcomson/russia-china-internet_b_9841670.html, accessed on 07 July 2016.
48. Charlie Fripp, Here are the details of SA's ICT deal with China, 11 June 2015, URL- http://www.htxt.co.za/2015/06/11/here-are-the-details-of-sas-ict-deal-with-china/, accessed on
49. http://jia.sipa.columbia.edu/online-articles/cyberspace-rise-brics/
50. *Alex Grigsby, Do India and Brasil really moderate China and Russia's Approach to Cyberspace Policy?*, Aril 26, 2016, URL - http://blogs.cfr.org/cyber/2016/04/26/do-india-and-brazil-really-moderate-china-and-russias-approach-to-cyberspace-policy/, accessed on 23 Aug 2016
51. Kaul Mahima, "Lessons from BRICS: Developing an Indian Strategy on Global Internet Governance", 06 Sep 2014, URL- http://cyfy.org/lessons-from-brics-developing-an-indian-strategy-on-global-internet-governance/, accessed on 17/Aug/2016
52. https://www.icann.org/resources/press-material/release-2015-06-22-en
53. Kaul Mahima, "Lessons from BRICS: Developing an Indian Strategy on Global Internet Governance", 06 Sep 2014, URL- http://cyfy.org/lessons-from-brics-developing-an-indian-strategy-on-global-internet-governance/, accessed on 17 Aug 2016.
54. Joint Communiqué of the 14th Meeting of the Foreign Ministers of the Russian Federation, the Republic of India and the People's Republic of China, URL - http://www.mea.gov.in/bilateral-documents.htm?dtl/26628/Joint+Communiqu+of+the+14th+Meeting+of+the+Foreign+ Ministers+of+the+Russian+Federation+the+Republic+of+India+and+the+Peoples+Republic+of+China, accessed on 18 Aug 2016.

PART II
BILATERAL RELATIONS

8

China-Brazil Bonhomie

Shaheli Das

As a formal group, BRICS (Brazil, Russia, India, China and South Africa) has markedly matured from being merely a dialogue mechanism at the time of inception to a cooperation mechanism today. Over time, the body has evolved into a locomotive of global economic recovery that has altered the configuration of international economic growth, which was previously reliant on the steam of the United States (US) and the European economies.[1] Commonly defined as a club of the leading developing countries, the BRICS nations have fundamentally trailed the path of established powers in terms of pursuing their national interests.

Despite effective strategies of the West to preserve its power, the status quo of the international order is gradually evolving to accommodate China as a great power. Like China, the other rising powers principally acknowledge the liberal features of the prevailing global order, and are likely to uphold them. However, they may bid to modify the hierarchy in which the system is embedded.[2] In this context, the BRICS holds critical importance in the 21st century.

Essentially, the BRICS group underscores reform of the existing international economic order in a fair, just and rational direction. They prioritise the following matters in their agenda: (a) consolidating representation and the voice of the emerging nations in the international economic order; (b) instituting a predictable, stable and pluralistic international monetary system; and (c) firm resistance to trade protectionism.[3] With these objectives in place, China—as a great power and a developing nation—has been a proactive member of the group.

It maybe affirmed that China's deeper engagement with the group will, in due course of time, enable the country's leadership to develop a discourse—enunciating the interests of the developing nations—to draw the contours of the evolving international institutional framework. Further, articulating the concerns of the emerging powers would enable the country to cultivate and magnify its influence in the prevailing international institutional framework as well. In this context, BRICS must undoubtedly be considered a significant platform. It must be reiterated that China, Brazil as well as the other emerging powers have established new institutions; such as the BRICS-led New Development Bank (NDB), not to revamp or fundamentally amend the global norms but to institutionalise their newfound power. As for Brazil, inadequate infrastructure has been the chief cause behind the country's low productivity, insufficient domestic market integration, languishing export performance and weak growth potential.[4] Thus, the NDB is of critical importance in terms of channelling funds for sustainable and infrastructure development projects, thereby narrowing the infrastructure gap in the country.

Precipitating from the international financial crisis in 2008, the BRICS represented a realignment of power in the global order. To add to it, the institution of the body demonstrated China's bilateral ties with the developing world in general, and its relationship with Brazil in particular. Robust bilateral ties with Brazil have always been a focal point of China's "South-South" strategy.

Brazil is the largest developing nation in the Western hemisphere, and China is the largest developing country in the world. Both the powers identify themselves as developing nations, and are pivotal states in their own right. After three successive decades of economic reform, China may be termed as a quasi-super power. As the second-largest economy of the world with an expeditiously modernising military, Beijing is undeniably a force to reckon with. Brazil, on the other hand, is not precisely in the league of the People's Republic of China (PRC). It is the 10th largest economy in the world, but comprises a modern industrial complex and substantial resources.[5] While China, at present, is in the course of amending its foreign policy in order to address issues of global concerns and legitimately promote 'Chinese solutions', Brazil is a 'peaceful rising power' that seeks to obtain the status of a rising great power from Latin America[6] Given their respective powers and the complementarity of interests, China and Brazil have been attracted towards each other at the BRICS platform.

Further, based on their bonhomie at the BRICS grouping, these two nations have cooperated at several international forums as well. They have converged on identical decisions to promote the interest of the developing nations as well as to tender support to each other at such platforms. Brazil has repeatedly endorsed the one-China policy, supported Beijing on the question of Tibet and has asserted its denial to recognise Dalai Lama as a political representative.[7] Thus, Beijing first resumed its core national interest in its relations with Brazil as a pre-condition for multilateral engagement. It is, however, not clear if China had accepted Brazil's core national interests.

The BRICS grouping is one of the strongest brands of the new world order. Interestingly, the group is distinctly diverse in nature. However, it is the political and the economic complementarity of the member states that has triggered its rise at the international stage. After seven annual summits, a decisive pattern of a South-South alliance has surfaced in the group. Although BRICS has, today, gained recognition as a multilateral organisation, there are bilateral and trilateral relationships within the group.[8]

It is in this context that the chapter analyses China's bilateral engagements with Brazil at this multilateral platform. It addresses the following questions: why is the BRICS important to China? Why is China interested in fostering closer ties with Brazil at the BRICS? What are Brazil's objectives in fostering a flourishing relationship with Beijing? What are the areas of discord between these two developing countries?

Background

Since the end of the Cold War and the collapse of the Soviet Union, it became a challenging task for international relations analysts to predict the dynamics of a unipolar world. Much debate took place in the late 1980s regarding the characterisation of the international structure (*guoji geju*), that was considered to be bipolar during the Cold War era. Contrary to the anticipation of the Chinese leaders, a multipolar world failed to emerge in the post-Cold War scenario. By the end of the 1990s, the Chinese strategists advocated that although multipolarity had been the trend, the new world order would constitute of 'one superpower and several major powers' (*yichaoduoqiang*).

In the 21st century, the US continues to be the sole superpower. Yet the global financial crisis of 2008-2009 and the global war on terrorism did dwindle its predominance to a considerable extent. Above all, the global financial crisis had questioned the international financial architecture piloted by the US.[9] However, Chinese analysts consider it too early to reckon the US to be on the path of decline, but they do acknowledge the "newly emerging powers" (*xinxing daguo*) as a formidable force in international politics. Thus, the BRICS grouping—essentially constituted of rising powers—is of special significance to China. At present, the BRICS constitutes 43 per cent of the world population, 37 per cent of the world GDP and 17 per cent of world trade.[10] Further, it is interesting to note that two BRICS nations are P-5 members of the United Nations Security Council, one is a G-8 member, and the others are participants in the Outreach Five.[11]

The 18th Congress of Chinese Communist Party (CCP) had identified the BRICS group as an important multilateral forum for China. The fact that the group consists of developing nations makes it critically important to Beijing. Since the time of its inception, the PRC has considered fostering ties with the developing nations as a cornerstone of its overall foreign policy. Two key factors have contributed to such relations: First, Beijing and a majority of the developing nations share similar or identical history. As Premier Zhou Enlai had stated at the first Asia-African Conference held at Bandung in 1955: "most of the countries of Asia and Africa, in varying degrees, have been subjected to colonial plunder and oppression; and, have thus, been forced to remain in a stagnant state of poverty and backwardness. Suffering from the same cause and struggling for the same aim, we Asian and African peoples have found it easier to understand each other, and have long had deep sympathy and concern for one another." This has been one of the chief rationales behind China's policy towards the developing nations. Second, as a socialist nation with Marxism as its guideline, Beijing argues that it adheres to the principle of blending patriotism and Marxist internationalism in its foreign policy. This denotes that China ascertains its position on international affairs based on the merit of each case, and in keeping with the fundamental interests of the people of PRC and the world as a whole. In fostering its ties with the developing nations, Beijing argues that it has always championed its obligation to endorse the righteous struggle of the beleaguered nations, and the necessity to preserve their national independence and ambition to advance their national interests.[12] Given these principles that are deeply embedded in the Chinese foreign policy, the BRICS group serves as a stage where China could fulfil its long-coveted dream of projecting itself as the leader of the "Third World".

According to ambassador Zhang Jun, director general of the Department of International Economic Affairs and China's Sous-Sherpa for BRICS Affairs, the BRICS is a "new paradigm of inter-governmental cooperation featuring openness, inclusiveness and common development".[13] It is a mechanism that has successfully preserved world peace through constructive approaches, and shared positions on key international issues such as counter-terrorism, issues in Ukraine and Syria; boosting global partnership in areas such as sustainable development; poverty alleviation; energy security and climate change; upgrading global economic governance by bracing the multilateral trading system; offering a thrust to issues of governance reform and International Monetary Fund (IMF) quota; collaborating with non-members to ensure common prosperity; and finally, ensuring an intra-BRICS cooperation.[14]

To China, apart from curtailing its dependence on the US and perhaps, to some extent, constricting the unilateralism of the latter, the BRICS has several other fruitful roles to play. Being a constituent member of the group, China has been able to consolidate its identity as a developing nation, preserve its international environment and, above all, coordinate with other BRICS members to maximise its leverage. Ensuring a peaceful international environment is critical to Beijing's rise, as the country now seeks to establish itself as a major power asserting immense influence on the international community. Chinese analysts such as professor Cao Heping of Peking University hopes that the BRICS would be "similar to the World Trade Organisation only on a smaller scale, and it will aim to resolve trade and commercial disputes" and that "it can also act as an administrative body if a Free Trade Zone is established under a BRICS mechanism".[15]

Given the fact that China has a sizeable population and is confronted with several challenges, it cannot be invalidated that the country invests a lot of its resources into the enhancement of the social security net, poverty alleviation and improvement of the industrial structure. However, it is true that Beijing continues to enjoy only a limited influence in the global decision-making process. Thus, in order to enhance its clout in the international sphere, China prefers to work within the BRICS framework because the members of the group share analogous interests. Indeed, contradiction of interest amongst member nations is an existing reality; however, resolution of such issues through cooperation in international forums would aid in containing the conflicts better. Further, the Chinese leaders consider that all BRICS members stand at a similar stage of development—engrossed in raising the standard of living of their people and in the process of industrialisation. Therefore, a 'coalition of interests' does exist in the group.[16]

Trade liberalisation and international financial interdependence are the fundamental trends of the 21st century. The world has also witnessed a shift in Beijing's foreign policy strategy from a marked decline in the country's use of force or military power to resolve international disputes to its reliance on soft power. Through China's cultivation of soft power and the country's dynamic engagement with the BRICS, the Chinese leadership endeavours to diminish the 'China threat' theory and construct a harmonious world order. Such engagements would not only strengthen China's status, but also promote its commercial ties with other nations in the evolving international institutional framework.

Bilateral Comparison

Essentially, BRICS is a group that represents the developing nations of the world. The yardstick to qualify as an emerging nation is a country with a large population and territory. The chart below indicates the share of the BRICS nations in the world territory:

Fig. 8.1: Share of BRICS Countries in the World Territory, 2013 [%]

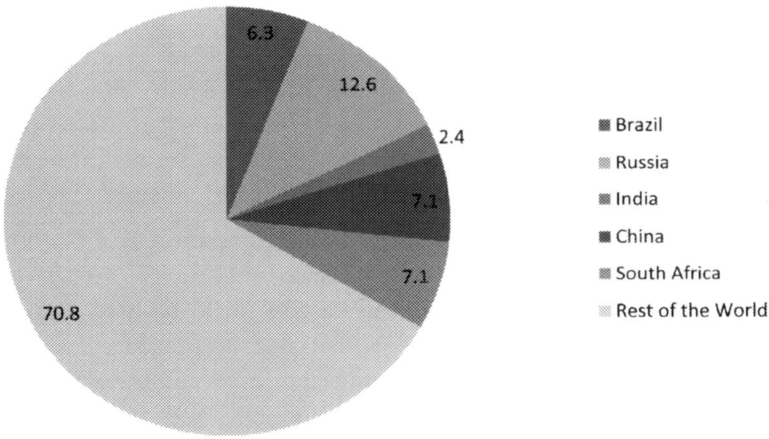

Source: BRICS Joint Statistical Publication 2015.

This calls for a bilateral comparison between China and Brazil. With a total area of 8516 sq km, Brazil is the biggest country in South America. China, on the other hand, comprises a total area of 9600 sq km, and is the third largest country in the world. With reference to population, as of 2014, Brazil has a total population of 202.8 million people, whereas China with a population of 1364.3 million people is the most populous nation in the world. Such statistics clearly indicate that both China and Brazil qualify to be termed as emerging powers in the global arena today. The chart below reflects the share of BRICS countries in world population.

Fig. 8.2: Share of BRICS Countries in World Population, 2013 [%]

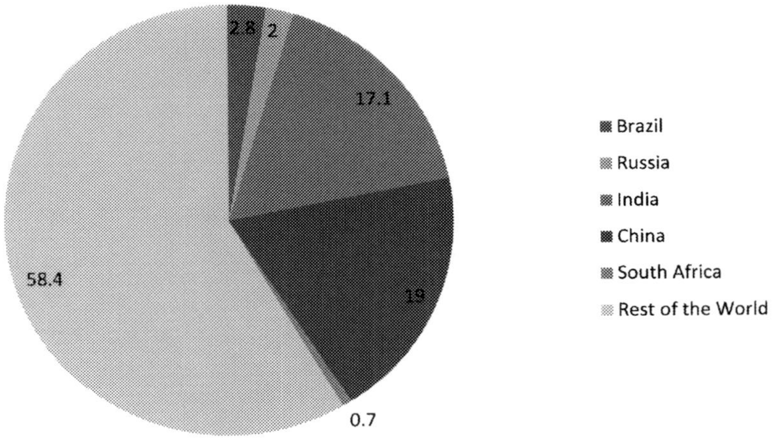

Source: BRICS Joint Statistical Publication 2015.

Interestingly, 65.5 per cent of the population of Brazil is economically active in comparison to 56.5 per cent of the population in China. However, unemployment rates in Brazil and China are 6.1 per cent and 4.1 per cent respectively. Despite a higher number of economically active people in Brazil, there are definitely certain limitations in terms of a gap in the production efficiency, presence of inadequate infrastructure, together with deficiency in education, governance and technological innovation that have contributed to the country lagging behind China. Further, Brazil has an infant mortality rate and maternal mortality rate of 14.4 per cent and 11.3 per cent in comparison to 9.5 per cent and 23.2 per cent in China respectively. However, Brazil has a life expectancy of 75.1 years while China lags behind a little at 74.8 years. These socio-economic indicators decisively reflect the stage of development of the country, and do not emphasise on economic growth alone. In terms of industrial production, Brazil has a total output of 96.7 per cent whereas China has an output of 108.3 per cent.[17] The graph below demonstrates the share of Gross Domestic Product (GDP) allotted by both China and Brazil to the primary, secondary and tertiary sectors of the economy.

Thus, a bilateral comparison between China and Brazil highlights that both the countries are well qualified to be termed as developing nations and ideal members of the BRICS grouping. With the varying degree of investment by the two countries in the different sectors of the economy, they have developed a pattern of complementarity amongst themselves within the framework of the BRICS.

Fig. 8.3: Comparison of Share of GDP Allotted by China and Brazil in Various Sectors of the Economy

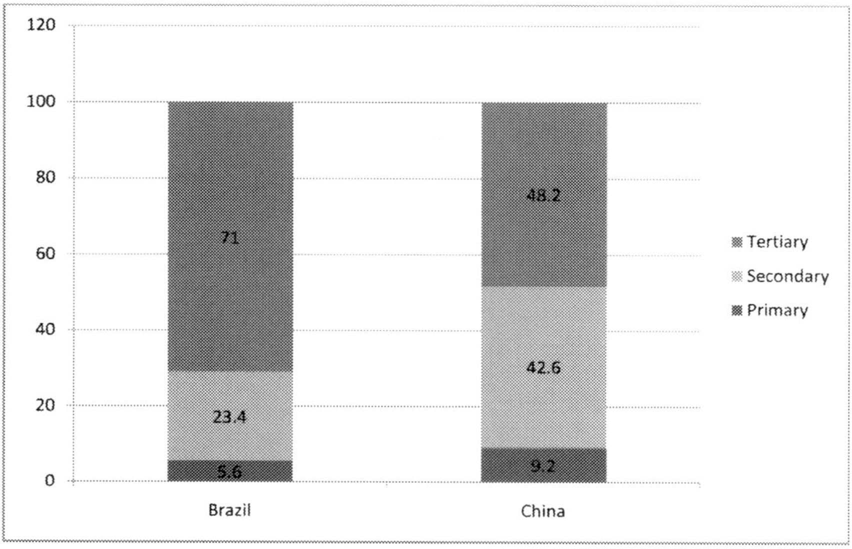

Source: Inspired by BRICS Joint Statistical Publication 2015.

China-Brazil Interactions

The re-emergence of China, over the past three decades, as a significant global economic power has been a major event in international politics. Since the 1980s, China's GDP has increased by more than 9 per cent per year. Over time, China has overtaken Japan to rank as the second largest economy of the world, after United States. Apart from its amplified integration into world trade, China is also growing in terms of its global financial resources. With foreign exchange reserves exceeding US $3 trillion—the highest in the world—the country has emerged as a major outward investor.[18] Brazil, on the other hand, stands out in the BRICS group as one of the least daunting powers in the bloc. It is less populous to both India and China, has a slower growth rate than China, Russia or India and is one of the two powers in the group that does not possess nuclear weapons. Of late, Brazil has gained recognition as a distinguished actor in world politics. Such a phenomenon derives its origin from the inclusion of the country by Goldman Sachs in its study of investment opportunities in "BRICS countries".[19]

China's interaction with Brazil is shaped by a number of interrelated as well as conflicting factors, namely: the Chinese perception of the world and destiny, which is largely derived from the country's national experience and

Communist ideology, long term and short term national interest and resources and domestic condition of the PRC.[20]

Generational leaders from Jiang Zemin and Franco to Cardoso, Lula and Hu Jintao have unswervingly promoted their political will to consolidate bilateral strategic partnership between China and Brazil. The shared identities of being leading regional players and major developing nations with the competence to play foremost roles in international politics has drawn the two countries towards each other at the BRICS platform. Away from constraining or balancing other powers, the Sino-Brazilian strategic partnership is a new kind of partnership in the post-Cold War era that is non-exclusive in nature. The relationship has facilitated both the countries to maintain their pre-eminence in their respective regions.

As BRICS members, both China and Brazil have enticed immense individual attention across the globe. Yet, they consider amplification of their international role through the framework of collaboration with other emerging powers. Apart from BRICS, these two developing nations share membership in several multilateral forums such as BASIC (Brazil, South Africa, India and China) and the G5 (Mexico, Brazil, China, India and South Africa) Summit.[21]

China's association with Brazil is distinctly different from that of the other BRICS members like Russia and India. Geographically, Brazil has been distant from China, sharing no historical conflict, security threats or territorial disputes. In a way, Brazil and India share certain similarities in their major power strategies, striving to improve the bargaining leverage of the developing countries as well as to improve their global economic influence. China's association with Brazil dates back to the early 19th century, when hundreds of tea growers from China were relocated as labourers to Brazil. By the middle of the century, Brazil was keen to import workers from China so as to make up for the dearth of labour, following the practice of slave emancipation in Brazil. The country proposed to establish diplomatic ties with China when it was under the Qing rule. In 1880, the two countries signed a treaty of friendship, pledging the institution of diplomatic ties.[22] However, diplomatic contact was finally established as late as in 1974. In 2004, during President Hu's state visit to Brazil, the relationship was elevated to that of an "all weather strategic partnership". Further, the year 2014 marked the 40th anniversary of Sino-Brazilian diplomatic relations and the 21st anniversary of their strategic alliance. The robust nature of the relationship is qualified by Confucius' celebrated statement, "One should have no more doubts when he is 40".

On the occasion of the 40th anniversary, President Xi had remarked, "Over the past 40 years, the two countries adhere to mutual respect, mutual benefit and win-win results, mutual assistance, and communication and mutual learning. The China-Brazil relations have gained long-term and stable development, and constantly reached new highs. With the political and strategic mutual trust reaching an unprecedented high and the interests being unprecedentedly closely tied, the two countries have become a community of common destiny."[23]

As one of the largest developing countries with an emerging market economy in the Western hemisphere, Brazil was the first country amongst the developing nations to institute strategic alliance with Beijing, and the first Latin American nation to foster a comprehensive strategic partnership with China.[24]

The government-to-government relations between China and Brazil from 1974 till date have principally been governed by three values: equality, win-win cooperation and non-interference. In the BRICS grouping, the two countries have primarily cooperated at three levels. First, they have boosted their strategic collaboration on important international issues, and in dealing with global challenges such as climate change, international financial crisis, and to uphold the interest of the developing nations. Second, both Brazil and China have endeavoured to set up regular mechanisms of exchanges in the fields of science and technology, energy, space, economy and trade. Third, as developing nations, Sino-Brazilian strategic partnership in international politics has generated far-reaching implications.[25]

Brazil, being one of the least imposing members of the BRICS, seeks to engage with China due to a number of reasons. First, Brazil, too, like China patronises the idea of multipolarity as it is key to establishing its status as an emerging power. The establishment of a more just and democratic multipolar world order is a source of idealistic appeal to both small as well as medium-sized developing nations. Second, like India and South Africa, Brazil seeks a permanent membership in the United Nations Security Council (UNSC). Since China is the only P-5 member in the BRICS group possessing a veto power, therefore, Brazil seeks to foster stronger ties with the country. Third, both China and Brazil appreciate the idea of multilateral diplomacy. Moreover, they seek a platform which would enable them to engage in a dialogue with the West on equal terms.

But why does China want to engage with Brazil at BRICS? In 2015, on the sidelines of the 7th BRICS Summit, President Xi Jinping compared the robust Sino-Brazilian ties and expanding strategic influence to a "luxuriant tree". He mentioned, "China is willing to work together with Brazil to cement multi-faceted exchanges, constantly improve economic and trade cooperation, optimise trade structure, facilitate constant and stable growth of bilateral trade, and enhance industrial investment cooperation in sectors such as infrastructure construction, oil and gas, electricity, clean energy, equipment manufacturing, as well as agriculture and cement financial cooperation."[26]

As December Green and Laura Luehmann have aptly mentioned, the prophecy that China would be the next superpower is barely new. In such a case, Russia and India stand to contest China's dominance at the international and regional realms respectively. The accomplishment of such an objective rests on military and economic power. Engagement with Brazil would be advantageous to China in three ways: (a) until recently, Brazil does not possess the capability to contend China on the global platform; (b) Brazil has maintained a fair stature of itself as an economic power (economic collaboration with Brazil is a constructive preference for China); and (c) with regard to the gradual decline of the Monreo doctrine, rising Chinese penetration in the Latin American region, and the fact that Brazil and China are strategic partners—the two powers may stake out positions that are largely unpopular to the West.

On the political front, China anticipates that a constructive relationship with Brazil would, in all likelihood, exert a decisive influence in the Latin American region, facilitating the institution of a China-Latin American Cooperation Forum as well as deepening China's cooperative partnership with the countries of the region. Brazil became increasingly conspicuous for China in the BRICS due to its political and economic features—namely the fact that it is an agricultural powerhouse, possesses enormous resource endowments, constitutes a sizeable domestic market and most importantly, enjoys significant regional influence.

The fact that Brazil shares territorial borders with most countries in South America and is a constituent member of regional alliances such as the Union of South American Nations (UNASUL) and the Southern Common Market (MERCOSUL) certainly makes the country a focal point for China's economic and diplomatic access to Latin America.[28]

In diplomatic terms, China seeks Brazil's support on its "One China Policy", and in its bid for membership to the Inter-American Development Bank (IADB). Brazil, in turn, seeks China's endorsement for a permanent seat in the UNSC.

Fig. 8.4: Brazil comprises of land for forests, agriculture and freshwater resources[27]

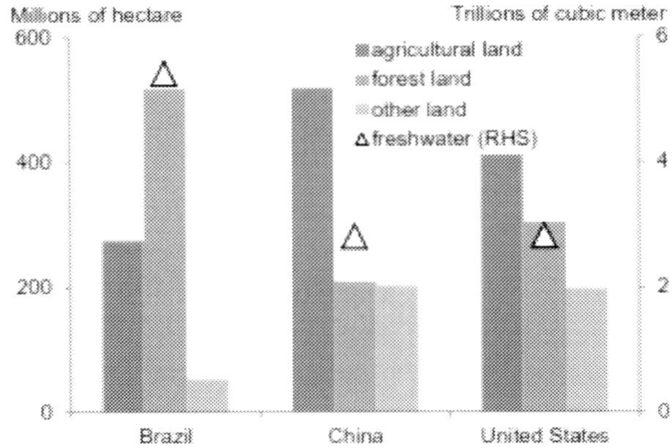

Note: Data for 2011.
Source: FAO; WB staff calculations.

China and Brazil are keen to enunciate regulations within international institutions. The principle objective behind this shared stance is to reform international political and economic institutions, so as to ensure that the developing countries have a greater voice in the decision-making process at these forums. The two countries seek to utilise the BRICS platform to jointly spearhead the transformation of the existing global governance, i.e. reformation of prevailing bodies like the UNSC and International Financial Institutions (IFIs).

With regard to the reformation of the UNSC, China and Brazil stand on different grounds. In an official statement made by the Chinese government on UNSC reform, it is stated, "Priority should be given to address the under-representation of the developing countries. Membership of the Council should not be judged by the benchmark of national wealth. Any formula of reform that discriminates against the developing countries will not work. Measure should also be taken to improve the working method of the Security Council with a view to enhance the efficiency and transparency of the Council's work."[29] In this case, China may be viewed as a status quo power, while Brazil may be deemed as a revisionist power. Since China is already a permanent member at the UNSC, it would seek reasonable reforms so as to preserve the present UNSC framework with a greater representation of the developing world. Brazil, on the other hand, is a revisionist power that has aligned with the G4 nations (Brazil, India, Germany and Japan) and the L69 Group to push its bid for membership in the body.

However, with respect to the reform of International Financial Institutions (IFIs), China and Brazil adhere to a shared stance. China had secured its seat at the executive board of the International Monetary Fund (IMF) in the early 1980s. Beijing has utilised its seat at this Bretton Wood body to principally demand a reform in the board to permit greater number of developing nations as well as emerging market economies at the table. China has frequently called for amendments in the IMF policies that go beyond the neoliberal model that the body presently embraces. The IMF imposes the principles of conditionality on countries that borrow money from it. Most importantly, China's stance on governance reforms comprises justifying the need to diversify the candidate pool used to elect the IMF managing director.[30]

In accordance with its stance to ensure a shift in international institutional power towards the emerging powers, China has depended profoundly on constructing coalitions with other emerging powers and groups such as the BRICS. In line with such an objective, China views Brazil as a significant partner. In fact, in this context, both China and Brazil act as revisionist powers which seek a greater voting share for developing nations at the IMF. In January 2016, the long-pending reforms finally came into effect, whereby the voting rights of China and Brazil were upped to 6 per cent and 2.25 per cent respectively.

The Sino-Brazilian bonhomie that strengthened at the BRICS forum has found resonance in various quarters. A case in point is the occasion when Robert Azevedo from Brazil was appointed the director general of the World Trade Organisation (WTO) in 2013. As the new DG, Robert Azevedo appointed Yi Xiaozhun, Beijing's permanent representative to the Organisation, as one of his four chief deputies[31] Such personnel arrangement clearly demonstrates the degree of cooperation that may be expected in future from China and Brazil in terms of their call for reforms in the WTO.

With regard to the issue of climate change, both China and Brazil acknowledge the fact that cooperation on climate change will accomplish co-benefits in advancing energy security, sustainable development and environment protection.[32] Further, as members of BRICS, they have also synchronised their approach to offset the US objectives at the Climate Change Conference of 2009 in Copenhagen, Denmark. The two countries usually coordinate their efforts through the mechanism of China-Brazil-High-Level Coordination and Cooperation Committee (COSBAN). To add to it, China and Brazil also recognise the importance of enforcing the outcomes of the

Bali Road Map. This would not only raise the pre-2020 ambitions but would also safeguard mutual trust amongst the countries.

Appreciating the China-Brazil Global Partnership, in 2015, the two sides have concluded a joint statement on climate change. Additionally, these two developing countries have consented to further bolster the multilateral process and the high-level bilateral dialogue on domestic climate policies. Both China and Brazil have continuously reiterated their commitment to conclude a comprehensive, balanced, ambitious and equitable agreement under the United Nations Framework Convention on Climate Change (UNFCCC). They have been working closely with other parties, especially the BASIC (Brazil, South America, India, and China) members, to attain this objective through the principles of 'equity, common but differentiated responsibilities and respective capabilities'.

China seeks to offer a full play to the complementary advantages of both the countries in areas such as agriculture, energy, mining and infrastructure construction.[33] For instance, in the field of scientific research, Brazil possesses profuse know-how on agricultural science and technology, whereas China has greater proficiency in industry—a realm in which Brazil has a relatively weaker foundation. Further, China's 13th Five Year Plan (2016-2020) seeks to emphasise on green economy. As US economist Laurence J. Brahm has rightly pointed out to Russia's Sputnik News Agency, "Creating a new 'ecological civilisation' rather than focusing on the GDP growth will become a new priority of the Chinese government toward 2020"[34].

However, although the CCP upholds the objective of instituting a green economy, as much as 80 per cent of Beijing's energy is secured from coal. In fact, the poor quality of air in the country is a clear reflection of China's dependence on coal. Evidently, Beijing seeks to alter such state of affairs. As a developing nation, not only does China seek to use energy efficiently, but also aspires to conserve the environment. Consequently, Brazil's experience and success of using bioethanol has fascinated China. Therefore, the urge of Beijing to foster close ties with Brazil on multilateral forums such as BRICS is profound.

The two countries have also engaged in a mutually beneficial relationship in the infrastructure sector. Brazil seeks to incur greater Chinese investment for ports, highways, railways and airport projects, while the Chinese leadership views infrastructure development as a key factor to boost bilateral cooperation. To endorse such infrastructure projects between China and Latin American countries like Brazil, the China-Latin American Cooperation Fund was instituted in January 2015 with an initial capital of USD 10 billion.[35]

China had once described the BRICS as an "adhoc political club" of the constituent developing economies that was constituted to address the interests and concerns of emerging markets.[36] Since economic governance is a key objective of the group, China's vision to engage with Brazil at the BRICS has a glaring economic facet to it. In fact, after the institution of diplomatic ties, the first official accord between the two nations was economic—the Sino-Brazil Government Trade Agreement, signed in 1987.[37]

Sino-Brazilian trade boom had ensued since late 1990s. In 2002, China outranked Japan as the largest trading partner of Brazil in Asia. Soon after in 2009, China substituted the United States as the chief trading partner of Brazil—a position enjoyed by the US for more than seven decades. According to the Ministry of Development, Industry and Trade of Brazil, bilateral trade between the two countries quintupled from 2000 and 2004, surpassing the USD12 billion mark in 2004.[38] Further, in 2014, bilateral trade between the two countries stood at USD86.67 billion.[39]

Fig. 8.5: China's Top Imports from Brazil in 2015

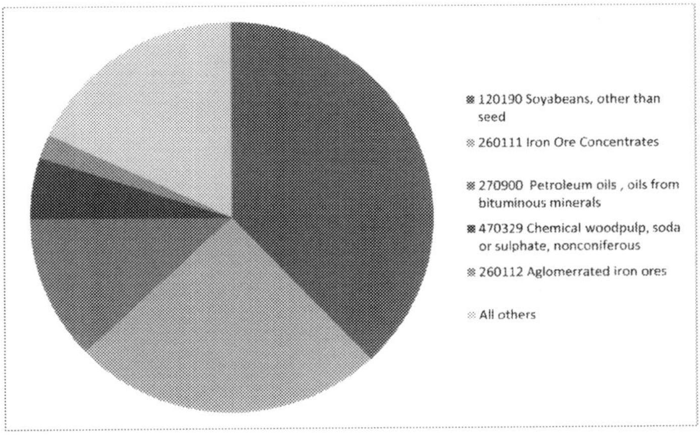

Source: Datamyne.

Brazil is host to abundance of natural resources—an essential prerequisite for China to sustain its rapid economic development. Clearly, Brazil requires capital to sustain, strengthen and develop its infrastructure and natural resources, which would in turn revamp their domestic investment environment. China, on the other hand, possesses foreign exchange reserves exceeding USD3.21 trillion, and explores appropriate investment outlets. Thus, in a way, an economic complementarity exists between the two countries.

Fig. 8.6: In per capita terms, Brazil's resources are abundant when compared to China[40]

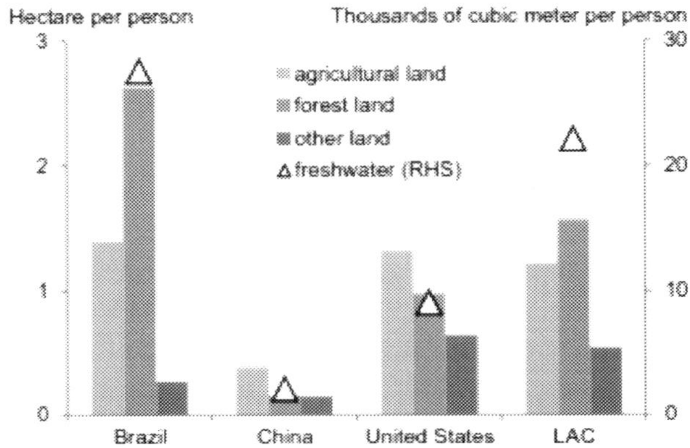

Note: Data for 2011. LAC= Latin America and the Caribbean region.
Source: FAO; WB staff calculations.

Further, as both the Chinese and Brazilian economies undergo economic reforms, there is a continued process of market liberalisation. Brazil cannot afford to disregard the huge market potential of China. Over time, China has evolved as Brazil's largest destination of exports and second largest source of imports.

One of the chief factors that charms China towards this Latin American country is its reserve of food, raw materials and energy. In May 2009, China approved to lend USD10 billion to Petrobras, Brazil's State-owned oil giant, in lieu of guaranteed supply of oil over the next decade. Given the challenges posed by the global economic crisis, Beijing deems it necessary to diversify its foreign assets in order to heighten security. In this regard, China considers investing in Brazil as a constructive alternative. China imports 16 per cent of its iron ore concentrates and 30 per cent of soya beans from Brazil. Beijing prefers the genetically unmodified soya beans from Brazil to the modified ones available in the United States. The robust sale of such items has led to Brazil enjoying a trade surplus with China.[41]

Fig. 8.7: Top ten sectors in which China and Brazil Enjoy Comparative Advantage[42]

Sectors in which Brizil has the greatest RCA			
Sector	*Sector Description*	*RCA of Brazil*	*RCA of China*
17	Sugars & sugar confectionery	16.7	0.2
12	Oil seeds, misc. grains, medicinal plants, straw	12.7	0.2
26	Ores slag & ash	12.4	0.03
9	Coffee, tea, mate & spices	11.1	0.3
47	Pulp of wood, waste & scrap of paper	9.1	0.03
2	Meat & edible meat	8.4	0.1
23	Residues from food industries, animal feed	6.5	0.3
24	Tobacco and manufacturing tobacco substitutes	5.4	0.3
41	Raw hides & skins & leather	4.8	0.2
20	Preps of vegetables, fruits, nuts, etc.	4.2	0.9
Sectors in which China has the greatest RCA			
Sector	*Sector Description*	*RCA of Brazil*	*RCA of China*
66	Umbrellas, sun umbrellas, walking sticks, whips, riding-crops & parts	0.01	6.6
67	Prepared feathers, human hair & articles thereof, artificial flowers	0.01	5.7
95	Toys, games & sports equipment, parts & accessories	0.02	5.4
46	Manufacturing of straw, esparto, or other plaiting materials, basket ware and wickerwork	0.05	4.7
65	Headgear & other parts		
42	Articles of leather, saddler & harness, travel goods, handbags, articles of gut	0.07	4.4
50	Silk, including yams & woven fabrics thereof	1.1	4.2
64	Footwear, gaiters & the like	1.2	4
62	Articles of apparel & clothing accessories--not knitted or crocheted	0.02	3.6
63	Made-up textile articles nesoi, needlecraft sets, worn clothing, rags	0.3	3.4

Note: RCA = revealed comparative advantages = the proportion of the country's exports in a given product category divided by the proportion of world exports of that category in total world exports. A comparative advantage is 'revealed' if RCA > 1.

Source: UN Comtrade: World Bank staff calculations.

With regard to Sino-Brazilian military cooperation, it may be stated that both these developing nations benefit from military exchanges, even though China's choices are fewer. It may be reiterated that Brazil is the only country in the BRICS grouping that possesses an aircraft carrier, proficient in launching and recovering conventional aircraft as well and keen or able to guide the PLAN personnel. Undoubtedly, Beijing benefits from naval training; and Brazil on its part earns international recognition as a global force, especially when it aids a country as dominant as China.[43] Further, China has purchased anti-air missiles, anti-tank and avionics from Brazil.[44] There have also been instances of cooperation in the satellite industry, nuclear energy development and in nuclear technology research.

There has also been substantial collaboration in the sphere of space and aeronautics, especially in the area of earth resource satellites. Both the countries have jointly constructed remote sensor satellites that were designed for the purpose of space imaging, and were championed as a model of South-South cooperation. Further, in the domain of science and technology, Brazil's Ministry of Science and Technology and the Ministry of Education, together with Beijing's Ministry of Education, had concluded the *Memorandum of Understanding to Carry Out "Science Without Borders" Program in China*. The ministries of science and technology of the two nations have signed documents on instituting the China-Brazil biotechnology centre and joint meteorological satellite centre.[45]

Finally and most importantly, as members of the BRICS, both China and Brazil bestow pivotal importance to the issue of cyber security. The 2013 Durban Declaration emphasised on the "critical positive role the Internet plays" and reiterated at the BRICS conviction that "it's important to contribute to and participate in a peaceful, secure and open cyberspace". However, there is a clear divergence on the cyber strategies that maybe adhered to within the group. This is evident in the lack of a joint BRICS proposal on the institution of a new Internet governance body or laying down of a code of conduct on cyber security. Although all the five members contest the US dominance on cyber space, they stand divided on the subject. While China and Russia have mobilised the Shanghai Cooperation Organisation way back in September 2011 to establish an 'International Code of Conduct for Information Society', India, Brazil and South Africa, at the first summit of the IBSA Dialogue Forum (2006), recognised 'information society' as a foremost issue of collaboration. In the context of Internet governance, Brazil along with India and South Africa has acted as 'swing states'. This signifies that although these three nations project pro-activeness in the international debate on global governance, they do not engage either with the Sino-Russian initiatives or the US.[46] Therefore, cyber security remains an issue of convergence as well as divergence between the two sides.

It is these comparative advantages that draw China towards Brazil at the BRICS grouping. However, the relationship has not been able to steer clear of a few daunting impediments, that in a way have constricted the bilateral ties from thriving at the international stage.

Areas of Discord

Generally speaking, commercial ties with China have been advantageous to Brazil, with the country experiencing trade surplus in most years between 2001 and 2012. Subsequently, the successive governments in Brazil have embraced a pro-China agenda and endorsed several big Brazilian companies to export to the Chinese market. Examples of such companies are EBX, Vale, BR Foods and Embraer. However, the key area of discord between the two nations is in the commercial sector. Brazilian officials have remained anxious about the overall quality of trade. Brazil exports iron ore, oil and soybeans but imports manufactured goods from China.[47] The trend of bilateral trade, on one hand, indicates Beijing's necessity of oil, raw materials and natural resources so as to sustain its booming economy; and on the other hand, it projects the demands of the rising middle class in Brazil for more inexpensive consumer products as well as the desire of the Brazilian government to accomplish trade diversification.

One school of thought articulates the presence of China in Brazil's industrial sector as a "threat". The rising trend of export of primary products has engendered a surge of protectionist sentiment in certain quarters of Brazilian industrial sector. Companies and pressure groups of the country, such as CNI (Confederation of National Industry) and FIESP (Federation of Industries of Sao Paulo) have underscored the necessity of additional governmental measures to prevent what they view as an "imminent invasion of Chinese products in Brazil".[48]

On the other hand, some scholars believe that since China has instituted a competitive industrial system, therefore countries that have adhered to a model intensive industrialisation (like Brazil) have been affected the most. This argument has given rise to the debate whether increasing Chinese demand for primary products and the subsequent flooding in of Chinese manufactured commodities in the Brazilian markets has led to de-industrialisation of the Brazilian economy.[49]

Consequently, the Brazilian government has adopted a two-pronged approach. On one hand, the government has adhered to a protectionist stance towards China launching several anti-dumping investigations. On the other hand, the Brazilian officials have preferred not to regulate and enforce the recognition of Beijing as a market economy that was decided upon with China in 2004. Seeking acknowledgement as a market economy from Brazil is imperative to China for it to obtain a similar status for its economy from other countries.

Second, the Brazilian government is also apprehensive of the increasing competition that the Chinese State-Owned Enterprises (SOEs) poses to Brazilian firms in Africa. Companies such as Camargo Correa and Vale have made heavy endowments in countries like Mozambique and Angola. However, competition from Chinese SOEs would definitely constrain the influence of the Brazilian companies in both, the private as well as the public sectors in Africa—something that Brazil deems strategic.

Third, in the political sphere, Brazil's voting record at the General Assembly and the Human Rights Council replicates a traditional interest in the principle of non-intervention and patronage for authoritarian regimes. However, in reality, Brazil is a democracy that prefers to debate about its stance on human rights. Therefore, in the long-term, it is likely that Brazil and China would adopt different grounds on the issue.

Fourth, although the two countries have commenced ambitious plans to uphold climate change negotiations, it may be expected that with the expansion of their respective economies, substantial differences in terms of environmental strategies is likely to occur.[50] While Brazil's greenhouse gas emissions are primarily due to deforestation, China's is an outcome of industrial output.

The Way Forward

In recent times, Brazil has been at the center of political, cultural, economic and social crisis. The economics and politics of the country have been confronted with significant turmoil. Moreover, the impeachment proceedings initiated against President Dilma Rousseff has been a recent blow to Latin America's biggest country. During the first tenure (2011-14) of the now-suspended Rousseff, the Brazilian economy grew merely by 2.2 per cent per year. However, a slowing Chinese demand for soy, iron ore as well as other commodities sparked off poor economic performance in her second term.[51]

This was one of the key factors that have contributed to her impeachment. Other factors being fiscal irresponsibility, illicit accounting manoeuvres to camouflage government deficit during the 2014 election and a corruption scandal with regard to the State oil company called Petrobras.[52] With the impeachment of the first woman President of Brazil by the Senate, her former deputy Michel Temer is presently in command of Brazil.[53]

China, on its part, has refrained from making official statements on the political turmoil and the new government in Brazil. Despite the disapproving tone of the new administration against the left-leaning nations and the deliberations about promoting democracy and human rights, Brazil's strategic ties with Beijing is expected to remain unaffected. Irrespective of the preference of the government, a robust investment and trade relationship with China is fundamental for the Brazilian economy. Moreover Beijing's support is critical for Brazil to pursue any international initiative. Therefore, from a foreign policy and commercial perspective, the ongoing projects would largely remain unhindered.[54]

China's proactive stance towards Brazil rests within the broader framework of China's 'Going-Out' strategy. Such an approach has been further institutionalised through China's association with this Latin American nation at the BRICS. Further, the intensity of China's engagement with Brazil at the BRICS Summits reflects the continuity in China's fascination to proclaim itself as the leader of the Third World. To add to it, China will continue to seek Brazil's patronage at the forum to legitimise institutions such as the BRICS-led NDB and Asian Infrastructure Investment Bank (AIIB). It is only through the accomplishment of these bodies that Beijing's infrastructure projects such as the 'One-Belt One-Road' and 'Twenty First Century Maritime Silk Route Economic Belt' would transcend into reality and grant the country geopolitical supremacy in the world.

For Brazil, the BRICS group will continue to be of critical strategic importance. BRICS membership would grant Brazil institutionalised access to the leadership of Beijing and New Delhi. Despite the slowing down of its economy, it is estimated that the Chinese economy would maintain a growth rate of 6 per cent in 2016 and 2017. Undoubtedly, Brazil's future would largely be dependent on Asia in general, and China in particular. In this context, BRICS offers far more than yearly presidential summits. It includes as many as 15 minister level meetings every year to promote intra-BRICS cooperation. Such summits would greatly contribute in bolstering Sino-Brazilian bilateral ties. Further, Brazil's membership in the BRICS group, its stature as a founding member of the AIIB and the NDB would reveal the country's global strategic presence in the international domain. Such a reputation would draw the attention and confidence of investors across the globe towards Brazil as an investor-friendly nation.[55]

However, a closer examination of the bilateral relationship demonstrates that both these developing nations have used the BRICS platform to collaborate in the domain of agriculture, aerospace, biotechnology, renewable energy sources, climate change, nanotechnology, global and regional affairs, and on the issue of currency. In a way, both China and Brazil have championed the interest of the Global South. In this regard, it is important to reiterate that BRICS is the ideal platform to promote such cooperation as unlike G-20, which is an adhoc association of developed and developing nations, BRICS comprises exclusively of developing countries. Thus, the Sino-Brazilian partnership at the BRICS forum elucidates a new path of 'South-South' cooperation—a relationship that is likely to strengthen in the forthcoming years, given the necessity of both the countries to foster deeper ties with the other.

END NOTES

1. Zhao, Mingwen (2011), "Rapid Development of the BRICS Cooperation Mechanism" in Qu Xing (eds.) *New International Environment and China's Peaceful Development*, Beijing :World Affairs Press
2. Stuenkel, Oliver (2016), "The BRICS: Seeking Privileges by Constructing and Running Multilateral Institutions", *Global Summitry*.
3. Cheng, Joseph Y.S. (2014), "China's Approach to BRICS", *Journal of Contemporary China*, 24(92): 370
4. Garcia-Escribano, Mercedes, Carlos Goes and Izabela Karpowicz (2015), "Filling the Gap: Infrastructure Investment in Brazil", *IMF Working Paper*, WP/15/180
5. Harta, Loro (2015), "Brazil-China Relations", *RSIS Working Paper*, No. 287, [Online:Web] Accessed 12 July 2016, URL https://www.rsis.edu.sg/rsis-publication/rsis/wp287/#.V6944Pl97IU
6. Pong, Zhongying (2015),"China, Brazil and Global Governance", in Yanan Song and David Ritchie (eds.) *Chinese-Lusophone Relations: China and Brazil*, Beijing: Social Sciences Academic Press
7. Mo, Honge (2006),"China, Brazil Strengthen Relations", *Xinhua*, [Online:Web] Accessed 10 July 2016, URL http://www.gov.cn/misc/2006-08/29/content_372510.htm
8. Lopes Jr, Gutemberg P. (2015), "The Sino-Brazilian Principles of Latin American and BRICS Context: The Case for Comparative Public Budgeting Legal research", *Wisconsin International Law Journal*, 33(1): 1-45.
9. Cheng, Joseph Y. S. (2014), "China's Approach to BRICS", *Journal of Contemporary China*, 24 (92): 357-375
10. "BRICS India 2016" [Online:Web] Accessed 10 July 2016, URL Brics2016.gov.in/content/innerpage/about-usphp.php (BRICS official page)
11. (2009) "Address by Foreign Secretary Shivshankar Menon on BRICs in the New World Order", *Ministry of External Affairs*, [Online:Web] Accessed on 2 July 2016, URL http://www.mea.gov.in/Speeches-Statements.htm?dtl/1041/Address+by+Foreign+Secretary+Shivshankar+ Menon+on+BRICs+in+the+New+World+Order
12. Yang, Fuchang (2002), "China's Relations with Developing countries", in Yang Fuchang (eds.) *Contemporary China and its Foreign Policy*, Beijing: World Affairs Press
13. (2014), "BRICS adds new Dynamism to International Relations", *Ministry of Foreign Affairs of the People's Republic of China*, [Online:Web] Accessed 9 July 2016, URL http://

www.fmprc.gov.cn/mfa_eng/wjbxw/t1170274.shtml
14. Ibid.
15. Wu, Jiao (2013), "BRICS 'Set to be a Global Force'", *China Daily*, [Online:Web] Accessed 13 July 2016, URL http://europe.chinadaily.com.cn/china/2013-03/27/content_16351114.htm
16. Cheng, Joseph Y. S. (2014), "China's Approach to BRICS", *Journal of Contemporary China*, 24(92): 360
17. BRICS Joint Statistical Publication 2015, [Online: Web] Accessed 19 August 2016, URL http://www.gks.ru/free_doc/doc_2015/BRICS_ENG.pdf
18. Jenkins, Rhys (2015), "IS Chinese Competition Causing De-industrialization in Brazil", *Latin American Perspectives*, 42(6): 42-63.
19. Armijo, Leslie Elliot and Sean W. Burges (2010), "Brazil, The Entrepreneurial and Democratic BRIC", *Polity*, 42(1): 14-37
20. Ratcliff, William E. (1972), "Communist China and Latin America", *Asian Survey*, 12(10): 846-863
21. http://www.scielo.br/scielo.php?script=sci_arttext&pid=S0034-73292010000300011
22. Jiang, Shixue (2015), "Demystifying the China-Brazil Relations" in Yanan Song and David Ritchie (eds.) *Chinese-Lusophone Relations: China and Brazil*, Beijing: Social Science Academic Press
23. (2014),"Xi Jinping Holds Talks With President Dilma Rousseff of Brazil, Inheriting the Past and Ushering in the Future to Forge More Splendid Future for China-Brazil Relations", *Ministry of Foreign Affairs of People's Republic of China*, [Online:Web] Accessed 15 July 2016, URL http://www.fmprc.gov.cn/mfa_eng/wjb_663304/zzjg_663340/ldmzs_664952/gjlb_664956/3473_665008/3475_665012/t1176222.shtml
24. (2014), "Ministry of Foreign Affairs Holds Briefing for Chinese and Foreign Media on President Xi Jinping's Attendance at Sixth BRICS Summit, Visits to Brazil, Argentina, Venezuela and Cuba, and Attendance at China-Latin America and the Caribbean Summit", *Ministry of Foreign Affairs of People's Republic of China*, [Online:Web] Accessed 16 July 2016, URL http://www.fmprc.gov.cn/mfa_eng/zxxx_662805/t1172783.shtml
25. Qiu, Huafei (2013), "Chinese Multilateral Diplomacy", in Qiu Huafei (eds.) *Contemporary Chinese Foreign Affairs and International Relations*, Beijing: Current Affairs Press
26. Xie, Huanchi (2015), "China-Brazil Ties Develop Vigorously: Xi", *Xinhuanet*, [Online:Web] Accessed on 11 July 2016, URL http://news.xinhuanet.com/english/2015-07/10/c_134398433.htm
27. (2014), "Implications of a Changing China For Brazil: A New Window of Opportunity?", *World Bank*, [Online:Web] Accessed on 16 July 2016, URL http://www19.iadb.org/intal/intalcdi/PE/2014/13978.pdf
28. Mendes, Carmen Amado and Daniel Cardoso (2015), "Diversifying Channels in China-Brazil Relations: The Multilateralization of the Bilateral relationship", in Yanan Song and David Ritchie (eds.) *Chinese-Lusophone Relations: China and Brazil*, Beijing: Social Sciences Academic Press
29. "Security Council Reform", *Permanent Mission of the People's Republic of China to the UN*, [Online:Web] Accessed 18 July 2016, URL www.china-un.org/eng/chinaandun/zzhgg/t29435.htm
30. Momani, Bessma (2015), "China at the IMF", in Domenico Lombardi (eds.) *Enter the Dragon:China in the International Financial System*, Canada: Centre for International Governance Innovation
31. Zhongying, Pang (2015), "China, Brazil and Global Governance", in Yanan Song and David

Ritchie (eds.) *Chinese-Lusophone Relations: China and Brazil*, Beijing: Social Sciences Academic Press

32. (2015), "Joint Statement on Climate Change Between the Government of People's Republic of China and the Government of the Federative Republic of Brazil", [Online:Web] Accessed 15 July 2016, URL http://en.ccchina.gov.cn/archiver/ccchinaen/UpFile/Files/Default/20150521102001198192.pdf
33. (2013), "China, Brazil Vow To Boost BRICS Cooperation", *Xinhua*, [Online:Web] Accessed on 14 July 2016, URL http://www.globaltimes.cn/content/808868.shtml
34. (2015), "5 Year Plan offers green Model of development", *China Daily Asia*, [Online:Web] Accessed 3 July 2016, URL http://www.chinadailyasia.com/chinafocus/2015-11/09/content_15342041.html
35. Huaxia (2016), "China-Brazil Infrastructure Cooperation Mutually Beneficial", *Xinhua*, [Online:Web] Accessed 11 July 2016, URL http://news.xinhuanet.com/english/2016-01/23/c_135038960.htm
36. (2011), "BRICS no anti-US bloc: China", *Economic Times*, [Online:Web], Accessed 17 July 2016, URL http://articles.economictimes.indiatimes.com/2011-03-23/news/29178220_1_bric-countries-brics-unsc
37. Wang, Jianwei and Zou Jing (2015), "Sino-Brazil Relations in the Context of China's Policy towards Latin America" in Yanan Song and David Ritchie (eds.) *Chinese-Lusophone Relations: China and Brazil*, Beijing: Social Sciences Academic Press
38. Jiang, Shixue (2006), "Recent Development of Sino-Latin American Relations and Its Implications", *Estudios Internacionales*, 38(152): 19-41.
39. (2016), "Brazil To See Better Ties With China In Trade, Investment", *Xinhua*, [Online:Web] Accessed on 14 July 2016, URL http://www.china.org.cn/business/2016-05/16/content_38462532.htm
40. (2014), "Implications of a Changing China For Brazil: A New Window of Opportunity?", *World Bank*, [Online:Web] Accessed on 16 July 2016, URL http://www19.iadb.org/intal/intalcdi/PE/2014/13978.pdf
41. Dominguez, "China's relations with Latin America: Share Gains, Asymmetric Hopes", *Working Paper*, pp. 27-28
42. (2014), "Implications of a Changing China For Brazil: A New Window of Opportunity?", *World Bank*, [Online:Web] Accessed on 16 July 2016, URL http://www19.iadb.org/intal/intalcdi/PE/2014/13978.pdf
43. Qiu, Huafei (2013), "Chinese Multilateral Diplomacy", in Qiu Huafei (eds.) *Contemporary Chinese Foreign Affairs and International Relations*, Beijing: Current Affairs Press
44. Shambaugh, David (2013), *Tangled Titans: The United States and China*, United Kingdom: Rowman & Littlefield Publishers Inc, [Online: Web], Accessed 11 July 2016, URL https://books.google.co.in/books?id=NN3BcORpwQIC&pg=PA335&lpg= PA335&dq=china+has+been+buying+anti-tank,anti-air+missiles+and+avionics+from+brazil+-&source=bl&ots=LwhI8R3DOq&sig=Vu9GJYrwG0TC_2pfh_N8PPNKh10&hl=en&sa=X&ved=0ahUKEwick_Ty-7nOAhUIpI8KHddcDHcQ6AEIGzAA#v=onepage&q=china%20has%20been%20buying%20anti-tank%2Canti-air%20missiles%20and%20avionics%20from%20brazil%20-&f=false
45. *China's Foreign Affairs, 2013*, Beijing:World Affairs Press
46. Maurer, Tim and Hannes Ebert (2013), "Cyberspace and the Rise of the BRICS", *Journal of International Affairs*, [Online:Web] Accessed 15 July 2016, URL http://jia.sipa.columbia.edu/online-articles/cyberspace-rise-brics/
47. Farah, Ana Gabriela Verotti (2013), "Largest Trading Partners of Brazil", *The Brazil Business*, [Online:Web] Accessed 18 July 2016, URL http://thebrazilbusiness.com/article/largest-

trading-partners-of-brazil

48. Mendes, Carmen Amado and Daniel Cardoso(2015), "Diversifying Channels in China-Brazil Relations: The Multilateralization of the Bilateral relationship", in Yanan Song and David Ritchie (eds.) *Chinese-Lusophone Relations: China and Brazil*, Beijing: Social Sciences Academic Press
49. Barbosa, Alexandre de Freitas, Maria Cristina Cacciamali, Angela Cristina Tepasse and Marina Neves Biancalana (2015), "Brazil-China Ecnomic Relations:Trade Pattern and China Investment Profile in Brazil" in Yanan Song and David Ritchie (eds.) *Chinese-Lusophone Relations: China and Brazil*, Beijing: Social Sciences Academic Press
50. Pereira, Carlos and Joao Augusto de Castro Neves (2011), "Brazil and China: South-South Partnership or North-South Competition?", *Brookings*, 26: 9
51. Barlett, John (2016), "Brazil's Economy is in the Mire. But Why? And When Will It Get Better?", *The Bubble*, [Online: Web] Accessed 18 August 2016, URL http://www.thebubble.com/brazils-economy-is-in-the-mire-but-why-and-when-will-it-get-better/
52. "Brazil in Upheaval After Rousseff Impeachment Vote", *China Daily*, [Online:Web] Accessed 19 July 2016,URL http://www.chinadaily.com.cn/world/2016-04/19/content_24646769.htm
53. Saxena, Shobhan (2016), "B Out of BRICS? Brazil Makes Dangerous U-Turn t Murkey Past", *The Wire*, [Online:Web] Accessed 20 July 2016, URL http://thewire.in/63273/b-out-of-brics-brazil-makes-a-dangerous-u-turn-to-its-murky-past/
54. Mothe, Stephan (2016), "What President Dilma Rousseff's Impeachment Means for Brazil-China Relations", *Cries*, [Online:Web] Accessed 14 July 2016, URL https://medium.com/@CRIESLAC/what-president-dilma-rousseffs-impeachment-means-for-brazil-china-relations-45737ae0afc5#.qew2rw90s
55. Stuenkel, Oliver (2016), "Why Brazil Shouldn't Turn Its Back on the BRICS", *Americas Quarterly*, [Online:Web] Accessed 17 July 2016, URL http://www.americasquarterly.org/content/why-brazil-shouldnt-turn-its-back-brics

9

China-Russia Relations

Sakshi Anand

Introduction

China's deviation from its long practice of isolationist approach is both refreshing and vital to shape regional and global world order. To hold its strong position in the world China is continuously opening up to the world and increasing its stakes in major areas of the world. Considering the fact that China stresses upon the need for a more equitable, transparent and inclusive world order, it becomes imperative for China to have proactive role in BRICS.[1] China's interest in BRICS includes:

(a) *reforming the multilateral institutions*: BRICS includes countries which share the feeling that emerging countries are being treated unfairly in the institutions such as the International Monetary Fund (IMF) and World Bank regarding voting power and the leadership selection process.[2] These countries also come together and speak collectively in Group of 20 (G20). Thus it creates the image of BRICS not as bystanders but as rule settlers.[3]

(b) *cooperation with developing countries*: President Hu Jintao's speech during BRICS Summit held in New Delhi in 2012 and that of President Xi Jinping's speech during Ufa Summit in 2015 both highlights that China seeks to cooperate with developing countries so as to add weight to the voice of BRICS nations.[4] This has benefitted China on the issue of climate change and in raising China's voting rights. This policy is as per current requirements of China. China's first generation of leaders led by Mao Zedong adopted the "leaning to one side" strategy and joined the Soviet Union. It not only helped China economically but also raised international status of China. Similarly, the second generation of leaders led by Deng Xiaoping realized the strategic intent of getting richer by actively integrating into the western society. In this regard, China's cooperation with BRICS once again signifies an adjustment of Chinese foreign strategy.[5]

(c) *increasing economic cooperation*: Increasing trade with emerging countries of BRICS is an important opportunity for China to diversify trade and decrease dependence on (United States) US. These countries are important raw materials suppliers as well as also a future market for China to achieve a stable and sustainable growth. These are vital areas for China to promote "Silk Road Economic Belt" project and also practice its "going out" strategy.[6]

(d) *recasting its image as a responsible global player and not as a free rider*: China also tries to present itself as a responsible player of the world by taking initiatives such as establishment of New Development Bank (NDB) and Contingent Reserve Agreement (CRA). Thus active participation in BRICS is China's new diplomacy in this century and the role played by China is a reflection of the reality of China's economic strength.[7] This shows China is gradually projecting itself as a responsible player and an important contributor in the world.

(e) *avoiding frictions*: Collaborating with these emerging influential countries allows China to put forward its demand without directly confronting the US and other leading developed countries. China is well aware of the fact that taking unilateral actions to put forward its voice may prove ineffective and also too costly. It does not want to repeat the historical conflict which rising powers of Germany and Japan had with US.[8] BRICS cooperation not only helps China avoid conflicts with US but also dilutes contradictions and conflicts of interests which China and other BRICS countries have at bilateral level.[9] The fear that US would try to get closer to BRICS countries in containing China is also a factor why China is actively participating in the BRICS group.[10]

Cooperation with BRICS countries in which India and Russia are its powerful neighbours having a capacity to threaten China helps to stabilise China's neighbouring and international environment.[11]

On a broader level, BRICS mechanism helps China raise its international status, deal with the current economic slowdown and its goal of reforming the current global order. China also considers itself to be the most important member of BRICS. Zhao Kejin, an international relations expert of Qinghua University believes that China plays a crucial role within the BRICS framework and it is due to China's involvement that BRICS cooperation has achieved success in such a short span of time.[12] However, there are views which suggest that it is difficult for BRICS to become as successful like the European Union, North Atlantic Treaty Organisation (NATO) etc. in a short span of time because of the diverse objectives and interests that the nations of the group pursue. Some of them see BRICS as a "coalition of issues" while others see it as "coalition of interests".[13] BRICS cooperation is sometimes also referred as a talking shop owing to their differences in economic level, political culture, strategic aspirations and policy goals.[14] Existence of issues among BRICS members such as the border disputes between China and India, mutual mistrust between China and Russia, the geographical position of Brazil etc. have somewhat reduced their combined influence.[15] However, despite of these differences they are moving in a positive direction. Coordinating their position in areas of common interest also allows them to maximise their bargaining leverage with western powers. Sharing ideas and experiences also help them find new ways to deal with challenges such as food security, agriculture, disease, foreign aid, energy, and global warming etc.[16] There is an increasing voice on expanding coordination among the BRICS members for a greater strategic coordination so that the group is not merely seen as a collective. The BRICS countries should be empowered to deal with more efficiency the common challenges that the developing countries of the world face.[17]

Similarly, Russia dissatisfied with the western hegemony, dwindling economy and a wish to regain its great power status, has to turn itself towards the east. BRICS therefore clearly remains one of the most important platforms for Russia. Although China and Russia are members of other multilateral organisations like Shanghai Cooperation Organisation (SCO), Conference on Interaction and Confidence Building Measures (CICA), East Asia Summit (EAS), but BRICS is important due to the overall power and influence of the group. Although the group does not include advanced countries of the west, but it is more important because despite being geopolitically diverse, it is much more inclusive, that has extended support to Russia when its economy was suffering due to western led sanctions. The present study, therefore, intends to analyse the behaviour and prospects of the two major powers working to counter the US hegemonic influence.

China-Russia Partnership

Russia's partnership with China occupies a special place since Russia remains one of the most influential strategic partners of China. Issues both of regional, domestic as well as global nature push them closer towards each other. Russian President, Vladimir Putin had included a trip to China during his first foreign visit in 2012. Likewise, Xi Jinping also chose to first visit Russia after becoming President of China. Besides, there is also a bilateral consultation mechanism along with regular visits at the higher level. In the year 2013, there were five meetings, three telephonic conversations and sixteen exchanges of messages between the presidents of Russia and China.[18] The following year they had five meetings.[19] Apart from this, they have frequent exchanges at the level of Prime Minister, legislatures, military etc. They hold regular talks on issues related to security, military, and energy.[20] In spite of these high level talks, mutual mistrust still persists. Russia is afraid of China's increasing economic clout and some sections also perceives rising China as a threat. Russia is also unhappy to see China's increasing influence in Russia's traditional area of influence of Central Asia and fears demographic expansion of the Chinese in its Far East. Similarly, Chinese often talks about Russia's imperial behaviour. They are very careful to not shape their partnership into an alliance. However, scholars do believe that Russian and Chinese attitudes towards each other are more positive than it was 20 years ago.[21] This could be substantiated by the recent increasing trend in trade relations between them, with only exception of 2015, during which sanctions were imposed by western world.

Fig. 9.1: Russia-China Bilateral Trade

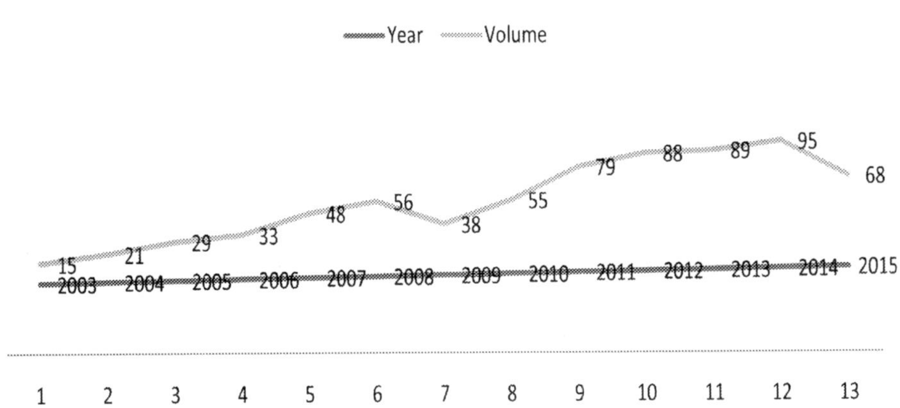

Source: UN Comtrade.[22]

Current changes in the international scenario, compels them to work together, keeping aside their differences. China and Russia are keen on promoting their respective economic developments and also face similar internal and external challenges. Thus, their cooperation becomes important towards managing the problems, achieve a stable and peaceful neighbourhood and to focus on other key issues of strategic and economic importance. The bilateral cooperation between the two has caught much attention worldwide after the Russian pivot to Asia, signing of the 30 year old gas deal, agreement on supply of sophisticated defence equipment and agreement on linking of Silk Road Economic belt and Eurasian Economic Union. This momentum is likely to continue for some years. China therefore views Russia as:

(a) A strong partner against the west—China and Russia has long opposed Western hegemony, western policy of interference in internal affairs of a country and western criticism of their record on democracy and human rights.[23] The two countries formed strategic partnership in 1996 which came up with Taiwan Strait crisis and NATO's eastward expansion as the background. After this they together opposed US abrogation of Anti-Ballistic Missile Treaty, western humanitarian intervention in Kosovo and criticised democratization campaign by the west and colour revolution in areas of Central Asia. Recent US announcement of its rebalancing towards the Asia-Pacific and Russia's 'Pivot to East' has again given them an opportunity to come closer together and it also gives China leverage against fighting the western hegemony. Some even points out that convergence of threat perceptions regarding the US and policies of US towards China and Russia has pushed them together to form a "soft alliance".[24] Russia plays an important role in agenda setting in BRICS and China recognizes the active role played by Russia in BRICS to establish the appropriate mechanism for cooperation and expressing their position and views on important international position and views.[25]

(b) Energy supplier—Russia has also become an important energy supplier for China. China has become world's largest consumer of oil and gas. Energy has played an important role in China's growth and so smooth supply of energy is essential for continued economic development of China. Russia being one of the world's largest producers of energy becomes an important partner of China in this aspect. China's heavy dependence on energy makes it look not only for additional supplier of energy, but also cheap, clean and secure supply. At current scenario Russia fits in all these aspects. Russia is one of the most secure suppliers of energy at a situation when Middle East is unstable and China need to diversify its trade route away from Malacca Straits. The 30-year natural gas deal worth $ 400 billion reached after so many years of negotiations will play an important role in improving the deteriorating environment of China and would also serve the demand for natural gas in its eastern region. Further they agreed to increase crude oil supply through oil pipelines and maritime transport.[26] Russia became the second largest oil supplier to China in the year 2015 and first in the first half of the year 2016. Over 22 million tons of oil was exported to China from January to May 2016.[27] They are also involved in several joint venture projects exploiting natural gas such as the Yamal LNG plant. Russia has also shared energy related technologies such as nuclear energy technology with China and there are further prospects for cooperation in the field of new energy technology.[28] Multi-directional energy cooperation between them will increase China's speaking right in international energy trade. The gas deal between them will play a great role in shaping the global price of Liquified Natural Gas (LNG) by offering China more competitive price than other countries such as Australia.[29]

(c) Defence partner—Russia has been China's most important defence partner since the end of Cold War. Military-Technical cooperation with Russia has played an important role in modernising backward Chinese military and enhancing China's aerial and naval capabilities which was in urgent need of advanced technologies after the western arms embargo in the backdrop of Tiananmen massacre incident in 1989. Recently Russia agreed to supply its important state-of-the-art weapons like Su-35 and S-400 Air Defence System further adding up to the military strength of China. Chinese military also learn from experiences they get during military training and military exercise with Russia. This cooperation gets even more strengthened by high-level military visits and military training from China and Russia, thus raising confidence and mitigating mutual mistrusts. Military exercises have further taken up their cooperation to a higher level. Chinese learns a lot from Russian army having significant experiences in combat operations. During May 2016, PLA and Russian Army performed a five-day computer simulation for a joint response to ballistic missile attack in Central Institute for Air and Defence in Moscow.[30]

They have even held their exercises in regions of East China Sea and are planning to conduct a military exercise in the South China Sea in September 2016 raising concerns of China's neighbour. They also have common stance in militarisation of outer space and even their technical cooperation also extends to the area of outer space. Defence cooperation with Russia has helped China's military modernisation, enhanced China's power projection capabilities and thus in coping up with possible military threat from the west.

(d) A partnership for regional issues—China recognises Russia as an important player in dealing with regional issues like the threat of terrorism, separatism and extremism affecting its provinces of Xinjiang and Tibet. In this regard, cooperation with countries of Central Asia where Moscow enjoys leverage due to its historical, cultural and political influence is important. Lo (2016) believes that Beijing's relation in Central Asia depends on achieving some level of accommodation with Moscow.[31] Russia is also important to constrain US from expanding its interests in Central Asia and curbing US destabilising role in Central Asia through democratic revolutions. Moreover, Russia is also a partner on dealing with the issues like piracy and other non-traditional threats.

Challenges

Despite Russia's increasing strategic importance for China in the areas of defence, energy and other regional and global issues, many Chinese see Russia as a weak country. Dmitry Trenin highlights that Post-Soviet Russia is unattractive to many Chinese and most of them see Russia as a disorganized, backward and uncivilized country.[32] It no longer remains attractive for the Chinese to study in Russia as was the case in the past, when they preferred studying there due to high standards of its education.[33] Many Chinese also pointed out why Russia has rarely proposed economic cooperation among BRICS countries is because the overall competitiveness of Russia in comparison to China, and other BRICS members, is weak and its attempt to promote political and security cooperation is a reflection of Russia's attempt to overcome the weakness.[34]

The bitterness among the Chinese owing to historical baggage vis-à-vis Russia still persists. The damage done to the mutual trust during the Cold war has left deep imprint and it continues to influence China-Russia relations.[35]

China still perceives Russia as a threat in the region. Russia's supply of arms to India and south-eastern countries is criticised and is viewed as a way of containing China.[36] Beijing is extremely careful that any problems with Russia may create problems in its neighbourhood and can also force Russia in the lap of west to join a hostile coalition against it. Although Russia supports China in their core interest of Taiwan, Tibet and Xinjiang, but China has modest expectations from Russia as it believes that the state of their bilateral relation depends on Russia's relations with the West.[37] Russia does not support internationalization of South China Sea issue, but it is out of Russia's general approach to territorial disputes in the region. Russia supports non-interference not only in Asia but also in other parts of the world. An article in Global Times mentioned that Sino-Russian relations are important but it should not be exaggerated. It goes on to say that countries like Russia won't make much difference in the face of Western pressure and therefore, China should not depend emphasise on an active diplomacy towards Russia, instead focus on good governance and in mobilising domestic as well as external support.[38] Even within the BRICS framework, some experts views Russia's participation as Russia's way of balancing western pressure. They even argue that it is likely for Russia to balance BRICS by participating in G8.[39]

Russia is described as the most important strategic partner by the current leadership of China and some important military and energy deals have further strengthened prospects for bilateral cooperation, but Russia's image of a weak and unfaithful partner cannot be overlooked. This is a reflection of Russia's current reality and historical legacy. Although, China has greatly helped Russia by helping Russia to come out of diplomatic and economic isolation from the west, but the relationship is gradually moving towards an asymmetrical interdependence due to the degree of inequality between the two partners.[40] However, this does not mean that China's interest for Russia has diminished. Russia still occupies influence in Eurasian and Central Asian Region which are the main areas for the Chinese "One Road, One Belt" initiative. Linking up of Eurasian Economic Union (EEU) and Silk Road project will accelerate the pace of these projects. Russia's defence cooperation is important to counter the US rebalancing in the Asia-Pacific. Moreover, Russia's support is important to counter any western led initiatives against China in United Nations Security Council (UNSC). In addition, increasing dependence may allow Russia to become more flexible in commercial cooperation, supply of sophisticated armaments etc.[41] Therefore, Russia is perceived by some as a weak and unfaithful partner. However, Russia's isolation under current global scenario may bring more opportunities for China and Russia's flexible attitude might also help in assuaging its concerns about Russia's intentions.

Towards Multipolarity

Multipolarity is a common position advocated both by China and Russia in different multilateral institutions. This has emerged out of common concerns against Western hegemony.[42]

Multipolarity opposes hegemony and aims at the establishment of a fair and reasonable world order. This gives the people all over the world the right to choose their own system, values, and road to development according to their own national condition and thus justifies that interference in internal affairs of any country is unacceptable. It promotes dialogue and consultation as the means to sort out differences. Majority of developing countries including China and Russia are not satisfied with the current world order led by the US and they believe that developing countries are an important force promoting multilateralism and thus, BRICS becomes important platform to promote multipolarity. Acting as a bridge between developing and developed countries, China and Russia under BRICS framework represents the position of developing countries.

In May 2015, the state councillor Yang Jiechi said that BRICS countries should cooperate to promote equal relations in the world to protect the interests of developing nations to lay a solid foundation for multi-polarity tendencies.[43] Zhang Guojun points out that at a time when western economy is in crisis, BRICS countries have become an engine for world's economic recovery and these countries will work together to set the global governance agenda. He further points out that pragmatic cooperation of BRICS countries has promoted South-South cooperation and has led to the shifting of political and economic rights from north to south. This is helpful in the building of new international and political order.[44] Thus, the combined strength of BRICS countries makes it an important platform for China and Russia to promote multipolarity. China-Russia cooperation at bilateral as well as in multilateral forums will strengthen their call for a multipolar world even stronger. Therefore, they also promote democratization of international relations and greater role played by the UN. It is one of the ways through which both Russia and China can contain USA's domination and establish their prominence in the globe.[45]

The debate on multipolarity has intensified after the relative decline of the US as the sole superpower in the years following the financial crisis and this debate has often involved BRICS countries. Emerging economies of BRICS and especially China plays a prominent role in advocating multipolarity in economic institutions such as IMF and World Bank. Since the decline of unipolarity is reflected strongly in the economic order, therefore, it is the most important area where emerging powers are challenging the unipolar world order.[46] The economy of BRICS countries reached $16 trillion in 2014 and their contribution in global economic growth exceeded 50 per cent in the last decade, strengthening their demand for increasing representation in international economic institutions.[47] Dissatisfied with the west led rules of these institutions, they came up with initiatives such as the establishment of NDB and CRA inside BRICS reflecting their growing capabilities.

Economic growth alone cannot drive multipolarity. This to a large extent depends on the position of BRICS countries on politics and security related issues.[48] Therefore, China-Russia also tries to contain the unipolar world order through diplomatic and political cooperation. At a time when western world imposed economic sanctions on Russia, China not only attended 70 years of victory of the Second World War, but also sent troops to participate in the parade at Red Square. China and Russia backed Syria against western resolution for human rights violation and political transition by using the veto power in UN. However, in the backdrop of promotion of multipolarity, several initiatives for regional integration have also been taken by China and Russia and China's increasing influence has often been seen as interference in Russia's area of interests. For example China comes with the idea of "Silk Road Economic Belt" project in Central Asia was geographically overlapping with Russia's "Eurasian Economic Union". Moreover, Chinese perception of multipolarity does not intend to directly challenge the western led world order, but to improve the current international order, unlike Russia which is more vocal in opposing west and transforming the current international order.

Security challenges such as terrorism and cyber security are also discussed among BRICS. All of them raise concerns against US surveillance activities. In other institutions such as Shanghai Cooperation Organisation (SCO) and CICA, China promotes New Security Concept which advocates multilateral dialogue, confidence-building measures, arms control and non-proliferation and expanded economic cooperation that will reduce international tensions. It denounces the use or the threat of use of force to settle political disputes and calls for equal treatment of all countries.[49] It also helps China in assuring the region that it intends not to dominate its neighbours.

In spite of their shared belief in multipolarity, there are differences among them depending on their interests. Although Chinese and Russian call for multipolarity is a result of their growing dissatisfaction with US and western hegemony but this does not indicate an alliance formation against the US. To alleviate such rising concerns, China, in the year 2003, declared that the view on multipolarity is not targeted at any third and neither is it aimed at restaging the old play of contention for hegemony in history.[50] Thus, through the following means, Beijing not only also justifies its expansionist forays but also strengthens its multipolarity agenda in the international system.[51] United States is still the largest trading partner in China with an estimated $659.4 billion trade in 2015.[52] However, trade with Russia only accounted to $68 billion in the same year.[53] Even Russia initially wanted to cooperate with the US after the end of cold war, which did not prove successful and compelled Russia to turn towards the east.[54] It again tried to go closer to the US after the September 11 attack, to the extent that Russian Foreign Policy Council advised Putin to drop the "multipolarity emphasis" in foreign policy and acquiesced the US position on missile defence to relieve itself of some of the Soviet-era debts and also an opportunity to join NATO.[55] Russia needs west for modernisation, technology, capital and in dealing with other challenges such as terrorism.[56] At the same time it also needs China's help to check western hegemonic actions. China's arms procurement and building defence capabilities are justified by Russia in the name of establishing a multipolar world order.[57]

China's active involvement in multilateral institutions arose due to the Chinese need to develop knowledge of global politics, international organisations and foreign policies of other states and at that time its approach was of "not taking the lead". Therefore, it adopted a wait and watch approach in these places. It gradually began actively participating in these institutions indicating that they would no longer remain passive within the institutions it has joined.[58] China finds that the rules of the game of international engagement are often enforced by the western countries and they protect the interest of these countries.[59] China expressing its dissatisfaction with the US hegemony is a reflection of its discontent against unipolar world. To project itself as one of the responsible player and a strong pole in multipolar world, it provides public goods in the form of finances to the IMF quota subscriptions and by purchasing IMF bonds.[60] Although Russia's initiatives is far below China in providing financial assistance, but it does play a significant role in combating other global challenges such as the issue of Syria, when China and Russia jointly vetoed four resolutions against it.

Engaging in the BRICS

China and Russia are two most important countries of BRICS and also of the world. Russia is the largest country in terms of geographical size while China ranks number one in terms of population. BRICS accounts for 40 percent of the world's population in which China constitutes 19 percent and

Russia constitutes 2 percent of the same. Area wise, BRICS occupies around 30 percent of world's territory in which China occupies 7.1 percent and Russia occupies 12.6 percent territory of the world.[61] Apart from this, China is the second largest economy while Russia has one of the strongest military in the world. Both are also permanent members of UNSC and other important multilateral institutions of the world such as SCO, CICA, Asia Pacific Economic Council (APEC), East Asia Summit (EAS) etc. The two have upgraded their strategic partnership to the level of comprehensive strategic partnership at the bilateral level and continue to discuss issues of common concerns at the multilateral level. Cooperation with emerging economies of the world further strengthens their regional influence. Thus, their combined strength makes the two strong and influential countries of the world. The Joint Statement of BRICS Summit 2015, showed that BRICS include discussion on wide ranges of issues such as the need for comprehensive, transparent and efficient multilateral approaches to addressing global challenges, and increasing role of UN in solving these challenges, safeguarding a fair and equitable international order, condemning military interventions and economic sanctions, intensifying financial and economic cooperation, enhancing economic partnership, coordination on the G20 agenda, expanding the use of national currencies in transaction, strengthening coordination in combating terrorism, prevention of arms race in outer space, cooperation in outer space for peaceful use and preventing misuse of Information and Communication Technology for mass electronic surveillance and data collection of individuals, peaceful settlement of the Syrian conflict, and other regional issues of Iran, Afghanistan etc.[62] Thus, BRICS discussion has not only remained limited to economic issues, but also includes political, security and social issues.

Convergences

Reforming the current international system forms an important component of Chinese and Russian diplomacy in BRICS. Promoting loans in local currencies and establishing a currency exchange system aims to reduce reliance on the US dollar and lower trade risks.[63] Similarly, the purpose of establishing New Development Bank (NDB) was established with the purpose of serving common needs without any string attached. This would help in mobilising resource for infrastructure and sustainable development projects in the BRICS and other developing countries. For Russia, it would be helpful in solving its economic problems at a time when its economy is suffering due to western sanctions. The rouble-denominated bonds by Russia would help the NDB to finance infrastructure and sustainable development projects in Russia.[64] Recently NDB approved the funding of $100 million small scale energy project in Karelia in Russia.[65] This would also help in regional integration of the Russian Far East. Vice President of NDB, Zhu Xian in a statement termed the Russian economy as resilient with high potential for development.[66] However, it will be difficult for Russia to emerge as one of the most important sponsors as it is far behind other members in terms of economy.[67] A recent report from the UN agency United Nations Conference on Trade and Development (UNCTAD) have also found that falling oil prices, geopolitical tensions and restrictions on foreign media viewership have resulted in the slowing down of FDI in Russia.[68] While China ranks no 2 in the world for FDI inflows and it also remained the largest investing country worldwide in 2015.[69] China's share of funding of US $ 41 billion in the CRA far exceeds Russia having a share of $18 billion. Beijing, on the other hand, gains experience through cooperation with other countries in the implementation of developmental projects by playing leadership rather than auxiliary role. This helps in promoting Yuan as one of the reserve currencies.[70]

China-Russia cooperation in BRICS is important for China to provide support to China's "One Road, One Belt" initiative in Asia and Eurasia and further extend it to Africa and Europe. Li Xing and Cheng Zhijie argues that China, Russia and India can form a troika in the construction of "One Road, One Belt" in Asia and Eurasia. In this, China and Russia will be the core and Brazil and South Africa would be the periphery.[71] Collaborating with Russia in the BRICS and at other levels, helped China to expand its voting rights from 3.8 percent to 6.43 per cent in the IMF.[72] Coordination at other multilateral forums apart from BRICS was also highlighted in President Putin's speech during BRICS summit 2012 when he emphasised to take advantages of the association to strengthen position at G20.[73] BRICS highlights Russia as a global leader and a respectable member of BRICS, unlike G7/G8 where it is uncomfortable with the partial integration.[74] Reforming the international institutions also includes reform of the UN Security Council. Although the joint statements mention the need to reform UN by inclusion of more developing countries like Brazil, India in the UNSC, they do not explicitly support their inclusion.[75] Opposing western hegemony and interference in internal affairs of the country has been another major challenge for China and Russia and this is being addressed in BRICS as well. Xi Jinping while attending a BRICS leader' meeting on the side-lines of the recently concluded G20 Summit in Hangzhou, urged the BRICS members to join equity, justice and build a peaceful and stable environment for development.[76] Russian

Foreign Minister Sergei Lavrov, on the other hand, has emphasised the need to promote political cooperation and align approaches towards key international problems.[77]

China and Russia are against supporting any military intervention in the UN Security Council. Both the country have altogether vetoed six times in UNSC and are quite successful in coordinating with BRICS countries in advocating peaceful resolution of the issues related to Libya, Syria and Iran etc. Recent Chinese decision to strengthen military exchanges and cooperation with Syria is another instance of more active coordination with Russia in the international affairs. This can also be said to Chinese reciprocation of Russia agreeing to perform military exercise with China in the disputed region of South China Sea which also includes countries like Vietnam, one of the oldest and important friends of Russia.

In another stance, Russia also agreed to support China's position on not to recognise decision of the Hague-based permanent court of arbitration while emphasising the fact that the support is legal and not political.[78]

However, the support is not shared by other members of BRICS such as India which called on all parties to show "utmost respect" for the United Nations Convention on Laws of the Sea (UNCLOS).[79] In the case of Crimea, though, China and is aware of the fact that Russia's role in Crimea and earlier in Georgia undermines its own principle of territorial integrity and non-interference in the internal affairs of a country and can have implications on Taiwan, China and other BRICS members abstained from the UN General Assembly resolution criticising the Crimea referendum. Chinese Foreign Ministry spokesperson Hong Lei said: "we hope that the Crimea issue will be appropriately handled and resolved through political dialogue as soon as possible while the reasonable concern and legitimate rights of all sides are respected."[80] Thus, abstention does not mean that China support Russia's actions in the region.

Energy has remained important for the economic development of both the countries. To further strengthen energy cooperation, Russia proposed the formation of BRICS Energy Association in 2014. It includes the idea of creating a fuel reserve bank and institute of energy policy which will help in strengthening energy security of BRICS member states.[81] Russia and Brazil being energy producers and China and India being energy consumers can greatly complement each other. Chinese scholars have also talked about energy cooperation between both as a way of US containment strategy as today west enjoys a key speaking right in energy which can help in countering US rebalancing strategy.[82]

BRICS energy cooperation is also seen as a way of attaining the goal of "low carbon status", friendly interaction, energy security and development and global economic growth and construction.[83] However, China has not coordinated with Russia regarding climate change as with BASIC countries. A political analyst and critic of President Putin, Stanislav Belkovsky said that the president believes that "there is no global warming, that this is a fraud to restrain industrial development of several countries including Russia".[84] It is yet to be seen if this association becomes a reality but it would definitely play a role in consolidating Chinese and Russian speaking right on energy at international level.

China, Russia and BRICS members share concern on security issues, especially the problem of global terrorism. BRICS members have even called for setting up a counter terrorism front to deal with the menace.[85]

China-Russia and China-India have also been practicing bilateral counter-terror exercise. Notwithstanding the fact that China, Russia and India are the worst sufferers of terrorism, BRICS cooperation on terrorism is not as successful as in the case of SCO, due to the existing differences between China and India on the issue of Pakistan sponsored terrorism.[86]

Besides terrorism, China and Russia also raise the issue of enhancing cyber security coperation and condemn USA's surveillance activities. A joint cyber security working group was established in 2013.[87] In addition to it, there was also a plan to lay internet cables for BRICS to avoid routing internet traffic through the US.[88] However their position on framing a cyber law is different. China and Russia promotes international code of conduct on information security and their pursuit of the issue allows content control from the state. However, democratic countries like Brazil, India and South Africa face domestic pressure on the issue of state controlled internet. Although they identify "information society" as a priority for collaboration,[89] the political differences resulted in the stalling of BRICS undersea cable.[90]

Divergences

BRICS cooperation, especially its relation with China in the forum, provides an important and much-needed support for Russia owing to the economic deterioration and isolation from the western world after the Ukraine crisis. It not only reduces the impact of western isolation, but also gives psychological support to Russia. However, BRICS is not the only priority for China. China cannot afford to lose its relationship with the west which still occupies an important place in terms of economic and trade partnership in comparison to the BRICS countries. BRICS importance to China continues to be less than other international institutions like UNSC, the World Bank, G-20, APEC and the EAS.[91]

In addition to it, China's contribution to the NDB is 10 billion which is even less than its bilateral loans and investment to some individual countries like Kazakhstan and Silk Road projects. China has also created its own organisations like AIIB which suggests that China views BRICS as one among its many alternatives and possess relatively lower confidence in the efficacy of BRICS.[92]

With respect to its relationship with the US, Russia reveals that BRICS countries are not satisfied with the western dominance in international economic and security institutions and also the frequent use of force by US and its allies. Therefore, Russia views the BRICS as a geopolitical power and considers it to be one of the most significant of this century.[93] However, China does not want BRICS to acquire a geopolitical identity and has resisted Moscow's driving the group in an anti-American direction.[94] Chinese scholars point out that Moscow's BRICS power diplomacy is a reflection of its traditional balance of power approach.[95] But, China is not interested in directly challenging the US and the current world order led by it. Stressing the importance of BRICS, does not mean that China wants to "set up a separate kitchen" and establish an alternate revised order, but to enhance and develop cooperation with developing countries and to promote a fair and equitable system.[96] It suffers from several domestic challenges and therefore, lacks both the willingness and support to directly challenge the US. This is also a reason why China does not oppose the current international order, but want to improve it, unlike Russia which perceives BRICS as an instrument to overturn the existing world order.[97] Moreover, there are voices which advocate China to build a strong partnership with the west in order to bring about reforms in the global governance.[98]

Thus, cooperation with BRICS countries provides an important multilateral forum for China to counter the widespread view of "China threat" among its neighbours and other countries.[99]

Russia, on the other hand, hopes to reform its former great power status with the help of BRICS.[100] Despite twenty years of efforts, Russia has not been able to regain its past glory. It currently wants to achieve this through BRICS which would entail lower domestic risks and costs for Russia.[101]

Conclusion

China and Russia are the two important and strongest players of the BRICS. Their bilateral cooperation which has reached up to the level of 'Comprehensive Strategic Partnership' shapes their nature of engagement at various multilateral levels. BRICS is another important international institution after SCO where they coordinate their positions on key global issues. Besides, the group which is also represented by democratic countries like India, Brazil and South Africa has helped China and Russia to avoid criticism that BRICS is led by non-democratic powers as in the case of SCO. The Chinese and Russian commitment towards multipolar world could be envisaged through the strengthening of regional blocks. In this vein, role of China and Russia becomes critical in consolidating developing countries of BRICS. Their cooperation within BRICS also coincides with their bilateral cooperation in areas, including trade, defense, technology etc. Economic growth remains a priority both for Russia as well as China, as these two countries are grappling with worst effects of the crisis. In this regard, cooperation with BRICS countries provides an important opportunity to find market and source investment. With regard to terrorism, these countries there have their own priorities and interests and necessarily do not share a common perspective, as promoted under the BRICS agenda. An overall assessment of their relation in BRICS, indicate that they prefer cooperation over competition as it would enable them to jointly counter the Western hegemonic domination as well as increase their economic and strategic activities. China being the second largest economy in the world has more to offer Russia than vice versa.

END NOTES

1. Bo, Yongguang (2013), "国际政治中的多边主义及其困境", guojizhengzhizhong de duobianzhuyijiqikunjing, Multilateralism in international politics and its dilemma, *Journal of Shanxi Datong University*, 27(1): 5-10, Bo Yongguang pointed out that multilateralism often proves to be ineffective due to difference in domestic policies of various countries. Important multilateral institutions like United Nations failed to prevent Iraq war. He also points out that institution like IMF to a large extent is serving western interests. Similarly "Kyoto Protocol" was not ratified by United States due to its own bilateral considerations. Zhao, Fahua (2011), 双边主义与多边主义的博弈, shuangbianzhuyiyuduobianzhuyi de boyi, "The Game of Bilateralism and Multilateralism", *Dongjiang Journal*, 28(1): 95-99 Zhao Fahua also talks about the complex nature of multilateral cooperation in Northeast Asia and pointed out that international relations in this part is still bilateral in nature. Some of the bilateral cooperation such as US-Japan, US-South Korea, China-North Korea are often built during the cold war and are of military and strategic significance. Promoting multilateralism in the region requires China to make effort to come out with existing bilateralism and advocating multilateralism on the basis of common interest.
2. Niu, Haibin (2015), "A Chinese Perspective on the BRICS in 2015", *Council of Councils*,

[Online: web], Accessed 03rd August 2016, URL: http://www.cfr.org/councilofcouncils/global_memos/p36088?cid=rss-fullfeed-a_chinese_perspective_on_the, _b-020615

3. Zhou, Yuyun (2012), "Deepen Practical Cooperation of BRICS and Expand Common Interests", *International Understanding*, p. 10.
4. Hu Jintao said "We believe that the development of developing countries to improve the productivity of human society as a whole, more balanced world economy, international relations, global governance more effective, more lasting world peace and the international community should focus on the current, long-term perspective and jointly developing countries to create a favourable environment for development."Speech during BRICS Summit, New Delhi, March 29, 2012, Accessed on September 05, 2016, URL: http://www.gatewayhouse.in/strengthen-mutually-beneficial-cooperation-create-better-future/;Ministry of Foreign Affairs of People's Republic of China, Xi Jinping attends 7th BRICS Summit and Delivers Important Speech, [Online:web], Accessed September 05th 2016, URL: http://www.fmprc.gov.cn/mfa_eng/topics_665678/xjpcxjzgjldrdqchwhshhzzzcygyslshdswchy/t1280846.shtml
5. Zhao, Kejin (2014), "中国国际战略中的金砖国家合作", Zhongguo Guoji Zhanlve zhong de jinzhuan guojia hezuo, BRICS Cooperation in China's International Strategy, *Chinese Academy of Social Sciences*, [Online: web], Accessed 21st August, URL: http://wap.mediaresearch.cn/zzx/201407/t20140708_1245339.shtml
6. Yue, Cui (2013), "Why the BRICS?: A Chinese View, *Culture Mandala: The Bulletin of the Centre for East-West Cultural and Economic Studies*, 10(1):51-58, p. 57.
7. Ibid, p. 56.
8. Glosny, A. Michael, (2010) "China and the BRICs: A Real (but Limited) Partnership in a Unipolar World", *Palgrave Macmillan Journals*, 42(1): 100-129, p. 104.
9. Joseph Y.S. Cheng (2015) China's Approach to BRICS, *Journal of Contemporary China*, 24(92), p. 359.
10. Ibid, p. 371.
11. Glosny, A. Michael, (2010) "China and the BRICs: A Real (but Limited) Partnership in a Unipolar World", *Palgrave Macmillan Journals*, 42(1): 100-129, p. 111.
12. Zhao, Kejin (2014), "中国国际战略中的金砖国家合作", Zhongguo Guoji Zhanlve zhong de jinzhuan guojia hezuo, BRICS Cooperation in China's International Strategy, *Chinese Academy of Social Sciences*, [Online: web], Accessed 21st August, URL:http://wap.mediaresearch.cn/zzx/201407/t20140708_1245339.shtml
13. Ibid, p. 3; Joseph Y.S. Cheng (2015) China's Approach to BRICS, *Journal of Contemporary China*, 24(92), 357-375, p. 360.
14. Lo, Bobo (2016), "The Illusion of Convergence-Russia, China and the BRICS", *Institut francais des relations internationals*, 92, p. 6.
15. Zhou, Hongtao (2012), "试析俄罗斯与金砖国家的关系", Shixi Eluosi Yu JinzhuanGuojia de Guanxi, An Analysis of the Relationship Between Russia and BRICS, *Siberian Studies*
16. Glosny, A. Michael, (2010) "China and the BRICs: A Real (but Limited) Partnership in a Unipolar World", *Palgrave Macmillan Journals*, 42(1): 100-129, p. 112.
17. Zheng, Yu (2015), "世界多极化趋势的加强与中俄关系", ShijieDuojihuaqushi de jiaqiangyuzhongeguanxi, The Strengthening of World's Multipolarisation Trend and China-Russia Relations, *Russian, East European, and Central Asian Studies*, p. 7.
18. Ministry of Foreign Affairs of People's Republic of China, China and Russia, [Online: web], Accessed August 30 2016, URL: http://www.fmprc.gov.cn/mfa_eng/wjb_663304/zzjg_663340/dozys_664276/gjlb_664280/3220_664352/
19. "China's Foreign Affairs" (2015),Ministry of Foreign Affairs of People's Republic of China, *World Affairs Press*, p. 280.

20. "China's Foreign Affairs" (2014), Ministry of Foreign Affairs of People's Republic of China, *World Affairs Press,* p. 261.
21. Lo, Bobo (2010), "How the Chinese See Russia", *IFR*I, [Online:web] Accessed on August 08th 2016, page 8-11 URL: https://www.ifri.org/sites/default/files/atoms/files/rnr6chinaloengdec2010.pdf
22. UN Comtrade, [Online: web], Accessed 14 september, 2016, URL: available at http://comtrade.un.org/data/
23. Lo, Bobo (2010), "How the Chinese See Russia", *IFR*I, [Online:web] Accessed on August 08th 2016, page 8-11 URL: https://www.ifri.org/sites/default/files/atoms/files/rnr6chinaloengdec2010.pdf
24. Feng Huiyun (2015), "Will China and Russia Form an Alliance against United States", *Danish Institute for International Studies,* page 5[Online:web] Accessed on 24th August 2016, https://www.diis.dk/files/media/publications/publikationer_2015/diis_report_07_the_new_geostrategic_game_web.pdf
25. Ma, Bin (2015), "**俄罗斯的金砖国家合作战略构想浅析**", Eluosi de Jinzhuan Guojia Hezuo Zhanlve Gouxiang Qianxi" An Analysis of Russia's Strategic Cooperation in BRICS", *China Economic and Social Council,* [Online: web], Accessed on August 29th 2016, URL: http://www.china-esc.org.cn/c/2015-11-09/617099.shtml
26. "China's Foreign Affairs" (2014), Ministry of Foreign Affairs of People's Republic of China, *World Affairs Press,* p. 262.
27. "Russia Overtakes Saudi Arabia as China's topmost energy supplier", [Online: web], Accessed September 03rd 2016, URL https://www.rt.com/business/348826-russia-china-oil-exports/
28. Shi, Ze (2016), "Building Strong China-Russia Energy Strategic Partnership", *China Institute of International Studies,* [Online: web], Accessed September 03rd 2016, URL: http://www.ciis.org.cn/english/2015-12/02/content_8422032.htm
29. Paton, James and Guo, Aiping (2014), "Russia, China Add to $400 Billion Gas deal With Accord", *Bloomberg,* New York, November 10, 2014, [Online:web], Accessed September 10, 2016, URL: http://www.bloomberg.com/news/articles/2014-11-10/russia-china-add-to-400-billion-gas-deal-with-accord
30. Clover, Charles (2016), "Russia and China learn from each other as military ties deepen", *Financial Times,* June 24th 2016 [Online:web], Accessed September 03rd 2016, URL: https://www.ft.com/content/a3e35348-2962-11e6-8b18-91555f2f4fde
31. Lo, Bobo (2010), "How the Chinese See Russia", IFRI, pp. 17 and 27, [Online:web], Accessed on August 08th 2016, URL: https://www.ifri.org/sites/default/files/atoms/files/rnr6chinaloengdec2010.pdf
32. Trenin, Dmitri (2012), "True Partners? How Russia and China See Each Other", Centre for European Reform, [Online:web], Accessed on August 07th2016 URL: http://www.cer.org.uk/publications/archive/report/2012/true-partners-how-russia-and-china-see-each-other
33. Lo, Bobo (2010), "How the Chinese See Russia", IFRI, [Online:web], Accessed on August 08th 2016, URL: https://www.ifri.org/sites/default/files/atoms/files/rnr6chinaloengdec2010.pdf
34. Ma, Bin (2015), "**俄罗斯的金砖国家合作战略构想浅析**", Eluosi de Jinzhuan Guojia Hezuo Zhanlve Gouxiang Qianxi" An Analysis of Russia's Strategic Cooperation in BRICS", *China Economic and Social Council,* [Online: web], Accessed August 29th 2016, URL: http://www.china-esc.org.cn/c/2015-11-09/617099.shtml
35. Lo, Bobo (2010), "How the Chinese See Russia", IFRI, [Online:web] Accessed on August 08th 2016, URL: https://www.ifri.org/sites/default/files/atoms/files/rnr6chinaloengdec2010.pdf

36. Qiao Xinsheng (2015),中俄关系的发展必须有战略思维, Zhonge Guanxi de Fazhan Bixu you zhanlue Sixiang, Development of China-Russia Relation Must have Strategic Thinking, [Online: Web] Accessed 20 Aug, 2016, URL: http://www.aisixiang.com/data/90855.html
37. Lo, Bobo (2010), "How the Chinese See Russia", IFRI, [Online:web] Accessed on August 08th 2016, page 13 and 16, URL: https://www.ifri.org/sites/default/files/atoms/files/rnr6chinaloengdec2010.pdf
38. Han, Kedi (2016), "Russian Suspicions of China Hold Back Ties", *Global Times*, Beijing, 24th July 2016, [Online:web], Accessed on September 7, 2016, URL: http://www.globaltimes.cn/content/996163.shtml
39. Xiao, Huizhong (2012), "试析俄罗斯金砖国家外交中的几个问题", Shixi Eluosi Jinzhuan Guojia Waijiao Zhong de Jig e wenti, *Analysis of Some of the problems in Russia's BRICS Diplomacy*, Foreign Affairs Observer, [Online:web], Accessed August 29th 2016, URL: http://www.faobserver.com/NewsInfo.aspx?id=7616, p. 8.
40. Gabuev, Alexander (2016), "Friends with Benefits? Russian-Chinese Relations After the Ukraine Crisis", Carnegie Moscow Center, p. 30.
41. Ibid, p. 31.
42. Sino-Russian Joint Statement in 1997, [Online:web], Accessed 25th August 2016, URL:http://www.cctv.com/lm/1039/21/88285.html
43. "China Urges BRICS partners to develop equal security concept", *Russia Beyond the Headlines*, Moscow, May 26th 2015, [Online:web], Accessed on September 10, 2016, URL: http://rbth.com/news/2015/05/26/china_urges_brics_partners_to_develop_ equal_ security_concept_46353.html
44. Zhang, Guojun (2013), "金砖国家合作意义的国际政治经济分子", Jinzhuan Guojia hezuo yiyi de guoji zhengzhi jingji fenxi", The Political and economic analysis of the significance of BRICS cooperation, *Finance Overview*
45. Ambrosio, Thomas (2001), "Russia's Quest for Multipolarity: A Response to US Foreign Policy in the Cold War Era", *European Security*, 10(1), p. 61.
46. Zheng, Yu (2015), "世界多极化趋势的加强与中俄关系", Shijie Duojihua qushi de jiaqiang yu zhonge guanxi, The Strengthening of World's Multipolarisation Trend and China-Russia Relations, *Russian, East European, and Central Asian Studies*, page 4
47. Scott, Malcolm, "Reason Why the BRICS Summit Here is a Big Deal", *Bloomberg*, New York: July 7 2015, [Online: web], Accessed September 1, 2016, URL: http://www.bloomberg.com/news/articles/2015-07-06/here-s-the-17-trillion-reason-why-the-brics-summit-this-week-is-a-big-deal; "BRICS Becomes Important Building Block of World's Economy", *China Daily*, Beijing: July 07 2015, [Online:web], Accessed September 15, 2016, URL: http://www.chinadaily.com.cn/business/2015-07/07/content_21203077.htm
48. Zheng, Yu (2015), "世界多极化趋势的加强与中俄关系", Shijie Duojihua qushi de jiaqiang yu zhonge guanxi, The Strengthening of World's Multipolarisation Trend and China-Russia Relations, *Russian, East European, and Central Asian Studies*, page 2
49. "China's Pitch for a Multipolar World: The New Security Concept", *Asia Pacific Center for Security Studies*, 2(1), [Online: web], Accessed September 20, 2016, URL: http://apcss.org/Publications/APSSS/ChinasPitchforaMultipolarWorld.pdf
50. Jing Men (2007), "Changing Ideology in China and its impact on Chinese Foreign Policy", Shijian Guo and Shiping Hua, *New Dimensions of Chinese Foreign Policy*, New York: Lexington:Rowman and Littlefield Publisher
51. Turner, Susan (2009), "Russia, China and a Multipolar World Order: The Danger in the Undefined, *Asian Perspective*, 33(1), p. 169.
52. "US-China Trade Facts, Office of the United States Trade Representative", [Online:web],

Accessed September 09, 2016, URL: https://ustr.gov/countries-regions/china-mongolia-taiwan/peoples-republic-china

53. UN Comtrade, [Online: web], Accessed 14 september, 2016, URL: available at http://comtrade.un.org/data/

54. Turner, Susan (2009), "Russia, China and a Multipolar World Order: The Danger in the Undefined, *Asian Perspective*, 33(1), p. 165.

55. Ibid.

56. Zakaurtseva, Tatiana, "The Current Foreign Policy of Russia", [Online:web], Accessed September 10 2016, URL: http://src-h.slav.hokudai.ac.jp/coe21/publish/no16_1_ses/05_zakaurtseva.pdf

57. Turner, Susan (2009), "Russia, China and a Multipolar World Order: The Danger in the Undefined, *Asian Perspective*, 33(1), p. 172.

58. Lanteigne, Mark (2009), "*Chinese Foreign Policy*", Oxon: Routledge, p. 5.

59. Chan, Gerald (2013), "The Rise of Multipolarity, The Reshaping of Order: China in a Brave New World", *International Journal of China Studies*, 4(1), p. 7.

60. Ibid, p. 10.

61. "BRICS Joint Statistical Publication" (2015), page 17, [Online:web], Accessed September 05th 2016, URL: http://www.gks.ru/free_doc/doc_2015/BRICS_ENG.pdf

62. "Ufa Declaration", 9 July 2015, VII BRICS Summit, [Online:web], Accessed on September 12, 2016, URL: http://www.brics.utoronto.ca/docs/150709-ufa-declaration_en.html

63. Ding, Ying (2012), "Banking on Other Options", *China and Africa,* [Online:web], Accessed on September 14, 2016, URL: http://www.chinafrica.cn/china_report/txt/2012-04/27/content_449298_2.htm

64. "Bonds in Ruble to Allow BRICS Bank to Step up Operations in Russia", Sputnik International, Moscow: September 8 2016, [Online:web], Accessed on September 11, 2016, URL: https://sputniknews.com/world/20160908/1045085873/brics-bonds-ruble-bank.html

65. "BRICS Bank to Allocate $100 million for Financing Small-Scale Energy Project in Karelia", TASS, Moscow: July 20 2016, [Online:web], Accessed on August 15, 2016, URL: http://rbth.com/news/2016/07/21/brics-bank-to-allocate-100-mln-for-financing-energy-project-in-karelia_613613

66. "BRICS Bank Considers Russian Economy Resilient with High Potential", Sputnik International, Moscow: September 9 2016, [Online:web], Accessed September 10, 2016, URL: https://sputniknews.com/russia/20160901/1044843867/brics-bank-russia-economy.html

67. Movchan, Andrey (2015), "Why Do Brazil, Russia, India, and China Need BRICS", *Carnegie Endowment for International Peace*, [Online:web], Accessed September 05th 2016, URL: http://carnegieendowment.org/2015/07/08/why-do-brazil-russia-india-and-china-need-brics/id96

68. "Russia's Share of Global Investment Amongst BRICs Falls Sharply", [Online:web], Accessed September 10 2016, URL: http://www.intellinews.com/russia-s-share-of-global-investment-amongst-brics-falls-sharply-104107/

69. World Investment Report (2016), United Nations Conference on Trade and Development, New York and Geneva, [Online:web], Accessed on September 1, 2016, URL: http://unctad.org/en/PublicationsLibrary/wir2016_Overview_en.pdf

70. Gabuev, Alexander (2015) "Why Do Brazil, Russia, India, and China Need BRICS", *Carnegie Endowment for International Peace*, [Online:web], Accessed September 05, 2016, URL: http://carnegieendowment.org/2015/07/08/why-do-brazil-russia-india-and-china-need-brics/id96

71. Li Xing and Cheng Zhijie (2015), "金砖合作机制是推动"一带一路"建设的强大助力",

Jinzhuan Hezuo jizhi shi tuidong "yi dai yi lu" jianshi de qiangda zhuli, BRICS Cooperation Mechanism is an Strong Force in the Construction of "One Road, One Belt", *The Journal of Humanities,* p. 27.

72. "China's IMF Voting Rights Soar Nearly 60%", *Asia Times,* Hong Kong, December 29th 2015, [Online: web], Accessed on August 13, 2016, URL: http://atimes.com/2015/12/chinas-imf-voting-rights-soar-nearly-60/

73. "Russian President's Address at BRICS Summit", New Delhi, March 29, 2012, [Online:web], Accessed September 14, 2016, URL: http://en.kremlin.ru/events/president/transcripts/14870

74. Roberts, Cynthia (2010), "Russia's BRICs Diplomacy: Rising Outsider with Dreams of an Insider", *Palgrave Macmillian Journals,* 42(1), p. 71.

75. Niu, Haibin (2013), "BRICS in Global Governance: A Progressive and Cooperative Force", *Friedrich Ebert Stiftung,* page 3, [Online:web], Accessed September 05th 2016, URL: http://library.fes.de/pdf-files/iez/global/10227.pdf

76. "Xi urges BRICS to safeguard int'l fairness, justice", *Xinhua,* Beijing, September 4, 2016, [Online:web], Accessed September 14, 2016, URL: http://news.xinhuanet.com/english/2016-09/04/c_135659766.htm

77. "BRICS to Promote Political Cooperation-Lavrov", *Russia Beyond the Headlines,* Moscow, August 15, 2016, [Online: web], Accessed September 2, 2016, URL: http://rbth.com/news/2016/08/15/brics-to-promote-political-cooperation-lavrov_621083

78. "Russia Support China's Stance on South China Sea", *Sputnik International,* Moscow: September 5 2016, [Online:web], Accessed September 09, 2016, URL: https://sputniknews.com/world/20160905/1044988523/russia-china-putin.html

79. Malik, Mohan (2016), "India's Response to the South China Sea Verdict", *The American Interest,* Washington D.C., July 22 2016.

80. "China Reiterates Call for Crimea Political Dialogue", *Xinhua News,* Beijing, March 18 2014, [Online:web], Accessed August 23, 2016, URL: http://news.xinhuanet.com/english/china/2014-03/18/c_133195555.htm

81. "BRICS Energy Association to Formed in 2016", *Russia and India Report,* [Online:web], Accessed 07 September 2016, URL: https://in.rbth.com/news/2015/11/20/brics-energy-asociation-to-be-formed-in-2016_542583

82. Su, Yina and Xu, Jinghua (2015), "俄罗斯能源近况与中俄能源合作前景", Eluosi Nengyuan Jinkuang yu Zhonge Nengyuan Hezuo Qianjing, Russia's Energy Status and Prospects of China-Russia Energy Cooperation, *Resources and Industries,* 17(3), 27-31

83. Ye, Jianmei (2015), "金砖国家能源问题和路径", Jinzhuan Guojia Nengyuan Wenti he Lujing" Issues and Solution for BRICS Energy Cooperation, *Legality Vision.*

84. Kuzmin, Andrey (2015), "Russian Media take Climate Cue from Skeptical Putin", *Reuters,* London: October 29 2015, [Online:web], Accessed September 05, 2016, URL: http://www.reuters.com/article/us-climatechange-summit-russia-media-idUSKCN0SN1GI20151029

85. "BRICS for Universal Front to Deal With Terrorism", *Economic Times,* Mumbai, November 15, 2015, [Online:web], Accessed on August 28, 2016, URL: http://articles.economictimes.indiatimes.com/2015-11-15/news/68297065_1_brics-leaders-brics-countries-imf-quota-reforms

86. Jash, Amrita (2016), "China's Response to Counter-Terrorism Under the BRICS Framework", *BRICS Information Sharing and Exchange Platform,* [Online:web], Accessed September 11 2016, URL: http://www.brics-info.org/chinas-response-to-counter-terrorism-under-the-brics-framework/

87. "BRICS Announce Joint Cybersecurity Group", *The BRICS Post,* [Online:web], Accessed

September 11, 2016, URL: http://thebricspost.com/brics-announce-joint-cyber-group/#.V9VXn1t97cc

88. Stevens, Tin (2015), "BRICS Set Out Vision for International Inforamation Security", *Thesigers,* [Online:web], Accessed on August 20, 2016, URL: http://thesigers.com/analysis/2015/7/3/brics-set-out-vision-for-international-information-security
89. Ebert, Hannes and Maurer Tim (2013), "Cyberspace and the Rise of the BRICS", *Journal of International Affairs,* [Online:web], Accessed on September 11 2016, URL: http://jia.sipa.columbia.edu/online-articles/cyberspace-rise-brics/
90. Lee, Stacia (2016), "International Reactions to the U.S. Cybersecurity Policy: The BRICS Undersea Cable, [Online:web], Accessed on September 11 2016, URL: https://jsis.washington.edu/news/reactions-u-s-cybersecurity-policy-bric-undersea-cable/
91. Lo, Bobo (2016), "The Illusion of Convergence-Russia, China and the BRICS", *Institut francais des relations internationals*, 92, p. 10.
92. Ibid, p. 21.
93. "Concept of Participation of Russian Federation in BRICS ", [Online:web], Accessed on August 28th 2016, URL: http://static.kremlin.ru/media/events/eng/files/41d452b13d 9c2624 d228.pdf, p. 2
94. Lo, Bobo (2016), "The Illusion of Convergence-Russia, China and the BRICS", *Institut francais des relations internationals*, 92, p. 22.
95. Xiao, Huizhong (2012), "试析俄罗斯金砖国家外交中的几个问题", Shixi Eluosi Jinzhuan Guojia Waijiao Zhong de Jig e wenti, *Analysis of Some of the problems in Russia's BRICS Diplomacy*, Foreign Affairs Observer, [Online:web], Accessed August 29th 2016, URL: http://www.faobserver.com/NewsInfo.aspx?id=7616, p. 1.
96. Zheng, Yu (2015), "世界多极化趋势的加强与中俄关系", Shijie Duojihua qushi de jiaqiang yu zhonge guanxi, The Strengthening of World's Multipolarisation Trend and China-Russia Relations, *Russian, East European, and Central Asian Studies,* p. 5.
97. Lo, Bobo (2016), "The Illusion of Convergence-Russia, China and the BRICS", *Institut francais des relations internationals*, 92, p. 13.
98. Niu, Haibin (2015), "A Chinese Perspective on the BRICS in 2015", *Council of Councils*, [Online: web] Accessed 03rd August 2016 URL: http://www.cfr.org/councilofcouncils/global_memos/p36088?cid=rss-fullfeed-a_chinese_perspective_on_the, _b-020615
99. Lo, Bobo (2016), "The Illusion of Convergence-Russia, China and the BRICS", *Institut francais des relations internationals*, 92, p. 10.
100. Sergunin, Alexander, "Understanding Russia's policies towards BRICS: Theory and Practice", [Online:web], Accessed August 28th 2016, URL: http://web.isanet.org/Web/Conferences/GSCIS%20Singapore%202015/Archive/55c376c8-7911-42be-b13d-22867ff8ea2a.pdf
101. Xiao, Huizhong (2012), "试析俄罗斯金砖国家外交中的几个问题", Shixi Eluosi Jinzhuan Guojia Waijiao Zhong de Jig e wenti, *Analysis of Some of the problems in Russia's BRICS Diplomacy*, Foreign Affairs Observer, [Online:web], Accessed August 29th 2016, URL: http://www.faobserver.com/NewsInfo.aspx?id=7616, page 9

10

China-India Relations

Sriparna Pathak

Introduction

In the 21st century, after the collapse of the former Soviet Union, the traditional Westphalian system underwent a shift as the demise of the international order characterised by a tight bipolarity between the US and the USSR was quickly substituted by a more multipolar system. Within this framework, the center of global politics and economics has seen a shift eastward and southward, and the BRICS (Brazil, Russia, India, China and South Africa) has emerged as a significant grouping. BRICS has become a vanguard in expressing this concern, asking for bigger 'representation of Southern values and interests' in various global multilateral forums and financial institutions[1]. The focus of the BRICS has been addressing issues such as financial legitimacy, accountability and social justices, among others. These issues are closely related to the functioning of multilateral institutions like the WTO, the International Monetary Fund, World Bank and the United Nations. Given the issues it seeks to address, the BRICS has become a potent voice in bridging the North-South divide in international relations. In the prevailing situations, particularly after the global financial crisis of 2008, the importance of the grouping increases even more[2].

Disclaimer: The author is a Consultant in the Policy Planning and Research Division of the Ministry of External Affairs, New Delhi. The views expressed are personal and do not reflect those of the Ministry or of the Government of India.

The BRICS Countries

In 2001, Jim O'Neill, the then chief economist of Goldman Sachs, coined the acronym BRIC for Brazil, Russia, India and China. South Africa became a member of the group later in 2010. He had expected these countries to grow faster than the developed countries. These countries have indeed grown faster than the rest. In the last 15 years, Brazil, Russia and India have caught up with the smallest G7 economy (Italy) in terms of nominal GDP, while China has overtaken Japan and become the second largest economy in the world. Together, BRICS' nominal GDP is similar to that of the EU or US, and is likely to overtake both in the coming few years[3].

If a quick look is taken at the growth rates of these five countries in the last decade—and is compared with the growth rate of the global economy—it becomes clear that for most of these countries, the rate has been higher than that of the world's.

Graph 10.1: Growth Rates of the BRICS Countries and the World's

Unit %

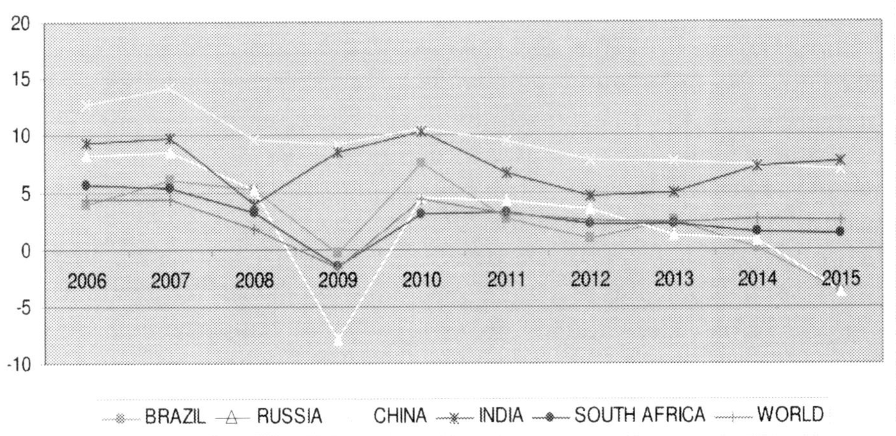

Source: World Bank data base.

As seen in graph 10.1, with the exception of Russia in 2009, no other BRICS country has seen a significant drop in growth rates below that of the global rate. Zhang Guo You studied the world's top 500 enterprises in 2009, and stated that large enterprises from the BRIC countries have emerged as important players. While large enterprises from these countries grow slowly, they are still in dominant positions and will play an important role in leading the global industry to higher rates of development. He adds that over the long run, the group of large enterprises from the group will maintain structure advantage of industry over others[4].

The point to note is that in 2009, when the global financial crisis was spreading across the globe with the growth rates of all the other countries in the grouping witnessed negative growth rates, the exceptions were India and China—which registered growth rates of 8.5 per cent and 9.23 per cent respectively. Overall, India and China have been the two better performing countries in the group.

India and China Relations: An Introduction

Even beyond the BRICS, the economic growth rates of India and China, particularly in the 21st century, have also led to the coining of the term "Asian Century". India and China, both have emerged as significant players in the international system; and beyond their own positions in the system, they are also shaping discourses at the international level through their individual capacities as well as through multilateral regimes that they are part of.

However, their similar stances on several issues and their mere geographical location within Asia do not mean the bilateral relations between the two are not fraught with tensions. Beyond the boundary dispute, imbalance in trade relations is a persistent irritant in bilateral relations. While the boundary dispute is a left-over from history, trade deficit has become a relatively newer yet constant feature of Sino- Indian relations—particularly in the past decade. In 2003-04, the gap between imports and exports was USD1098.13 millions, with the balance tilting in China's favour. In 2013-14, the deficit has grew to USD 36,210.26 millions, and the balance still tilts in China's favour. The growth in deficit for India therefore in a span of ten years has been 319.74 percent. If the current situation persists, India will experience an unsustainable trade deficit of USD60,000 million. The high trade imbalance, therefore, is a major concern.

In order to understand where the relationship is headed, it first becomes pertinent to take a brief look at how the nature of the relationship has been in the past, the areas of cooperation between the two and the areas where the potholes of the relationship lie. This chapter is an attempt at understanding the relationship between the two countries, with a focus on the positives of cooperation between the two; followed by the two thorny issues of trade deficit in general, and the boundary dispute in particular. The last section looks at the latest issues of contention that have arisen between the two in 2016.

Cooperation between India and China

While both India and China share similar developmental challenges, fact remains that China has been a better performer in most indices of development than India. However, even though extremely less in number, there are segments in which India performs better than China. Therefore, experience sharing and cooperation could definitely facilitate better outcomes for both. The following table compares India and China in a few select indicators:

Table 10.1: Comparing India and China

Indicator	*India*	*China*
Gross Domestic Product (GDP) (current USD) [2015]	2.074 trillion	10.866 trillion
Population	1.311 billion	1.371 billion
Carbon Dioxide Emissions (metric tons per capita) [2011]	1.66	6.71
Life expectancy [2014]	68	75.8
GNI per capita (current USD) [2015]	1590	7820
Growth rate [2015]	7.6%	69%
Trade per capita USD (2012-14)	822	215390
Trade to GDP Ratio (2012-14)	53.6	46.9

Source(s): World Development Indicators Database, World Bank' World Trade Organization statistics

In the context of understanding the areas of cooperation between India and China, the then Prime Minister Dr. Manmohan Singh's speech at the Central Party School in Beijing in October 2013[5] becomes important. The areas of cooperation he had outlined briefly are as follows:

- Expansion and modernisation of infrastructure.
- Efficient management of the process of mass urbanisation. City administrators in the two countries should share experiences and seek solutions in dealing with the physical, social, environmental and human challenges of mobility.
- Drawing upon China's strength in the manufacturing sector, which is vital for provision of mass employment. India has strengths in services, innovation and certain manufacturing sectors which can benefit China.
- Intensification of cooperation in energy security as well as joint development of renewable energy resources, along with working together in third world countries.
- Working together to impart stability to the global economy and sustaining growth.

- Working together to make the international economic environment more conducive.
- Joining hands to ensure that the international response to climate change does not constrain our growth.
- Cooperation in the eradication of terrorism. Ensuring maritime security in the Pacific and Indian Ocean respectively.

In the light of the areas outlined by Dr. Singh, it can be held that in the last two years, India and China have struck common ground—be it at the Nairobi talks of the WTO, on the issues of special and differentiated treatment (SDT), the special safeguards mechanism to protect farmers from import surges from developed countries or in Paris at the Conference of Parties (COP) 21. In the context of Chinese investment, data reveals that Chinese investment in India increased to USD2.3 billion in the past three months against USD1.3 billion in 2000-16. The investment of more than USD2.3 billion has been in four Indian companies, which include ad tech start up Media.net, drug maker Gland Pharma and electrical equipment maker Diamond Power Infrastructure Ltd. In contrast to USD2.3 billion investment announced in the past three months, China routed only USD1.35 billion in India by way of Foreign Direct Investment (FDI) between April 2000 and March 2016[6,7].

In the context of infrastructure creation, in 2016, China Railway Construction Corporation—one of the largest countries in the world—has shown interest in bidding for Rs. 35000-40,000 crore worth of highway contracts in India[8]. In the realm of addressing concerns of urbanisation, waste disposal and creation of smart cities, the following has taken place between India and China:

- Agreement between Guangdong and Maharashtra on cooperation in the smart city mission.
- Visit of Chinese delegation to Solapur for its development as a smart city.
- A Memorandum of Understanding (MoU), pledging investments worth Rs 19,000 crore to build a new smart city in Gujarat was signed between Gujarat government and China Small and Medium Enterprise Investment Limited (CSMEI) in 2015.
- MoU signed for bio-waste and city-waste based power projects in Gujarat.
- Guangdong's Richwood Group and iNDEXTb signed an MoU for developing hospitality and tourism infrastructure at Gandhinagar, transport infrastructure in Surat and logistic parks at Kandla port,

and Dahej Petroleum Chemicals and Petrochemical Investment Region (PCPIR).

- Another MoU signed between Gujarat government and Gao Xia, chairman, Hong Bang Finance and Investment Ltd. for infrastructure projects.

Climate change, which has emerged as one of the major sources of concern in the international system, has also seen better cooperation between India and China. The Agreement on Cooperation on Addressing Climate Change was signed between India and China in 2009. An MoU between the governments of the two countries on Cooperation on Green Technologies was signed in 2010. In a joint statement issued during Prime Minister Narendra Modi's visit to China in 2015, the two sides stressed the importance and urgency of implementing the outcomes of the Bali Road Map in order to increase the pre-2020 ambition and build mutual trust amongst countries. The two sides also urged the developed countries to raise their pre-2020 emission reduction targets and honour their commitment to provide 100 billion US dollars per year by 2020 to developing countries[9]. In 2014, India and China as part of the BASIC countries (Brazil, South Africa, India and China) in a meeting in New Delhi expressed disappointment over a "continued lack of any clear roadmap for providing USD100 billion a year by developed countries by 2020". In particular, the countries demanded "immediate and substantial capitalisation" of the Green Climate Fund, which is seeking to raise USD15 billion by the end of the year[10]. Thus, India and China have been collaborating actively on the issue of climate change not just at the bilateral level, but at the multilateral level as well.

Ahead of the BRICS summit last year in 2015, Chinese President Xi Jinping stated, "China and India should work together to build a closer, more comprehensive and firmer partnership among the BRICS countries". He added, "China and India, both as staunch supporters and active builders of the BRICS mechanism, work together to forge a closer, more comprehensive and firmer partnership within the emerging-market framework so as to enable the BRICS countries to play a positive and constructive role, and contribute more to world peace and development"[11]. Similarly, in August this year, PM Modi, during his meeting with Chinese foreign minister Wang Yi in New Delhi, stated that he cherishes friendship with Chinese leaders and looks forwards to exchanging views on further development of India-China ties with Chinese leaders on occasions including the G20 Summit and the BRICS Summit[12].

Within the ambit of the BRICS grouping as well, cooperation has taken place between the two. The purpose of foreign minister Wang Yi's visit to India just before the G20 Hangzhou Summit and the 8th BRICS Leaders Meeting, for example, was strategic communication with India. According to reports from the Press Trust of India, both sides agreed that the two countries have far more common interests than differences, far more aspects of cooperation than competition, and thus should place specific differences at a proper position in bilateral relations so as not to impact the overall friendliness[13]. On August 20, Lok Sabha speaker Sumitra Mahajan inaugurated the BRICS Women Parliamentarian Forum, where discussions were also held on implementation of the Sustainable Development Goals[14]. A rose garden has also been dedicated in New Delhi to the BRICS grouping[15]. In July, BRICS policy planning dialogue was conducted successfully in Patna, as there were fruitful exchanges of strategic assessments of prevailing international conditions and the regional situation of each member country[16]. Dialogues and communication through the BRICS platform, as seen in these mentioned cases, has also been a movement in the positive direction for Sino-Indian relations.

However, despite the seeming bonhomie, camaraderie and intent for cooperation, the bilateral relations remain at best a mix of cooperation and conflict, with conflict at times outweighing the positives of cooperation. The following sections trace the causes of the conflict to lay out a better understanding of the relationship between the two.

The Boundary Dispute

China, with the third largest territory in the world, also has the largest number of neighbours—14 to be precise; and India is its third largest neighbour. The two share about 3488 km land border[17]. Currently, China claims 92,000 square kilometers of Indian territory, which can be divided into the eastern, middle and western sectors. The eastern sector includes the McMahon Line which runs from the tri-junction between India, China and Bhutan from the West to Brahmaputra River in the East, largely along the crest of the Himalayas. The dispute in this sector is in the Indian state of Arunachal Pradesh. It occupies an area of about 90,000 km[18]. The middle sector starts from the tri-junction between the south-western of Ngari Prefecture, Tibet, La Dwags and Punjab to the tri-junction between China, India and Nepal. Its border is about 450 km long, with about 2,000 km of land under dispute. The disputed area in the middle sector on the other hand is much smaller, involving only several pockets. The western sector starts with the pass of Karakoram in the North to the tri-junction between Tibet's Ngari Prefecture, La dwags and Himachal Pradesh, running along 600 km. The disputed area, known as Aksai Chin to the outsiders, occupies about 33,500 km of land, and is under Chinese control.

The boundary dispute is a complex historical issue, and till date remains unsolved largely because neither side can agree to border delimitation. When India came under British rule, it began to advance the two countries' traditional border to the Chinese side[19]. In 1913-1914, a tripartite conference was held, which included representations from the Tibetan side and the Chinese side respectively, along with Sir Henry McMahon, the foreign secretary of the British-Indian government.

On July 3, 1914, Tibet and India signed the Simla Convention that gave birth to the McMahon Line, separating Tibet from India in the eastern sector. Although the Convention recognised that 'Tibet forms part of Chinese territory', the then Chinese authorities did not sign the Convention as they objected specifically only to Article 9 of the said Convention, that laid down the boundaries between Inner and Outer Tibet. Other than that, the Chinese authorities made it amply clear, on several occasions, that they did not object to any other Article, including that which showed the McMahon Line.

From the time of the signing of the Simla Convention in July 3, 1914 till January 23, 1959 when Prime Minister Zhou wrote a letter to Prime Minister Nehru, the Chinese never raised any formal objections to the McMahon Line; even though they had many opportunities to do so. In his letter dated January 23, 1959—Zhou, for the first time ever, made the following points to Nehru[20]:

- Firstly, that the Sino-Indian boundary had never been formally delimited and that no treaty or agreement had been concluded between the Chinese Central Government and the Government of India.
- Secondly, that the McMahon Line was a product of the British policy of aggression against the Tibetan Region of China.
- Thirdly, Zhou admitted that the Tibetan local authorities had signed the Convention but were dissatisfied with the 'unilaterally drawn' line. Nevertheless, Zhou asserted that 'the Chinese government finds it necessary to take a realistic attitude towards the McMahon Line'.

Today, China maintains that the McMahon Line effectively sees India occupying some 90,000 square kilometres of its territory in the Indian state of Arunachal Pradesh. India, on the other hand, claims that China is 'occupying 38,000 square kilometres of land in Aksai Chin in the North-eastern corner of Jammu and Kashmir' and a further '5180 square kilometres of land in Kashmir ceded to it by Pakistan in 1963'[21].

In terms of attempts made to resolve the boundary dispute, it first becomes pertinent to mention the Sino-Indian skirmish of 1962, which led to a break down of diplomatic relations between the two sides. It was only in 1976 that diplomatic relations were re-established, with ministerial-level exchanges beginning in 1979. From 1981 to 1987, the Indian government and Chinese government conducted eight rounds of border negotiations.

Rajiv Gandhi's visit to Beijing in 1988 was a turning point in Sino-Indian relations because this was the first Prime Minister visit, 34 years after Nehru's visit in 1954[22]. This visit successfully de-escalated the tension over border issues, and established an Indian-Chinese Joint Working Group that organised six round of talks to solve border disputes from 1988 to 1993. It also led to an increase in the high-level exchanges in the 1990s. In 1991, Chinese Premier Li Peng reciprocated a visit to India—31 years after Premier Zhou Enlai. Then, in 1992, the first ever Indian defense minister Sharad Pawar went to Beijing for broader cooperation. When Prime Minister Narasimha Rao visited China in 1993, he signed the Agreement on the Maintenance of Border Peace and Tranquility, which provided as guiding principles over border issues. In return, in 1994, Chinese defense minister Chi Haotian came to New Delhi for extensive talks with high-level Indian trade and defense officials. One result of Chi's meeting was troop reduction along the Himalayan frontier. Two years later, Chinese President Jiang Zemin's India visit resulted in the signing of the Agreement on Confidence Building Measures, which reiterated the guiding principles such as demilitarisation on border issues. These political interactions between leaders in the two governments steadily improved the Sino-Indian relations from 1976 to the early years of the 20th century. Cumulative outcomes of nine key visits in recent times have been transformational for Sino-Indian ties. These were that of Prime Minister Vajpayee [2003], of Premier Wen Jiabao [2005 and 2010], of President Hu Jintao [2006], of Prime Minister Manmohan Singh [2008 and 2013], of Premier Li Keqiang [2013], of President Xi Jinping [2014] and of Prime Minister Narendra Modi [2015][23,24].

The 19th round of border talks between the two sides was held in 2016. National Security Advisor Ajit Doval held the annual talks with Chinese counterpart Yang Jiechi to discuss the road ahead to resolve the dispute, which has bedevilled bilateral ties. In recent years, there has been a marked increase of confidence building measures between China and India, including establishing the Working Mechanism, which is tasked with resolving any issues that arise on the border. In lieu of any border incidents to resolve and seemingly unable to make any progress on resolving the border, the 19th SRM appeared to turn its focus on efforts to smooth over other bilateral concerns[25].

While the Sino-Indian border is placid as compared to the Indo-Pakistani border for example; fact remains that border transgressions and/or incursions have been a regular feature of this dispute. According to statistics from the Ministry of Home Affairs, the number of transgressions from 2010 are as follows:

Table 10.2: Year-wise Transgressions by PLA into India

Year	*Number*
2010	228
2011	213
2012	426
2013	411
2014 (till August)	334

Source: Ministry of Home Affairs[26], New Delhi.

Beyond transgressions, there are issues of aggressive border patrols and incursions too[27]. Both sides interpret the border differently. A transgression for India means that Chinese troops cross over into Indian territory and eventually retreating into their own side. Intrusion, on the other hand, means crossing over the boundary and staying put in Indian territory. However, India has maintained that there has been no intrusion by the Chinese Army since 2010. China, on its part, refers in general only to occurrences of "isolated incidents" on the border[28]. China also states that India is transgressing along the line of the Line of Actual Control (LAC), and the number may be more than the number stated by India. The point to which both sides agree is that differing perceptions lead to continuing border tensions.

A Brief History of Economic Ties

A quick cursory glance at bilateral trade between the two sides in the last 30 years reveals that the relationship went through an initial slow growth in the first two decades, and then increased in the third decade. Growth in bilateral economic relations was minimal from 1981 to 1993. Even though the two sides concluded a comprehensive trade agreement and a mutual bestowal of Most-Favored-Nation (MFN) status in 1984, the bilateral trade remained negligible in the 1980s. The signing of Agreement on the Maintenance of

Border Peace and Tranquillity in 1993 propelled the economic relationship to a new stage. At this point, the political agreement over border issues encouraged bilateral trade to grow. Another plausible explanation for the increase in that period is that India and China, at the time, possessed competitive rather than complementary economic structures[29]. From 1993 to 2003, the bilateral trade showed signs of steadying growth. The following graph shows the bilateral trade between the two:

Graph 10.2: Bilateral Trade between India and China: 1994-2014

Unit: USD10,000

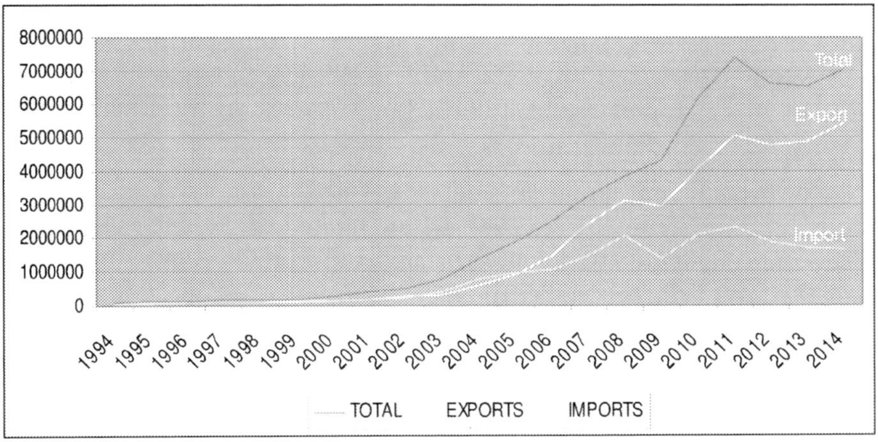

Source(s): China Statistical Yearbooks; 1995-2015.

As seen in graph 10.2, bilateral trade between the two has been extremely low in the 1990s, especially when seen in contrast with the decade of the 2000s—which sees a gradual but steady pick up. Additionally, this period also coincides with the two countries' respective domestic policies of reforms and liberalisation. The renewed focus of both on the forces of globalisation to integrate their own respective domestic economies with the global economy also had at least a small role in ushering closer economic relations between India and China. After India liberalised its market in 1991 and went through structural adjustments, its total foreign trade began to grow in the 1990s, and grew much more rapidly after 2000. Meanwhile, China experienced an increase in its total foreign trade after it opened the market in 1978. Especially after Deng Xiaoping's Southern Tour to Shenzhen Economic Zone in 1992, China developed its manufacturing power, and become an exports-led economy. In 2003, the visit of the then Indian Prime Minister Atal Behari Vajpayee to China accelerated the momentum for economic integration. The visit led to a pragmatic decision by both sides to cultivate economic ties without being constrained by the unresolved border dispute. After this, the two sides set up a joint study group to examine how India and China could expand trade and cooperation.

With increasing trade between the two, the importance of the two in their respective lists of largest trading partner has also undergone drastic changes. In 1993 for example, China was at rank 13 in India's list of trading partners. In 2015, China ranks at 1 in the same list. However, the reverse is not true, i.e. India does not figure in the most important trade partners for China. China's largest trading partners include the US, the EU, South Korea, Taiwan and ASEAN. In 2001, Japan was China's largest trading partner, followed by the US, the EU, Hong Kong, ASEAN, South Korea and Taiwan. In 2013, it was the US which ranked at 1, followed by Japan, South Korea, Taiwan and Germany. The constant feature is India's absence in this particular list.

However, the importance of India is particularly high in China's trade in South Asia. India's total trade with China ranked the top among all South Asian countries' trade with China. The Sino-Indian trade is seven times greater than the Sino-Pakistani trade, the second biggest trade in 2010. Although India only counts about 2 per cent of China's foreign trade so far, it is an increasingly important market and vital trading partner to China in South Asia. The following graph shows China's trade with South Asian countries:

Graph 10.3: China's South Asia Trade

Unit: USD 10,000

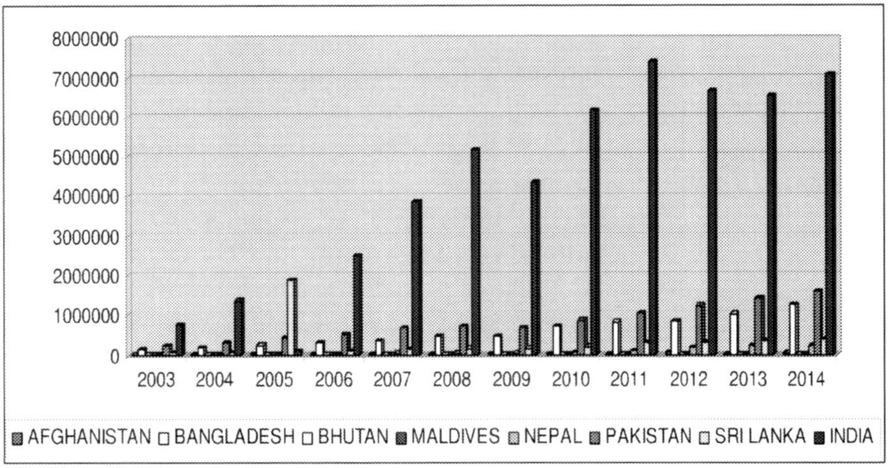

Source(s): China Statistical Yearbooks.

The case of China's total trade with South Asia (including that with India) is extremely dismal. China's exports to the region accounted for 1.59 per cent of China's total exports in 2001 and 3.44 per cent in 2012. In 2001, China's imports from South Asian countries accounted only 0.95 per cent of China's total imports, and in 2012, the ratio was merely 1.29 per cent. This is the case when trade with India is also included. If the component of total trade with India is excluded, then it is seen that in 2013, China's total trade with South Asian countries accounted for only 0.106 per cent of China's global trade. In short, imports and exports from South Asian countries (with the exception of India) are of minimal importance to China's overall trade profile. However, within China's South Asia trade relations, those with India become pertinent. In 2013 for example, China's total trade with SAARC stood at 92.99 billion, and trade with India represented 70.32 per cent. In this context, India stands as a bright spot in China's trade relations with South Asian countries.

The Persistent Trade Deficit

In 2008, China replaced the US as India's largest trading partner. China has an edge over India in terms of manufacturing exports more than India does. With an increase in the two-way trade between the two, what has also been witnessed is an exponential increase in the trade deficit for India. While the uncovered trade gap was reported at USD602 million in 1998, it increased alarmingly to USD39.2 billion in 2012[30] and to USD48 billion in 2015[31]. The following graph shows the trade deficit for India in the last five years:

Graph 10.4: The Trade Deficit

Unit: USD millions

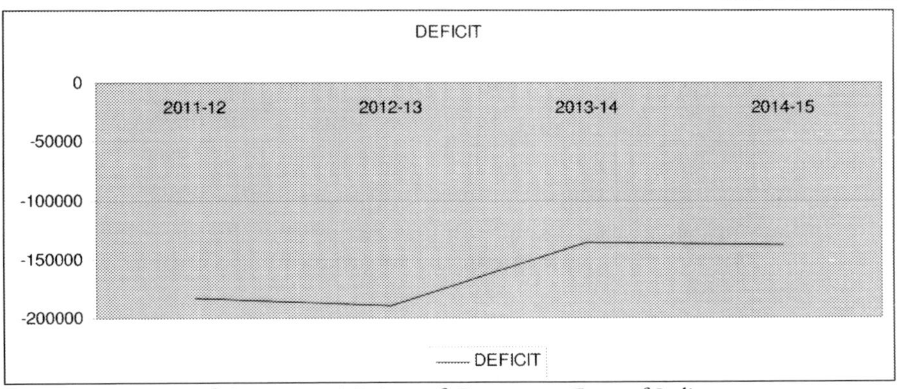

Source: Department of Commerce, Ministry of Commerce, Govt. of India.

As seen in graph 10.4, the worst trade deficit in the more recent past has been in the year 2012-13. While the trade deficit reduced in 2013-14, it is far from being a sustainable one for India. In 2014-15, India's exports to China stood at USD11.95 billion while imports were USD60.39 billion[32].

China's New Normal and Implications for India

After years of double digit GDP growth rates, the Chinese economic model which was primarily reliant on exports and investment is now attempting a shift to a model based on internal consumption as a growth driver, along with reinforcing the tilt towards services sector. The 'New Normal' also means a growth rate of 6.6 per cent, which has been made a target in the country's 13th five year plan. Given that China is the world's largest manufacturer and trader, a top commodity buyer, a significant outward investor and inward FDI (Foreign Direct Investment) destination, and a huge emerging market, management of its slowing economy bears crucial implications for the shape of the global economy in the future. As an increasingly integrated member of the global economic community and a large economy in its own right, India is also likely to feel the impact[33].

India's export basket (exports to China) is dominated by commodities like cotton, copper, cement and mineral fuels, and these are commodities the prices of which are likely to remain subdued. Exports to China are not likely to hold up in the next few years. As stated by Sharmila Kantha of the Confederation of Indian Industries, unfortunately, exports of machinery and electrical equipment—which also figure in the top 10 exports from India to China—have also failed to maintain their volume and value[34]. In a situation where China wants to spur its own domestic consumption and address its own problems of prevailing oversupply, import reduction is not unimaginable. In fact, imports have already begun to shrink, and India is likely to see its trade deficit with China rising in the near future. The only way that the slowdown in China may impact India positively is that it may bring more investment for India; as there is a movement of global FDI out of China and into India; and secondly, through increasing Chinese investments in India. Increasing FDI from China is one of the most favourable ways to address the trade deficit.

Addressing the Trade Deficit

The reason as to why India does not fare in the list of top trading partners is because of its lack of comparative advantage in producing goods, especially in comparison with countries such as the US, Japan and Taiwan for example. However, in the goods in which India does have a comparative advantage, pharmaceuticals for example, there exists tariff as well as non-tariff barriers for Indian products in China.

While licences and registration timelines for Chinese APIs are granted by the Indian Drug Regulatory Authority in about four months, it takes roughly about five to six years for established Indian pharma firms to register their products in China[35].

Even in the case of IT/ITES and agricultural commodities, there exist a series of non-tariff barriers for Indian exports. Indian IT services are unable to make a breakthrough in China's opaque State-controlled and State-owned enterprises. Additional issues faced are those of banking and foreign exchange remittance procedures, lack of intellectual property standards and the lack of transparency. A series of Memorandums of Understanding have been signed in the past on allowing more bovine meat, IT services and pharmaceuticals from India to enter China. However, ground realities are that no progress has taken place at all. Despite assurances given by China several times to address the trade deficit, nothing has taken place so far. Given the slowdown in the Chinese economy amidst the New Normal, demand from China is only set to decrease, and signals a worse spell of trade deficit for India as far as bilateral trade is concerned.

A plausible way to address the trade deficit is through increasing levels of foreign direct investment (FDI) in India. In 2015, according to reports from FDI intelligence, a division of Financial Times, India emerged as the top destination for FDI, replacing China—which had been at the position for several years in a row. An increase in the number of investment projects in coal and power in India helped in surpassing China[36]. As far as investment from China is concerned, it ranks at 17th in India's list of countries which have foreign investment in India. Chinese investment in India, as of September 30, 2015, were to the tune of USD1.24 billion, which is 0.47 per cent of the total FDI inflow in India in 2015[37]. The following graph shows the FDI received from China from 2000-01 to 2015-16 (up to September) (graph 10.5):

As seen in graph 10.5, FDI has been close to zero largely up to 2007-08, after which it has shown a very weak take off. The low levels of FDI get highlighted further when contrasted with the total FDI inflow received by India, as shown in graph 10.6.

Graph 10.5: FDI Inflow from China

Unit: USD millions

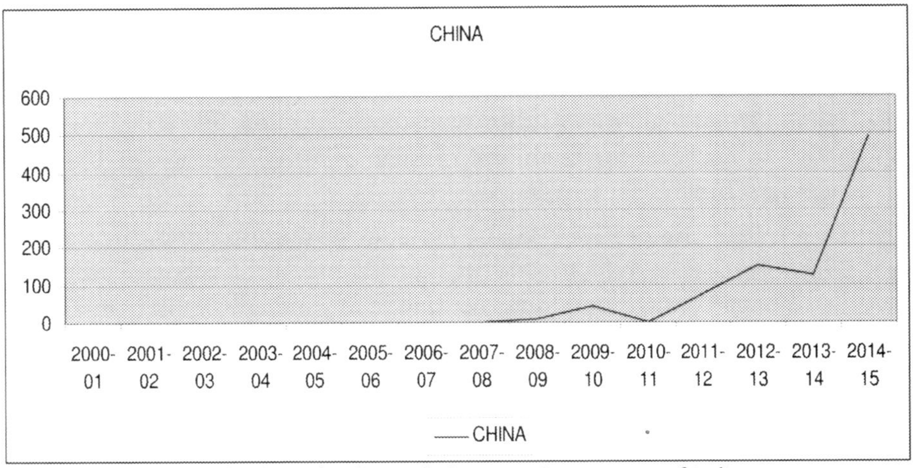

Source: Department of Industrial Policy and Planning, Government. of India

Graph 10.6: FDI Inflow from China versus Total Inflow

Unit: USD millions

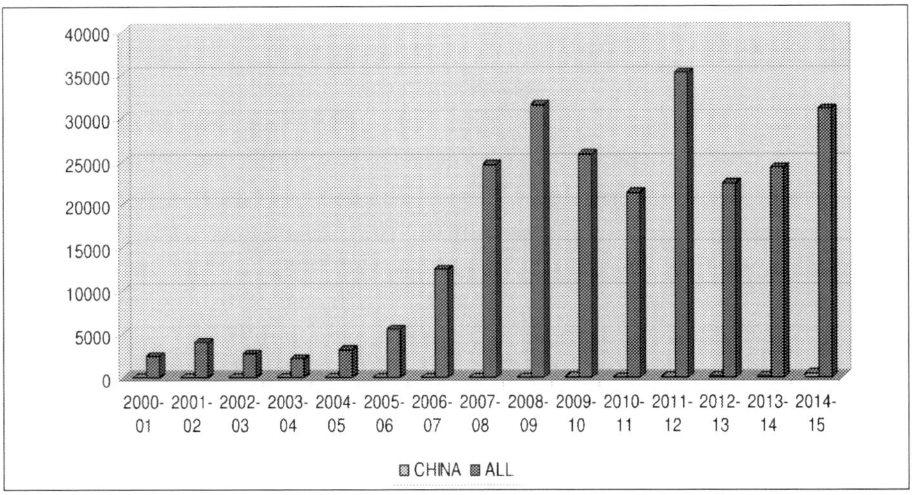

Source: Department of Industrial Policy and Planning, Government. of India.

Even in 2014-15, while the total FDI inflow for India amounted to USD30,931 million, India received only USD494.75 million as FDI from China. The maximum FDI equity flow from China was in the financial year of 2011-12. The previous high was in the financial year of 2008-09. Between

2011-12 and 2012-13, the decline in FDI inflow from China was of 56.62 per cent. The increase in trade deficit in the same time period was that of 3.96 per cent. Overall, the period only saw declines, which have not been in India's favour. Therefore, in case the persistent trade balance actually has to be rectified, an urgent look at increasing FDI from China needs to be stressed.

Additional Thorny Issues in 2015-16

While the number of tensions in the relationship between India and China are already outweighing the positives, additional issues to worsen the relationship arose in 2015-16. The most problematic issues were in the form of Chinese ambiguous response to the United Nations Security Council (UNSC) reforms, China blocking India's NSG bid, Chinese refusal to blacklist JEM leader at the UN, and India initially issuing a visa to exiled Uyghur activist Dolkun Isa.

UNSC Reforms and China's Stance

The group of four or G4, comprising India, Germany, Brazil and Japan, have been trying to get a text-based negotiation in the UN General Assembly. However, so far, this has not met with any success.

The new facilitator of the inter-governmental negotiations (IGN), Courtenay Rattray of Jamaica, promised a working text which would be the basis for international negotiations on how to reform the UNSC. In March 2015, Rattray shared a framework document in the General Assembly which is supposed to segue into a negotiating text. China's ambassador, Liu Jieyi, opposed the text. Since then, China has mounted a strong diplomatic offensive against text-based negotiations in various capitals of the world, either through demarches or by visiting various capitals in the world—according to sources, they have been very active in African capitals and among the Pacific islands to "sensitize" them about the Chinese position. Diplomats from different countries have said that China wants most countries to go slow on these processes[38].

In September last year, China came out with a guarded and ambivalent reaction to a call by G4 nations, including India, for their inclusion as permanent members in the UN Security Council, saying it supports the reforms to improve the Council but with widest possible consensus. Chinese Foreign Ministry spokesman Hong Lei said, "China supports the UN Security Council reform so as to enhance its authority and effectiveness". He added that the UNSC reform should give priority to the representation and voice of the developing countries"[39].

The problem with an attitude ranging from ambiguity to outright hostility while stating the need for more voices from the developing countries in the international order leaves no scope for trust or cooperation, and statements on "win-win" and "mutual benefit" become mere rhetoric.

China Blocks India's Bid to Ban Masood Azhar

In April this year, India approached the UN to include Pakistan-based terror master mind Masood Azhar on the list of globally designated terrorists. As stated by India, it is a great anomaly that the Jaish-e-Mohammed (JeM) is listed in the 1267 Sanctions Committee, but not its leader. However, the attempt failed because of China's last minute opposition.

The 1267 Sanctions Committee was a result of the UN Resolution on October 15, 1999. As the 1267 Committee officially takes decisions on the basis of consensus, the permanent five can exercise veto powers by placing a proposal on "technical hold", which is exactly what China did in the Masood Azhar case. This delays the case for three months. A listing of terror outfits/ individuals leads to an asset freeze, a travel ban and an arms embargo[40].

China stated technical reasons for its stance on listing Masood Azhar, and as stated by Chinese Foreign Ministry spokesperson Hua Chunyin, China "encourage(s) all parties related to the listing matter of Masood Azhar to have direct communication and work out a solution through serious consultations". She added, "China is willing to continue with its communication with all the relevant parties," signalling Beijing's intent to stay diplomatically engaged on this subject, and achieve results based on consensus[41]. The deadlock over the issue continues. Previously in 2015, China had put the Indian request to question Pakistan on the release of 26/11 mastermind Zaki-ur Rehman Lakhvi on "technical hold", and China stated that India had not provided "sufficient information" in support of its case[42].

What is pertinent to note here is that terrorism is not consensus-based, and a global attempt to reduce the impact of terrorism, if not completely eradicate, is needed. China and India, both fully understand the consequences of terrorism, and shielding terrorists and terror organisations in the name of adherence to technical details is definitely not the right approach when it comes to dealing with the ever-pertinent issue of terrorism.

The Dolkun Isa Visa Issue

Roughly coinciding with China's opposition to India's attempts to put Masood Azhar on the list of globally-designated terrorists came about the issue of granting of visa to Uyghur activist Dolkun Isa to attend a conference in India. The Indian government had initially given Mr. Isa a tourist visa. However, after China's displeasure, the visa was revoked. As stated by India, the visa was revoked because the purpose for which the visa was granted was tourism; however, the purpose of Mr. Isa's planned visit was attending a conference. India has also suggested that Interpol's red corner notice was one of the reasons for the cancellation.

While there have been several speculations on whether the initial granting of visa was retaliation against China's opposition to list Masood Azhar on the global list of terrorists or not, or whether India cowed down to China or not—fact remains that India attached importance to concerns raised by the Chinese side. Isa is the chairman of the Germany-based World Uighur Congress. China has been battling Uighur separatism in Xinjiang since the 1990s, and began labelling separatists there as "terrorists" since 2001 to get global support—even as its stringent policies have been fuelling militancy further[43].

In the context of maintaining cordial, if not friendly bilateral relations, it is pertinent that mutual recognition of each other's concerns is undertaken. A relationship based on the principles of classical realism alone in the 21st century will not lead to any peaceful outcome.

India's Failed Bid at NSG Membership

At the Plenary Meeting of Nuclear Suppliers Group (NSG) in Seoul in South Korea, India failed to gain entry into NSG. She has been trying for NSG membership since 2008. The group had earlier failed to reach a consensus on New Delhi's membership application after several members of the 48-member group insisted on adhering to Non Proliferation Treaty (NPT) conditions for admission. While the common perception is that it was China that blocked India's membership, fact remains that there were other countries which were grappling with the question of admission of non-NPT signatories to the NSG as well. Besides China, the other countries that opposed India's membership included Switzerland, Brazil, Turkey, Austria, Ireland and New Zealand.

Technically, the requirement for NSG membership does require signing the NPT, fact also remains that China itself has undertaken proliferation despite being a signatory[44]. According to Kan, between the 1990s and 2000, the Bush and Clinton administrations faced the issue of whether to impose sanctions on PRC entities or state owned enterprises (SOEs) for transferring M-11 short range ballistic missiles or related technology to Pakistan. However, sanctions were waived in return for another non-proliferation promise from Beijing. However, proliferation continued and in September 2011, the Bush administration imposed sanctions for PRC proliferation of missile technology to Pakistan, denying satellite exports to China[45].

In the current context, it becomes pertinent that proliferation of weapons indeed gets curtailed. While adherence to technical details on non-proliferation is correct, an attempt to ensure non-proliferation actually becomes a reality that is required.

BRICS and the Scope for Cooperation

The BRICS grouping is seen as an important organisation in the context of South-South cooperation. Composed of leading emerging economies, the BRICS is now entering the domain of development assistance. According to an agreement signed by the five members at the Sixth BRICS Summit in 2014, the organisation developed a New Development Bank (NDB) and a Contingent Reserve Agency (CRA). Unlike the Bretton Woods Institution which require large amount of collaterals over and above structural economic reforms, the NDB will help in infrastructure development of all countries.

Beyond the establishment of NDB, the grouping also has significance in terms of providing a platform for deliberations and discussions. Since the first summit, the BRICS countries (BRIC at that time) have called for a more multilateral world order, which is based on cooperation, coordinated action and collective decision making of all the the States. Hence, they started to form a strategic alliance to reform, for the 21st century, the institutions of global governance such as the World Bank, IMF and the UNSC—which have remained largely unchanged since 1945. The BRICS, as a group, are expected to step up their role and extend to pressing peace and security challenges—from terrorism, piracy and nuclear non-proliferation to regional security in North Africa and the Middle East[46]. Speaking at a seminar titled BRICS-upon-BRICS for a Stronger BRICS: Challenges and Opportunities, held in August this year, Shakti Sinha, a former bureaucrat, stated that BRICS plays a pivotal role as "no country can alone respond to impacts of globalisation".

Even though he was skeptical of how far the group can help in resolving disputes between India and China, he said that through group reforms in sectors like e-commerce, agriculture and climate change could be looked at[47].

What remains to be witnessed is the level of coordination among these five countries in setting the global agenda. The lack of coordination is witnessed even in the setting up of the BRICS University. The BRICS Network University (BRICS-NU) was first mooted in March 2015, and was scheduled to be launched in 2016. But the member countries—Russia, China, India, Brazil and South Africa—are yet to find common modalities for the unique venture. Several technical issues like curriculum, language differences among the students of member countries and the nature of infrastructure are yet to be resolved. These issues are likely to be taken up by the education ministers of the member-countries of BRICS during the upcoming summit in Goa, India[48].

The BRICS platform as such provides an immensely valuable platform for identifying issues that are of global concern, and which need a more concerted effort to tackle. Terrorism or the global economic slowdowns are examples of issues that affect not just these five countries but the world at large. In order to be a more potent force in international affairs, the grouping could identify the issues for deliberation so as to present a more concerted effort. Cooperation in the form of the setting up of the NDB and the CRA has already been witnessed, and this clearly implies that the grouping does have immense scope for deliberations and arrival at consensus on issues of concern. In the post Brexit world for example, developing countries need a judicious mix of fiscal, monetary and structural policies, as stated by India's finance minister Arun Jaitley at the first annual meeting of the board of governors of the New Development Bank of BRICS, held in July this year[49]. It is such issues which can be better addressed through groupings which represent the Global South, and the BRICS is the best platform for this.

For both India and China, the BRICS grouping definitely is a valuable forum to hammer out thorny issues in order to move at least a step closer to a win-win outcome. However, a movement forward at the multilateral level would mean reducing the thorns at the bilateral level so that actual cooperation and not mere lip service can take place.

END NOTES

1. Fen Osler Hampson and Paul Heinbecker, 'The "New" Multilateralism of the Twenty-First Century', Global Governance, 17, 2011, p. 299.
2. 黄荣斌 (2012), "后危机时代" 金砖国家的投资合作, "后危机时代" 金砖国家的投资合作, Vol. 28, No. 2, pp. 67-76. (Huang Rong Bin, "BRICS' Investment Cooperation in the Post crisis

Era", International Economics and Trade Journal)

3. Sergei Guriyev, "Five Questions About the BRICS Countries", World Economic Forum, URL: https://www.weforum.org/agenda/2015/07/five-questions-about-the-brics-nations/ Accesses on September 1, 2016.
4. Zhang Guo You (2010), "金砖四国"与"金柱四国"间大公司势力状态比较" (A Comparative Research of Large Enterprises Between in BRICs and in FGPCs) Economic Management, Vol. 32, No. 12.
5. *The Hindu*, October 24, 2013, "Manmohan Singh's speech on India-China relations at the Central Party School, Beijing", URL: http://www.thehindu.com/news/resources/manmohan-singhs-speech-on-indiachina-relations-at-the-central-party-school-beijing/article5268097.ece Accessed on September 1, 2016.
6. Keshav Sunkara (2016), "Chinese investment in India shoots to $2.3 bn in past 3 months against $1.35 bn in 2000-16 , August 30, 2016, URL: http://www.vccircle.com/news/economy/2016/08/30/chinese-investment-india-shoots-23-bn-past-3-months-against-135-bn-2000-16 Accessed on September 1, 2016.
7. A latter section of this chapter deals with the issue of Chinese foreign investment in India in greater detail.
8. Rajat Arora, *Economic Times*, "Chinese corporation to bid for Rs 40,000 crore highway contract in India, July 13, 2016, URL: http://economictimes.indiatimes.com/news/economy/infrastructure/chinese-corporation-to-bid-for-rs-40000-crore-highway-contract-in-india/articleshow/53183652.cms Accessed on September 1, 2016
9. Narendra Modi, 2015, "Joint Statement on Climate Change Between India and China During Prime Minster's Visit to China", May 15, 2015, URL: http://www.narendramodi.in/joint-statement-on-climate-change-between-india-and-china-during-prime-minister-s-visit-to-china-63630 Accessed on September 1, 2016.
10. *Climate Change News*, August 8, 2014 "BASIC Countries Urge Rich Countries to Act on Climate Change", URL: http://www.climatechangenews.com/2014/08/08/basic-group-urges-rich-countries-to-act-on-climate-change/ Accessed on September 1, 2016
11. *Xinhua*, 2015, "BRICS: Xi seeks Sino-Indian efforts", July 9, 2015, URL: http://www.chinadailyasia.com/nation/2015-07/09/content_15287703.html Accessed on September 1, 2016
12. *Xinhua*, August 14, 2015, China, India agree on mutual support to successfully host G20, BRICS summits URL: http://news.xinhuanet.com/english/2016-08/14/c_135594231.htm Accessed on September 1, 2016.
13. *Navhind Times* (2016), "India China Agree Not to Let Differences Affect Ties", Beijing, August 18, 2016, URL: http://www.navhindtimes.in/india-china-agree-not-to-let-differences-affect-ties/ Accessed on September 12, 2016
14. *The Indian Express* (2016), "Lok Sabha speaker Sumitra Mahajan to inaugurate BRICS Women Parliamentarian Forum", Jaipur, August 17, 2016, URL: http://indianexpress.com/article/india/india-news-india/brics-women-parliamentarian-forum-meet-in-jaipur-2981173/ Accessed on September 12, 2016
15. *NDTV* (2016) "Delhi Gets Rose Garden Dedicated To BRICS Summit", August 10, 2016, New Delhi, URL: http://www.ndtv.com/delhi-news/delhi-gets-rose-garden-dedicated-to-brics-summit-1442716 Accessed on September 12, 2016
16. *Times of India* (2016), "BRICS policy planning dialogue ends on a successful note: MEA", July 26, 2016, Patna, URL: http://timesofindia.indiatimes.com/city/patna/BRICS-policy-planning-dialogue-ends-on-a-successful-note-MEA/articleshow/53400199.cms Accessed on September 12, 2016

17. Ministry of Home Affairs, Department of Border Management, Government of India, http://www.mha.nic.in/hindi/sites/upload_files/mhahindi/files/pdf/BM_Intro_E_.pdf Accessed on August 8 2016
18. Vivek Raghuvanshi, 2015, "India China Border Talks Make No headway", URL: http://www.defensenews.com/story/defense/policy-budget/leaders/2015/05/23/india-china-border-dispute-summit-talks-lac-tibet-pakistan/27601373/ Accessed on August 7, 2016
19. M. Neville, Forty Years of Folly: What Caused the Sino-Indian Border War and Why the Dispute Is Unresolved, «Critical Asian Studies», vol. 35, no. 1, 2003, pp. 99-112.
20. S. Kalha, 2014, "The McMahon Line: A hundred years on", Institute of Defence and Strategic Analyses", URL: http://www.idsa.in/idsacomments/TheMcMahonLine_rskalha_030714, Accessed on August 6, 2016
21. Tsering Topygal, 'Charting the Tibet Issue in the Sino-Indian Border Dispute', *China Report*, Vol. 47, No. 2, 2011, page 120
22. John Garver, "Sino-Indian Rapprochement and the Sino-Pakistan Entente," *Political Science Quarterly*, (111:2), Summer 1996, 546
23. India-China Relations (2016), Ministry of External Affairs, New Delhi
24. See Annex 1 for the latest visits and outcomes of the visits between 2013-16.
25. Stephen Westcott, *The Diplomat*, "The Ongoing Saga of the China-India Border Talks", May 2, 2016, URL: http://thediplomat.com/2016/05/the-ongoing-saga-of-the-china-india-border-talks/ Accessed on August 3, 2016
26. Kamaljeet Kaur Sandhu, 2016, "How China Is Provoking India: 250 Soldiers Intrude into Arunachal, Beijing Blocks India's NSG Bid", URL: http://indiatoday.intoday.in/story/china-transgression-arunachal-pradesh-india-nsg-bid/1/690662.html, Accessed on August 10, 2016
27. For notable Chinese intrusions and events pertaining to the disputed Sino Indian border, see Annexure 2 at the end of the chapter
28. D.S. Rajan, April 2015, "Chinese Intrusions into India's Borders Ever End?", URL: http://www.southasiaanalysis.org/node/1758#_ftn5 Accessed on August 8, 2016
29. John Garver, "Sino-Indian Rapprochement and the Sino-Pakistan Entente," *Political Science Quarterly*, (111:2), Summer 1996, 326.
30. S.K. Mohanty, January 2014, Study Prepared for Reserve Bank of India, "India China Report", Page 42, RIS, URL: http://www.ris.org.in/sites/default/files/pdf/India%20china%20report.pdf
31. *The Hindu*, May 13, 2015, "India China Trade Deficit Swells from 34 to 48 Billion, URL: http://www.thehindu.com/news/national/indiachina-trade-deficit-swells-34-to-48-billion/article7201545.ece Accessed on 7 August 2016
32. *The Hindu*, May 13, 2015, URL: http://www.thehindu.com/news/national/indiachina-trade-deficit-swells-34-to-48-billion/article7201545.ece
33. Sharmila Kantha (2016), "What does China's 'new normal' mean for India?" 17 June 2016, URL: http://www.ideasforindia.in/article.aspx?article_id=1648 Accessed on September 1, 2016
34. Ibid.
35. *Economic Times*, September 16, 2014, "China Should Open Up to Indian Generic Drugs: Experts", URL: http://articles.economictimes.indiatimes.com/2014-09-16/news/53983182_1_indian-companies-indian-pharmaceutical-apis Accessed on August 7, 2016
36. Huang, Zheping and Karnik, Madhura, Quartz India, "India Attracted More FDI than China in 2015", April 22, 2016, URL: http://qz.com/667598/india-attracted-more-fdi-than-china-in-2015/ Accessed on August 7, 2016
37. "FDI Synopis on Country China", Department of Industrial Policy and Planning, New Delhi, URL: http://www.dipp.nic.in/English/Investor/China_Desk/FDI_Synopsis_China.pdf Accessed on August 7, 2016

38. Indrani Bagchi, "China emerges as principal opposition to UNSC reforms", August 1, 2015, New Delhi, URL: http://timesofindia.indiatimes.com/india/China-emerges-as-principal-opposition-to-UNSC-reforms/articleshow/48303032.cms Accessed on September 1, 2016
39. Press Trust of India, "China ambivalent on G4 call for UNSC reforms", September 28, 2015, URL: http://economictimes.indiatimes.com/news/defence/china-ambivalent-on-g4-call-for-unsc-reforms/articleshow/49137968.cms Accessed on September 1, 2015
40. United Nations, "Sanctions Measures", URL: https://www.un.org/sc/suborg/en/sanctions/1267 Accessed on August 7, 2016
41. Atul Aneja, "China urges India, Pak. to hold talks" *The Hindu*, April 26, 2016, New Delhi, URL: http://www.thehindu.com/news/china-nudges-india-and-pakistan-to-establish-direct-contact-on-masood-azhar/article8524358.ece Accessed on August 7, 2016
42. Sushant Singh, "Behind the news: Lakhvi, UNSCR 1267, and China's 'technical hold'," *The Indian Express*, New Delhi, June 25, 2015, http://indianexpress.com/article/explained/behind-the-news-lakhvi-unscr-1267-and-chinas-technical-hold/ Accessed on August 7, 2016
43. Harsh Pant, 2016, The Dolkun Isa Visa Affair : India Mishandles China Once Again, The Diplomat, http://thediplomat.com/2016/04/the-dolkun-isa-visa-affair-india-mishandles-china-once-again/ Accessed on August 7, 2016.
44. Devirupa Mitra, June 24, 2016, The Wire, New Delhi, "India Stumbles at NSG Door, Blames 'One Country' for Tripping It Up", URL: http://thewire.in/45678/india-stumbles-at-nsg-door-blames-one-country-for-tripping-it-up/ Accessed on August 7, 2016.
45. Shirley A. Kan, "China and Proliferation of Weapons of Mass Destruction and Missiles: Proliferation Issues", January 5, 2015, p. 6, Congressional Research Service. URL: https://www.fas.org/sgp/crs/nuke/RL31555.pdf
46. "The BRICS Forum: The Evolving Role of BRICS in a Changing World", April 28, 2015, http://www.gdforum.org/balkanssecurity-2-2/ Accessed on August 7, 2016.
47. *The Indian Express* (2016), "BRICS yet to broker peace between India and China: Former bureaucrat", August 12, 2016, Panaji, URL: http://www.newindianexpress.com/nation/BRICS-yet-to-broker-peace-between-India-and-China-Former-bureaucrat/2016/08/12/article3576387.ece Accessed on September 12, 2016.
48. *The Hindu* (2016), "Technical issues delay launch of BRICS university", August 12, 2016, New Delhi, URL: http://www.thehindu.com/news/national/technical-issues-delay-launch-of-brics-university/article8975336.ece Accessed on September 12, 2016.
49. *The Indian Express* (2016), "Developing economies need judicious mix of policies in post-Brexit scene: India", Shanghai, July 21, 2016, URL: http://www.newindianexpress.com/business/news/Developing-economies-need-judicious-mix-of-policies-in-post-Brexit-scene-India/2016/07/21/article3540563.ece Accessed on September 12, 2016.

Annex 1: Important Visits 2013-16

Month/Year	*Details of Visit*	*Outcome (s)*
May 2013	State visit of Premier Li Keqiang to New Delhi	• 8 agreements signed • Joint statement issued, which included proposals to designate 2014 as the Year of Friendly Exchanges between India and China and hold the first High Level Media Forum
Oct 2013	Former Prime Minister Dr. Manmohan Singh paid an official visit to China	• Agreements relating to border, trans-border rivers, establishing service centres for servicing power equipment in India, road transport and Nalanda University signed. • Also signed were three agreements establishing sister-city partnership between Delhi-Beijing, Kolkata Kunming and Bangalore-Chengdu.
June 2014	Vice president Shri Hamid Ansari paid a visit to China	• Three agreements related to industrial parks, training of public officials, and exchange of flood season data on the Yarlung Zangbu River were signed. • The two Vice presidents also jointly released the English and Chinese versions of the Encyclopedia of India-China Cultural Contacts.
Sept 2014	President Xi Jinping paid a State visit to India	• 16 agreements were signed during the visit in various sectors including, commerce and trade, railways, space-cooperation, pharmaceuticals, audio- visual co-production, culture, establishment of industrial parks, sister-city arrangements etc. • MoU signed to open an additional route for Kailash Mansarovar Yatra through Nathu La. • The Chinese side agreed to establish two Chinese Industrial Parks in India and expressed their intention to enhance Chinese investment in India.
Feb 2015	External affairs minister, Smt. Sushma Swaraj paid an official visit to China	• External affairs minister inaugurated the 2nd India-China High-Level Media Forum • Attended launch of Visit India Year • Participated in the 13th Foreign Ministers' Meeting of Russia-India-China Trilateral.
May 2015	Prime Minister Narendra Modi visited China	• 24 agreements signed on the government-to-government side • 26 MoUs on the business-to-business side • Two joint statements, including one on climate change.

Month/Year	*Details of Visit*	*Outcome (s)*
June 2015	External affairs minister, Smt. Sushma Swaraj met foreign minister Wang Yi on the sidelines of the international donors' conference in Kathmandu	
Sep 2015	Minister of state for external affairs Gen. (Dr.) V.K. Singh (Retd.) visited China	• Met with foreign minister Wang Yi • Attended the SCO HOG Meeting in Zhengzhou on 14th December, 2015.
Oct 2015	Minister for environment and forest Sh. Paraksh Javdekar visited China	• Attended the 21st BASIC Ministerial Meeting on Climate Change
Nov 2015	Prime Minister Narendra Modi met with Premier Li Keqiang on the sidelines of the ASEAN Summit in Kuala Lampur	
Nov 2015	Home minister of India Sh. Rajnath Singh visited China	• Met with minister of public security of China.

Source: Ministry of External Affairs, New Delhi.

Annex 2: Notable "Transgressions" and Incidents Related to the Sino Indian Border

Month/Year	*Incident*
February 1997	Subsequent to then President Jiang Zemin's visit to India in 1996, the PLA transgressed 6 kms into Himachal Pradesh.
April 2003	PLA helicopters hovered around Chumar area in Nyoma sector of eastern Ladakh and dropped food cans, cigarette packets and hand-written notes.
June 2003	At the time when the then Indian Prime Minister Atal Behari Vajpayee was on a visit to Beijing, the PLA "transgressed" in the Asaphila region of the upper Subansiri District of Arunachal Pradesh.
May 2005	Following the then Chinese Prime Minister Wen Jiabao's visit to India in April 2005, the PLA "transgressed" into Asaphila again.
November 2006	On the eve of Chinese President Hu Jintao's visit to New Delhi in November 2006, Beijing's ambassador to India, Sun Yuxi, told an Indian television channel that "the whole of the state of Arunachal Pradesh is Chinese territory. And Tawang is only one of the places in it".
October 2009	Chinese Foreign Ministry protested the then Indian Prime Minister Dr Manmohan Singh's visit to Arunachal Pradesh.
December 2010	Beijing denied visa to India's Northern Army Commander and began issuing stapled visas to residents of Jammu and Kashmir.
February 2012	Chinese Foreign Ministry protested the visit to Arunachal Pradesh by the then Indian defence minister A.K. Antony.
November 2013	The Chinese Foreign Ministry protested Indian President Pranab Mukherjee's visit to Arunachal Pradesh.
April 2013-May 2013	Prior to Premier Li Keqiang's first visit to India, the PLA "transgressed" into Daulat Beg Oldi (DBO) in the Ladakh region, and Depsang plains of Aksai Chin. Additionally, the PLA also intruded in Chaglagam area in Arunachal Pradesh.
June 2014	The PLA made a two-pronged simultaneous entries by sending its troops into Indian waters in the Pangong lake (Ladakh) as well as five kilometres deep into Indian territory through the land route in the same area.
September 2014	Just prior to Chinese President Xi Jinping's visit to India in September, Chinese troops "transgressed" in Chumar area of Ladakh.1000 Chinese troops intruded 3 kms inside India's Chumar territory.
January 2015	Chinese Foreign Ministry protested Japanese foreign minister Fumio Kishida's recognition of Arunachal Pradesh as part of India.
February 2015	China protested Prime Minister Narendra Modi's visit to Arunachal Pradesh.
March 2015	PLA "transgression" in Burtse and Depsang in Northern Ladakh.
July 2016	Chinese PLA "transgressed" into the Chamoli district of Uttarakhand.

Source(s): News reports, various issues.

11

Guanxi, Interests and Mutual Trust

Zhang Yang

Introduction

Alongside their fast economic growth and rise in the global economic hierarchy, China and India, in the recent decades, have been engaging with each other to mitigate the fallouts of accidental bilateral friction, and to tackle the asymmetric treatment meted out to them in the West-dominated international order. These two countries have played a crucial role in advocating reforms in international institutions as well as in the larger global governance. Post financial crisis, especially China has taken an active lead in stabilising the world economy. The emerging economies of India, China and Brazil, although affected by the financial crisis, could manage to come out of it because of their strong economic foundations. In this backdrop, Jim O'Neill, the senior economist in Goldman Sachs, predicted the rise of BRIC in 2001.[1] He argued, "the global economy in the coming decades would be propelled by the growth of four populous and economically ambitious countries: Brazil, Russia, India and China" along with the United States and Japan". The idea influenced the national leaders of the four countries, prompting them to make BRIC a reality in 2009. Soon, it became BRICS after South Africa joined in 2011.

This chapter, therefore, seeks to analyse India-China relationship purely from a Chinese perspective. The aspects that the chapter discusses are: *guanxi* (relationship), interests and mutual interests. The idea of BRIC was timely to shape a new platform for China and India to have greater *guanxi*, common interests and create deeper mutual trust[2]. The common interests actuated the BRICS countries to establish multilateral *guanxi*. Meanwhile, the interaction between BRICS countries has facilitated greater mutual trust, especially between China and India, by expanding their scope of cooperation.

Guanxi (relationship)

Talking about China-India relations in BRICS, the official statements highlight deepening of the "strategic cooperative partnership"[3]. The Chinese approach to BRICS relations can also be understood from '*guanxi*' perspective. *Guanxi*—which is influenced by the Chinese cultural ideal— indicates harmony among people, *Jiahe Wanshixing* (Harmony brings wealth). This cultural idea reflects the nation's attitude and behaviour towards the outward world.[4] During the Seventh BRICS Summit, discussing the global political and economic issues, China's President Xi Jinping stressed that "BRICS nations should build a new type of state-to-state relations (*guanxi*) with win-win cooperation at the core." Xi Jinping made four proposals:

> "To build a partnership maintaining world peace; to forge a partnership promoting common development; to build a partnership carrying forward diversified civilisations; and to forge a partnership advancing global economic governance."[5]

On May 26, 2016, in a meeting with the President of India Pranab Mukerjee, China's President Xi Jinping highlighted that "both China and India agreed to deepen the peaceful and flourishing 'strategic cooperative partnership'."[6] China has many kinds of "partners"[7]: "cooperative partner", "comprehensive-cooperative partner", "strategic (cooperative) partner" and "comprehensive strategic cooperation partner". The bilateral relationship between China and India was defined as a "comprehensive cooperation" relationship by the two governments in 2003, when former Indian PM Atal Behari Vajpayee visited China[8]. The relationship of these two nations was elevated to "strategic (cooperative) partnership for peace and prosperity"[9] in 2005, when former China's Premier Wen Jiabao visited India. From Cui Xiaosu's article in News of Communist Party of China, "comprehensive" refer to the field of cooperation, including politics, economy, culture and military etc., while "strategic" refer to the higher level of cooperation which means the entirety, and that overall situation and core interests—all should have consistency[10]. With regard to the *guanxi* with India, China has shifted all aspects of its bilaterals; politics, economy, culture and military with India ("comprehensive cooperation") to a higher level of cooperation, in which BRICS could provide a platform for China and India to catch these "entirety, and that there is a greater alignment of core interests between the two countries".

Guanxi and Power

Chinese constructivist scholar Qin Yaqing points out "correlativity" as one of the four key elements in Chinese culture, which suggests that Chinese have a lot of emphasis on *guanxi* (relationality)[11]. Qin argues that in China's foreign policy-making, this element (correlativity) demonstrates Chinese "value relational governance which tend to build up a good atmosphere and manage well the relational network."[12] This explains China's good neighbourly policy, in which it seeks to establish cordial relations with its neighbouring countries and its counterpart-like developing countries and emerging powers. Another factor that explains why Chinese government emphasizes *guanxi* is due to Chinese understanding about power. China's society is a *guanxi* society, *guanxi* is "[an important factor] in the Chinese socio-cultural context and a key concept of Chinese political philosophy"[13]. In Chinese thought, the one who has greater *guanxi* will be relatively superior in society. *Guanxi* also leads to accumulation of power[14]. While reflecting this thought in international affairs, "processual constructivism" suggests "relational networking in international society that helps nation states to establish their identities and produces international power" with "conceptualising relationality and treating it as the core assumption".[15] China's national leader Xi Jinping's statement explains China's *guanxi* idea: "It's not the best way to work alone. Only through cooperation and building global partnership, and working together will we achieve the expected result."

Building *Guanxi* with Developing Countries Through BRICS

To understand China's approach/expectation in BRICS, it is also necessary to know its self-recognition. China keeps emphasising that its per capita GDP is below average level; although its economy is world's second largest, it is slowly moving away from the developing countries league into the developed powers club.[16] However, it is lying low in international affairs front, and still associates herself with the developing countries. Its foreign policy, therefore, is oriented towards enhancing the relations with developing countries. The BRICS is, thus, a specific platform to develop *guanxi* with those emerging markets and developing nations which are also a part of the *guanxi wang* (relational network) of China. President Xi Jinping's speech during the Seventh BRICS Summit also indicates the same[17]:

> "The BRICS countries should join hands to forge a closer economic partnership, push forward the construction of the headquarters and the African regional centre of the New Development Bank of BRICS nations simultaneously, and earnestly implement the BRICS Economic Partnership Strategy. The BRICS nations should also safeguard the common interests of emerging markets and other developing nations on such major issues concerning global development as post-2015 development agenda and climate change. [...] The BRICS countries should stick to openness and inclusiveness, actively carry out dialogue and exchanges with other countries and international organisations, strengthen solidarity and cooperation with other emerging markets and developing nations, and boost the representation and influence of the BRICS countries."

Through an analysis of the importance of *guanxi* in China's foreign relations, it can be understood that the delicate characteristics of Chinese approach to a macro level frame, which provides the larger context to the speeches by the Chinese national leaders, often criticised by the West as "same tedious socialist rhetoric"[18]

Circuitously Consolidating the State-*Guanxi* Level

Although discordant episodes happen between China and India, i.e. "NSG episode"—as portrayed by India as "China stalling India's bid for membership of the NSG at the plenary meeting of the 48-nation grouping in June", [19] the attitude of their national leader, however, shows that the *guanxi* of the two states is circuitously consolidating instead of being easily influenced by the "disputes". Although it was believed that China blocked India's bid to enter the NSG, the Indian government has underlined that the process of engaging Beijing will not be affected by it.[20] During the August 2016 meeting of Indian PM and Chinese Foreign Minister Wang Yi, one of the purposes behind the visit was to review the arrangements for Chinese President Xi Jinping's October visit to India for the BRICS Summit; the Indian PM has extended cooperation, reflecting positive bilateral *guanxi*. The Chinese foreign ministry reported that the Indian side has expressed satisfaction about how the bilateral relations have made all-dimensional development in the recent years and how India "highly values promoting India-China relations."[21] Indian PM believes "its stance of viewing and dealing with China remains unchanged. Strengthening cooperation between India and China will inspire all developing countries and bring hopes to them."[22]

Interests

Push Yuan into Becoming an International Currency

China became a full participant in world economy by joining the World Trade Organisation (WTO) in 2001, facing trade rules which benefitted developed countries more. Now, China hopes to push the internationalisation of RMB (Renminbi) via the BRICS platform[23]. It is hard task for China to negotiate with developed countries in the existing international financial system. With representation of interests of the developing countries, BRICS is the forum in which China needs to balance developed countries in the international financial system. As the position and demands are different for different countries, to frame an inclusive financial system that satisfies all countries' needs could be difficult. To push the internationalisation of RMB, China needs help from emerging markets like India. Although China and India are in the WTO (World Trade Organisation), G20 (Group 20), and SCO (Shanghai Cooperation Organisation); still, BRICS platform has a "more crucial role in exchange of information, agenda setting, reducing conflict and developing a common idea".[24]

BRICS called for reforming the international financial institutions in every joint statement since 2009: "a stable, predictable and more diversified international monetary system"[25] to "reflect the changes in the world economy".[26]

The aim is to "increase the voice and representation of emerging economies and developing countries".[27] There have been allegations by the West that China has deliberately undervalued its currency, which has been vehemently opposed by the Chinese scholars.[28] In this context, China needs BRICS to push the internationalisation of its currency under the broader agenda of approaching a new international monetary system.

Facility Between Rupee and Chinese RMB

Bank of India started to offer trade settlement facility between Rupee and Chinese RMB from Hong Kong since 2011[29]. It was recognised as "intense persuasion by the China Banking Regulatory Commission, which is trying to gain acceptance of the RMB as an international currency"[30]. For China-India trade, it has improved the efficiency when compared to using US dollars, which usually takes three working days. It was facilitated by an MoU signed between the Reserve Bank of India and the China Banking Regulatory Commission (CBRC) to enhance banking relationship.[31] This facility provided real time settlement with buyers and sellers across all over China. It is part of "a campaign by Hong Kong Monetary Authority, which has persuaded 100 foreign banks to enter into arrangements with Chinese banks for trade settlement in RMB".[32] There are some new steps in currency cooperation between China and India. According to the Embassy of India in Beijing, the State Bank of India have authorisation to conduct local currency (RMB) business at its branch in Shanghai, and it is only Indian bank which enjoys this right at present.[33]

Although it may not be the direct outcome of BRICS mechanism, the BRICS generating an overall willingness to cooperate cannot be ruled out.

The New Development Bank

One of the important achievements that China, India and other BRICS countries have done to balance developed countries[34] is the establishment of the New Development Bank BRICS (NDB BRICS) established at the Fifth BRICS Summit in Durban, South Africa in 2013. According to the statement leading to the creation of NDB, BRICS states agreed upon this multilateral development bank "as an alternative to the existing US-dominated World Bank and International Monetary Fund" with "an objective of funding infrastructure projects in the developing countries, and meet the aspirations of millions through sustainable development."[35] In the first Xi Jinping's biography in Russian[36], the Russian expert on China, Yuri, points out that some political commentators have found many similarities between NDB and World Bank—which is considered the mainstay of American financial hegemony. Despite outlining the similarities, they view that NDB cannot be equated with the other mainstay of "American dollar empire". Although one of the biggest multilateral development bank with both the capital and emergency capacity of US$ 100 billion, NDB has been criticised to be just a virtual insurance system, lacking in proper institutionalisation[37].

Multilateral and Bilateral Banking Links between China and India

The first round of loans by NDB, a US$ 811 million has been issued for clean energy projects in Brazil, China, India and South Africa on April 18, 2016.[38] Of these, China's Shanghai Lingang Hongbo New Energy Development Co. got US$ 81 million loan to fund 100 megawatts of rooftop solar power while India's Canara Bank got a US$ 250 million loan with US$ 75 million earmarked for 500 megawatts of renewable-energy projects. It clearly shows that NDB is carrying out its promise to make clean energy a part of the bank's core focus.[39] Many Indian banks have established their branches or representative offices in the main financial cities of China like Shanghai, Tianjin, Guangzhou, Shenzhen and Beijing in last few years, and the first branch of the mainland China bank ICBC (Industrial and Commercial Bank of China) started banking operations in Mumbai, India, in 2011.[40] Six protocol and MOUs were signed between the two governments from 1992 to 2014 for border trade, bilateral banking cooperation and setting up of industrial parks.[41] Even as it remains nearly impossible to build a bilateral bank between these two nations in contemporary times, the BRICS NDB is opening possibilities for China and India to work closer via a multilateral platform for the interests of their sustainable development.

Improving Investment Ties

Well-known economist Justin Yifu Lin argues that China will become the largest economy in 2025. He believes that the economic development of BRICS countries is related to the incomplete recovery of developed countries from the financial crisis. As the 'steady' growth of developed countries will probably continue for a while in the future, the export from developing countries to developed countries will be restrained. Lin suggests the best arrangement for BRICS countries is to develop their domestic demand and improve the infrastructure investment and in this context; the One-Belt One-Road initiative could be a commendable engagement.[42] To be able to smoothly invest in India is arguably linked with China's national agenda, and matches with the common development goal of BRICS as well.

Mutual Trust: "Speak with One Voice" in BRICS

While facing the limitation of fund shares and the right to vote in the international economic institutions, China and India share similar agenda in their dealing with global governance. Considering the interests the two developing countries share, the BRICS mechanism would, therefore, be a good platform for these two nations to improve mutual trust.[43] Although it is a complex issue for China and India to build mutual trust, it is necessary for the two nations to voice a strong argument on issues pertaining to the countries.

One of the major distrusts affecting the bilateral is the unequal trade between the two countries. Although China's GDP reached US$ 10.866 trillion in 2015, India's GDP was US$ 2.071 trillion (World Bank 2016), and the bilateral trade did not reach up to the level it was supposed to be. Despite

China being the largest trade partner of India since 2007, China faces serious scrutiny from India's bureaucracy due to concerns related to trade deficit, anti-dumping[44]and visa issues. However, there involves greater benefits in cooperation between the two countries, which was stated by Xi Jinping during his meeting with India PM Narendra Modi at the Sixth BRICS Summit in Fortaleza, Brazil:[45]

> "[...]that as two biggest developing countries and emerging markets, both China and India are in a great historical process of realising national rejuvenation; thus, what the two countries value most is peace and development, and the ideals and goals of the two countries are linked closely. Both China and India are important poles in the world and share a number of strategic integrating points. If China and India speak with one voice, the whole world will listen; and if China and India join hands in cooperation, the whole world will watch. Whether from a bilateral, regional or global perspective, China and India are long-term strategic cooperative partners instead of competing adversaries."

For seeking common points, it is crucial to build mutual trust based on the idea of obtaining a win-win situation. The formation of BRICS can help reconstruct the global international order[46] based upon mutual trust. In the BRICS forum, Xi Jinping aspired to reduce the influence of bilateral tensions and pay more attention on discussing the detail of the necessary condition for the development of the two nations and other developing countries[47],

> "It meets our greatest common interest to join hands to realise peaceful development, cooperative development and inclusive development so as to provide a better life for the 2.5 billion people of the two countries, and to fortify strength of peace and development for the region and the world at large. [...] China and India should strengthen cooperation in multilateral fields, and jointly participate in the formulation of international rules so as to strengthen the voice of the developing countries. [...]Both sides should control and handle differences in an active and forward-looking attitude, and find fair and reasonable solutions to the boundary issues acceptable to both sides as soon as possible through friendly consultations. Prior to the final settlement, both sides should jointly safeguard peace and tranquility in the border areas."

Diversified Cooperation

While shaping BRICS mechanism to a diversified forum, the cooperation area is expanding and venturing into new avenues. For example, corruption was proposed as one of the "new areas of cooperation" in the Fifth BRICS

Summit in 2013.[48] China expects to expedite the construction of anti-corruption mechanism with BRICS countries in order to continually improve the negotiating power of emerging markets and developing countries in the international anti-corruption field.[49] The anti-corruption cooperation between BRICS was put into practice by:

1) Holding meeting of BRICS experts on Anti-Corruption Cooperation during the Sixth BRICS Summit. The statement mentioned:

> "We recognise that corruption negatively affects sustainable economic growth, poverty reduction and financial stability. We are committed to combat domestic and foreign bribery, and strengthen international cooperation, including law enforcement cooperation in accordance with multilaterally established principles and norms, especially the UN Convention Against Corruption." [50]

2) Creating a BRICS Working Group on Anti-Corruption Cooperation in the Seventh BRICS Summit. The statement read:

> "We are convinced that corruption is a global challenge which undermines the legal systems of states, negatively affects their sustainable development and may facilitate other forms of crime. We are confident that international cooperation plays a pivotal role in countering and preventing corruption. We reaffirm our commitment to make every effort to that end, including mutual legal assistance, in accordance with the UN Convention Against Corruption (UNCAC) and multilaterally established principles and norms. In this regard, we look forward to the success of the sixth session of the Conference of State parties to the UNCAC, which will take place in St. Petersburg on between November 2 and 6, 2015. In that context, we decided to create a BRICS Working Group on Anti-Corruption Cooperation."[51]

Although the issue of anti-corruption is different between China and India, the new tendency of BRICS cooperation—including BRICS Public Diplomacy Forum, BRICS State-Owned Companies/Enterprises, National Agencies Responsible for Drug Control, BRICS virtual secretariat, BRICS Youth Policy Dialogue, Sports and Mega Sporting Events and so on[52]—will lead these two nations to develop a deep and systemic network of relationship and contribute to the mutual trust. It was argued in the Party School of the Central Committee of CPC-owned newspaper that the decline in world economy will not change the trend of BRICS cooperation.[53] Except the cooperation on economy, with expanding and deepening the cooperation area, BRICS could be a vast platform for China-India cooperation in different area in the future.

Friendship States/Cities

In BRICS, not only the national relations have improved but also state-to-state, and city-to-city ties among the BRICS countries are getting better. During the first Forum of BRICS Friendship Cities and Local Governments Cooperation on December 2, 2011, former vice chairman of Standing Committee of the National People's Congress (NPC) Lu Yongxiang mentioned International Friendship Cities event as an important event for China to develop the bilateral relationship with other countries; Lu highlighted "the forum is expected to create a platform to boost communication between local governments and further promote ties between BRICS sister cities" as well.[54] Chinese cities have established 1,817 sister-city agreements with foreign cities and states, but only 167 were from the BRICS countries.[55] Thus, BRICS mechanism directly or indirectly has promoted the dialogue and cooperation at the state and city level among these countries.

From October 2013, China and India established friendship cities between Beijing and New Delhi, Chengdu and Bangalore and Kunming and Kolkata. Till May 2015, there are 10 pairs of friendship states/cities between China and India. Other friendship cities/states are Guangdong and Gujarat, Shanghai and Mumbai and Guangzhou and Ahmedabad, for which an MOU was signed in September 2014 during Chinese President Xi Jinping's visit to India.[56]

The provincial partnership between Sichuan and Karnataka and sister-city relationship between Chongqing-Chennai, Qingdao-Hyderabad and Dunhuang-Aurangabad were established in May 2015, during the first State/Provincial Leaders' Forum (or the Forum of Leaders of the Regions) of China and India when Indian PM Narendra Modi visited China.[57] The establishment of this Forum was inspired by "noting the increasing role played by Indian States and Chinese Provinces in advancing the bilateral relationship".[58] Thus, the friendly states/cities initiative in BRICS has also impacted positively the bilateral cooperation, and could be seen as a prospective channel to improve mutual trust between China and India.

Conclusion

> "*One, who wishes to be successful, seeks to help others to be successful. One, who wishes to be understood, understands others.*"
>
> —Confucius (it was cited by Chinese President Xi Jinping in his speech when he visited India in 2014)

Based on their common interests, China and India have established *guanxi* in BRICS to boost diversified cooperation, for greater gains and towards facilitating sustainable development in the two countries. The BRICS mechanism indicates that good *guanxi* and common interests are key to facilitating the enlargement of cooperation between the countries in the same region. Thus, three elements, i.e. *guanxi*, interests and mutual trust, form the basis of interaction in the bilateral and multilateral relations. With these kind of interactions, the BRICS "have surpassed most expectations in recent years in forming a nascent political grouping".[59] However, with regard to India-China relations, there are differences and divergences which hinder the coming close of the two countries in multilateral foras, such as BRICS. Chinese demand largely drives BRICS which is asymmetrical and not sustainable, says Indian scholar Manoj Pant.[60] Talking about the intra-BRICS competition, Pant argues "it is essential for the four countries of India, Brazil, South Africa and Russia to balance the excessive economic dominance of China", which is evident from the intra-BRICS and inter-BRICS trade figures and GDP shares, and "only this can make the BRICS bloc an effective economic bloc".

END NOTES

1. Jim O'Neill (2001), "Building Better Global Economic BRICs", Goldman Sachs Global Economics Paper, No. 66, November 2001.
2. Trust was highlighted in Confucius thought and paid important attention in the society and diplomacy of China. It is also analysed in International Relations Studies through theoretical perception. See Yang Yang (2012), "Theory of Trust in the International Relations Viewed from Sociological Perspective—With an Eye to Mutual Trust in the East Asia Cooperation", Pacific Journal, Vol.20, No.7, pp.26-34. Yin Jiwu (2008), "Trust and Alliance Trust in International Relations", *International Forum*, Vol 10, No 2, pp. 55-61. Zhu Liqun (2003), "Trust and Cooperation among Nations: On Current Sino-American Relations", World Economic and Politics,Vol 1, pp.16-20. Aaron M. Hoffman (2002), "A Conceptualization of Trust in International Relations", European Journal of International, Vol.8 No.3, pp.375-401.
3. Zhang Yan (2012), "Powering the world: Fourth BRICS summit in Delhi: expectations and ambitions", Embassy of the People's Republic of China in the Republic of India, Accessed on 19 August 2016, URL: http://in.china-embassy.org/eng/embassy_news/t918098.htm.
4. Shang Huipeng (2016), 人,文明体与国家：国际关系理论的心理文化学路径 [Human, Civilized Community and Nation: Psychoculturological method of International Relations Theory], p120.(Forth coming). See Shang Huipeng (2013), "人、文明体与国家间关系" [The Relations among Human, Civilized Community and Nation], The Journal of International Studies, Vol 4 No50, pp.3-19. It is not only for Chinese or new idea to emphasize the importance of the "Guanxi(relations)" in human-being activities. In Lawrence and Nohria's research (2002), they found the "Social Network", which means "the need to bond with others in long-term, caring, committed relationships", is one of the four basic drives in human nature.
5. Ministry of Foreign Affairs of the People's Republic of China (2015), "Xi Jinping Attends

7th BRICS Summit and Delivers Important Speech", 9th July 2015, Accessed on 15 August 2016, URL:http://www.fmprc.gov.cn/mfa_eng/topics_665678/xjpcxjzgjldrdqchwhshhzzzcygyslshdswchy/t1280846.shtml.

6. Du Yifei (2016), "习近平同印度总统慕克吉举行会谈: 双方同意加强中印全面合作, 将两国战略合作伙伴关系推向新高度"[Xi Jinping met President of India Mukherjee: Both sides agreed to strengthen China and India comprehensive cooperation and carry the Strategic Cooperative Partenership to a new height.], People's Daily, Accessed on 18 August 2016, URL:http://www.ccps.gov.cn/theory/picnews/201605/t20160530_79818.html.
7. Cui Xiaosu (2015), "全天候战略合作伙伴"是啥样的铁关系?"[What kind of Tie Guanxi(strong relationships) is the All-weather Strategic Cooperative Partners?], News of Communist Party of China, (The most comprehensive and systematic website about the Communist Party of China), Accessed on 18 August 2016, URL:http://cpc.people.com.cn/xuexi/n/2015/0421/c385474-26879902.html.
8. Ministry of External Affairs, Government of India(2003), Declaration on Principles for Relations and Comprehensive Cooperation Between the Republic of India and the People's Republic of China, URL:http://www.mea.gov.in/in-focus-article.htm?7679/Declaration+on+Principles+ for+ Relations+and+ Comprehensive+Cooperation+Between+the+ Republic+ of+ India+and+the+Peoples+Republic+of+China.
9. Ministry of Foreign Affairs of the People's Republic of China (2005), "Premier Wen Jiabao Meets with Journalists, Talking about 3 Achievements of His Visit to India", 12 April 2005, Accessed on 6 September 2016, URL:http://www.fmprc.gov.cn/mfa_eng/topics_665678/wzlcfly_665842/t191621.shtml.
10. China is having constructive cooperative partnership(Jianshe xing huoban guanxi) with the USA, comprehensive strategic collaborative partnership (Quanmian zhanlue xiezuo huoban guanxi) with Russia, all-weather strategic cooperative partner(Quantianhou zhanlue huoban) with Pakistan and strategic reciprocal relations(Zhanlue huhui guanxi) with Japan(Cui 2015).
11. Qin Yaqing (2011), "Chinese Culture and Its Implications for Foreign Policy-making", International Studies, vol 5:25-27. Qin argued that "the four key elements in the Chinese culture-contextuality, correlativity, complementarity and changeability, suggest that Chinese have a lot of emphasis on shi(megatrend), guanxi (relationality), he (harmony), and bian(changeability)".
12. Ibid., p. 25.
13. Qin Yaqing(2009), "Relationality and Processual Construction:Bringing Chinese Ideas into International Relations Theory", Social Sciences in China, Vol 3:6.
14. Qin Yaqing(2011), "Chinese Culture and Its Implications for Foreign Policy-making", pp.26-27.
15. Qin Yaqing (2009), "Relationality and Processual Construction:Bringing Chinese Ideas into International Relations Theory", p. 5.
16. Liu Xiaoyan and Meng Xue (2014), "A Brief Analysis of the dynamics of China and India to joint the BRICs Cooperation Mechanism" [浅析中印参与"金砖国家"合作机制的动因], South Asian Studies Quarterly, Sum No. 158, No.3, 2014, p. 104.
17. Ministry of Foreign Affairs of the People's Republic of China (2015), "Xi Jinping Attends 7th BRICS Summit and Delivers Important Speech", 9th July 2015, Accessed on 15 August 2016, URL:http://www.fmprc.gov.cn/mfa_eng/topics_665678/xjpcxjzgjldrdqchwhshhzzzcygyslshdswchy/t1280846.shtml.
18. Elizabeth C. Economy, "Ten Fascinating Facts About China's President Xi Jinping",15 October 2014, The National Interest, URL:http://nationalinterest.org/blog/the-buzz/ten-fascinating-facts-about-chinas-president-xi-jinping-11475 (Accessed on 9 September 2016).

19. Rajya Sabha TV (2016), "After Chill Over Nsg Episode, Beijing Calls On New Delhi", 13 August 2016, URL: http://www.rajyasabhatv.com/chinese-fm-calls-pm-modi-holds-talks-swaraj.html (Accessed on 9 September 2016).
20. United News of India, "NSG issue not to affect India-China engagement: MEA, 2 July 2016,URL: http://www.uniindia.com/nsg-issue-not-to-affect-india-china-engagement-mea/india/news/540305.html (Accessed on 13 September 2016).
21. Ministry of Foreign Affairs of the People's Republic of China (2016), "Prime Minister Narendra Modi of India Meets with Wang Yi", 13 August 2016, Accessed on 24 August 2016, URL:http://www.fmprc.gov.cn/mfa_eng/wjb_663304/wjbz_663308/activities_663312/t1389330.shtml.
22. Ibid.
23. Liu Xiaoyan and Meng Xue (2014), "A Brief Analysis of the dynamics of China and India to joint the BRICs Cooperation Mechanism", p. 105.
24. Liu Tong(2012), "An Brief analysis of the BRICS' role and issue in the Global Governance", Foreign Investment in China, No.14, pp. 214-215.
25. BRICS (2009), Joint Statement of the BRIC Countries Leaders, URL: http://brics2016.gov.in/upload/files/document/57566ee059e181stdec.pdf, pp.3. BRICS(2010), II BRIC Summit - Joint Statement, URL: http://brics2016.gov.in/upload/files/document/5763e23d75e512nd.pdf, pp.10,13.
26. BRICS (2011), Sanya Declaration,http://brics2016.gov.in/upload/files/document/57566e28a911e3rd.pdf, p. 15.
27. Ibid.
28. Liu Xiaoyan and Meng Xue(2014), "A Brief Analysis of the dynamics of China and India to joint the BRICs Cooperation Mechanism", pp.105.
29. Dasgupta, Saibal (2011), "Bank of India becomes first to offer trade settlement in yuan", *Times of India*, 24 February 2011, Accessed on 4 August 2016, URL:http://timesofindia.indiatimes.com/world/china/Bank-of-India-becomes-first-to-offer-trade-settlement-in-yuan/articleshow/7565143.cms.
30. Ibid.
31. Ibid.
32. Ibid.
33. Embassy of India in Beijing, China (2016), "Economic and Trade Relations", Accessed on 21 April 2016, URL:http://www.indianembassy.org.cn/DynamicContent.aspx? MenuId=97& SubMenuId=0.
34. Although the BRICS had criticised the World Bank and IMF(International Monetary Fund) did not provide enough voting right for developing countries, it was argued by BRICS that the establishment of the New Development Back BRICS is to provide a new loan channel for the developing countries instead of competing with World Bank and IMF. BBC Zhongwen Net: "The New Development Bank of BRICS in Shanghai officially open for business" [金砖国家在上海的新开发银行正式开业], 21 July 2015, URL: http://www.bbc.com/zhongwen/simp/business/2015/07/150721_brics_bank (Accessed on 12 September 2016).
35. The New Development Bank BRICS, URL:http://www.ndbbrics.org/za.html.
36. Wang Shu (2016), "给习近平写传记，这位作者啥来头?"[What is the derivation of the author who wrote biography for Xi Jinping?], The Beijing News, 17 August 2016, URL: http://www.bjnews.com.cn/news/2016/08/17/413758.html (Accessed on 12 September 2016).
37. Yuri Taffpetrovsky 尤里·塔夫罗夫斯基 (2015)《习近平：正圆中国梦》[Xi Jinping, Reading China Dream] translated by Study Time, URL:http://www.ccps.gov.cn/theory/rdgz/201603/t20160317_75245_1.html

38. New Development Bank, "BRICS Bank Gives $811 Million in First Round Green Energy Loans", 18 April 2016, URL: http://www.ndb.int/brics-bank-gives-811-million-in-first-round-green-energy-loans.php#parentHorizontalTab1 (Accessed on 12 September 2016).
39. Bloomberg News, "BRICS Bank Gives $811 Million in First Round Green Energy Loans", 18 April 2016, URL: http://www.bloomberg.com/news/articles/2016-04-18/brics-bank-gives-first-china-loan-to-solar-project-daily-says (Accessed on 12 September 2016).
40. Embassy of India, Beijing, China, "India-China Bilateral Relations: Economic and Trade Relations", URL: http://www.indianembassy.org.cn/DynamicContent.aspx?MenuId=97&SubMenuId=0 (Accessed on 21 May 2016).
41. Ibid.
42. Su Rongrong (2015), "Lin Yifu: China will be the largest economy in 2025", 9th September 2015, URL: http://news.wenweipo.com/2015/09/09/IN1509090056.htm (Accessed on 8th August 2016).
43. Liu Xiaoyan and Meng Xue (2014), "A Brief Analysis of the dynamics of China and India to joint the BRICs Cooperation Mechanism", p. 106.
44. It was reported India has so far initiated 322 anti-dumping cases out of which 177 cases involve China. PTI(2016), "India-China trade deficit at $44.7 billion in April-January", *The Economic Times*, 2 March 2016, URL: http://economictimes.indiatimes.com/news/economy/foreign-trade/india-china-trade-deficit-at-44-7-billion-in-april-january/articleshow/51223260.cms (Accessed on 14 September 2016).
45. Ministry of Foreign Affairs of the People's Republic of China, "Xi Jinping Meets with Prime Minister Narendra Modi of India", 15 July 2014, URL:http://www.fmprc.gov.cn/mfa_eng/topics_665678/xjpzxcxjzgjldrdlchwdbxagtwnrlgbjxgsfwbcxzlldrhw/t1175135.shtml(Accessed on 9 September 2016).
46. Liu Jianfei (2016), The Reform of International Order in the Global Governance [全球治理中的国际秩序变革], *Study Time*, Assessed on 16 August 2016, URL: http://www.ccps.gov.cn/xxsb_jx/201607/t20160704_81798_1.html.
47. Ministry of Foreign Affairs of the People's Republic of China, "Xi Jinping Meets with Prime Minister Narendra Modi of India",15 July 2014.
48. BRICS (2013), "BRICS and Africa: Partnership for Development, Integration and Industrialisation", Durban, South Africa, 27 March 2013,http://brics2016.gov.in/upload/files/document/5763be1c4da6e5th1.pdf, pp.13.
49. Huang Shuxian (2016), "Spread the Tight Encirclement of Fight against Corruption to the World: in-depth study of General Secretary Xi Jinping's important discourse on anti-corruption international cooperation, pursuit evasion and recover botty" [把惩治腐败的天罗地网撒向全球——深入学习习近平总书记关于反腐败国际合作和追逃追赃工作的重要论述], Qiushi Journal (Organ of the Central Committee of the Communist Party of China), 2016, Vol 11, URL: http://www.ccps.gov.cn/designated_topics/lxyzxxjy/xxljh/201606/t20160612_80442.html. The author is the Deputy Secretary of the Central Commission for Discipline Inspection of PRC.
50. BRICS (2014), "Sixth BRICS Summit:Fortaleza Declaration", *Fortaleza,* Brazil, 15 July 2014, URL: http://brics2016.gov.in/upload/files/document/57566d35a13456 declaration.pdf, pp.14,17.
51. BRICS (2015), "VII BRICS Summit:Ufa Declaration",Ufa, the Russian Federation, 9 July 2015, URL: http://brics2016.gov.in/upload/files/document/5763c20a72f2d7th Declarationeng.pdf, pp.13-14.
52. BRICS (2013), "BRICS and Africa:Partnership for Development, Integration and Industrialisation", Durban, South Africa, 27 March 2013, p.13.

53. Bao Zheng (2016), "Is BRICS really fading?" [金砖是否真的在"褪色], *Study Times* (Website of the Party School of the Central Committee of C.P.C-owned Newspaper)Accessed on 16 Aug 2016, URL:http://www.studytimes.cn/zydx/DDSJ/HUANQLW/2016-05-02/5482.html.
54. Embassy of PRC in India (2011), "First BRICS Friendship Cities and Local Gov'ts Cooperation Forum Opens in S. China", 2 December 2011, http://www.fmprc.gov.cn/ce/cein/eng/zgxw/t883651.htm (Accessed on 31 Aug 2016).
55. Ibid.
56. Ministry of Foreign Affairs of the Peoples's Republic of China, "China and India relations", February 2016, URL: http://www.fmprc.gov.cn/web/gjhdq_676201/gj_676203/yz_676205/1206_677220/sbgx_677224/ (Accessed on 13 September 2016).
57. Press Information Bureau, Government of India, Prime Minister's Office, Joint Statement between the India and China during Prime Minister's visit to China, 15 May 2015, URL:http://pib.nic.in/newsite/PrintRelease.aspx?relid=121755 (Accessed on 13 September 2016).
58. Ibid.
59. Michael A. Glosny (2009), "China and the BRICs: A Real (but limited) Partnership in a Unipolar World", Polity, Northeastern Political Science Association, 2009, p. 109.
60. Manoj Pant (2011), "India and the BRICS countries: Issues of Trade and Technology", URL: http://wtocentre.iift.ac.in/FA/India%20and%20the%20BRICS%20Countries-Issues%20of%20Trade%20and%20Technology.pdf.

12

China-South Africa Relations

Abhishek Kumar Darbey

Introduction

China-South Africa relations are on the upswing recently, both in the bilateral and multilateral forums such as the BRICS. The bilateral ties between China and South Africa gradually began to strengthen after 2009, largely after the South African foreign policy orientation shifted towards China with the expansion of trade and economic engagements between the two countries. Although, the first formal summit of BRIC grouping was held on 16 June 2009, South Africa joined the group on December 24, 2010 at the invitation of then Chinese President Hu Jintao, and the with consensus of the other BRIC members.[1] On the concept proposed by Jim O'Neill of Goldman Sachs in 2001 in his research paper titled The World Needs Better Economic BRIC,, the leaders of the four countries, namely the Federative Republic of Brazil, the Russian Federation, the Republic of India and the People's Republic of China (PRC), came together to form a group in 2009 to discuss the contemporary situation in global economy and other pressing issues of global development.[2] The discussion in the summits following 2009 has mainly focused on major issues of the international agenda—broadly on global governance and international economy and finance.[3] The common vision of the BRICS members is to transform global governance towards a more multipolar, equitable and democratic world order, and expresses strong commitment for the concerns of the developing countries[4] In this regard, the representation of the African continent became a must for this grouping, and the agendas BRICS proposed during its formation have direct relevance with the continent. Subsequently, South Africa was invited in December 2010 to join the group as part of the objective to have an African representation. There were a host of factors in favour of South Africa to get the membership of BRIC, and among them, one of the most significant factors was strengthening China-South Africa bilateral relations.

Understanding China-South Africa Relations

In December 1997, the Government of China and the Republic of South Africa signed Joint Communique after their agreement on relevant issues regarding the establishment of diplomatic relations.[5] The South African government affirmed its position to strictly follow the 'One China Policy'. The diplomatic relations between China and South Africa were established on January 1[s], 1998. The diplomatic ties between the two States advanced gradually under the Chinese leadership of Jiang Zemin, Hu Jintao and Xi Jinping, and South African leadership of Thabo Mbeki and Jacob Zuma. In their early phase of diplomatic ties, the former South Africa President Thabo Mbeki followed a cautious approach to China and later, from 2009, President Zuma's regime, it shifted to a more pragmatic policy. South Africa was affected by the international financial crisis and to mitigate the effects of the crisis, the new government stepped in in May 2009 and adopted 'Look East Policy' to expand cooperation with emerging market.

Since 2009, the economic ties accelerated significantly, thereby making China the largest trading partner of South Africa in 2013. A high-level Bi-National Commission (BNC) was set up by signing the 'Pretoria Declaration on the Partnership' between the PRC and South Africa in April 2000 under the respective leadership of Jiang Zemin and Thabo Mbeki.[6] The declaration publicly states the common guiding vision and fundamental principles in strengthening the bilateral relations. The BNC aimed to guide and coordinate government-level relations between China and South Africa, and to consult each other on bilateral or multilateral issue of mutual interests. The Pretoria Declaration's common guiding vision and fundamental principles can broadly be summarised as: commit to constructive dialogue, creation of wealth for their peoples, safeguarding of their national sovereignty, safety and integrity; secondly, within the context of South-South Cooperation, strengthen and diversify their economic relations; thirdly, to support the African continent in its endeavour to seek peace, stability and development, and promote its interests in the multilateral forums; and fourthly, support each other to create a new international political and economic order. The BNC also facilitated high-level visits and bilateral cooperation in all areas. The frequent exchange of high-level visits between the two countries has gradually consolidated their political and economic ties since 1998.

Bilateral Visits

Prior to 1998, the Chinese leader's visit to South Africa was less frequent—unlike the present leader's—but it was significant in consolidating a foundation for establishing formal diplomatic relations between the two States. The visit of Qian Qichen, then CPC Politburo member and Shanghai Municipal Party secretary to South Africa in December 1997, was significant as the visit followed the signing of Joint Communique for establishing diplomatic relations between the two states. Some of the important Chinese leaders' visit prior to 1998 are: Li Shujing, deputy director of the China Liaison Department (July 1992); Tian Zengpei, deputy foreign minister (February-March 1994); Xie Bangding, deputy director of the China-Africa Friendship Associations (May 1994); Liu Shuqing, director of the Chinese People's Institute of Foreign Affairs (February 1995); Jie Peiding, assistant foreign minister (January 1996); Wu Yi, minister of Foreign Trade and Commerce (April 1996); Hu Qili, minister of Electronics Industry (April 1996); Qian Qichen, deputy premier and foreign minister (December 1997); Shi Guangsheng, deputy minister of Foreign Trade (November 1997); Jie Peiding, assistant foreign minister (January 1997); and Hu Jintao, CPC Politburo member and Shanghai Muncipal Party Secretary (July 1998).[7]

In 2000, Chinese President Jiang Zemin visited South Africa, which witnessed the signing of Pretoria Declaration on Partnership and setting up of BNC. From the South African side, President Nelson Mandela (in 1999) and Thabo Mbeki (in December 2001) visited China, followed by President Jacob Zuma, who has made four State visits to China since August 2010. During Zhu Rongji's visit, both sides declared 'China-South Africa Partnership', adding depth to the bilateral ties. In 2008, the China-South Africa relations were upgraded to the strategic dialogue partnership and later, in August 2010, they signed the 'Comprehensive Strategic Partnership'. Since then, the number of high-level official visits and exchanges between two sides increased significantly, reflecting the importance both sides attach to each other. In March 2010, Jia Qinglin, chairman of the Chinese Political Party Consultative Conference (CPPCC) visited South Africa to sign contracts worth more than USD300 million between the two sides. In December 2014, President Jacob Zuma visited China along with his government ministers and

100 South African business delegates. During the visit, concerns were raised over trade imbalances, the Chinese impact on South African industries and China's influence over South Africa's domestic and international affairs.[8] In October 2010, Max Sisulu, speaker of the National Assembly of South Africa, visited China. The former Chinese Vice-President Xi Jinping visited South Africa in November 2010, and met with his South African counterpart Motlanthe—and both side signed a host of bilateral cooperation agreements on areas such as energy, trade statistics and banking regulation.[9] In May 2010, the Chinese Politburo member Wu Bangguo paid an official goodwill visit to South Africa. In September 2011, a South African trade delegation to Beijing was led by Vice-President Kgalema Petrus Motlanthe and an MOU was signed between the two sides on geological exploration and mineral resources. An agreement worth USD2.5 billion was also signed between the China Development Bank and the Development Bank of South Africa.[10] In July 2012, President Jacob Zuma, along with a South African delegation including International Relations minister Maite Nkoana-Mashabane, minister of Trade and Industry, Rob Davies and minister of Presidency, Collins Chabane visited Beijing to attend the 5th Forum on China–Africa Co-operation (FOCAC).[11]

In July 2015, Cyril Ramaphosa, deputy president of South Africa led a trade and economic delegation to China.[12] He held talks with the Chinese Premier Li Keqiang and emphasised that South Africa highly values its relations with China as well as Sino-Africa relations. He said that South Africa is willing to learn from the Chinese experience in industrialisation and economic zone development, and promote bilateral cooperation in ocean economy and energy. Li Keqiang said, "China is ready to strengthen political trust and win-win cooperation with South Africa, enhance coordination in global and regional affairs, and work with other African countries to set an example for South-South cooperation".[13] In December 2015, Chinese President Xi Jinping made a State visit to South Africa and emphasised on pushing forward China-South Africa Comprehensive Strategic Partnership to new highs.[14] Along with the frequent bilateral visits and exchanges, the governments of both sides promoted events such as 'South Africa Year in China' in 2014 and a 'China Year in South Africa' in 2015 as part of public diplomacy campaign to promote better understanding of their relations.

The bilateral trade between China and South Africa started in early 1990s. After the establishment of diplomatic ties in 1997, the economic exchanges and cooperation increased between them. In October 2000, Yu Xiaosong, president of the China Council for the Promotion of International Trade (CCPIT) attended South African International Trade Exhibition along with a Chinese delegation. On October 16, 2000, the first meeting of the Joint Science and Technology Committee was held in Beijing. In February 2001, China Construction Bank's branch was opened in Johannesburg. On May 18, 2001 the South African Chinese Business Council was established. In 2002, the trade volume between China and South Africa reached to USD2.58 billion, which grew rapidly to USD45.4 billion by 2011. By the end of June 2002, 96 Chinese enterprises were approved by the Chinese government to invest in South Africa and the contract volume was about USD190 million. South Africa approved for 205 investment projects in China with contract value of USD130 million. In December 2015, during the Chinese President Xi Jinping's visit to South Africa, both sides signed deals and loans of worth USD6.5 billion, focusing on building infrastructure in South Africa.

Table 12.1: Comparison of the Chinese Economy and the South African Economy

Index	*China*	*South Africa*
GDP	USD10866 billion	USD312.80 billion
GDP Annual Growth Rate	6.70	0.60
GDP Per Capita	USD 6416 billion	USD7575.24 billion
Unemployment Rate	4.05	26.60
Inflation Rate	1.80	7.00
Govt. Debt to GDP	43.90	50.10
Labour Population	USD1374.62 million	USD54.96 million

Source: Trending economics, 2016.

Table 12.2: China-South Africa Trade 2015

China's Total Export in 2015	USD 2.15 trillion
China's Total Import in 2015	USD 1.58 trillion
South Africa's Total Export in 2015	USD69631 million
South Africa's Total Import in 2015	USD79591 million
South Africa's Export to China in 2015	USD5803 million
South Africa's Import from China in 2015	USD14603 million

Source: wits.worldbank.org 2015.

Bi-National Commission (BNC) and Strengthening of Bilateral Ties

The regular working of BNC has played a significant role in expanding the Sino-South Africa ties in political as well as economic spheres. The plenary session of the BNC was inaugurated by South African President Thabo Mbeki in December 2001, and the ministries and departments of foreign affairs,

Table 12.3: Export, Import and Total Trade between China-South Africa, 2007-2015

Year	*South Africa's Export to China (USD million)*	*Partner Share (%)*	*South Africa's Import from China (USD million)*	*Partner Share (%)*	*Total Trade (USD million)*
2015	5,802	8.33	14,603	18.35	20,405
2014	8,680	9.58	15,449	15.47	24,129
2013	12,046	12.67	16,006	15.47	28,052
2012	10,337	10.46	14,611	14.03	24,948
2011	12,495	11.57	14,195	13.82	26,690
2010	8,095	9.80	11,480	13.84	19,597
2009	5,670	10.57	8,325	13.06	13,995
2008	4,310	5.83	9,909	11.31	14,219
2007	4,170	6.51	8,563	10.72	12,733

Source: wits.worldbank.org

science and technology, economic cooperation, trade and energy, including department of tourism from both sides, conducted their meetings. So far, there have been five BNC meetings since 2001, and the 5th Plenary Meeting of the BNC was held in China from October 27 to 30, 2013. The meeting was co-chaired by the South African deputy president Kaglema Motlanthe and the Chinese vice president Li Yuanchao. During the meeting, South Africa expressed her desire for greater participation of the Chinese companies in the sectors such as renewable energy, mining, banking, manufacturing and rail infrastructure.[15] In the 2nd Plenary Meeting of the BNC in 2004, it was announced that the South African Customs Union would enter into free trade negotiations with China. In the meeting, a common concern was raised for further deepening of South-South cooperation to safeguard the rights and interests of the developing countries in multilateral forum such as WTO and the United Nations. In the meeting, both sides emphasised on mutual support in the regional forums of Africa such as the Forum on China-Africa Cooperation (FOCAC) and the New Partnership for Africa's Development (NEPAD). During the meeting, South African deputy president Jacob Zuma highlighted a shared common perspective on "restructuring of the UN, the reform of the global trading system and enhanced South-South cooperation". The BNC meeting is actually providing a mechanism for both sides to reiterate their common diplomatic sentiments and organise the dialogue for investment and business cooperation.

Both sides are striving to realise the comprehensive strategic partnership envisaged in 2010, and this is reflected in their deepening economic cooperation and closer international cooperation in the multilateral forum such as G-20 and BRICS.[16] The impact of the China-South Africa relations can be felt in the regional as well as global affairs indicating the level of cooperation achieved. It is to be noted that President Jacob Zuma held bilateral talks with the Chinese President Xi Jinping ahead of the Sixth BRICS Summit held in Fortaleza and Brasilia in July 14-16, 2014.

In January 2013, Maite Nkoana-Mashabana, International Relations and Co-operation minister of South Africa expressed gratitude to the Chinese foreign minister Yang Jiechi, as South Africa was honoured to assume co-chair of FOCAC and that South Africa looks forward to work with China to address Africa's developmental challenges in the next six years of their co-chairship. On the behalf of the South African government, he also thanked China in supporting South Africa's membership of BRICS. The Chinese foreign minister acknowledged the fact that China-South Africa relations have been making huge strides, and experienced comprehensive and rapid growth in the past 15 years, with numerous high-level exchanges and enhanced political mutual trust. He further admitted to the expansion of business between the two along with an increase in people-to people exchanges.

African Continent and the Bilateral Ties

With regard to Africa, South Africa and China are seeking for convergence in their diplomatic engagement in the continent. China-South Africa relations constitute a prominent relationship in the context of Africa, which has gained momentum through both, bilateral exchanges and various multilateral frameworks. The BRICS and the FOCAC are the two major multilateral platforms for China and South Africa to push their interests forward in the African continent. South Africa has a leadership role at the African Union (AU) and FOCAC, and it has always tried to balance its position in the bilateral, regional and multilateral relations. Mostly, it is the regional agenda that drives South Africa's China policy in the continent. South Africa has played an important role in drafting the African Union's 'Common African Position' on the post-2015 development agenda, which comprises the guidelines for the development of China. The BRICS and FOCAC becomes a significant forum for South Africa to negotiate with China.

South Africa is the largest economy and one of the big powers in Africa, and its companies are established throughout the African continent. South African companies hold a strong position in Africa across various sectors such as finance, power generation, telecom, construction and agriculture. South

Africa has already developed its market in the member countries of Southern African Development Community, where it has pushed 85 per cent tariff-free commodities. The other BRICS members are also eager to access the African market, and so, China needs South Africa's cooperation to establish itself fully in the African market.

At the UN Security Council, both countries have cooperated closely for further expanding peacekeeping activities in Africa. Xi Jinping's initiative of a new 'Maritime Silk Road' is aligned with the Chinese approach to Africa's infrastructure development—which is parallel to South Africa's commitment to pursue regional infrastructure development. For the regional commercial competition in services and trade in Africa, both sides promote a high-level diplomatic engagement; and pertaining to the controversial cases in Africa such as Sudan and Zimbabwe, the two countries, however, differ in their positions. In 2015, South Africa hosted the 6th Summit on FOCAC was a major event on its diplomatic calendar. South Africa is seen as a genuine partner of China, and through mutual consultations, formulates positions on the UN Security Council. In the China-South Africa relations, there are nuances that can potentially affect their other 'strategic partnership'. For instance, in BRICS, the countries would make calculated decisions while giving priority to other partners; and also South Africa's regional identity and affinities with India and Brazil would be crucial in shaping its orientation on global issues.[17] Although China is credited for South Africa's inclusion in BRICS in 2010, now South Africa is provided with a privileged platform, from where it can articulate its position on the world stage.[18]

South Africa's Inclusion in BRICS

The inclusion of South Africa in BRICS can be seen as an initiative to change the dimension of the international multilateral institutions through a more unified voice against existing arrangement of global political and economic order. The addition of South Africa to BRICS is also part of China's efforts to promote South-South cooperation, in setting up a new economic and political order in the African continent and also at the global level. South Africa can serve as a gateway to Africa for China in expanding their roles in the continent.[19] In 2010, China, as rotating chairperson of BRIC, proposed for inclusion of South Africa; and then, based on agreement reached by the other members of the group, it became a member in December 2010. In the 3rd Summit of BRICS in Sanya, Hainan, with the inclusion of South Africa, major declaration was seen in context to Africa such as support for the African Union High-Level Panel Initiative on Libya and development in Africa within the framework of NEPAD and support for South Africa to host 2011 United Nations Climate Change Conference COP-17 in Durban. South African President Jacob Zuma said that BRICS is an important group of emerging economies, and its member states have a major role to play in restructuring political, economic and financial institution, and making them more equitable and balanced.[20] He believes that inclusion of South Africa in BRICS means the participation of over one billion African people.

Earlier, the emergence of BRICS was thought of as a group of prominent rising economies of the world; and looking at their impressive growth forecasts and expected economic dominance, it was also speculated that the group is going to be a new political power. The members of the BRICS originally linked solely through economic likeness and investment potential, but gradually began to encompass global political agenda to translate a combined economic power into international political alliance. The diplomatic strategy and geopolitical consideration for engagement with Africa is a significant factor to include South Africa. For the BRICS' effort in fair dealing of an issue at the global system and in making an equally distributed multipolar world, it was necessary to involve African representative to strengthen its voting power at the international forums such as the UN and WTO.

On the other hand, formulation of BRICS can be seen as combination of new emerging regional powers in the Global South, and their aspiration to redefine power structure in the international system. In this context, the South African minister of International Relations and Cooperation, Maite Nkoana-Mashabane, pointed out that the inclusion of South Africa in BRICS is an effort to fulfill the commitment and aspiration of balanced global platforms and multilateralism as well as enhancing South-South cooperation. He further added that since President Jacob Zuma has assumed his office in May 2009, he has visited all the BRIC nations and the South African government has "lobbied very hard" to join the group.

She believes that BRICS will provide South Africa a big platform to engage with major countries of the Global South, and in particular, its economic cooperation with BRICS countries will give access to investment and trade opportunities. On diplomatic grounds, South Africa can think of crucial support of BRICS countries on any issue of international concern at the United Nations and WTO. The element of cooperation on international issues at the global level seen in the past between China and South Africa has set the ground for the later inclusion in BRICS. The other possible reason is that the inclusion of South Africa in BRICS will change the relations between the two countries at bilateral as well as multilateral level. In August 2010, during President Jacob

Zuma's State visit to China, the relations between two countries were upgraded from 'strategic partnership' to 'comprehensive partnership'; and in December 2010, South Africa was officially invited to join BRICS. In the 3rd BRICS Summit in Sanya in 2011, soon after South Africa's inclusion in the group, President Jacob Zuma—while addressing at the Plenary Session of BRICS — said, "We are now equal co-architects of a new equitable international system".

Hany Besada, researcher at Institute of African Studies, Carleton University, argues that with the inclusion of South Africa in BRICS, it is reinforcing neoliberalism in Africa and the markets are being liberalised, trade and investment are given priority in the continent but that there is least concern about the social and environmental protection. He believes that South Africa is the regional hegemon in Africa. He suggests South Africa is the largest economy in sub-Saharan Africa and the third largest stakeholder of the African Development Bank while also being the largest donor for South African Development Community.[21] In the international political sphere, South Africa presides as an African leader. The South African government lobbies for the African interests because it is a member in major multilateral forums such as G-20, African Union, SADC and BRICS. South Africa is a major contributor to the peacekeeping operations conducted by the United Nations and the African Union. [22]

Critics are of view that the addition of South Africa to BRICS is an 'unnatural fit' on the basis of their consideration on relatively smaller size in economy, population and state. The critics were of belief that inclusion of South Africa will be of limited gain for the rest of the BRICS members because they are bigger economic powers, sharing common economic characteristics; they also suggested that there are other countries with fast economic growth such as Mexico, Turkey, Indonesia and South Korea, who merit the membership of BRICS. Jim O'Neill, then chairman of Goldman Sachs Asset Management International, said, "South Africa's economy is very small," and "for South Africa to be treated as part of BRIC doesn't make any sense to me; but South Africa as a representative of the African continent is a different story." But contrary to Jim O'Neill, Martyn Davies, chief executive officer of Johannesburg-based Frontier Advisory, said, "South Africa as a country is small, but if we go there as a regional market, that's a different story," and "for South Africa, it's nice to be associated with the big boys".[23]

The membership of South Africa was questioned because it does not match to fellow BRICS members in production with similar investment and financial indicators, and so it is placed far below in global fiscal ranking compared to other members of the group. The critics believe that South Africa's participation and role is intertwined with her bilateral relations with China. South Africa shares good relations with other BRICS countries, particularly Brazil and India; but still, its understanding and cooperation with China in the grouping is higher. In 2011, South Africa, India and Brazil were non-permanent members at the UN Security Council, and China and Russia are the permanent members of the UNSC. So the inclusion of South Africa had increased the voting power of China at the United Nations. All the BRICS countries are also member of G-20, which provides them with an option to band together as a pressure group on an issue of common concern at the international organisation. The critics are of view that a *quid pro quo* dynamic was being played in the background of China-South Africa relation. They believe that with the expansion and deepening of economic cooperation with China, South Africa largely votes in favour of China at the multilateral forums, overlooking the principles of human rights and democracy; for instance, South Africa, during its first tenure on the UNSC, failed to uphold perceived principles congruence with international expectation that sparked widespread criticism. South Africa joining BRICS will create a more inclusive international economic system, in which the opinion of the developing countries will influence policy making.[24] Van Den Bosch says that South Africa's inclusion in BRIC will not be beneficial for the country as such, but that the merger could probably allow the other member states to exploit the region. According to some analysts, South Africa's membership in BRIC will allow its participation in global governance, conflict resolution and security, and will add to the process of democratisation of the international system.[25]

In recent years, China and South Africa have worked on strengthening bilateral ties at all levels, including parliamentary level. On September 28, 2004, then chairman of the Standing Committee of the National People's Congress Wu Bangguo and then Chinese Premier Wen Jiabao visited South Africa and met with then vice-president of South Africa, Jacob Zuma. At the meeting, Wu Bangguo pointed out that both sides have worked to successfully develop and establish sound cooperative relations between the National People's Congress (NPC) and the National Assembly of South Africa—which has influenced the development of bilateral-friendly cooperation. He said that the Chinese government wishes to strengthen exchanges and cooperation between the NPC of China and the National Assembly and the National Committee on Provincial Affairs of South Africa to further deepen the bilateral ties. Understanding at the parliamentary level signify cooperation at policy making decisions which, at times, can influence their interests at the global economic and political forums. On the official good will visit of the Chinese top legislator Wu Bangguo to South Africa in May 23-28, 2011, Sanusha Naidu, senior researcher of the Africa and Global South Unit of Cape Town office of Human Sciences Research Council (HSRC), said in an exclusive interview with Xinhua news, "It is a critical feature of diplomacy because it does not stay at State level, but goes further in agenda—much more important relations that come off parliament terrain.[26] The parliament, especially in South Africa, is an important legislature (as) it plays override role (in national affairs)." She added, "Firstly, we need to see what (China's) strategic relation to South Africa is; in terms of South Africa's foreign policy, BRICS' membership becomes a cornerstone to South Africa's foreign policy." She is of the view that the strengthening of relations and cooperation between China and South Africa is aimed at reforming international financial institutions and the global political order. "Strategically, at the global level, China and South Africa try to pursue common ideology and common identity with regard to their common interest in reforming international system— doing it through the platform of BRICS, G20, United Nation Security Council (UNSC), and of course, also promotes South-South cooperation in the process as well," she added. She believes that the deepening of cooperation between the two countries at multilateral institutions such as BRICS and G-20 will promote African agenda and support Africa's integration into global economy. During the visit, Chinese leader Wu Bangguo met with President Jacob Zuma, and said that China is willing to strengthen her close coordination in key international issues with South Africa, and mutual cooperation in areas such as green economy, manufacturing, agriculture as well as bilateral visits and exchanges at the government and parliament level. He pointed out that China is aiming to promote South-South cooperation, and willing to coordinate with South Africa at multilateral institutions such as the UN, WTO, G20 and BASICS on regional and international issues in order to set up a new international, political and economic order. Wu Bangguo reiterated that China supports South Africa's initiative to host 2011 United Nations Climate Change Conference in Durban. President Jacob Zuma affirms South Africa's commitment to China by speaking highly of China's role in international affairs and said that South Africa attaches great importance to its bilateral ties with China. He assures South Africa's cooperation with China in bilateral as well as multilateral frameworks, and strengthens their coordination on regional and international issues to jointly safeguard and promote the interests of the developing countries. It is to be noted that the first regional office of the New Development Bank is in Johannesburg, South Africa, and its headquarters are in Shanghai, China.[27] The New Development Bank is a multilateral bank established by BRICS on July 15, 2014 at the 6th BRICS Summit held in Fortaleza, Brazil. According to Ross Anthony, director of Center for Chinese Studies, Stellenbosch University, in context of international political economy, China "talks left and walks right". He suggests that China is a dominant player in global capitalism with its integration into global market system, the rise of a consumer-oriented middle class and its outward-bound commodity forays. Moreover, China's engagement with Africa is an extension of this process. In the context of the New Development Bank, he believes that the Chinese-driven Asian Infrastructure Investment Bank that has major global players, including South Africa, has eclipsed the BRICS New Development Bank and it has presented itself as a champion of the Global South.

In the framework of BRICS, the China-South Africa relations exhibit a trend of changing order in the distribution of power in political and economic dimensions at the international level. The BRICS give an international platform for the cooperation between the two countries on global issue, and has further broadened their ties, that challenges the monopolised domination of international agendas by the Western developed countries. The inclusion of South Africa in BRICS also indicates that the Northern countries are no longer sole economic and trade partner of the many emerging economies; and the relations between the two countries is also an exemplary case of South-South cooperation. Dawn Mokhobo, chairperson of African International Advisor, commented on the 5th BRICS Summit in South Africa, that the awareness among the global communities about the potential of the BRICS has been raised with South Africa hosting the Summit this year, and the main theme was to build a mutually and highly beneficial partnership for development, integration and industrialisation of the African continent. The eThekwini Declaration under the theme 'Unlocking Africa's Potential: BRICS and Africa Cooperation on Infrastructure' was signed by the all members of the group during the Summit to reaffirm their commitment to promote intra-BRICS solidarity, and looking at new ways of contributing positively to development, economic cooperation, peace and stability.[28] She added that now, the challenge is to reap the undoubted benefits for South Africa and African continent from the membership of BRICS. She suggests that South Africa should tap the opportunities for economic development and cooperation in support of the National Development Plan, and attract new foreign investments to boost her major infrastructure development projects in order to create new strategic joint business ventures.

According to Dr. Rob Davies, minister of Trade and Industry of South Africa, the country has benefitted substantially after the BRICS membership; its export trade with fellow members of the group increased from 6.2 per cent of the total export in 2005 to 16.8 per cent at the end of 2011, and its imports from the BRICS countries has increased from 13.6 per cent of the total imports in 2005 to 20 per cent in 2011. He emphasised that the trade between South Africa and the fellow BRICS countries has increased by 29 per cent. But in the case of Africa, according to a report issued by the United Nations Conference on Trade and Development (UNCTD), Africa attracts merely 4 per cent of combined BRICS Foreign Direct Investment (FDI) outflow. However, the investment is one fourth of the continent's total inflows for 2012.[29] He also pointed out the advantage of using their own currencies in trade among the BRICS countries, which will protect them from volatile international convertible currencies, namely the US dollar.

Although, China shares healthy bilateral ties with most of the African countries, it has only invited South Africa to join BRICS in 2010 as a representative of African continent. China's proposal for South African membership in BRICS is due to various factors, favourable for China as well as for the fellow BRIC members. The relations between China-South Africa have already experienced a greater strategic cooperation in bilateral and multilateral spheres. South Africa is a reliable member of multilateral institutions such as G8 outreach 5, G20, BASIC and IBSA, and was a non-permanent member of UN Security Council in 2011-2012 as a representative of Africa regional group. The South African companies are active in more than half of the African countries with a much diversified economy. In terms of history and economic trajectory, South Africa is different from the other BRICS member states. Although it is not similar to other African countries, it does share the major concerns of the continent such as poverty and unemployment, law and order issues, social and cultural diversity, democracy, economic inequality etc.[30] In all the major international forums, South Africa is already the voice of the African continent. In addition to the geopolitical factor and African representative, South Africa is one of the largest economies in Africa, and it can serve as a gateway to the continent for the BRICS members, given the rich mineral resources of the region. South Africa has vast reserves of platinum, gold and diamond, it has well-established infrastructure, corporate footprints, easy access to finance for business, an advance banking system, a culture of innovation, a stable macro and micro financial climate and functioning regulatory frameworks.

The issues of the Middle East and North Africa have also been part of the discussions during the BRICS meetings, which can be understood as a consolidated move by the BRICS nations to define their stance on pressing international issues. South Africa has acted as a mediator in the settlement of Darfur conflict, which would accrue it political mileage to pursue trade relations with both, North and South Sudan. And this will have immense economic implications for BRICS members, especially China. China-South Africa relations, despite being upgraded to a comprehensive strategic partnership, carry with it an element of competition at a bilateral, continental and multilateral level. Since 2009, there is a constant deepening and expansion of economic and trade relations between the two countries, and therefore, it becomes imperative for South Africa to balance cautiously its bilateral, regional and global interactions with China. In this context, inclusion of South Africa in the BRICS came at a time when the relationship needed further boost—an additional multilateral dimension to diversify the engagement.

During the tenure of President Thabo Mbeki, the foreign policy was not very encouraging about its relation with China, whereas in Jacob Zuma's administration since 2009, China is given high priority. In 1996, Dalai Lama visited South Africa to meet Nelson Mandela, and was warmly welcomed by the South African government.[31] In March 2009, Dalai Lama was denied visa to attend the 80th birthday celebration of Desmond Tutu, and this may be the beginning of a new era in the China-South Africa bilateral ties.[32] Throughout his regime, Africa has been very explicit about preserving South Africa's enhanced engagement with China. It is also argued that South Africa's foreign policy has acquired an international stature after its integration into BRICS, and sometimes, it might be faced with tricky situations which could cost it global embarrassment because of China. For instance, in 2009, on the denial of visa to Dalai Lama, the South African government officials said that his visit would distract the audience of the Football World Cup in 2010.

China has favoured South Africa for its inclusion in BRICS in order to fulfill its major interests. For instance, China has huge financial stakes in various sectors such as banking, infrastructure, mining, transport and renewable energy in South Africa. In October 2011, Dalai Lama was denied visa by the South African government when he wished to attend the birthday celebration of fellow Nobel Laureate Desmond Tutu, once again.[33] In this context, Dawn Mokhobo, chairperson of African International Advisor, has commented that China's interest as part of BRICS is to look at the Southern Hemisphere for potentially lucrative business and joint venture opportunities, and the leveraging South Africa's position on the African continent to explore commercial opportunities and areas of future economic interest in Africa.

Conclusion

There are few factors in BRICS which directly impact the China-South Africa relations. In fact, regional and bilateral aspects remain crucial to their evolution of relation in BRICS. The change in Chinese leadership in 2012 has further strengthened the mutual trust and economic cooperation. In case of South Africa, the change of leadership in 2009 has influenced the bilateral ties—taking it to the level of comprehensive strategic partnership in 2010. The other aspect of Sino-South Africa relations is the understanding between the African National Congress (ANC) and National People's Congress (NPC). At present, the ANC is the ruling political party in South Africa, and it is alleged that China had funded ANC heavily in the last 2014 presidential election. China has always emphasised on party level cooperation, so that even if the leader changes, the bilateral ties relations remain unaffected. Secondly, China is also concerned about changes in the ruling party of South Africa, which may possibly affect their ties at government level as well as leadership level. So, any form of difference at the party, government and leadership level will hold consequences for the bilateral relationship, subsequently influencing China-South Africa relation in BRICS. BRICS as an international multilateral forum that deals with issues like energy and international trade gives China and other members a platform of opportunity to enter into Africa. Owing to China's closer ties with South Africa, and South Africa being the African representative in BRICS, China has the advantage in terms of market and natural resource access in Africa. So, China-South Africa relations is a key factor for the Chinese government in BRICS. Since South Africa represents the African continent at major international forums, it is highly advantageous for China to handle any political and economic issue in Africa. Besides, the China-South Africa lobby in BRICS, also affects the interests of Russia, Brazil and India, and holds implications for other African countries in terms of resource and consumer exploitation.

END NOTES

1. Seria, Nasreen (2010), South Africa to Join BRIC to Boost Emerging Markets, *Bloomberg Market,* New York City, December 24, 2010, http://www.bloomberg.com/news/articles/2010-12-24/south-africa-asked-to-join-bric-to-boost-cooperation-with-emerging-markets
2. Jim O'Neill (2001), Building Better Global Economic BRICs *Global Economics*, Goldman Sachs, Paper No: 66
3. Ministry of External Relations Brasilia (2010), Government of Brazil, *BRICS Second Summit: Joint Statement,* Brasilia.
4. Mathola, Miller (2012), SA in BRICS: collaboration for growth, *SouthAfrica.info, March 28, 2012,* http://www.southafrica.info/global/brics/miller-matola-280312.htm#.V9krSFt97Mw

5. Ministry of Foreign Affairs (2010), Government of the PRC, *China - South Africa Relations,* Beijing, http://www.fmprc.gov.cn/ce/ceza/eng/zghfz/zngx/t165290.htm
6. Ministry of Foreign Affairs (2004), Government of the PRC, *Pretoria Declaration,* Beijing, http://www.fmprc.gov.cn/ce/ceza/eng/zghfz/zngx/t165286.htm
7. Ministry of Foreign Affairs (2015), Government of the People's Republic of China, *China's Foreign Affairs,* World Affairs Press, Beijing.
8. Ensor, Linda (2014), Zuma, ministers and business to visit China, *Investors Monthly,*November 28, 2014, http://www.bdlive.co.za/national/politics/2014/11/28/zuma-ministers-and-business-to-visit-china
9. South Africa, China sign trade and industry deals, *SouthAfrica.info,* 4 December 2015, http://www.southafrica.info/business/Chinese-South-Africa-trade-041215.htm#.V9uMXVt97Mw
10. South Africa, China seal new deals, *SouthAfrica.info*, September 30, 2011, http://www.southafrica.info/news/international/china-300911.htm
11. SA, China to 'expand mutual investment', *SouthAfrica.info,* July 19, 2012, http://www.southafrica.info/news/international/china-190712.htm#.V9kuvVt97Mw
12. Shange, Naledi, Ramaphosa on state visit to China, *News24,* Johannesburg, July 13, 2015, http://www.news24.com/SouthAfrica/News/Ramaphosa-on-State-visit-to-China-20150713
13. Chen Jimin (2014), The Evolving Dynamic of China-Africa Relations, May 16, 2014, http://thediplomat.com/2014/05/the-evolving-dynamic-of-chinafricaa—relations/
14. South Africa: President Zuma to Host President Xi for State Visit, *AllAfrica,* Pretoria, December 2, 2015, http://www.sanews.gov.za/south-africa/president-zuma-host-president-xi-state-visit
15. The Presidency (2013), Government of Republic of South Africa, *Media statement on conclusion of the Fifth Bi-National Commission between South Africa-The People's Republic of China,*Pretoria.
16. SAA makes first non-stop flight to China, *SouthAfrica.info,*February 1, 2012, http://www.southafrica.info/travel/saa-china.htm
17. Alden, Chris and Yu Shanwu (2014), South Africa Institute of International Affairs, *South Africa-China Relations: Evolving Cooperation, Collaboration and Competition,* Johannesburg.
18. Everett, Cath (2014), Chinese business deals trump Nelson Mandela commemoration for South Africa's President Jacob Zuma, *International Businesstimes,* South Africa, December 5, 2014, http://www.ibtimes.co.uk/chinese-business-deals-trump-nelson-mandela-commemoration-south-africas-president-jacob-zuma-1478091
19. Major Chinese bank opens SA office, *SouthAfrica.info,* November 29, 2011, http://www.southafrica.info/business/investing/cpticbc-291111.htm
20. Besada, Hany & Tok, Evren (2014), 'South Africa in the BRICS: Soft Power Balancing and Instrumentalization.' Journal of International and Global Studies 5:2, pp. 76-95.
21. Leclercq, François (2014), BRICS: building education for the future; priorities for national development and international cooperation Paris: UNESCO, 2014, 91p. ISBN: 978-92-3-100047-8.
22. Tharoor, Shashi (2015), India, China and the Rest of the BRICS Will No Longer Wait for a Seat at the Table, *The World Post,* June 22, 2015, http://www.huffingtonpost.com/shashi-tharoor/india-china-brics-world-power_b_7633684.html
23. De Wet, Phillip (2015), SA and China: A love founded on state control, *Mail & Guardian,* Pretoria, 21 August, 2013, http://mg.co.za/article/2015-08-22-sa-and-china-a-love-founded-on-state-control
24. Hao Feixiong (2012), *China South Africa Relations in the Context of BRICS*, Maters Thesis, South Africa: University of Witwatersrand.
25. Besada, Hany&Tok, Evren (2014), 'South Africa in the BRICS: Soft Power Balancing and Instrumentalization,' *Journal of International and Global Studies* 5:2, pp. 76-95.

26. Wang Guanchun (2011), Top Chinese legislator starts visit to South Africa, *Xinhua,* Cape Town, May 24, 2011, http://www.sanews.gov.za/south-africa/top-chinese-legislator-starts-visit-sa
27. Aneja, Atul (2016), South Africa to host BRICS office, *The Hindu,* July 27, 2016, http://www.thehindu.com/todays-paper/tp-international/south-africa-to-host-brics-office/article8908400.ece
28. Mokhobo, Dawn, Reaping the benefits of BRICS membership for South Africa, *Wesizwe Platinum,* Johannesburg, http://www.wesizwe.co.za/reaping-the-benefits-of-brics-membership-for-sa.php
29. Begbie, Yolaan,(2014), BRICS: What's In It For Africa?, Africa.com.http://www.africa.com/brics-whats-in-it-for-africa/
30. MaiteNkoana-Mashabane (2013), South Africa's Role in BRICS, and Its Benefits to Job Creation and the Infrastructure Drive in South Africa, Department of International Relations and Cooperation, Republic of South Africa, University of Toronto.
31. Dalai Lama visit to SA hangs in the balance, *Mail & Guardian,* Pretoria, 28 September, 2011, http://mg.co.za/article/2011-09-28-dalai-lama-visit-to-sa-hangs-in-the-balance
32. South African minister: Refusing visa to Dalai Lama "a matter between states", *Xinhua,* Johannesburg, 27 March 2009, http://news.xinhuanet.com/english/2009-03/27/content_11085970.htm
33. Gerardy, Justine (2011), Tutu turns 80 amid Dalai Lama dithering, *Mail &Guardian,*Pretoria, 2 October, 2011, http://mg.co.za/article/2011-10-02-tutu-turns-80-amid-dalai-lama-dithering

ANNEXURES

ANNEXURE 1

BRICS Chronology

November 30, 2001: Jim O'Neill, Senior Economist at Goldman Sachs coined the acronym BRICs. Sachs as part of an economic modeling exercise to forecast global economic trends over the next half century used the acronym in the Global Economics Paper No. 66, "The World Needs Better Economic BRICs".

November 30, 2001: Jim O'Neill launched the big idea: Building Better Global Economic BRICs. He predicted "over the next 10 years, the weight of the BRIC and especially China in world GDP will grow in line with these prospects; world policymaking forums should be reorganized".

September 14, 2002: An informal luncheon meeting between the Foreign Ministers of India, China, and Russia took place on the margins of the 57th session of the UN General Assembly in New York. The convergence of economic interests and the imperative of mutual cooperation, however, provided the context of the meeting.

October 01, 2003: The economic report "Dreaming with BRICs: The Path to 2050" by Goldman Sachs was released. By 2035, China could overtake the US to become the largest economy in the world, and by 2039 the combined GDP of the BRIC economies could become bigger than that of the G7.

September 15, 2004: President Kalam visited South Africa, the first by an Indian President. The visit was part of the country's continuing "Focus Africa" policy and reaffirmation of the time-tested relations between the two countries and their peoples.

April 18, 2005: BRIC's representation at the G7 Finance Ministers Meeting. Since then China became greatly involved in the G7 finance ministers' process. The discussion focused on fiscal and monetary policies, Asian economy and exchange rate stability.

July 18, 2006: President Vladimir Putin had a trilateral meeting with President of China Hu Jintao and Prime Minister of India Manmohan Singh in St. Petersburg. The first trilateral meet with focus on major regional and international issues. They also explored the scope of expanding cooperation among themselves.

September 21, 2006: The first meeting of BRIC Foreign Ministers held in St.Petersburg on the margins of the G8 Outreach Summit. The grouping was formalized during the 1st meeting of BRICS Foreign Ministers on the margins of the UN General Assembly in New York.

September 5&6, 2006: The official visit of Russian President Vladimir Putin to South Africa, the first Head of the Russian state visit to Africa south of

Sahara. A number of intergovernmental agreements and contractual documents between large companies of both countries were also signed during the visit.

June 3, 2007: Brazilian President Luiz Inacio Lula da Silva visited India. He addressed the Indian captains of business and industry in a function jointly being organised by CII, FICCI and Assocham.

October 17, 2007: Prime Minister Dr Manmohan Singh, South African President Thabo Mbeki and Brazilian President Luiz Inacio Lula da Silva attened the IBSA summit. The leaders reiterated the importance of strengthening the global governance system and South-south cooperation.

May 16, 2008: The Foreign Ministers of BRIC held their meeting in Yekaterinburg. They emphasized the prospects of the BRIC dialogue based on mutual trust and respect, common interests, coincidence or similarity of approaches toward the pressing problems of global development.

July, 2008: Leaders of BRIC attended G8 meet in Japan. They decided to coordinate their moves on the key economic issues, including cooperation in finance and the food problem.

September 25, 2008: The fourth BRIC foreign ministers' meeting was held in New York, where the ministers took part in the 63rd UN General Assembly session. It discussed the financial crisis problems, and the question of interaction within the UN.

November 7, 2008: Heads of the BRICs financial agencies met in San Paulo for the first time on the eve of the financial G20 events. They issued a joint communiqué stating their common approaches to world economy problems, including the causes and ways of overcoming the global financial crisis. Agreement was reached to hold regular meetings of BRIC finance ministers, and contacts between their deputies.

November 25, 2008: Dmitry Medvedev on an official visit to Brazil. They pointed out that Russia and Brazil are developing along similar patterns and setting an example of what progress modern countries can make.

June 16, 2009: The 1st BRIC Summit was held in Yekaterinburg, Russia. The summit focused on methods of improving the global economic situation, reforming financial institutions and on improving co-operation between the nations.

October 27, 2009: The 9th trilateral meeting of the foreign ministers of Russia, India and China was held in Bangalore. They explored business opportunities in key sectors, including infrastructure and energy, mutually beneficially to the three countries in the region.

April 15, 2010: The 2nd BRIC Summit took place in Brasilia. The issues discussed included the world economic situation, the Group of 20, reform

	of global financial organizations, climate change and dialogue and cooperation among BRIC countries.
June 2, 2010:	President Zuma paid a State Visit to India. This was President Zuma's first state visit to Asia since assuming office as President of the Republic of South Africa. His talks with Prime Minister Mannoham Singh focused on deepening strategic partnership between South Africa and India.
August 5, 2010:	President Jacob Zuma visited Russia. His visit to Russia was part of his strategic initiative to open new trade and investment routes to the fast growing BRIC economies.
September 21, 2010:	BRIC Foreign Ministers at their meeting in New York and agreed to invite South Africa to join BRIC. They focused mainly on the problems of bolstering comprehensive cooperation between the BRIC nations, including within the G20 framework, and discussed key issues on the agenda of the current session of the UN General Assembly.
November 11, 2010:	South Africa applied to join BRIC at the G20 meeting of the world's leading economies in Seoul.
December 21, 2010:	Medvedev on a three-day state visit to India. The visit redefined the tenor of Russia-India relations beyond the traditional military-centric, buy-and-sell, hard-cash format, to a far more broad-based strategic partnership in tune with his resolve to revive Russia's stature as a global power.
December 24, 2010:	BRIC became BRICS with inclusion of South Africa. The group was renamed as BRICS, with "S" standing for South Africa.
February 14, 2011:	President Jacob Zuma led a South African delegation to India. Zuma thanked the Indian president for continued development support to South Africa.
April 14, 2011:	The 3rd BRICS Summit took place in Sanya, Hainan island of China. Topics discussed include the international situation, global economic and financial affairs, development issues, and cooperation within BRICS.
October 14-15, 2011:	South Africa hosted the 5th India-Brazil-South Africa (IBSA) Academic Forum at the Durban University of Technology. They contemplated increasing interactions in the research circles and formulating recommendations to be presented to the leaders during the Summit of 26-27 March 2013.
November 3, 2011:	A consultation meeting of the BRICS leaders was held on the margins of the G20 Summit.
November 24, 2011:	BRICS deputy foreign ministers issue communiqué on North Africa and Middle East. They underlined the legitimacy of the aspirations of the peoples of the region for greater political and social rights.

February 25, 2012: BRICS finance officials meet during the G20 finance ministers meeting, Los Cabos, Mexico

March 28, 2012: The 2nd Meeting of the BRICS Trade and Economic Ministers in New Delhi. The Ministers emphasised the need to resist protectionist tendencies and to promote international trade as an engine of economic growth and development, while respecting the WTO consistent policy space available to developing countries to pursue their legitimate objectives of growth, development and stability.

March 29, 2012: PM Manmohan Singh's address at the 4th BRICS summit. India reaffirmed its full commitment to work with BRICS.

April 13, 2012: Chinese Foreign Minister Yang Jiechi, Russian Foreign Minister Sergei Lavrov and Indian Foreign Minister S.M. Krishna attended the 11th China-Russia-India Foreign Ministers Meeting in Moscow, Russia.

August 27, 2012: DARE/ICAR hosted meeting of Experts on Agro Products and Food Security of BRICS. During the meeting, there was suggestion for making a "Framework document for establishing BRICS Strategic Cooperation Alliance on Agricultural Science and Technology" which had been circulated to all the BRICS countries (Brazil, Russia, China and South Africa) for their comments/ suggestion.

September 11, 2012: The first BRICS Wellness Workshop concluded in Bengaluru. Secretary level Officers and Traditional Medicine/wellness experts from the BRICS countries participated in the BRICS Wellness Workshop.

September 26, 2012: A BRICS Think Tank Forum was held in China. They reached consensus on creating a BRICS development bank to complement existing global financial institutions like World Bank.

October 11, 2012: G7 Finance ministers meeting in Tokyo at the Annual Meeting of the IMF & World Bank

October 29, 2012: Media statement by the DIRCO Mr Ebrahim Ebrahim, on developments in the international relations field. They focused on a few matters, including the meeting of the Indian Ocean Rim Association for Regional Cooperation, which South Africa attended; the 5th BRICS Summit etc.

January 01, 2013: State Councilor Dai Bingguo attended the third Meeting of BRICS High Representatives for Security Issues in India. On the sidelines of the meeting, State Councilor Dai had a bilateral meeting with Prime Minister Singh and presented a letter of CPC Central Committee General Secretary Xi Jinping to Prime Minister Singh.

January 11, 2013: The BRICS Health Ministers held the 2nd Health Ministers'

meeting in New Delhi, with a strong call for strengthened cooperation in the implementation of affordable, equitable and sustainable solutions for common health challenges. Reference was made to reaching one key HIV-related development goal by 2015.

January 17-18, 2013: The Heads of Revenue of BRICS Countries met in New Delhi. They identified seven areas of tax policy and tax administration, for extending their mutual cooperation.

February 15-16, 2013: Finance ministers and central bank governors meet at the G20 meet

February 17-23, 2013: Chinese Foreign Minister Yang Jiechi paid official visit to South Africa and Russia.

February 28, 2013: The Deputy Minister of DIRCO Mr Ebrahim Ebrahim, participated in a public debate organized by Action Aid, "BRICS: Paradigm shift or more of the same?"

March 13, 2013: BRICS Think Tanks Council established at DUT. Signed during the BRICS Academic Forum, the declaration served to indicate the common intention of BRICS academia to enhance co-operation in research, knowledge sharing, capacity building as well as policy advice.

March 17, 2013: Egypt President invited to attend Durban BRICS summit. President Morsi said he hopes Egypt will join the BRICS group so that one day the name becomes E-BRICS where "E stands for Egypt."

March 26, 2013: Toast by Jacob Zuma to the BRICS Gala Dinner, Durban

March 27, 2013: The 5th BRICS Summit took place. It concluded the first cycle of BRICS Summits and we reaffirmed our commitment to the promotion of international law, multilateralism and the central role of the United Nations.

September 05, 2013: BRICS Leaders met, ahead of the formal opening of the G20 Summit in St Petersburg. In light of the increase in financial market and capital flow volatility during recent months, the BRICS Leaders reiterated their concerns they had expressed in the Durban Summit in March, regarding the unintended negative spillovers of unconventional monetary policies of certain developed economies.

October 29, 2013: BRICS agriculture and agrarian development ministers declaration, Pretoria. the 3rd Meeting of BRICS Ministers of Agriculture and Agrarian Development on October 29, 2013 under the theme: "The negative effect of climate change on world food security".

November 05, 2013: The South African Minister of Higher Education and Training, Dr B Nzimande hosted the first meeting BRICS Ministers of Education in Paris, France, on the margins of the 37th session of

	the UNESCO General Conference. The meeting provided a platform for BRICS Education Minsters to explore areas of collaboration in the fields of education and training between their countries.
March 24, 2014:	BRICS foreign ministers meet in Hague. Minister Maite Nkoana-Mashabane convened a BRICS Foreign/International Relations Ministers' meeting on Monday, 24 March 2014, on the margins of the Nuclear Security Summit.
May 20, 2014:	BRICS health ministers statement on margins of the World Health Assembly, in which they committed to strengthen intra-BRICS cooperation for promoting health of the BRICS population. They resolved to continue cooperation in the sphere of health through the Technical Working Groups and the "BRICS Framework for Collaboration on Strategic Projects in Health".
July 14-16, 2014:	Brazil launches website for Fortaleza Summit
July 14, 2014:	BRICS trade ministers' joint communiqué. They reviewed the global economic situation and expressed concern at the slow pace of recovery, which continues to hinder trade and investment flows.
July 15, 2014:	BRICS Fortaleza Declaration and Action Plan; Treaty for the Establishment of a BRICS Contingent Reserve Arrangement & Agreement on the New Development Bank
November 15, 2014:	The BRICS Leaders met on the occasion of the G20 Summit in Brisbane. They underscored that the signing of the agreements establishing the New Development Bank (NDB) and the Contingent Reserve Arrangement (CRA) brought BRICS cooperation to a fundamentally new level with the creation of instruments to contribute to the stability of the international financial system.
December 05, 2014:	Fourth BRICS Health Ministers Communiqué. The Ministers underscored that the Declaration of Fortaleza and its Action Plan, adopted at the Sixth BRICS Summit, inaugurated a new cycle of BRICS coordination. The focus on social inclusion and sustainable development will contribute to the strengthening of intra-BRICS partnership, including cooperation in health.
April 01, 2015:	Russia launches official website for the Ufa Summit
April 22, 2015:	BRICS environment ministers issue first statement. reaffirm our commitment to implement the Rio Declaration, Agenda 21, the Johannesburg Plan of Implementation (JPOI), and the outcomes of the Rio+20 Conference in our respective countries, and through our cooperation within the framework of BRICS in accordance with the Rio principles, including the principle of common but differentiated responsibilities.
July 9, 2015:	Ufa Declaration and Action Plan, under the theme "BRICS

	Partnership – a Powerful Factor of Global Development".
October 28, 2015:	The Diplomatic Academy of the Russian Ministry of Foreign Affairs hosted a forum for young diplomats from BRICS countries in Moscow.
November 15, 2015:	The BRICS Leaders met on the margins of the G20 Summit in Antalya. The Leaders recommitted to strengthen cooperation among BRICS countries and with other nations in the fight against terrorism.
January 25-26, 2016:	BRICS Labour and employment ministers meet in Ufa, at the first BRICS Labour and Employment Ministers meeting to discuss new areas of cooperation in labour and employment, social security and social inclusion, public policies.
March 22, 2016:	India to host eighth BRICS summit in Goa announced. The theme of India's BRICS chairmanship is Building Responsive, Inclusive and Collective Solutions
April 14-16, 2016:	1st BRICS Friendship City Conclave held in Mumbai, which an international discussed and tackled urbanisation issues emerging in the cities of five developing BRICS nations.
July 1-3, 2016:	The second BRICS Youth Summit held in Guhawati. The summit focused on enhancing people to people contacts among BRICS member states.
September 2-6, 2016:	1st BRICS Film Festival was held in Delhi
September 4, 2016:	The BRICS Leaders met on the margins of the G20 Summit in Hangzhou. The the focus of the G20 summit was on the four I's of "innovative, invigorated, interconnected and inclusive." The Leaders held wide-ranging discussions on the G20 Summit Agenda and agreed to pursue issues of global and mutual interest to the BRICS countries at the G20.

Sources: http://www.brics.fudan.edu.cn/;http://www.brics.utoronto.ca/;http://thebricspost.com/; http://mea.gov.in/press-releases.htm?51/Press_Releases

ANNEXURE 2

BRICS Summits and Packages

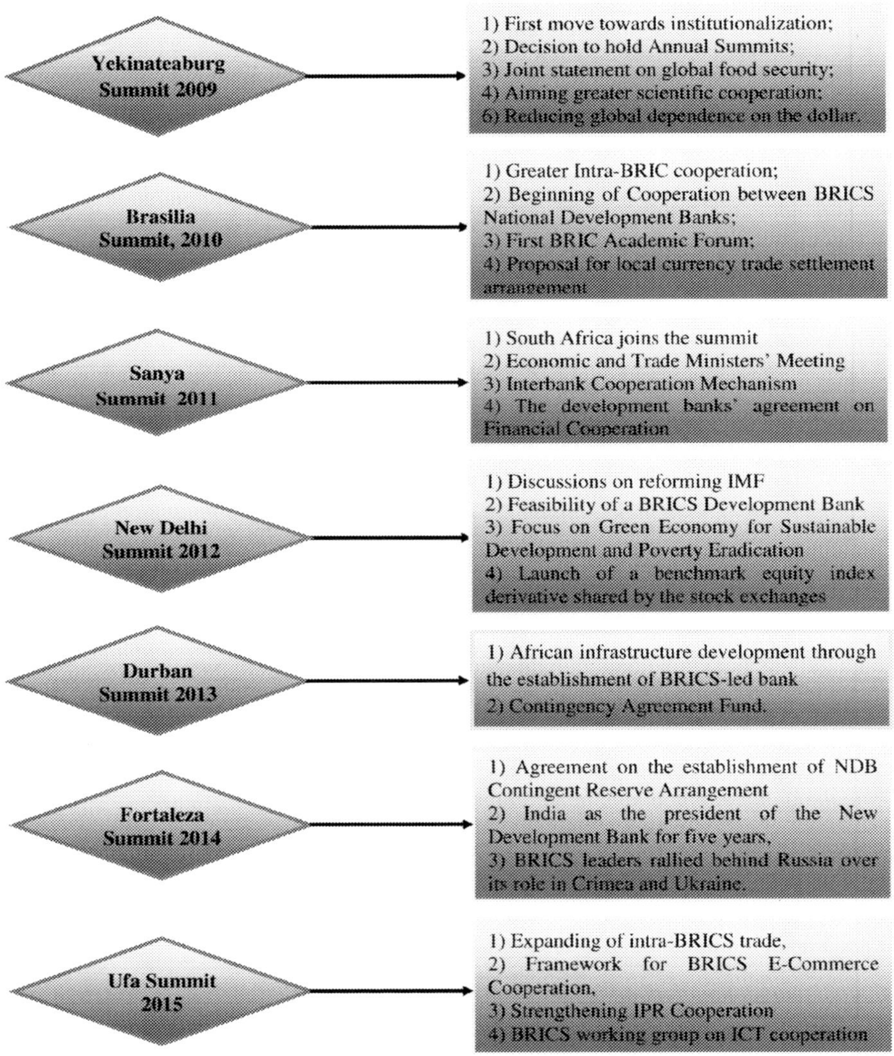

ANNEXURE 3

BRICS Summit Declarations and Highlights

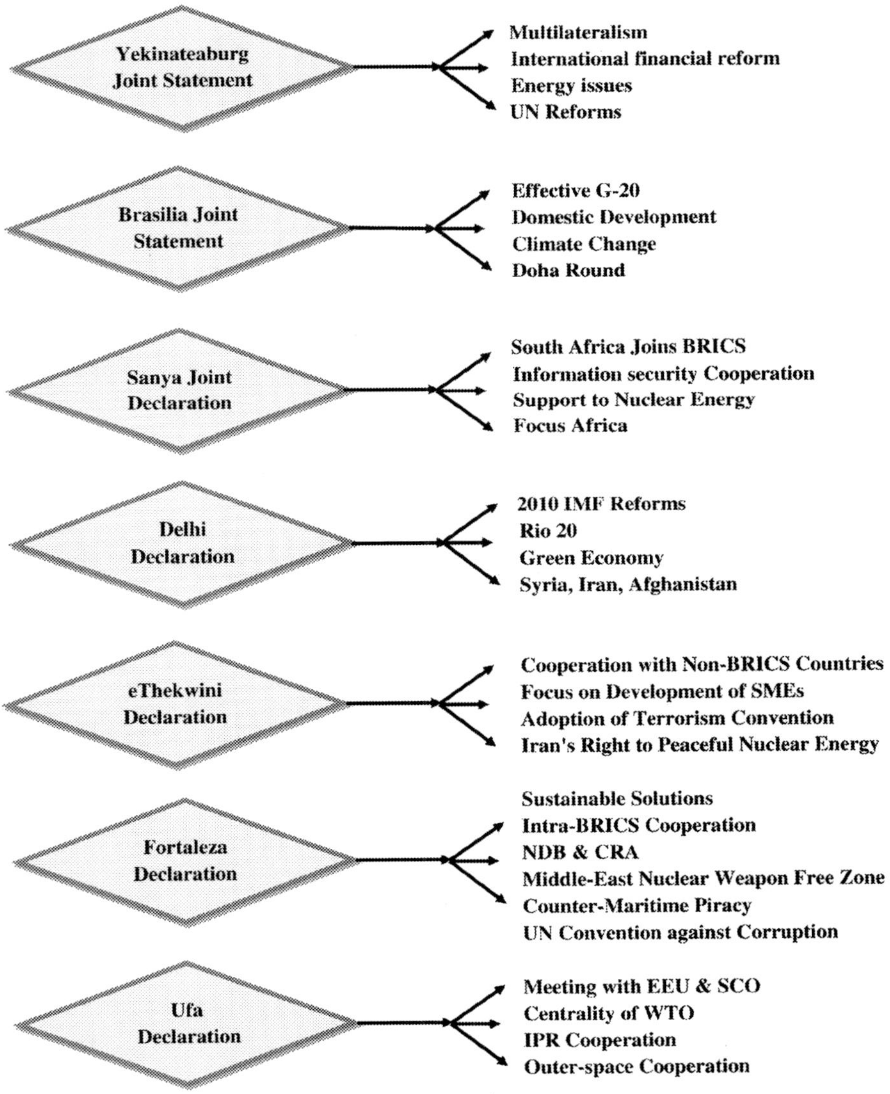

ANNEXURE 4

BRICS Summits and Mechanisms

Summits

2016: October 15-16	Goa	India
2015: November 15	Antalya	Turkey
2015: July 8-9	Ufa	Russia
2014: November 15	Brisbane	Australia
2014: July 15-16	Fortaleza	Brazil
2013: September 5	St. Petersburg	Russia
2013: March 25-27	Durban	South Africa
2012: June 18	Los Cabos	Mexico
2012: March 29	New Delhi	India
2011: November 3	Cannes	France
2011: April 14	Sanya	China
2010: April 15	Brasilia	Brazil
2009: June 16	Yekaterinburg	Russia
2008: July 9	Hokkaido	Japan

Ministers' Summits

Agriculture Ministers
2015: October 9, Moscow
2015: March 11-13, Brasilia, Brazil
2013: October 29, Pretoria, South Africa
2011: October 29-30, Chengdu, China
2010: March 26, Moscow, Russia

Culture Ministers
2015: June 17, Moscow

Education Ministers
2015: November 18, Moscow
2015: March 2: Brasilia
2013: November 5, Paris

Energy Ministers
2015: November 20, Moscow

Environment Ministers
2015: April 22: Moscow, Russia

Foreign Ministers
2015: September 29
2014: September 25
2014: March 24
2013: September 26
2012: September 26
2011: November 24
2011: September 23
2010: September 21
2009: September 24
2009: May 16
2008: September 25

Finance Ministers
2015: April 16: Washington DC
2014: September 9: Cairns
2014: July 15: Fortaleza
2014: April 11
2013: October 10
2013: April 19
2012: October 10
2012: April 19
2012: February 25
2011: September 22
2010: April 23
2009: September 4

Health Ministers
2015: October 30
2015: May 19
2014: December 2-5
2014: May 20

2013: November 7
2013: May 22
2013: January 10-11
2012: May 22
2011: July 11
2009: March 14
2008: November
Labour and Employment Ministers
2016: January 25-26, Ufa
Migration Authorities
2015: October 8, Sochi
Science, Technology and Innovation Ministers
2015: October 28
2015: March 17-18
2014: February 10
Trade Ministers
2015: December 16, Nairobi, Kenya
2015: July 7, Moscow, Russia
2013: July 14, Fortaleza, Brazil
2013: March 26, Durban, South Africa
2012: April 19, Puerto Vallarta, Mexico
2012: March 28, New Delhi
2011: December 14, Geneva, Switzerland
2011: April 13
2010: April, Rio de Janeiro

Meeting of the Officials

Anticorruption Officials
2015: November 1
Competition Authorities
2015: November 11-13, Durban
2013: India
2011: September 20-22, Beijing
2009: September 1, Kazan, Russia
High Representatives on Security/National Security Advisors
2015: May 26, Moscow, Russia
2010: October, Sochi, Russia
2010: April 15
2009: May, Russia
National Statistical Authorities
2014: November 17-19, Rio de Janeiro
2012: February 6-8: New Delhi
2011: March, Beijing
2010: April, Brazil
Science and Technology Officials
2011: September 15, Dalian, China
Tax and Revenue Authorities
2015: November 19, Moscow - Declaration
2013: January 17-18, Delhi - Communiqué

Other

Academic Forum/Track II
2015: May 22-23, Moscow
2014: March 18-19, Rio de Janeiro
2013: March 26-27, Durban
2012: March 5-6, New Delhi
2011: March, Beijing
2010: April 14-15, Brazil
2009: May, India
Mayors of BRICS Cities and Friendship Cities
2011: December 1-3, Sanya, China
Business Forum
2015: July 8, Ufa (BRICS Business Council)
2015: June 18, St Petersburg
2013: March 26, Durban
2012: March 27, Delhi
2011: April, Sanya
2010: April 14, Rio de Janeiro

ANNEXURE 5

BRICS Demographic and Social Indicators

General Information on BRICS Countries

BRICS Countries	*Area of Territory (Thousand sq. km)*	*Capital City*	*Mid-Year Population (Million persons)*	*Population Density (Person per sq. km)*	*Nation Currency*
Brazil	8516	Brasilia	203	23.8	Real - R$
Russia	17098	Moscow	146	8.4	Rouble - ₽
India	3287	New Delhi	1239	391	Rupee - ₹
China	9600	Beijing	1364	142.1	Renminbi - RMB
South Africa	1221	Pretoria	54	44.2	Rand – ZAR

Source: BRICS Joint Statistical Publication 2015.

Share of the BRICS Countries in the World Population, 2013 (%)

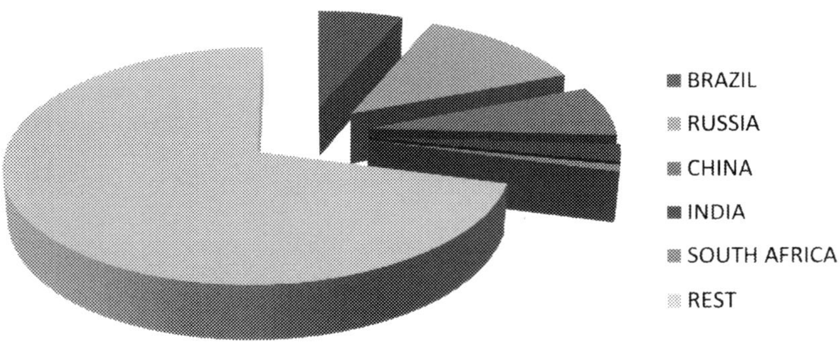

Share of the BRICS Countries in the World Territory, 2013 (%)

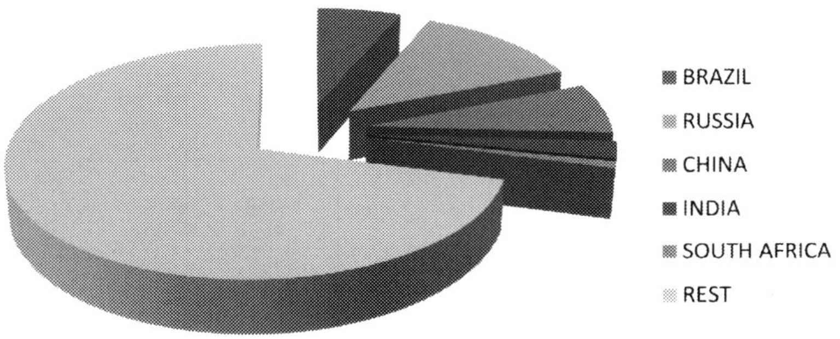

Economic and Social Indicators Comparison of BRICS Countries – 2013-14

BRICS Countries	*Economically Active Population (%)*	*Share Unemployment Rate (%)*	*National Accounts GDP (Current Prices/ Billion US$)*	*Public Expenditureon Education as (%) of GDP*	*Public Expenditureon Health as (%) of GDP*	*Gini Coefficient*
Brazil	65.5	6.5	2346	5.3	4.9	0.497
Russia	52.6	5.2	1881	4.3	3.5	0.416
India	55.6	3.4	2069	3.1	1.2	0.367
China	56.5	4.1	10362	4.3	5.6	0.469
South Africa	37.6	25.1	350	6.9	4.1	0.650

Source: BRICS Joint Statistical Publication, 2015.

Human Development Indicators of BRICS Countries

BRICS Countries	*Human Development Index*	*Rank*
Brazil	0.755	75
Russia	0.798	50
India	0.609	130
China	0.727	90
South Africa	0.666	116

Source: UNDP Human Development Report, 2015.

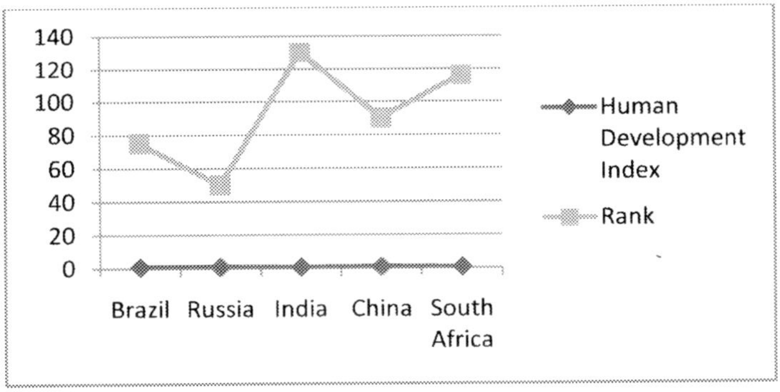

ANNEXURE 6

BRICS Inter and Intra Trade Value

Table 1: Evolution of Total BRICS Exports by Country (US$ Billions)

Year	*Brazil (value)*	*India (value)*	*Russia (value)*	*China (value)*	*South Africa (value)*
2006	138	121	302	969	53
2007	161	146	352	1,220	64
2008	198	182	468	1,431	72
2009	153	177	302	1,202	54
2010	202	220	397	1,578	83
2011	256	301	517	1,898	108
2012	243	290	525	2,049	99
2013	242	337	527	2,209	95
2014	225	318	498	2,342	91
2015	191	264	334	2,282	82

Source: Economics & Trade Statistics, BRICS Ministry of External Affairs, Brazil.

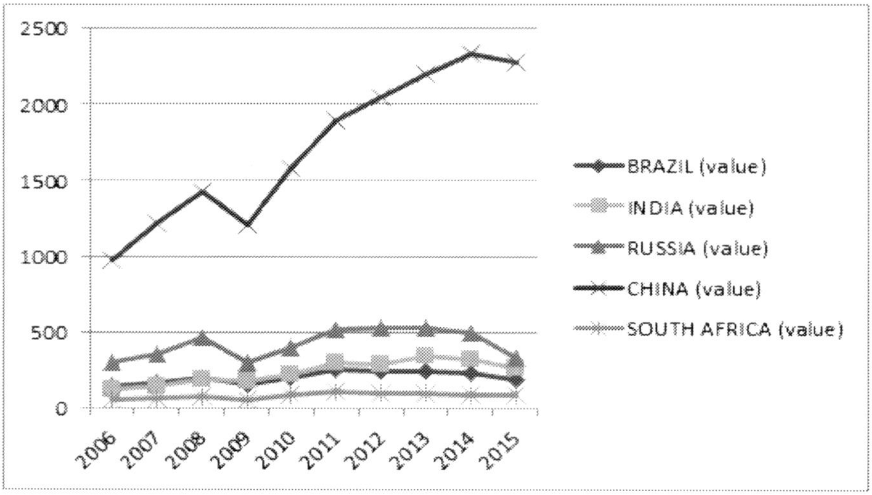

Table 2: Evolution of Total Imports by the BRICS Country (US$ Billions)

Years	*Brazil (value)*	*India (value)*	*Russia (value)*	*China (value)*	*South Africa (value)*
2006	91	178	138	791	68
2007	121	219	200	956	80
2008	173	316	267	1,133	88
2009	128	266	171	1,006	64
2010	182	350	229	1,396	83
2011	226	462	306	1,743	103
2012	223	489	316	1,818	104
2013	240	466	315	1,950	103
2014	229	459	287	1,958	100
2015	171	391	177	1,682	86

Source: Economics & Trade Statistics, BRICS Ministry of External Affairs, Brazil.

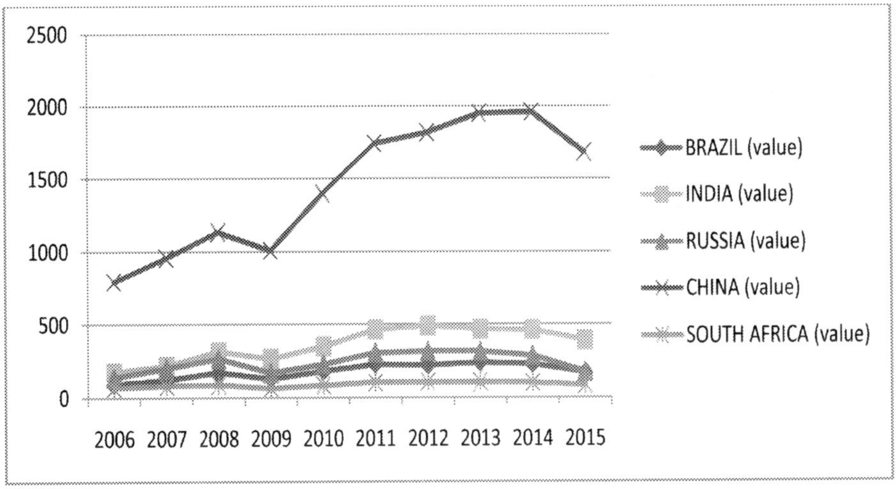

Table 3: Intra-BRICS Trade (US$ Billions)

Years	*Total*	*Value*
2006	1,582	93
2007	1,943	129
2008	2,352	169
2009	1,887	144
2010	2,475	211
2011	3,081	275
2012	3,205	281
2013	3,410	296
2014	3,473	295
2015	3,152	244

Source: Economics & Trade Statistics, BRICS Ministry of External Affairs, Brazil.

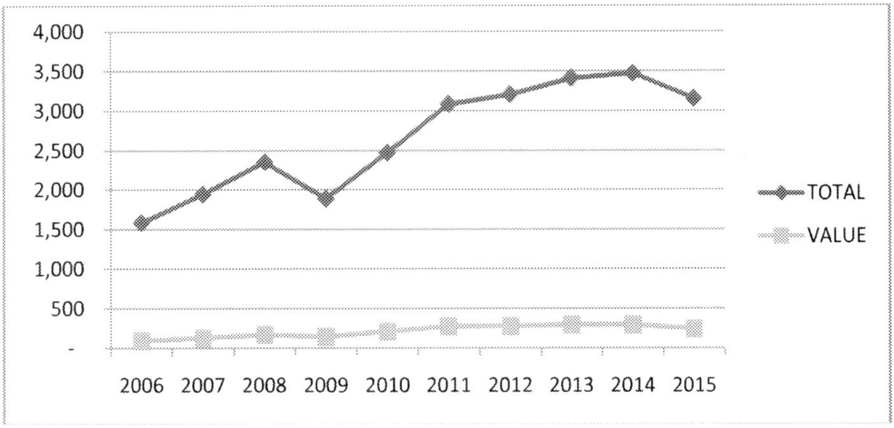

Table 4: Evolution of Intra-Block Exports Country-wise (US$ Billions)

Years	*Brazil*	*India*	*Russia*	*China*	*South Africa*
2006	14.2	12.3	19.4	43.6	3.4
2007	17.2	14.4	19.3	71.4	6.2
2008	24.0	16.9	28.5	92.1	7.5
2009	28.5	15.1	23.9	68.7	8.3
2010	39.7	26.2	27.0	105.8	12.1
2011	53.4	28.3	41.6	134.6	17.0
2012	51.7	28.0	45.9	140.5	15.3
2013	54.0	30.7	44.9	150.8	16.1
2014	50.5	28.5	44.4	158.5	13.4
2015	43.0	18.1	34.9	136.4	11.6

Source: Economics & Trade Statistics, BRICS Ministry of External Affairs, Brazil

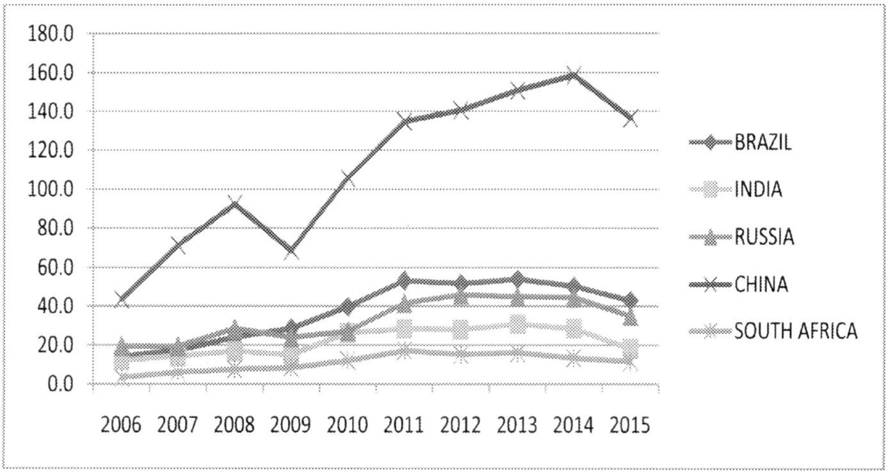

Table 5: Composition of Exports (Intra-BRICS) in 2015 (US$ Billions)

Products	*2015*	*Part (%) No Total*
Fuels	28.99	11.9
Electric Machines	28.41	11.6
Mechanical Machines	25.57	10.5
Grains & Seeds	16.33	6.7
Ores	13.22	5.4
Organic Chemicals	10.67	4.4
Fertilizers	7.42	3.0
Iron & Steel	6.80	2.8
Plastics	5.87	2.4
Automobiles	5.39	2.2

Source: Economic Data & Trade Statistics, BRICS Ministry of External Affairs, Brazil

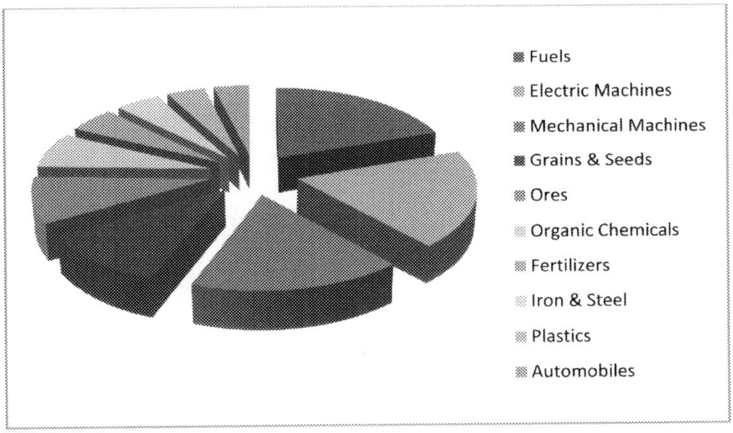

ANNEXURE 7

GDP Growth of BRICS Countries

GDP Growth of BRICS Countries (annual %)

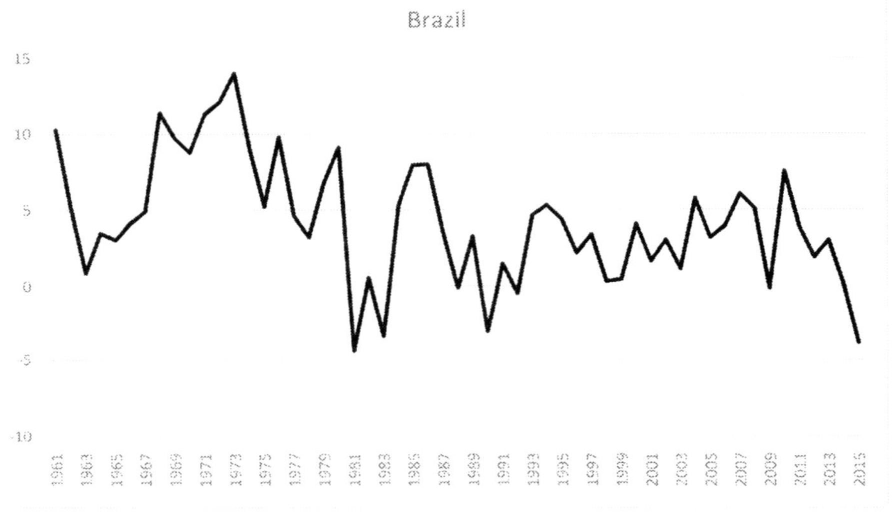

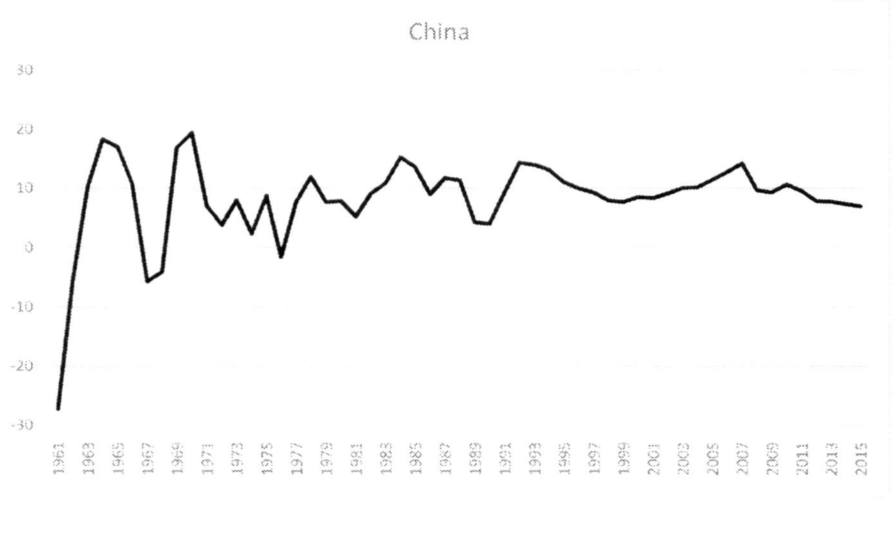

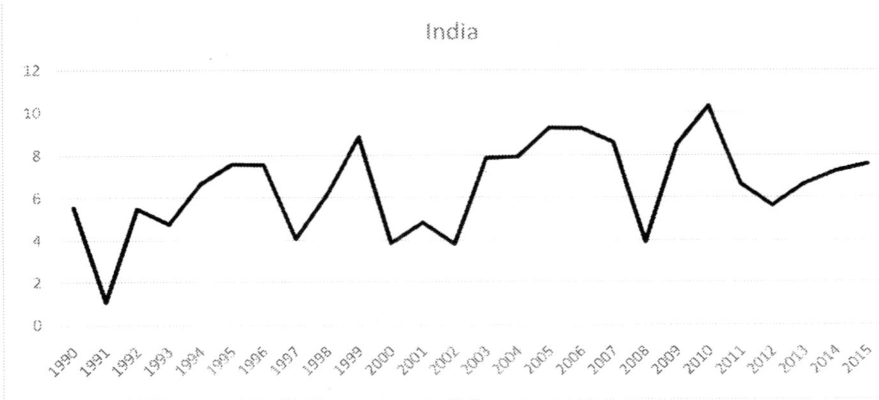

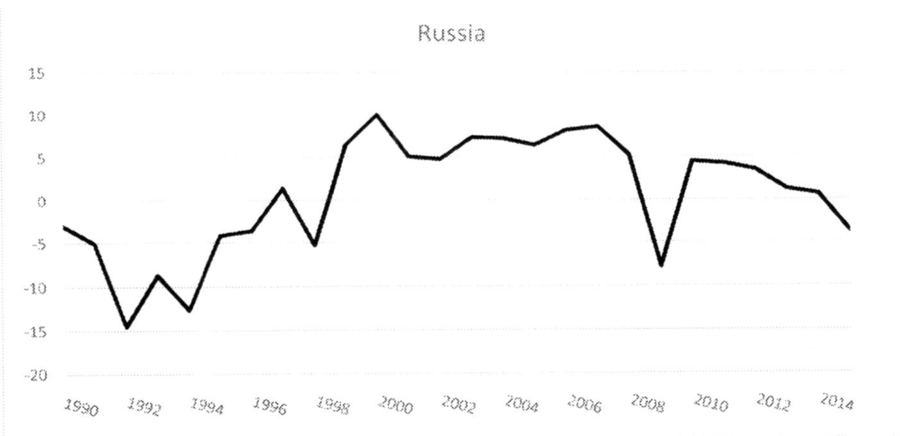

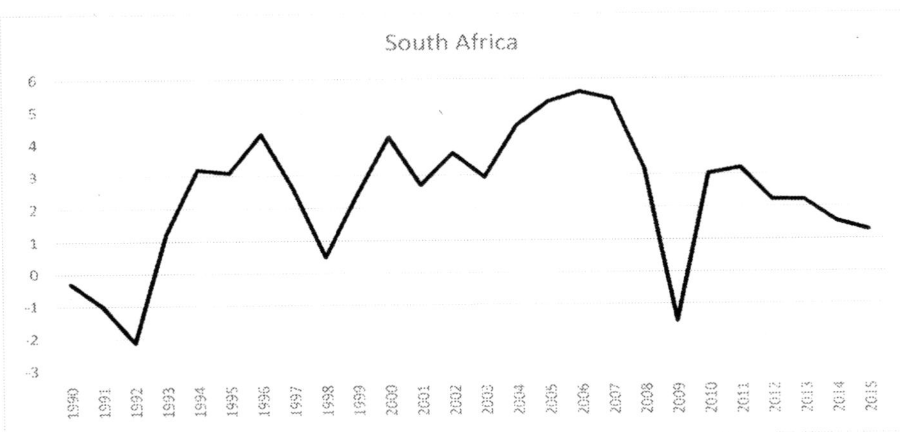

Source: World Bank.

ANNEXURE 8

Total Reserves of BRICS Countries

Total Reserves (including gold, current US$) of BRICS countries

Country	*1960 (million)*	*2015 (million)*
Brazil	349.85	356,464.98
China	NA	3,405,253.36
India	674.54	353,319.06
Russian Federation	NA	368,042.95
South Africa	272.20	45,887.06

Source: World Bank.

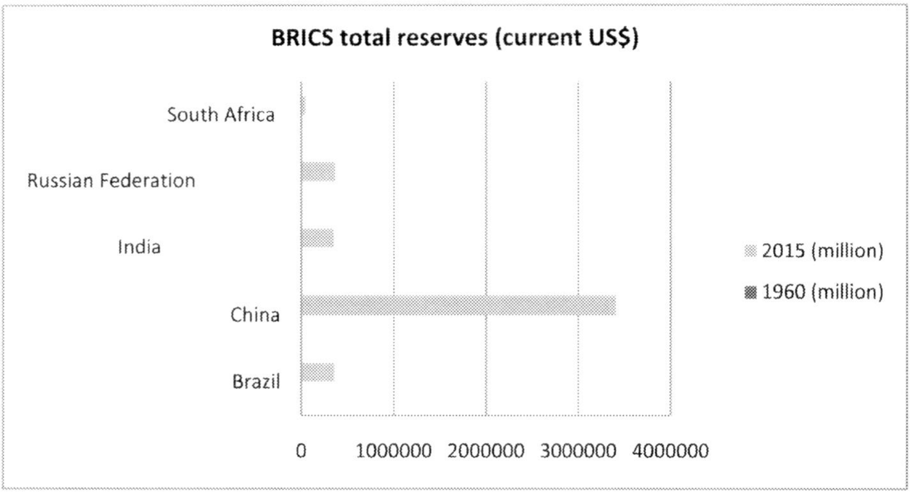

Index